PENNSYLVANIA COLLEGE OF TECHNOLOGY LIBR

5 0608 01085094 8

DATE DUE

MAR 1 9 2003		
MAY 9 2006		
OCT 1 2 2007		
DISCARDED		

Demco, Inc. 38-293

e of JSP

D1369701

Making Use of JSP

Madhushree Ganguli

Wiley Publishing, Inc.

LIBRARY

Pennsylvania College
of Technology

One College Avenue
Williamsport, PA 17701-5799

SEP 0 4 2002

Publisher: Robert Ipsen
Editor: Ben Ryan
Developmental Editor: Kathryn A. Malm
Managing Editor: Angela Smith
New Media Editor: Brian Snapp
Text Design & Composition: John Wiley Production Services

Designations used by companies to distinguish their products are often claimed as trademarks. In all instances where John Wiley & Sons, Inc., is aware of a claim, the product names appear in initial capital or ALL CAPITAL LETTERS. Readers, however, should contact the appropriate companies for more complete information regarding trademarks and registration.

This book is printed on acid-free paper. ♾

Copyright © 2002 by Madhushree Ganguli. All rights reserved.

Published by Wiley Publishing, Inc., New York

Published simultaneously in Canada.

No part of this publication may be reproduced, stored in a retrieval system or transmitted in any form or by any means, electronic, mechanical, photocopying, recording, scanning or otherwise, except as permitted under Sections 107 or 108 of the 1976 United States Copyright Act, without either the prior written permission of the Publisher, or authorization through payment of the appropriate per-copy fee to the Copyright Clearance Center, 222 Rosewood Drive, Danvers, MA 01923, (978) 750-8400, fax (978) 750-4744. Requests to the Publisher for permission should be addressed to the Permissions Department, John Wiley & Sons, Inc., 605 Third Avenue, New York, NY 10158-0012, (212) 850-6011, fax (212) 850-6008, E-Mail: PERMREQ @ WILEY.COM.

This publication is designed to provide accurate and authoritative information in regard to the subject matter covered. It is sold with the understanding that the publisher is not engaged in professional services. If professional advice or other expert assistance is required, the services of a competent professional person should be sought.

Library of Congress Cataloging-in-Publication Data:

ISBN 0-471-21974-6

Wiley also publishes its books in a variety of electronic formats. Some content that appears in print may not be available in electronic versions. For more information about Wiley products, visit our Web site at www.wiley.com.

Printed in the United States of America.

10 9 8 7 6 5 4 3 2 1

Contents

Introduction

The world seems to shrink each day, thanks to the ever-increasing power of the Internet. With the growth and popularity of the Internet, even distant areas across the globe seem closer today. It is indeed the era of fast communication and information exchange. To retain a commanding position in this changing world, organizations need to prepare themselves for the rapid development of Web-based applications that are platform-independent. As a result, organizations need to identify the tools required to emerge as a formidable force in the competitive world of Web-based applications. Java Server Pages, or JSP, a Sun Microsystems product, is one tool that is fast catching up as a preferred technology for creating Web-based applications.

JSP is based on the Java technology and is an extension of the Java Servlet technology. As a result, platform independence and extensibility of servlets are easily incorporated in JSP. In addition, using the Java server-side modules, JSP can fit effortlessly into the framework of a Web server with minimal overhead, maintenance, and support. The use of XML-like tags and Java-like syntax in JSP facilitate building Web-based applications with speed and ease as never before.

The power, extensibility, and portability of JSP are well described by the following statements from Sun Microsystems:

The JSP specification is the product of industry-wide collaboration with industry leaders in the enterprise software and tools market, led by Sun Microsystems. Sun has made the JSP specification freely available to the development community with the goal that every Web server and application server will support the JSP interface.

Future Direction
By working with a consortium of industry leaders, Sun has ensured that the JSP specifications remain open and portable. Over time, tool vendors and others will extend the functionality of the platform by providing customized tag libraries for specialized functions.

It is beyond doubt that JSP will rule the market in the future and become one of the most powerful languages for developing Web applications. The use of customized tags and libraries is gaining wide acceptance in the industry as a flexible mechanism that allows segregation of the work profiles of the page author and the programmer.

Along with conceptual information, this book will also provide extensive practical exercises for the reader to gain valuable real-life exposure in creating different types of applications. The aim of this book is to make learning an enjoyable and energizing process.

Overview of JavaServer Pages

Two friends, Gwen and Griffith, decide to enroll themselves in a short course during the fall break. While Gwen's choice is interior decoration, Griffith chooses a more professional course in secretarial practice. Both friends, being computer savvy, search the Internet and come up with the same site advertising their choices of short courses. As an afterthought, both Gwen and Griffith marveled that although their choice of courses was different, the same site displayed a list of details for the two completely different courses. How was the display of the courses linked and changed according to the search criteria? What actually ensued was a request-response cycle that displayed the result pertaining to the individual query. In other words, the Web application for the site received the requests and returned dynamic content in the form of the course details. In the world of the Internet, dynamism is part and parcel of Web applications. Technologies such as Hypertext Pre Processor (PHP), Active Server Pages (ASP), and Java Server Pages (JSP) are used to create dynamic Web applications.

This book will help you understand the JSP technology that can be used to create applications to generate dynamic content. Java Server Pages allows Web developers and designers to develop easily maintainable, information-rich, dynamic Web pages. Java Server Pages separates the user interface from content generation. This enables designers to change the layout of a Web page without altering the underlying dynamic content. As a result, the workload can be clearly separated into two categories, the graphical content created by a designer or a page author and the dynamic content created by the developer or the programmer. As a result, in simple words, JSP provides a simplified, faster way to create dynamic Web content.

History of JSP

Sun Microsystems was founded in 1982. Ever since its inception, Sun Microsystems has maintained a singular vision of "The Network Is The Computer." This vision has helped Sun Microsystems remain as one of the leading providers of industrial-strength hardware, software, and services to aid companies across the world. The company has a global presence in more than 170 countries with gross annual revenue crossing the $17 billion mark.

A significant year in the history of Sun Microsystems was 1995. This was the year when Sun received ISO 9001 certification for quality in all major country service organizations and ISO 9002 certification for all worldwide manufacturing operations. In the same year, the company unleashed Java technology, which was the first universal software platform designed for the Internet and corporate intranets. Java technology enabled developers to write applications once and run them on computers anywhere without any modifications. If we flip back the pages of the history of Java, we'll realize that the introduction of Java was more of an accident. In fact, you'll be surprised to know that Java was originally developed not for computers but for home appliances such as ovens, toasters, and refrigerators. The accident, though, has proved to be a boon in disguise—with the popularity of the Internet neither Sun nor Java has had to look back. Java has worked hard to be accepted and recognized as a favorite language for developing Web applications.

JSP is a part of the Java family that shares the key characteristics of the Java technology: "Write Once, Run Anywhere." It is a core component of the Java 2 Enterprise Edition. JSP has inherited most of the features and benefits of both Java and Servlet technology and is fast gaining acceptance as a standard tool for building dynamic Web sites.

Features of JSP

JSP provides an attractive alternative to other dynamic scripting languages by offering the following features:

Platform independence. The use of JSP adds versatility to a Web application by enabling its execution on any computer.

Enhanced performance. The compilation process in JSP produces faster results or output.

Separation of logic from display. The use of JSP permits the HTML-specific static content and a mixture of HTML, Java, and JSP-specific dynamic content to be placed in separate files.

Ease of administration. The use of JSP eliminates the need for high-level technical expertise, thereby helping Web developers, designers, content creators, and content managers to work together and develop Java-based applications in less time and with less effort.

Ease of use. All JSP applications run on major Web servers and operating systems, including Microsoft IIS, Netscape Enterprise Server, iPlanet Web Server, and Apache Web Server. These applications are also available on Windows NT, Windows 2000, and Solaris 7.

Users of the Product/Technology

By moving Web development into the twenty-first century, Java Server Pages technology enables faster product delivery time. Here are a few examples of enterprises that are using the Java Server Pages framework to deliver break-away business strategies for both themselves and their customers:

- Knight Ridder
- Delta Airlines

- Waterstone Consulting
- Axtive Software Corporation
- MetaMarkets.com, Inc.
- Cambridge Interactive
- NMG New Media Group
- Epicentric, Inc.
- PostalWorks LLC
- Flashline.com, Inc.
- TheWorksUSA.com
- Klicman Incorporated
- TouchNet Information Systems, Inc.
- Linnebank IT
- Tradiant

Competing Products across Platforms

Competing products include Active Server Pages (ASP), Hypertext Pre Processor (PKP), and JavaScript.

JSP versus ASP. ASP is the immediate competing technology from Microsoft. The dynamic content of JSP is written in Java, in contrast to that of ASP, which is written using an ASP-specific language, such as VBScript. As a result, complex applications can use the power of Java to reuse and embed Java components in JSP applications. Second, JSP is portable to other operating systems and servers in contrast to the allegiance of ASP to Windows NT/2000 and IIS.

JSP versus PHP. PHP is similar to ASP and JSP to a certain extent. PHP is a free, open-source, HTML-embedded, server-side scripting language. With basic HTML knowledge, however, a VBScript programmer can write ASP applications and a Java programmer can create JSP applications, whereas PHP requires learning an entirely new language. Second, by virtue of the power of Java, JSP has access to an extensive API for networking, database access, and object distribution.

JSP versus JavaScript. JavaScript is a programming language that is totally different from the server-side HTML and Java-based JSP technology. JavaScript is a client-side programming language used to build parts of HTML Web pages while the browser loads a document. As a result, the pages generated in JavaScript create dynamic content that is solely based on the client environment. JSP applications, by virtue of its being a server-side scripting language, use mechanisms such as hidden fields, session objects, cookies, and URL rewriting to access all request data transmitted during a request-response cycle. Equipped with only cookies as aids to provide request data, the client-side JavaScript routines are unable to access the HTTP request data. Although JavaScript can be used on servers as a scripting language for IIS, JSP backed by the reliability, flexibility, and portability of Java is a more powerful technology by far.

How This Book Is Organized

This book differs from the traditional content-based approach and uses the problem-based approach to deliver the concepts of JSP. Problems used in the book are presented against the backdrop of real-life scenarios. The problem is followed by a task list that helps to solve the given problem, in the process explaining the concepts and their implementation. This practical approach will help readers understand the real-life application of the language and its use in various scenarios. Moreover, to provide an appropriate learning experience, the concepts will be supported adequately by case studies that provide a frame of reference for the reader.

Chapter 1 is a guide to the basics of the Internet and discusses the World Wide Web environment, browser and server interactions, and the HTTP request-response cycle.

Chapter 2 is a getting-started guide that begins with a brief introduction to JSP. This is followed by a discussion on the JSP life cycle and concludes with the steps used for installing and setting up the environment to execute JSP applications.

Chapter 3 attempts to highlight the advantages incorporated in JSP as an extension of Java Servlet technology. The chapter begins with a discussion of the JavaServlet architecture and life cycle. The chapter concludes with an example of a simple servlet that is used to count the number of hits for a particular page.

Chapter 4 introduces concepts related to creating a JSP application. It discusses the various components of a JSP page by using the simple "Hello World" example. The difference between static and dynamic content is also discussed using appropriate examples.

Chapter 6 delves into the all-important concept of HTML forms. All user-specific input is transferred to the server by using various controls of the HTML page. The chapter begins with an introduction to HTML forms, followed by a discussion of the various types of HTML controls that can be added to a form. Next, the mechanisms of retrieval and transfer of form values in JSP are discussed using a simple example. The chapter concludes with a JavaScript-aided client-side validation for ensuring user input in a form control.

Chapters 6, 7, and 8 discuss the different JSP-specific components one by one. Chapter 5 discusses implicit objects, including such implicit objects as request, response, session, application, and config. This is followed by a brief discussion of the importance of the scope of implicit objects.

Chapter 7 discusses two JSP components, directives and action elements. The chapter begins with the types and uses of the page, include, and taglib directives. Next, the various JSP standard actions are discussed with suitable examples. In the concluding section of the chapter, examples are used to show the difference in the usage of the include directive and the include standard action.

Chapter 8 introduces the scripting elements of JSP that are primarily used to generate the dynamic content. It discusses the use of the three types of scripting elements: scriplets, expressions, and declarations.

Chapter 9 explains concepts relating to reusing Java bean components in a JSP page. The chapter begins with an introduction to JavaBeans, followed by a discussion on using JavaBeans in JSP. To aid a better understanding of using a bean component in a JSP page, the chapter concludes with an example that uses a Java bean instead of a direct use of JSP components to display dynamic content.

Chapter 10 moves on to discussing activities on the server side. This chapter assumes that the reader has a basic knowledge of databases, data storage in databases, RDBMS concepts, and their implementation. The chapter begins with a discussion of concepts pertaining to JDBC basics that include types of JDBC drivers, the various application architecture, and database access models. Next, the chapter explains the processes of accessing and manipulating a database by using SQL commands. Finally, a JSP application is used as a backdrop to implement database connectivity and discuss concepts such as connecting to a database, creating a table in a database, and inserting records in a database.

Chapter 11 combines the concepts of reusing bean components to implement database interactions in JSP applications. The chapter begins with an example of a login bean that is used to validate and authenticate a user. Next, the concept of connection pooling is discussed to highlight the importance of economizing the use of Web resources during a database interaction. The chapter then discusses the various classes and methods required to create a connection pool in a JSP application.

Chapter 12 delves into handling errors in JSP. The chapter begins with a discussion of error handling and the implementation of exception handling in JSP. Next, the translation and request time errors are discussed with examples.

Chapter 13 introduces another important concept of session tracking. The chapter begins by differentiating between a stateful and stateless session and the importance of the availability of session-related information in applications. It then discusses the methods of using cookies, hidden fields, session-tracking APIs, and URL rewriting for session tracking.

Chapter 14 further discusses the advanced Web programming concepts of using Simplified API for XML (SAX) and Extensible Markup Language (XML) in JSP applications. To start with, this chapter discusses the benefits of using XML. This is followed by a discussion of the SAX API and the use of various classes and methods of the SAX API to parse the contents of an XML document in JSP.

Chapter 15 delves into developing the relatively new concept of custom tags. This chapter discusses the need of custom tags in JSP to encapsulate recurring code snippets. The chapter uses examples to discuss in detail the various formats that can be adopted to add both simple and complex tags in a JSP application. In addition, the chapter also includes an example that uses a custom tag to initiate a database interaction for retrieving and displaying a particular record from the database.

Chapter 16, the final chapter, is a brief introduction to JavaMail and the importance of mailing services in our lives today. The chapter wraps up with an example that creates an application for sending a message by using the class and method declarations of the JavaMail API.

Who Should Read This Book

This book is a guide for readers with basic familiarity with HTML and the Java language. In this book the content will be covered using lucid examples, sample codes, and the appropriate use of visuals and demonstrations. The concepts will be supported adequately by case studies that will be formulated in such a way that they provide a frame of reference for the reader. Problems will be presented to the reader against the backdrop of real-life scenarios. The practical approach will help readers to understand the real-life application of the language and the use of JSP in various scenarios. In a nutshell, this book will provide a starting point for working with and creating applications in JSP.

This book is intended for programmers interested in developing dynamic Web sites by using JSP. The target audience for this book would include the following:

- Web application developers
- Technical support professionals
- Web site administrators

Novice developers of Web applications can use relevant real-world-oriented scenarios and exercises for the concepts covered as a guide to learn the basics of writing Java Server Pages.

Tools You Will Need

For performing the tasks in this book, you will need a Pentium or faster computer with a minimum 32MB RAM (64MB RAM recommended).

You will also need the following software:

Operating system: Windows NT 4.0 with Service Pack 6.0.

RDBMS: SQL 7.0.

Text Editors: Notepad or Edit Plus, for example.

Software: Java Development Kit (v 1.3).

Software: Java 2 SDK, Enterprise Edition (v 1.2.1).

What's on the Web Site

The following will be available on the site www.wiley.com/compbooks/makinguse:

- Java Development Kit (v 1.3)
- Java 2 SDK, Enterprise Edition (v 1.2.1)
- All the code snippets used in the book

Scenario

All problem statements in this book are based on the scenario of the Banco de Glendanthi. The following section elaborates on the setup of the Banco de Glendanthi and its future plans.

Banco de Glendanthi

Banco de Glendanthi was established 70 years ago in New York by Norman Cropper. Today, under the chairmanship of Marty Bates, the bank has spread across not only all states of the United States but also the world and has its regional headquarters in London, Paris, Istanbul, Cairo, Kuala Lampur, and Singapore. The bank activities have also increased in terms of the services offered and the volume of transaction.

Broadly, the bank offers the following three financial services: financial deposits, loans, and credit facilities. Customers can open both personal and business accounts with the bank. In addition, a customer can register and can use the loan facility when certain prerequisites are fulfilled. The bank also offers a credit card facility to keep up with the current trend of plastic money.

Banco de Glendanthi also has ATM (Any Time Money) centers in most of the business quarters of the cities where it has branches. The ATM facility is a useful addition to the bank's services. Customers can deposit or withdraw money at any of the ATM centers 24 hours a day.

Over the years, the bank has gained acceptance through dedicated and personalized customer service. The financial presentation in the last general body meeting has shown that the profits of the bank have increased manifold. The board members have decided to increase profits further by encompassing the latest technologies. As a result, the board has unanimously decided to make a foray into e-banking and make their presence felt on the Internet.

During the last board meeting presided over by Marty, the following developments were observed:

- Most of the competitors of Banco de Glendanthi either had their own Web sites or were in the process of launching online banking services.
- Customer feedback in recent years has shown that most professionals find it difficult to access their accounts while traveling.
- The transfer of accounts from one place to another is mostly delayed by lengthy administrative procedures.
- The sales team is unable to cater to the large number of people wanting to open accounts or apply for loans.
- Overhead is increasing because Banco de Glendanthi has to employ a number of people to handle the increasing business.

The head of the marketing department, Lisa Holley, after extensive research on current trends in the banking market, has proposed the following changes to overcome the current limitations:

- With the growth and popularity of the Internet, online banking is proving to be very successful.
- Most people prefer online banking because it saves time and is accessible irrespective of the customer's location.
- The Internet is an effective medium to reach new customers and will also hasten the otherwise delayed processes of new customer registrations.
- Online banking will help save resources because the automation of services will reduce team size and bring down errors.

At the end of the board meeting, the proposal to set up an online site for Banco de Glendanthi is unanimously supported. The task of creating the online site for the bank is given to an upcoming software organization, Business Software Solutions Inc. James McNamee, a senior analyst at Banco de Glendanthi, is assigned the task of coordinating the project.

The project has been code-named Banco de Glendanthi Online. Paul Karlson has been nominated as the project manager, heading a team of competent designers and Java programmers. A quality assurance team and a graphics team have also been assigned to support the development team.

According to the requirements furnished by James McNamee, the online bank site should do the following:

- Allow users to view different account types:
  - Personal Checking Accounts
    - Basic Checking
    - Checking Plus+

- Business Checking Accounts
  - Basic Business Checking
  - Business Checking Biz+
- Personal Savings Accounts
  - Student Savings
  - Money Market Plus
  - Certificates of Deposit
  - Club Account
  - Passbook Savings
- Commercial Savings
  - Glendanthi Biz
- Loan Products
  - Commercial Loan Products
  - Consumer Loan Products
  - Mortgage Loan Products
- Allow users to view loan details
- Allow a first-time user to register personal details
- Allow account holders and registered users to log on
- Enable account holders and nonregistered users to browse through the services offered
- Process registrations and send details to the sales department for further processing
- Display account information to valid account holders
- Display loan application status to registered applicants

During the next few months, it will be the team's endeavor to ensure zero-defect software development in line with client requirements. After the development of the online banking site for Banco de Glendanthi, customers will no longer have to visit the bank offices to use their accounts. They can simply log on to the Web site www. BancodeGlendanthi.com and carry out transactions. People who want to open an account or apply for a loan can browse through the site and register themselves.

As a part of future plans the bank also intends to facilitate the payment of bills through the site, a service that will save customers the ordeal of tracking payment schedules. Because the bank believes firmly in customer service first, the site will make provisions for accepting customer feedback.

Whether the bank functions online or otherwise, one thing that remains unchanged is that Banco de Glendanthi values customer relationship and is a reliable financial institution offering products and services to meet individual financial goals.

Introducing Web Development

OBJECTIVES:

In this chapter, you will learn to do the following:

- ✔ Identify the events that led to the beginning of the Internet era
- ✔ Describe the various terms and components associated with the Internet
- ✔ Identify the changes in the application architecture with the advent of the Internet
- ✔ Appreciate the World Wide Web environment

Getting Started

The origin of Web development is the result of man's continuous endeavor to gratify the basic need for communication. Both man and animals subsist as social beings and depend heavily on communication as a means of expression. Animals have their own system of social communication, which is specific to their individual species. Man, on the other hand, has used the postal services and inventions such as telephones to facilitate communication across geographical borders.

Communication through postal services, though, was slow. Telephones, on the other hand, did enable communication but were expensive because of the sizable geographical distances between locations. As a result, subsequent innovations aimed to overcome these shortcomings of time and money. Success finally came in the form of computers that not only provided the stepping-stones for a communication revolution, but also facilitated automation of tasks and storage-retrieval of information. Accordingly, the success of computers and subsequent research efforts in network technology provided a means of communication through computers that was both simpler and faster. This was just the beginning of an era, the era of the Internet that paved the way for computer-to-computer communication. The advent of this technology made it possible to access information and communicate at an unimaginable speed.

Justifying the popularity and success of the Internet today, this chapter begins with a look at the basic workings of the Internet. This is followed by a brief discussion of the evolution and history of the Internet. The next sections of the chapter discuss the various terms and tools associated with this technological revolution.

Internet Basics

During the early 1970s, computers still existed as islands (as they were popularly known) that diligently performed user-specific tasks. As the requirement for an alternative and faster mode of communication increased, the next best step was aimed at connecting these solitary computers so that they could communicate with each other. Picture the thrill and excitement that this view brought to the world of computers. For a moment, just visualize the expanse and the utilization of this technology! Because of computer-to-computer linking, a new channel of communication could be exploited that could link the world and facilitate the exchange of information. In 1973, the U.S. Defense Advanced Research Projects Agency (DARPA) initiated a research program whose objective was to investigate technologies and techniques that could be used for linking computers. Subsequent research resulted in the development of a system of networks, popularly branded as the Internet. In other words, this was just the beginning of an epoch that led to the phenomenal acceptance and success of networked computers.

Nevertheless, the last 20 years more so the early 1990s have largely contributed to the growth in the popularity of the Internet as a fast source of information and communication. And why not? The extent of the use of this technology is unlimited and needs no introduction. The following are a few examples that illustrate the use of the Internet:

- Away from home, homesick? Need more money? Need to submit assignments to the professor on short notice? Need data for a particular project? Correspondence today is efficient and fast, thanks to email. The versatility of email has no bounds, be it letters, greetings, textual assignments, anything! Email has proved to be a fast alternative to the traditional and slow postal mode of correspondence.

- Changing your job? Moving to a new city? Jittery about problems related to housing, schooling, and neighborhoods in the new city? Thanks to information available on the Internet, the process of relocating to a new town, state, or country is trouble-free. The Internet provides information that can be used to explore and weigh the possibilities of a change in location without having to leave home.

■ Thanks to the Internet, medical practitioners today can exchange requests and information that facilitate access to medical aid in remote areas. Not only that, but sharing information has opened doors to new research that has diagnosed and cured rare diseases.

■ Appeals from calamity-stricken and war-torn areas are immediately answered with medical and food supplies, thanks to the Internet newsgroups.

How are all these things possible? All the services offered by these examples are a part of the Internet. Before exploring the workings of the Internet, let's retrace the changes brought to communication in computers before and after the advent of the Internet.

Conventional stand-alone computers facilitated the housing of information for future reference and simplified tasks such as data manipulation and word processing. The DARPA research necessitated the study and exploration of computers as a means of communication. To ensure communication between two computers, say computers A and B, first, the computers have to be connected through a single wire. Next, A needs to send a signal to B, requesting permission to initiate the communication. Subsequently, the availability of B for counter-communication further needs to be given using a reply signal. Figure 1.1 represents such a conventional and simple computer connection.

Communication through computers cannot be restricted to only two computers. How would a dozen computers connect in order to ensure such a communication? The situation is complicated further by the isolated placement of computers—say, 5,000 miles apart. Nonetheless, can you connect computers in such a situation? If so, how? Well, the already existing telecommunication framework can be used to connect computers regardless of their location or distance. These complex sets of connections are wired using a networking system. In fact, this networking technique is the very basis for connectivity between computers. Sounds simple, doesn't it? Understand, though, that the term "Internet" describes a network of not two or a dozen computers, but thousands of computers spanning 65 countries. In fact, the Internet represents a network of networks.

With the advent of the Internet, there was a total change in the field of computing. At the macro level, the framework still consisted of two computers, but the application framework changed to keep pace with the expanse of the Internet network. From the very beginning, the principle behind the Internet was sharing of information. Therefore, keeping the architecture of the connected computers in mind, information could be made available to all computers within the network. As a result, computers A, B, C, and many more, known as clients, accessed a central repository of information, running on another system, which is known as the server. This approach founded the basis for client/server architecture. Figure 1.2 represents a sample Internet connection.

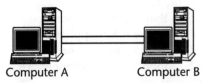

Computer A   Computer B

Figure 1.1 A simple computer connection.

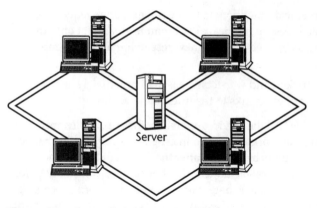

Figure 1.2   A sample Internet connection.

However, the growing acceptance of the Internet, and the subsequent increase in its spread, made a great impact not only on the architecture of application tools and databases but also caused a radical shift in the deployment of applications and the information repository or the database. This led to further changes in the application architecture. Let's now outline the cause of these architectural changes.

An application aiming to solve a specific problem can be defined as a program consisting of presentation and business logic. Presentation logic constitutes the user interface and the format of the program output while business logic, using various mathematical manipulations or computations, aims to deliver the required results. In addition, with the introduction of the Internet, another component in the form of the information repository was added to the application. This component, which was hosted on the server, was known as the database.

The various approaches to application development over the years can be categorized as follows:

- The traditional approach
- The client/server approach
- The component-based approach

In the traditional approach, a single application handled presentation logic, business logic, and database interactivity. These applications were also called *monolithic applications*. With no inherent advantages (being the only known method for application development), the drawback of this approach was that if even a minor change, extension, or enhancement was required in the application, the entire application had to be recompiled and integrated again. For example, a minor change in the database structure would require all functions or methods in the application to be changed. This made the cost of updating and redistributing the application very high.

The disadvantages of the traditional approach led to the introduction of the client/server architecture, which is also called the two-tier architecture. Subsequently, as the demand for faster and more efficient access to this information increased, further changes in application architecture provided a basis for the introduction of the three-tier architecture and the n-tier architecture. In the world of the Internet, two-tier, three-tier, and n-tier sound like complex terms, but they cannot be ignored. Therefore, let's understand these types of application architectures and their structures. Let's also understand the advantages of using different types of application architectures in Web applications before we move ahead in this chapter.

The Two-Tier Architecture

In this architecture, data is separated from the client side and is stored at a centralized location that acts as a server. Business logic is either combined with presentation logic in the form of applications at the client side, or business logic could be integrated into the database at the server side in the form of stored procedures. If business logic is combined with presentation logic at the client side, the client is called a *fat client*. Similarly, if business logic is combined with the database server, the server is called a *fat server*.

The use of the client/server architecture helped clearly segregate data from presentation or business logic. In other words, the data represented by the application is hosted on the client computer (the first tier) while the database is contained in the server computer (the second tier). Figure 1.3 represents the placement of the application and the database in the two-tier architecture.

There is no doubt that sharing resources and data was facilitated by the two-tier architecture; however, this approach also had a few drawbacks:

- The client computer was overburdened with the responsibility of performing all processing functionality while the server merely served as a traffic controller, facilitating the movement of data to and from the client and server computer. As a result, availability of resources was always a problem and the performance of the application suffered. Conversely, it could also be held that the server had to take the load of all the client applications trying to connect to the database in order to access or manipulate its data. Therefore, as we scale up the system by increasing the number of clients, we find a degradation in the performance of the server.

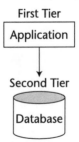

Figure 1.3   The two-tier architecture.

- Multiple data requests from the database increased network traffic. Often, bottleneck situations also led to a decline in application performance.

- Maintenance was another major issue. Any changes made to the application might necessitate considerable changes in the complete application architecture. In addition, every single client installation had to be synchronized with the others to ensure the use of the latest version of the application. This would necessitate recompilation of the application on each client. As a result, if the clients were spread far (in a wide area network), it also led to maintenance and deployment issues.

To address these problems and improve application performance and network traffic, the three-tier architecture was developed.

The Three-Tier Architecture

The only distinct change added to the three-tier architecture is the separation of presentation and business logic into two separate logical layers. As a result, this architecture is made up of three layers:

- The first tier or the presentation layer consists of the user interface to accept and post data sent by a user.

- The second tier or the business layer consists of the business logic that is essentially responsible for retrieval and processing of data.

- The third tier or the data layer consists of the database that functions as a data repository.

Figure 1.4 represents the placement of the three layers and the flow of data in a typical three-tier application architecture.

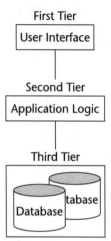

Figure 1.4 The three-tier architecture.

The preceding two types of application architecture were further enhanced with the introduction of the n-tier architecture. This type of architecture, as is evident from its nomenclature, incorporates further divisions of the middle-tier layer according to the application functionality. As a result, the application layer could be further divided to define presentation and business logic separately. Figure 1.5 represents the placement of the various layers in the n-tier application architecture.

The structure of n-tier architecture required the inclusion of multiple applications across different tiers. While n-tier applications on the one hand provided advantages in terms of low deployment costs, low database switching costs, low cost of business logic migration, and resource pooling and reuse, it also had problems in terms of degrading communication performance. This degradation was primarily due to the presence of too many tiers across which communication had to take place. In addition, the cost of maintenance in terms of significant increase in software installations, software upgrades, redeployment costs of applications, and administration costs was also very high. The component-based approach was designed to overcome these drawbacks of n-tier architectures. In the component-based approach, the middle tier was defined in terms of multiple business objects. In addition, generic interfaces were used to facilitate communication between these application objects. This approach to writing business objects using generic interfaces wherein an object is written to an interface is also known as interface-based programming. As a result, this type of architecture, called the component-based enterprise architecture, promoted standardization of business practices by the use of common business functions for the entire organization. The advantage of using such an architecture was that subsequent changes to the business rules did not affect the entire architecture, but only required changes to be made to

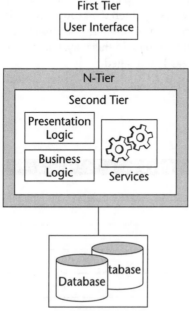

Figure 1.5 The n-tier architecture.

business objects and interfaces. Therefore, the enterprise architecture provided a foundation for the development of component technologies consisting of application-level, reusable business components.

Equipped with the basic knowledge of the Internet network and application architecture, let's look at the workings of the Internet.

How the Internet Works

The TCP/IP network protocol suite facilitates the exchange of information over the Internet. This suite is an amalgamation of Transmission Control Protocol (TCP) and Internet Protocol (IP) that provides the naming and addressing scheme for resources on the Internet. Because our aim is understanding Internet basics, we will not delve into the details of how TCP/IP protocols function. Because the naming and addressing scheme is a mandatory feature for accessing the Internet resources, let's understand its conventions and abbreviations.

The Internet Addressing Scheme

Today, the Internet is available not only at an organizational level but also to individuals from all lifestyles. The Internet is accessed and used by millions today, irrespective of age, caste, creed, and perspective. Considering the coverage, in terms of the vastness of its geographical area, the Internet is split into country-based domains. These domains control the functioning for a particular geography and are responsible for controlling, managing, and creating new domains within their boundaries. For example, the domain of Japan controls smaller domains, such as ac.jp and co.jp. As a result, if a group named VLSI needs a new domain named vlsi.ac.jp, then the group will seek permission from the governing ac.jp domain. Similarly, if the domain registration were for vlsi.co.jp, the domain providing permission would be co.jp. In this way, name conflicts are avoided and functioning of the domains is easily managed.

Table 1.1 describes some of the most commonly used worldwide geographical domain names.

Table 1.1   Common Geographical Domain Names

COUNTRY NAME	ABBREVIATION USED
Australia	au
Canada	ca
France	fr
The United Kingdom	uk
The United States of America	usa
India	in

Table 1.2 Classification of the Internet Domains

DOMAIN NAME	USED TO DESCRIBE A...
com	Commercial organization or a company
edu	Educational institution
mil	Military site
gov	Government organization or workgroup
net	Internet service provider or a network resource
org	Other nonprofit or noncommercial organization

In addition to this classification, domains are also allocated names based on their basic functioning. Table 1.2 describes some of the nongeographical domain names.

It is fairly simple to get connected to the Internet. Other than additional peripherals such as a modem and Internet-specific software, all that you need is to register with an Internet service provider (ISP). An ISP is a company that provides access to the Internet. The ISP usually provides the Internet-specific software. The common characteristics of a good ISP are these:

Accessibility. Because the preexisting telecommunication system is used to make an Internet connection, the ISP must have access to a local phone number. Provision for many numbers ensures easy availability of lines and avoids the frustration of redialing.

Software. The ISP should provide a CD-ROM used to install the software necessary to make a connection.

Support. The ISP should provide a 24-hour help line with the necessary technical support in case of problems or breakdowns.

Speed. The ISP should have a local access number to work with 28.8 Kbps, 33.6 Kbps, or 56 Kbps modems.

From the preceding discussion, we have understood that we need a computer, a modem, a telephone line, and the services of an ISP to connect to the Internet. Once we are connected, information on varied topics, such as technological guides, topic-specific data, and games are available at the click of a mouse button. Bear in mind that this information is stored in the form of documents spread over thousands of computers all over the Internet. How are these documents linked so that they are accessible on the Internet? They use the World Wide Web (WWW), an Internet service, as the architectural framework for accessing and linking these documents.

The World Wide Web

WWW is a common set of protocols that provides standards for computers to distribute documents on the Internet. As a result, the World Wide Web is composed of millions of information-holding documents or Web pages distributed on multiple servers popularly known as Web servers.

A Web page is a document created in HTML that includes text, graphics, hypertext links, and audio files. Hypertext Markup Language (HTML) was created as a subset of the Standard Generalized Markup Language (SGML) to serve documents over the Internet. HTML uses a simple textual format to create Web pages and contains commands in the form of tags. These tags specify the display format of the various elements of a document. A collection of Web pages under a specific individual or group is known as a Web site. Web sites are created to tender organizational information. Some other reasons for creating Web sites are these:

- The Internet provides an inexpensive but interactive mode of advertising for small businesses. All that you need to do is draw up some Web pages detailing the services provided by your organization. Thereafter, the address of the Web site, printed on business cards and brochure, acts as an excellent advertising medium. How does this help? Well, for one, it does save on time spent in verbal business promotion and advertising. Today, this task is taken over by the professionally designed text and images of corporate Web pages.

- Community groups use the Internet to offer information and recruit new members. A Web page can prove to be a useful way to reach out to a larger section of people. In addition, instead of arranging meetings, members can access internal updates about important events and schedules from a Web page.

- Personal or family pages provide glimpses of personal life that can include images of you at work, kids at play, personal possessions, and even pets. Can you think of a better way to ensure your grandma's participation at your birthday in absentia? All you need to do is create and host a Web page with pictures of the fun and frolic at the party.

NOTE To make a Web page available to everyone, you need to publish the site on a Web server. This is popularly known as Web hosting. Depending on the available financial resources and the size of your Web site, you can choose any of the following methods for publishing a site:

- You can use your own financial resources or the support of a strong financial partner/institution.

- You can acquire the services of your ISP to do the same. Most ISPs allocate some space to dedicated clients for a nominal fee.

- You can hire the services of a Web hosting service company to rent you Web space at reasonable rates.

The documents on the server are accessed through computers that use different platforms such as Unix, Windows 95, Windows 98, or Mac OS. As a result, applications at the client end use certain programs to facilitate the display of the Web pages in a standardized format. What aids are used to facilitate such standardization? Let's look at a new concept of Web browsers that facilitates a consistent display of Web pages.

Web Browsers

Web browsers are programs that communicate with the Web servers on the Internet, enabling the download and display of requested Web pages. Functionally, a Web browser interacts with both the Web server and the operating system of the computer on which it is running. As a result, the basic features of a Web browser call for a minimal understanding of HTML and the ability to display text. In recent years, with advances in the components of a Web page, the expectations from a Web browser have also increased multifold. As a result, a state-of-the-art Web browser today is able to provide support to complex Web pages with graphics, sound, video, and 3-D imaging.

The most popular Web browsers with the maximum industry support are Netscape Navigator and Microsoft Internet Explorer. Navigator supports a wide range of platforms such as Windows, Macintosh, and Unix. Internet Explorer, on the other hand, was originally designed for Microsoft products; but is also available for Macintosh and some Unix platforms today.

The display of the contents of a Web page depends solely on the choice of the browser. Therefore, Web applications need to support a standardized display of content regardless of the choice of the browser. As a result, an important feature of applications is *cross-browser support*, which ensures the uniform display of content independent of the browser or platform used. This feature of Web applications enables you to view pages in the correct format due to compatibility with both browsers, Navigator and Internet Explorer.

Because the browser runs on the client computer, it should contain components that facilitate the display of Web page contents. These components are a part of the browser window and are consistent in layout regardless of their brand. Let's look at the elements of a browser window.

Components of a Browser Window

The basic elements of a Web browser consist of the menu bar, toolbars, the address bar, the viewing window, and the status window. Most of you are familiar with universal elements, such as the menu bar, the viewing window, and the status bar, which are common to nearly all computer applications. The address bar is a browser-specific element that is used to specify the Uniform Resource Locator (URL) of the Web page. The URL contains the name and address of the requested Web page. Figure 1.6 depicts the contents of a Web page.

NOTE Observe and identify all the elements of the Web page. Notice the URL address specified in the address bar. It follows this format:

```
Protocol://host.domain.first-level domain/path/filename.extension.
```

As a result, in the preceding figure, the break up of the URL address http://www.microsoft.com/windows/ie/default.asp is as follows:

```
Protocol     =      http
Host         =      www
Domain       =      microsoft
```

```
First level domain    =    com
Path (directory)      =    windows
Filename              =    default.asp
```

We will discuss HTTP protocols in the later sections of the chapter.

How does a Web browser use a URL to access HTML documents? The process of accessing HTML documents (representing Web pages) is achieved through the following three steps:

1. The browser determines the protocol to be used.

2. The URL is used to contact the server.

3. The pathname and the filename are used to request the specific Web page from the server.

We now know that the client computer uses the browser to display the content of a Web page. We also know that when a Web page is hosted on the server, the client calls for a particular Web page on the server. When the Web server receives the client call, it responds by retrieving and sending the contents of the requested Web page back to the client. Can you visualize an ongoing interaction between the client and the server? Let's now look at the process of this interaction or information flow between the client and server by using a close-to-life example that'll help us understand the methodology adopted for a client/server communication in the Internet context.

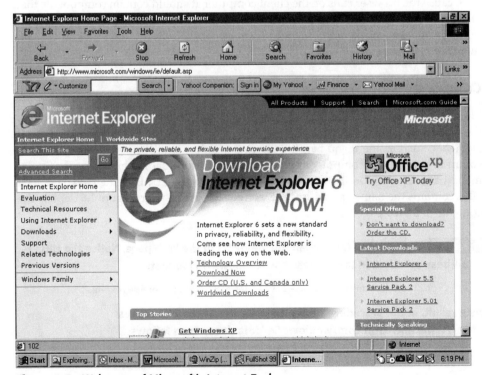

Figure 1.6   Web page of Microsoft's Internet Explorer.

Consider a situation in which you need to visit a snack bar near your office, in order to save the trouble of cooking dinner. To identify the steps of such an interaction, you need to list the events that take place in such an outlet. Let's sequentially list the process of ordering for a packed snack of a large burger with cheese and a soda.

1. You browse through the menu and then specify your choice of food to the attendant at the food counter.

2. Your order is communicated to the kitchen, which prepares and packs the requested food items.

3. Finally, you pay and take the pack home for your regular 5 o'clock snack.

Coming back to the computing scene, let's now relate this example to a client/ server interaction. The process of an interaction between a client and a server is not different from that of the preceding example. Let's sequentially list the steps of an interaction between the client and the server during an online call for a shopping site catalog.

1. The client represented by the browser requests information such as the shopping catalog to choose the items to be purchased.

2. The call for the catalog is communicated to the server.

3. The server uses the URL provided to search for the specific catalog.

4. The shopping catalog is retrieved by the server and sent back to the client for display in the browser window.

In both these examples, there was a precise *request* from the client end of the interaction, represented by the customer, that was duly communicated and answered in the form of a valid *response* from the server end.

In the case of Web applications, Hypertext Transfer Protocol (HTTP) is used to facilitate the exchange of information and data between the client and the server. HTTP is based on the request-response phenomenon in which the client (represented by the browser) sends a request to the server (represented by the Web server). A typical HTTP transaction between a Web browser and a Web server will take place in the following manner:

1. A TCP/IP connection is established between the client (browser) and the server.

2. The browser sends a request for a particular HTML page.

3. The server locates the file and sends a response in the form of the text content of the requested page.

4. The TCP/IP connection is closed.

Figure 1.7 depicts the interaction between a client and a server.

HTTP uses explicit methods and specifications to structure both the request and the response messages. Let's now look at the specifications used by the client and the server during an HTTP request-response cycle.

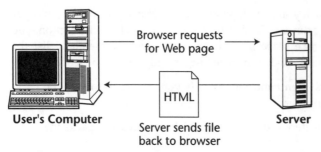

Figure 1.7   The HTTP request-response cycle.

The HTTP Request

The HTTP request is sent to the server along with the URL of the requested page, which is typed in the address location bar of the browser. The standard methods of HTTP 1.1 used to specify the type of user request are GET, POST, HEAD, OPTIONS, PUT, DELETE, TRACE, and CONNECT. Of these, with the Java Servlet and Java Server Pages perspective, only the former two are generally used.

The GET Method

The GET method is the simplest and most frequently used method to request a static resource with inert contents, such as an HTML page. This method is simple because merely typing the URL of the requested Web page while surfing the Net invokes the GET method. As a result, a statement such as `http://www.mysportspage/index.htm` is a request made using the GET method to fetch the specified page contents from the Web server. In addition to a simple page request, the GET method can also be used to include additional information. Such additional information is passed as a query parameter that is appended to the URL of the Web page. For instance, at any Web shopping site, have you ever noticed the URL string when you send your logon information for validation? Or, better still, have you noticed the change in the URL string on the status bar when you open your mailbox at the end of the day? The URL address is appended with a string set apart with a "?". The URL is something like this:

```
http://www.URLAddress.com?login=yourLoginName
```

The query parameter in such a case serves as a dynamic search criterion that is used to send parameter-specific content.

The POST Method

The POST method is used to request a dynamic resource that requires sending large amounts of data as request parameters for the server. Unlike the parameters in the GET method, the parameters in this method are contained within the body of the request.

Because a request parameter can contain any amount of text, the POST method can be used to upload even huge binary and text files.

An advantage of using the GET method, despite the restriction in the size of the parameter, is that such requests can be used as bookmarks, which can be saved for visits to the same site in the future. All through the book, we'll use these request modes to access pages and retrieve data according to specific parameters.

We have so far discussed Internet basics, application architecture, use of Web browsers, and the HTTP request-response model to help the exchange of data between the browser and the Web server.

Finally, before concluding the discussion on Internet basics, let's quickly recap Internet services. These services pave the way to endless hours of engrossed activity that could include most, if not all, of the following:

Browsing or surfing the Net.   This is an action that is related to a fun or educational spree that involves searching for specific pages of information, chatting, or participating in forum discussions.

Sending and reading mail messages.   This is a nonintrusive, instantaneous means of communication. It uses specific software that can be used to send and receive electronic mail (email) messages at leisure without any time restrictions. Both Navigator (using Messenger mailbox) and Internet Explorer (using Outlook Express) integrate email and provide email as freeware during installation.

Transferring files.   The File Transfer Protocol (FTP) service facilitates transfer of binary files in the form of programs or documents. FTP is mostly used as a protocol to upload or download files.

Downloading files.   This is the most popular form of file transfer, which involves simply clicking a link on a Web page. The link may be in the form of an icon or underlined, blue text that contains the URL of the Web site. A common downloading activity is implemented when acquiring copies of shareware, freeware, or specific software drivers.

Uploading files.   Such a methodology is adopted to place Web pages on the Internet and make them accessible to all Internet users. Before uploading files, you need have access to a Web server or host that provides the base directory to store your files. This method of transferring is used for files with complex and bulky contents, which cannot be transferred by any other means.

Shopping on the net.   This Internet service allows commercial enterprises to use the electronic media to facilitate business transactions. These transactions use the Electronic Fund Transfer (EFT) to conduct the day-to-day business of buying and selling various items and products such as gifts, stocks, software, and other consumer products.

Words cannot express the amount of information that is made available to all who link to this huge network of networks, aptly called the Internet. A network of connections, backed by computers, a few gadgets, and professional services, has made life more interactive and the world almost devoid of any physical boundaries.

Summary

With the growth and success of the Internet, almost everything is possible today. Mailing, searching for information, shopping, playing games, chatting with friends—name it and you have it at the click of a mouse button.

This chapter has primarily dealt with technologies, methodologies, and tools associated with the Internet. The chapter described the change-of-scene brought about by the advent of the Internet. We began by tracing the origin of Internet from the solitary stand-alone computer to the current gigantic network of computers. We learned how the Internet application architecture changed to facilitate the flow of information from the client to the server. The information stored on the Web server was in the form of documents known as Web pages that could be accessed by numerous computers linked to the Internet. Bearing in mind the disparity of platforms, browsers were used to standardize the display format of the Web page contents. In addition, standard protocols in the form of the HTTP request-response cycle further facilitated exchange of information across the client and server ends.

In addition to the early Internet applications, in the form of email and FTP, new Internet applications, such as Internet telephony and conferencing, have proved the marvel of technology in life today. Nonetheless, the wonder of the Internet and its popularity continue to attract people to their computers each day. People from far-off states, cities, towns, and villages, are today connected to each other via this network known as the Internet. At this juncture, it would not be incorrect to state that the Internet is an invention that is here to stay—and stay it will, for a very long time.

The topics in this chapter covered the basics of Internet and the working of the World Wide Web. The next chapter is an introduction to the Internet-and Java-based component technology called Java Server Pages.

CHAPTER

2

Introducing Java Server Pages

OBJECTIVES:

In this chapter, you will learn to do the following:

- ✔ Understand the role of Java Server Pages
- ✔ Identify the stages of the JSP life cycle
- ✔ Identify the advantages of using JSP
- ✔ Set up the J2EE environment

Getting Started

The marvel of the Internet needs no introduction. Nevertheless, the world definitely seems to be shrinking every day, thanks to the ever-increasing power of the Internet. People across geographical borders are now able to share and exchange ideas, views, and information by using the Internet. To keep pace with the "world at your doorstep" phenomenon, information on the Net needs to change in accordance with changes around the world. As a result, changes in stock prices, exchange rates, discount rates, and prices of daily-use items on the Net need to be constantly updated. With the advent of the Internet, the rather primitive, monolithic application architecture changed to the networked, component-based, multitiered, client/server architecture. As a result of this change, the need for server-side scripting gradually began to dominate aspects of Web programming.

Why was there a need for server-side scripting? The requirement can be substantiated in response to the following questions. Would you like to visualize the Internet as a dull, lifeless, and uninteresting medium, where you are forced to view Web pages in the same format and with the same content every day? Would you revisit sites on the Net that host such Web pages? Or, for that matter, evaluate the plight of organizations such as newspaper agencies whose core business is to monitor and print news events by the minute all around the world every day. Can you relate to the importance of dynamism in Web pages? Dynamism, which allows the incorporation of changes on a daily basis! To understand the need for this technology, let's consider the following example of a simple Web page.

Consider a Web interaction such as the process of registering on any Web site—say, for a free subscription to newsletters. The input information accepted from the customer is in the form of personal details, such as first name and last name, and details pertaining to the individual's organization. The customer is also simultaneously expected to choose an ID to use to log on to the Web site. After filling in the registration details, when the user clicks the submit button, the page along with the data in it is forwarded to the Web server for processing.

Understand that an infinite number of registrations are received each day. It is therefore important to validate the login ID as a part of processing. This will eliminate the possibility of assigning duplicate, invalid, or null values for the user ID. Data processing, though, need not be limited to such validations only. In addition to checking for the correctness of the ID format, validations also need to check for the authenticity of the ID. In such a case, comparing and matching the entered values against those contained in the database authenticate the user ID.

Even so, if the processes of validating and authenticating the login ID are to be managed by the server alone, the server is unnecessarily overloaded. An overloaded server, in turn, slows down processing speed, which slows down the network.

As a step toward reducing the overhead on the server and the network, validations such as checking for blank fields and negative or invalid values can be done at the client side itself. This type of processing on the client side is achieved through small programs written using client-side scripts. VBScript and JavaScript are two languages used for client-side scripting. On the other hand, due to the installation of the database on the Web server, or on a different tier, the process of authenticating the value of the ID needs to be done on the server side. Tasks such as this and those that require processing of data on the Web server are achieved through small programs written by using server-side scripts. Java Server Pages (JSP), Active Server Pages (ASP), servlets, PHP, and Perl are some examples of server-side scripting languages. In this way, continuing to boost the hype and success associated with the name "Internet," scripting languages helped to make Web pages of a Web application dynamic. The introduction of such scripting languages helped to reduce and simplify the complexities involved in the creation and management of dynamic Web pages.

Microsoft was the first to introduce Active Server Pages (ASP) in order to capture the market for server-side scripting. Subsequently, Sun introduced Java Server Pages (JSP), a core component of the Java 2 Enterprise Edition, to use the existing Java technology and further add functionality and flexibility to server-side Web applications. Sun Microsystems was founded in 1982, and from the very beginning, its watchword "The Network Is the Computer" has helped reiterate its stand on the importance of networking in computers. In keeping with its singular vision and constant endeavor of adding improvement and innovation to the Internet services, Sun introduced Java technology in 1995. This platform-neutral technology has enabled developers to write applications once and run the same application on any computer supporting the Java Virtual Machine (JVM). This became Sun's USP, which we all know as "Write Once, Run Anywhere" paradigm. With the introduction of JSP as a part of the Java technology, the functionality and extensibility of Web applications have increased multifold.

This chapter introduces the Java technology-based Java Server Pages, which has created quite a stir in the world of Web application development. The later sections of the chapter will discuss the life cycle of a JSP page, followed by a comparison of JSP with existing technologies. Throughout the book, we'll use a scenario-based, task-oriented approach to develop applications by using JSP. To support the creation and implementation of the applications, we'll need to set up the JSP environment. As a result, the final sections of this chapter discuss the JSP environment, the installation process, and the deployment of the server for executing JSP applications.

Java Server Pages

The preceding sections have highlighted that JSP has made the best use of the robust Java technology, which has facilitated the creation of platform-independent, dynamic server-side programs for Web applications. How is JSP different from other server-side scripting languages? What is the basic principle of a JSP page? Which is the foremost and basic feature of JSP that has contributed to its acceptance as a technology to develop faster and efficient Web applications? To understand and answer these questions, let's look at a typical Web page. Recall that the content of a Web page does not include only dynamic content. A typical Web application consists of two types of content, static and dynamic. Static content represents the presentation logic used to design the structure of a Web page in terms of the page layout, color, and text. Dynamic content represents the business logic that symbolizes the application's business rules and diagnostics in the form of financial and business calculations or data retrieval from a database. The nature of such computations and data retrievals could change from one point of time to another, thereby rendering them dynamic. Ideally, it is the job of a Web designer to code for the static presentation content by using HTML. The Web developer or programmer, on the other hand, uses Java and other programming languages to code for the dynamic business content.

While developing Web applications, time was often lost in situations where the developer, conversant with scripting languages, was required to write the code for the static HTML content. Similarly, imagine the plight of a designer whose basic HTML skills were put aside when he or she was expected to write Java code snippets for business logic. How can we optimize the disparate skills of designers and developers to the fullest?

No problem! The criterion behind the introduction of JSP was to use a technology that could minimize the diligent task of a programmer, whose skills are wasted in programming for both the static and dynamic aspects of content. This technology helped segregate the work profiles of the Web designer, who is responsible for static content generation, and the Web developer, who is responsible for dynamic content generation. As a result, each of them is able to use his or her expertise and add value to the content of the application. A Web designer could design and formulate the layout for a Web page by using HTML. A Web developer, on the other hand, working independently, could use Java code and other JSP-specific content to code for the business logic. The simultaneous construction of static and dynamic content added flexibility to application development and facilitated the development of quality applications with increased productivity.

Of course, the success of this approach to developing Web applications is drawn through the features of JSP that have helped application developers build rapid, platform-independent Web applications. The features of JSP that have contributed to its acceptance as an attractive alternative to other scripting languages are these:

Platform independence.   The use of JSP adds versatility to a Web application by enabling its execution on any computer.

Enhanced performance.   The compilation process in JSP, as discussed in the later sections, produces faster results or output.

Separation of logic from display.   The use of JSP permits the HTML-specific static content and a mixture of HTML, Java, and JSP-specific dynamic content to be placed in separate files.

Ease of development.   The use of JSP eliminates the need for high-level technical expertise, thereby helping Web developers, designers, content creators, and content managers to work together and develop Java-based applications in less time and with less effort.

Ease of use.   All JSP applications run on major Web servers and operating systems, including Microsoft IIS, Netscape Enterprise Server, iPlanet Web Server, and Apache Web Server. These applications are also available on Windows NT, Windows 2000, and Solaris 7.

JSP Life Cycle

JSP is an extension of the Java Servlet technology. This technology is based on the typical Internet application model; it uses Java objects to receive Web requests and subsequently builds and sends back appropriate responses to the browser. As a result, the compilation of an JSP page generates a servlet that incorporates all servlet functionality. If JSP incorporates the features of Java Servlet technology, why was there a need to reintroduce JSP technology?

NOTE Chapter 3, "Servlet Basics," is a brief overview of Java Servlet technology that will help you understand the features and workings of servlets.

The following example can be used to illustrate the need to introduce JSP and its advantages over servlets. Consider a servlet application whose development is interrupted due to a project-related decision that requires making changes to the application content. The main cause for this disarray is the fact that a servlet application consists of both static and dynamic content in a single file. Bear in mind that the business logic cannot be changed because changes in the embedded code will require recompilation. As a result, in such situations the developer is forced to make changes to the presentation logic. In contrast, if the same application were developed using JSP, the changes to the static content would call for the skills of a Web designer to turn out the required changes in the application. In addition, changes to the business content could also be put together, aided by the skills of the Web developer.

As a result of the segregation of work profiles or the functionality of the Web designer and the Web developer, JSP ensures the maximum utilization rather than a nonfruitful use of individual skills. Therefore, the developer responsible for coding the business logic does not necessarily need to review and refine the output of the static HTML content.

We have discussed the role of JSP in adding dynamism and efficiency to Web applications. How does the efficiency of an application improve by the use of JSP? To understand this, let's discuss the compilation process of a JSP page.

JSP architecture is quite similar to Web architecture. You may recall that the client or the browser in Web architecture sends a request to the server, and the server acknowledges the request and responds to it. Similarly, the compilation of a JSP page also builds a request and a response cycle that consists of two phases, the translation phase and the request-processing phase. When the client or the browser requests a particular JSP page (identified by the extension .jsp), the server, in turn, sends a request to the JSP engine. The translation phase is initiated, and the JSP engine, or the JSP container as it is called, compiles the corresponding translation unit (contains the JSP page and other dependent files, if any). Then, the JSP engine automatically generates a servlet. Internally, this results in the creation of a class file for the JSP page that implements the servlet interface. During the request-processing phase, the response is generated according to the request specifications. The servlet then sends back the response corresponding to the request received.

It is important to understand that the automatic servlet generation is responsible for improving the efficiency and speed of JSP applications. The speed of an application is proportional to the time taken to display the response content in the browser. It has been proven that this span of time is much less in the case of JSP applications because the first time a JSP page is called, the servlet code is generated, compiled, and loaded on to the server. The generated servlet is not destroyed at the end of the response but remains active and continues to process all the subsequent requests for the particular page. As a result, this methodology helps save time that is otherwise lost in reloading a servlet for each request and recompiling it every time that it is loaded. This is applicable only if no modifications are made to the source page. As a result, if the source JSP page is modified, it is automatically compiled and reloaded for the next request.

Figure 2.1 represents the flow of events that occur after a client requests a JSP page.

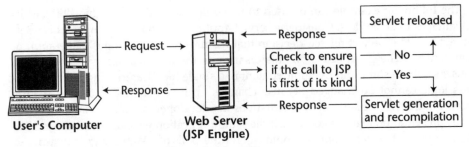

Figure 2.1   The request-response cycle for a JSP page.

Comparing JSP with Existing Technologies

JSP is Sun Microsystems' answer to server-side programming. Therefore, there is a general tendency to compare it with equivalent competitive products. Here is a brief comparative study of JSP-and servlets and JSP and ASP.

JSP and Servlets

A JSP file, when compiled, generates a servlet; however, despite their similarities, a JSP file is much easier to deploy because the JSP engine performs the recompilation for the Java code automatically. JSP also aims to relieve the programmers from coding for servlets by auto-generation of servlets during the compilation of a JSP page. As a result, servlets and JSP share common features, such as platform independence, creation of database-driven Web applications, and server-side programming capabilities. There are also some basic differences between servlets and JSP, though.

Performance

The following are the differences between the performance of a servlet and a JSP page:

- Servlets tie up files to handle the static presentation logic and the dynamic business logic independently. An HTML file is used for the static content and a Java file for the dynamic content. Due to this, a change made to any file requires the recompilation of the corresponding servlet.

- JSP, on the other hand, allows Java code to be embedded directly into an HTML page by using special tags. The HTML content and the Java content can also be placed in separate files. As a result, any changes made to the HTML content are automatically compiled and loaded onto the server.

Efficiency

The following are the differences between the efficiency of a servlet and a JSP page:

- Servlet programming involves extensive coding. Therefore, any change made to the code requires identification of static code content and dynamic code content for the designer and the developer to effect changes respectively. This facilitates the incorporation of the changes.

- On the other hand, a JSP page, by virtue of the separate placement of static and dynamic content, allows both Web developers and Web designers to work independently.

JSP and ASP

The comparison between JSP and ASP is rather interesting because these technologies are both similar and dissimilar in many respects. Both technologies provide a simple yet fast method to create dynamic Web pages. Both aim at separating static and dynamic content in order to segregate the work profiles of Web designers and developers. While JSP uses Java as a medium to write the code for dynamic content, ASP uses Visual Basic or other Microsoft-compatible languages. Java, by virtue of its acceptance as a Web application language, is more versatile, powerful, and a full-fledged programming language, and easier to comprehend. A major difference between the two technologies is that JSP is implemented as a part of J2EE while ASP uses the Internet Services Application Programming Interface (ISAPI). In addition to this, Java-based JSP is platform independent with respect to its compatibility with JVM-enabled operating systems and Web servers (non-Microsoft) while ASP is a solution for server-side scripting on the Windows platform.

Because we aim to learn to develop applications in JSP and to ease this rather precarious tug-of-war situation, let's list the main strengths of JSP.

Portability

The following are the differences between the portability of ASP and JSP applications:

- A portable application is flexible because it is machine, operating system and server independent. As a result, such applications can be shared between developers. The "Write Once, Run Anywhere" phenomenon offers JSP applications an inimitable, platform-independent reusability. Accordingly, JSP can be deployed on several servers, browsers, and tools.

- On the contrary, ASP is a Microsoft product that can be deployed mainly on Windows NT, and is therefore restricted in its scope.

Considering its support for the Apache Web Server, which hosts a major percentage of the world's Web sites, it is merely a matter of time before JSP is also able to use the strong Unix platform.

Performance

The following are the differences between the performance of ASP and JSP applications:

- The compilation or translation phase of a JSP page is such that once generated, the servlet class for a particular JSP page remains in the server memory. As a result, a subsequent request for the same JSP page does not require reloading and recompiling. The response time of a JSP page is therefore very short.

- On the other hand, a first-time or subsequent request for an ASP page requires continuous recompilation, which increases response time.

Deployment

The following are the differences between deployment of ASP and JSP applications:

- JSP components, such as JavaBeans and custom tags, help isolate the page design from the programming logic of a Web page. Such an approach to application development gives more leverage to the individual, skill-based profile of Web designers and developers. Just visualize the flexibility and extensibility that can be added to such applications, where designers concentrate on static content generation while developers program for the generation of the dynamic content.

- Although ASP is dependent on Microsoft's COM/DCOM components, developing such applications is quite a complex process as compared to the easy development and deployment of components (JavaBeans) using Java.

Though most of the features are similar in both ASP and JSP, a widely acclaimed fact remains that JSP does provide a sturdy and scalable platform for development of Web applications. The only major criterion, call it hurdle if you wish, is the Java expertise required to create these applications. Another point of view uses the strength of the enterprise as the basis for choosing between ASP and JSP. Accordingly, experts state that if an enterprise is small and the main programming expertise of its employees is in a language other than Java, then choose ASP. If the enterprise is large and the primary skill set of the employees is Java, then choose JSP. In this way, you can benefit from the features and advantages of this technology in the development of Web applications.

There is no need to reiterate that JSP provides a very exciting and productive working relationship between Web developers and designers. So immense is its acceptance that almost all major vendors of application servers have stood in firm support of this Java-based technology.

Let's now look at the platform that has provided the backdrop for the success and acclaim of JSP. Although Java, as a programming language, is rather new and young, it has always been associated with efforts to provide standards for the component-based, enterprise applications. As a result, one of the foremost technologies to be associated with Java is the Java 2 Platform, Enterprise Edition (J2EE). What exactly are the technologies provided by the J2EE platform for developing components? They are Web components, servlets, and Java Server Pages. The Web component technology includes a Web container and an EJB container, which provide the run time environment for application components. The Web container is used to host Java servlets and JSP pages. The EJB container, on the other hand, hosts the Enterprise JavaBean components.

NOTE Because this book is based on the JSP technology, we will not discuss the EJB container.

This book primarily involves deployment of JSP applications on the J2EE server. Let's now discuss the steps of setting up the J2EE environment.

Setting Up the J2EE Environment

Problem Statement

Kayson's Software Solutions and the members of the administrative body of Banco de Glendanthi had several discussions before they decided on the technology to be used for developing their Web application. In course of the brainstorming discussions to evaluate all available technologies, the technical team has decided to use Java Server Pages to develop the bank's Web site. All computers in the bank have the Windows NT 4.0 operating system.

Shane, a member of Kayson's technical team, has been delegated to help the technical executives of the bank acquaint themselves with the platform to be used to execute the developed Web application. To do this, a JSP environment needs to be set up on the banking premises. The first such environment will be set up at the office in New York. Let's identify the tasks to be performed to set up the JSP environment.

Task List

✔ **Verify the hardware configuration of the computers.**

✔ **Identify the components to be installed.**

✔ **Install the Java Development Kit.**

✔ **Install the server.**

✔ **Set up the environment.**

✔ **Test the server.**

Verify the Hardware Configuration of the Computers

Before beginning the installation, let's confirm the hardware configuration required to execute the Banco de Glendanthi application. Table 2.1 displays the machine specifications.

Table 2.1   JSP Machine Specifications

HARDWARE	SPECIFICATIONS
Processor	Pentium or faster processor
RAM	64MB of available RAM (128MB recommended) Acceptable performance was observed on a HP-Vectra VE corporate-class PC with a Pentium III processor (650 mhz.) and 256MB RAM.
HDD	128GB
Mouse	MS mouse or compatible
Monitor	SVGA monitor
Other hardware components	Video card displaying more than 256 colors and CD-ROM drive
Operating system	Windows NT 4.0 with Service Pack 6.0

Identify the Components to Be Installed

The following components need to be installed:

- Java Development Kit (v 1.3)
- Java 2 SDK, Enterprise Edition (v 1.2.1)

Install the Java Development Kit

Verify that JDK 1.3 is installed on the computers before installing the server. If JDK1.3 is not installed, use the Sun Microsystems site to download this freeware.

> **NOTE** Use the Sun site to download JDK 1.3 freeware from the following URL: http://java.sun.com/j2se/1.3/. Alternately, the software can also be installed from a CD. When using the CD for installation, double-click the setup icon and from the dialog boxes, then select the default settings.
>
> *Freeware* is software that is distributed by disk, through BBS systems and the Internet, free. There is no charge for using it, and it can be distributed freely as long as the use it is put to follows the license agreement included with it.

To install JDK from the Sun site, double-click the URL and simply follow the installation steps listed. On the other hand, to install from a CD, do the following:

1. Double-click the JDK1.3 icon.

2. Accept all default settings prompted by the dialog boxes that are displayed throughout the installation.

3. Complete the installation by clicking the finish button of the concluding dialog box.

Install the Server

Once the Java Development Kit is installed, you can download the Java 2 SDK, Enterprise Edition that will install the preferred J2EE server.

NOTE You can download JSP environments from the following site: http://java.sun.com/products/jsp/download.html. Alternately, the software can also be installed by using a CD.

The steps for the installation remain the same as those shown previously except for changes in the software icon and the appearance of the displayed dialog boxes.

Set the Environment

An important task faced by developers before implementing JSP applications is to set up the various environment variables. The environment variables that require settings are PATH, CLASSPATH, J2EE_HOME, and JAVA_HOME. These variable settings help to inform the server and the compiler about the placement of the JDK and J2SDKEE software components and the various Java and servlet classes. Any deviations from the standard formats of the environment variable settings result in errors and nonexecution of the application.

Table 2.2 displays the settings that need to be specified for various environment variables.

Table 2.2   The Environment Variable Settings

ENVIRONMENT VARIABLE	SETTING TO BE SPECIFIED	SPECIFIES
PATH	`%PATH%; C:\j2sdkee1.2.1\bin;`	The location of the downloaded or installed j2sdkee bundle.
CLASSPATH	`%CLASSPATH%; C:\j2sdkee1.2.1\lib\ j2ee.jar;`	The location of Java class files or Java classes. If unspecified, Java refers to the current directory and the standard system libraries for class references.
JAVA_HOME	`C:\jdk1.3.0_02;`	The absolute path of the installed JDK directory.
J2EE_HOME	`C:\j2sdkee1.2.1;`	The absolute path of the installed j2sdkee directory.

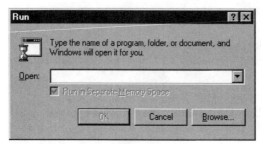

Figure 2.2   The Run dialog box.

It is important to remember that when specifying the values of the environment variable, you typically use two distinct symbols. The first symbol is the semicolon (;), which you use to separate directories when specifying multiple directories. The second symbol is the percentage sign (%), which you use if the variable is already set and you only need to append the current specifications. You can set the environment variables either from the command prompt or by using the System Properties dialog box. To set the properties at the command prompt, do the following:

1. Click Start, Run to open the Run dialog box. Figure 2.2 shows the Run dialog box.

2. In the Open text box, type **cmd**, which is the abbreviation for command prompt. Figure 2.3 shows the Open text box of the Run dialog box.

3. Click OK to open the DOS prompt window. Figure 2.4 shows the DOS prompt window.

4. Type each of the individual environment variable settings one after the other by prefixing each setting with the word "SET." For example, to set the PATH variable, type the following line at the DOS prompt:

```
SET PATH=%PATH%; C:\j2sdkee1.2.1\bin
```

5. Press Enter to save the setting and display the prompt once more.

To set the properties by using the System Properties dialog box:

1. On the desktop, right-click My Computer to display the shortcut menu.

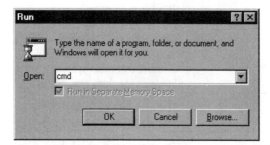

Figure 2.3   The Open text box.

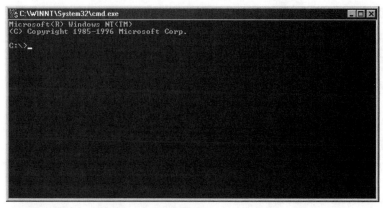

Figure 2.4   The DOS prompt window.

2. Select Properties to open the System Properties dialog box. Figure 2.5 shows the System Properties dialog box.

3. Select the Environment tab to display the list of system and user-defined variables.

4. Select any system variable; edit its name and value in the Variable and Value text boxes, respectively. If a particular environment variable is already defined, simply append the specific setting at the end of the earlier definition. Figure 2.6 shows the specification for the CLASSPATH setting in the System Properties dialog box.

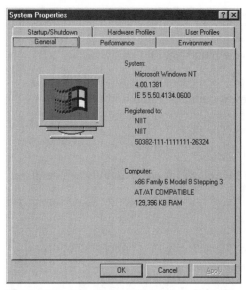

Figure 2.5   The System Properties dialog box.

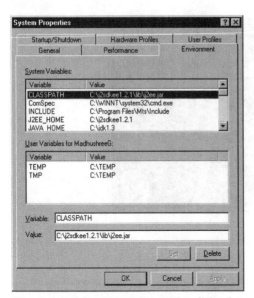

Figure 2.6   The System Properties dialog box with the CLASSPATH settings.

5. Type and set the values for each of the environment variables as specified in Table 2.2.

6. Click Apply to save the values of the settings.

7. Click OK to close the System Properties dialog box.

Alternately, you can also follow these steps in order to open the System Properties dialog box:

1. Click Start, Settings, Control Panel to open the Control Panel window.

2. Double-click the System icon to open the System Properties dialog box.

3. Type and set the value for each of the environment variables.

Test the Server

To test the installation of the server, type the following command at the command prompt:

```
start j2ee -verbose
```

The verbose option displays a list of all the steps that are executed at server startup. Figure 2.7 displays the executable steps of server startup.

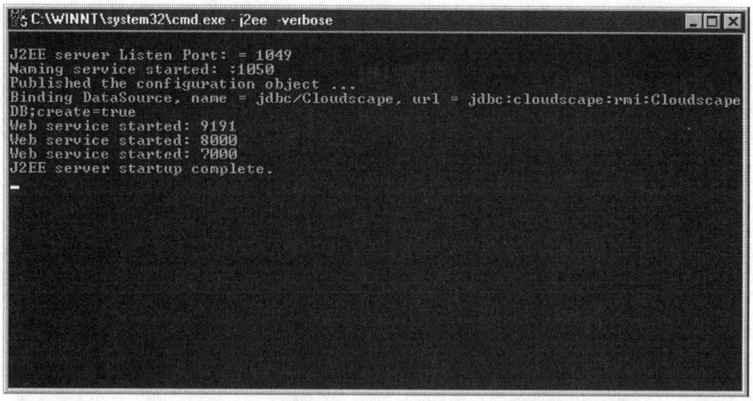

Figure 2.7 The j2ee server startup.

NOTE Please remember to shut down the server at the end of sessions. Merely closing the command prompt window does not shut down the J2EE server. Instead, at the command prompt, type the following line:

```
j2ee -stop
```

The JSP applications are allocated specific ports for execution, which are listed at server startup. Most programmers prefer to use the 8000 port. To check for the successful installation of the server and the settings of the environment variables, follow these steps:

1. Start Internet Explorer to open the Web browser.
2. In the address box, type:

```
http://localhost:8000
```

Figure 2.8 displays the default J2EE home page that signifies the successful server installation and startup. Congratulations! You are now ready to view the output of JSP applications by using the J2EE platform.

NOTE If you are working in a networked environment that uses a proxy server, you may encounter the "Page not found" error. In such a case, for the successful display of the J2EE default page, you'll need to change the Internet options to explicitly bypass proxy settings.

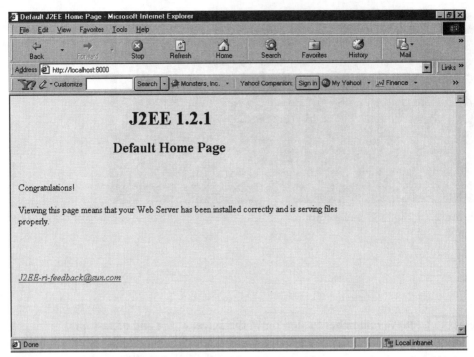

Figure 2.8 The J2EE default home page.

Summary

The popularity of the Internet and the e-business boom have resulted in an increase in the demand for fast and dependable Web applications. A powerful solution to meet and fulfill such a demand is JSP, the Java-based, JSP technology of Sun Microsystems.

The contents of this chapter have explicitly brought out the features of JSP, which have earned wide support from most vendors of application servers. We also discussed how the inclusion of servlet technology in the JSP compilation process has enhanced the speed, efficiency, and robustness of JSP applications. In addition, we used a comparative study of JSP and existing server-side technologies to highlight the advantages of using JSP for coding Web applications.

Installations for JSP require specific settings of environment variables. As a result, simply installing the necessary software components will not guarantee successful execution of a JSP application. Keeping this constraint in mind, we used a task-based, step-by-step installation guide for installing the JSP components and setting the various environment variables.

By the end of this chapter, most of you were all set and prepared to begin creating JSP pages. More so, because the only prerequisite required is the knowledge of HTML and Java. Nonetheless, for Java programmers, the shift from developing applications in Java to doing so in JSP calls for little HTML help in order to design the presentation part of the application.

JSP, as an extension of servlet technology, calls for a brief overview of the workings of servlets. As a result, in the next chapter, we will discuss concepts of servlet programming.

CHAPTER 3

Servlet Basics

OBJECTIVES:

In this chapter, you will learn to do the following:

- ✔ Identify the various components of the Java Servlet architecture
- ✔ Distinguish between the three phases of the servlet life cycle
- ✔ Create a servlet to display the hit count of a Web site

Getting Started

It is established beyond doubt that much of the speed and efficiency of JSP applications is due to the servlet generation that is implicit, internal, and automatic. As a result, JSP is often expressed as an extension of the servlet technology. Before we delve into an overview of servlets, let's try to recreate the Web scenario and the information flow from and to the browser to understand the need for servlets.

You'll agree that as Internet users, we tend to overlook the behind-the-scene complexities in a Web interaction. Complex, because these interactions do not merely involve sending requests and obtaining corresponding responses. In the preceding chapters, we discussed the importance of the request-response cycle in regulating information traffic between the browser and the server. Simultaneously, it is important to understand that although both the browser and the server are HTTP compliant, the formats of the browser request and the server response are different. The request sent from the browser is in HTML while the response is generated in HTTP. How then do the two sides interact on a common platform? What medium do they use to reach uniformity in the mode of communication? A simple example can explain the workings of and need for such an interface.

People from across the world speak different languages. Despite the diversity in language, communication has never faced a setback because people take the initiative to learn other languages or use the expertise of a translator. The translator helps to maintain communication between people speaking diverse languages. As a result, the translator serves as a resource or medium for interpreting one language to the other. Similarly, in the case of Internet communication, utilizing the services of a mediating component can facilitate such an interaction. The function of this component is to interpret the diverse formats into those understood by the browser and the server.

As a result, the request in HTML is converted to the server-understandable HTTP format while the HTTP response is subsequently converted to a browser-understandable HTML format. How and where does the format interchange between the browser programs and server take place?

It is interesting to note that the interpretation is facilitated by a standard phenomenon and takes place at the server side only. This standard, provided originally by the Common Gateway Interface (CGI), serves as a mediating interface that facilitates information exchanges between the client and the server. CGI is the technology used to overcome the difference between the HTML-supporting system (browser) and the HTTP-supporting system (Web server). Figure 3.1 illustrates the function of CGI in a typical request-response cycle.

Initially CGI programs were written in C, which is the traditional third-generation language. Subsequently, with advances in language availability, the choice of the language for CGI programs moved to another interpretable language, Practical Extraction and Reporting Language (PERL). PERL became the language of choice for server-side scripting because of its powerful text processing, pattern matching, and text parsing commands. Today CGI can be written in almost every language, including Java. With the help of available languages, CGI programs could synchronize the request-response communication format. Despite this, programmers were presented with problems that hampered both the speed and the efficiency of the applications.

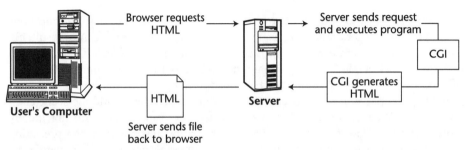

Figure 3.1 The CGI-based request-response cycle.

Speed. The processing of a browser request using the CGI model was slow. At the end of every request-response cycle the CGI program which was so far running as a process got terminated and de-allocated from the server memory and had to be restarted from scratch. Therefore, for every request from the browser, a corresponding new CGI program needed to be started. For example, a popular Web page is being accessed by thousands of browsers from different clients. It entails filling up a HTML form and then pressing the SUBMIT button. Pressing the SUBMIT button from each of these innumerable browsers results in a call to a server-side CGI script and each such call results in a separate executing instance of the same CGI script starting up in memory as a separate process. Imagine if a different set of browsers initiate a call to a different server-side CGI script. The result would be thousands of processes running in memory (they may actually be representative of a few CGI programs after all) and a stage would come when too many processes would clog up the memory on the server and increase the load on the server CPU. This in fact proved to be the proverbial millstone around the neck for CGI scripts. In addition, the tasks performed by the programs, such as opening database connections or establishing links with other resources, also had to be repeated. Calls made to a Web page requested earlier were also no exception to this type of processing.

Efficiency. The merging of static presentation logic and dynamic business logic proved to affect the turnout time for the application development. The Web designer primarily developed the static HTML content while the Web developer developed the dynamic code specific content. As a result, changes to any of the contents resulted in the need for changes to be made to both contents that had to be incorporated one at a time and executed individually to check for errors.

In order to ease these problems, subsequent changes were made to CGI programs. The aim was to enhance the processing speed and productivity of application development with the introduction of fast CGI; however, this too did not prove to be of much help. The problems were finally resolved by means of servlet technology and templating systems. The former helped to enhance request-processing speed while the latter helped to segregate HTML from business logic. Microsoft's Active Server Pages (ASP) and Sun Microsystems Java Server Pages (JSP) use templating as the basis to separate HTML content from business logic content in a Web application. The templating feature of JSP has already been dealt with in detail in the preceding chapter.

Sun's approach to enhance the speed of request processing is known as servlets. We will not discuss servlet programming in detail because the processing or compilation of a Java Server Page is achieved using a servlet and does not require detailed knowledge of servlet programming. Nonetheless, considering this link between JSP and servlets, before we delve into the intricacies of a Java Server Page development, let's look at the significance and functioning of servlets.

This chapter will begin with a brief introduction to the importance of servlets in Web applications. The functioning of servlets will thereafter be explained through Java servlet architecture and the various phases of its life cycle. In the later sections of this chapter, we will explore the world of servlets by creating a simple hit count servlet for the bank site.

Introduction to Servlets

Servlets are Java programs that can be deployed on a Java-enabled Web server to enhance and extend the functionality of the Web server. They are internal modules on the server side that load dynamically and are used to service requests from the Web server. In simpler terms, servlets can be used to incorporate server-side functioning and validations in applications.

Servlet architecture eliminates the need for reloading a servlet at every browser request. With servlets, the Java Virtual Machine stays running and handles each servlet request using a lightweight Java thread, and not a heavyweight operating system process, as is the case with CGI programs. This means that if a servlet is invoked N times, there would be N threads but only a single copy of the servlet class. This is in sharp contrast to the traditional CGI architecture. Servlets are widely used in Web application development and provide a well-organized, portable, and easy-to-use substitute for CGI. Before we discuss the features of servlets that have made it popular among programmers, let's understand the working of a servlet.

Workings of a Servlet

The functioning of a servlet is synonymous with the HTTP request-response cycle. Communication between a browser and a server is initiated because of a client or browser request by using the GET or POST methods. For a better understanding of this process let's assume that a request to the server invokes a servlet. In this case, the servlet can be invoked as a result of either clicking a user-interface HTML component, such as a submit button on a form, or following a hyperlink in a Web page. After the request is processed by the servlet (such as a login ID validation), the output is returned as an HTML page (message notifying a successful validation) to the client. Figure 3.2 depicts the execution of a Java servlet.

Let's follow the working of a servlet with the following request statement:

```
GET
http://www.Glendanthi.com/login.html?username="Carol"&passwd="3445H"
```

This URL is the personal mailbox address of an employee in Banco de Glendanthi, a banking organization. You'll observe that the client/browser request statement consists of the following components:

- The protocol specification for communication between the server and the client, such as HTTP

- The request types, which can be either GET or POST

- The URL of the document being retrieved or requested

- The Query string that contains additional information, such as login name, the password, and registration details

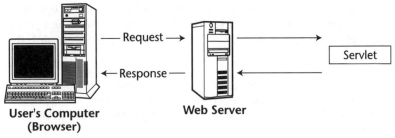

Figure 3.2 The execution of a Java servlet.

As a result of this servlet processing, the contents of Carol's mailbox are displayed. We have used words like efficient, easy-to-use, and powerful to describe servlets. Nevertheless, how are these features incorporated in servlets?

Characteristics of Servlets

As servlets are written using Java, they can make use of the extensive power of the Java API, such as networking, URL access, multithreading, database connectivity, internationalization, remote method invocation (RMI), and object serialization. The characteristics of servlets that have earned them widespread acceptance are as follows:

Servlets are efficient.   A servlet that is loaded once remains active in the server memory. As a result, the initialization code for a servlet is executed only once, and subsequent requests that are received by the servlet are straightaway processed. This helps to increase the efficiency of the server by avoiding re-creation of unnecessary processes.

Servlets are robust.   As servlets are based on Java, they integrate all the powerful features of Java, such as exception handling and garbage collection, which make them robust.

Servlets are portable.   Servlets are also portable because they are developed in Java. This enables easy transfer of servlets across Web servers.

Servlets are persistent.   Servlets help to increase the performance of the system by preventing frequent disk access. For example, after logging on to a site, the customer can perform many activities, such as checking for a balance, applying for a loan, and so on. At every stage, the customer needs to be authenticated by checking for the account number against the database. Instead of checking for the account number against the database every time, servlets retain the account number in the memory until the customer logs out of the Web site.

Until now we have understood that the power, efficiency and versatility of servlets help simplify the process of developing Web applications. Let's now look at how and where you fit in or add a servlet to use its features to the fullest.

A servlet easily fits into a Web application and is considered a very viable option. A practical use of servlets can be demonstrated by the following example. When developing an application for an online university, you can use servlets to accomplish the following tasks:

- A servlet can be used to create a catalog for the list of courses offered. The course details can be obtained from the university database. This catalog can contain a dynamically changing list of courses, and their prices can be presented to the customer (student) in an HTML format.

- A visitor to the university site can choose the course, then enter and submit data such as course name, price, and mode of payment to a servlet.

- On receiving the posted data, the servlet processes and updates the database with the relevant information.

The task ahead involves learning to write and execute the Web applications developed by using JSP. Because a JSP page ultimately generates a servlet, it makes sense to understand and appreciate the working of a servlet. An added advantage is that this will make writing a JSP page fairly easy. A servlet primarily uses Java as its programming language. Therefore, can it be referred to as Java servlets? As such, do servlets also use Java classes? What are the packages that a servlet class should implement? The answer to questions such as these and many more can be obtained by understanding the architecture of a servlet.

Java Servlet Architecture

Java servlet architecture or design consists of two main packages, `javax.servlet` and `javax.servlet.http`, that form the basic framework of servlet architecture. The classes of `javax.servlet` are generic, protocol independent, and implemented and extended by all servlets. The classes of the `javax.servlet.http` package are protocol-dependent and are explicitly used to create Web-specific or HTTP servlets. HTTP servlets provide output in the form of HTML pages.

The core of servlet architecture is the `javax.servlet.Servlet` interface. This interface uses the object-oriented approach that specifies the use of an interface as an intermediary during communication between two objects. As a result, two objects can communicate as long as the first object uses an interface to reference the second object, without the need to determine the name of the actual implementing class.

The five methods defined by the javax.servlet.Servlet interface are `init()`, `service()`, `destroy()`, `getServletConfig()`, and `getServletInfo()`. These methods control the basic functionality of a servlet starting from its initiation to its elimination. Of these, the following three are generally implemented during the life cycle of a servlet.

The `init()` method. On servlet instantiation, the `init()` method is invoked and the servlet performs the required initializations defined as part of the `init()` method. These initializations are completed before the servlet responds to an

HTTP request. After this method is invoked, tasks such as logging services or database driver registrations are performed.

The `service()` **method.** This method is invoked on receiving a browser request, after the completion of the initialization process. The application logic in a servlet is executed, request objects methods are used to access data, and the response object methods are used to build a response. This method is invoked as many times as the number of browser requests received for the servlet.

The `destroy()` **method.** This method is invoked prior to the removal of the servlet from server memory. Because no requests are routed to the server at the end of the `destroy()` method, all processes that are called as a result of the `service()` method are completed before the realization of the `destroy()` method. Typically cleanup tasks such as unregistering a database driver and closing links to a database are performed during this period.

As a result, it is imperative that all servlets implement the `javax.servlet.Servlet` interface either directly or indirectly (through inheritance by extending the GenericServlet class which by its definition implements the Servlet interface).

The two main classes of servlet architecture are the `GenericServlet` and `HttpServlet` classes. The GenericServlet class is an abstract class and implements the Servlet interface. All subclasses of this class, in turn, override the `service()` method. The class that is used to create HTTP servlets is called `HttpServlet` and is derived from the `GenericServlet` class.

Serialization is also made possible in servlets because `GenericServlet` implements the `java.io.Serializable` interface. *Serialization* is the process of writing an object into a persistent storage medium, such as a hard disk.

The hierarchies of classes that are used to create a servlet are shown in the text that follows.

Servlet Class Hierarchy

Table 3.1 describes some of the classes and interfaces that are used to create servlets.

Table 3.1 Servlet Classes and Interfaces

CLASS/INTERFACE NAME	DESCRIPTION
HttpServlet class	Provides an HTTP-specific implementation of the Servlet interface. This class extends the GenericServlet class, which provides a framework for handling other types of network and Web services.
HttpServletRequest interface	Provides methods to process requests from clients. For example, assume that the client browser consists of a form with two fields. When the values are submitted to the server for processing, they are extracted using the methods in the HttpServletRequest interface.

(continues)

Table 3.1 Servlet Classes and Interfaces *(Continued)*

CLASS/INTERFACE NAME	DESCRIPTION
HttpServletResponse interface	Response to the client is sent in the form of an HTML page through an object of the HttpServletResponse interface.
ServletConfig interface	Used to store the configuration values for servlets startup and the initialization parameters. The `getServletConfig()` method of the Servlet interface is used to obtain information about the configuration values of a servlet.

We have seen the various methods that are executed after invoking a servlet. It is quite evident from these methods that every servlet has a life span, which begins with its initiation and ends with its removal from the server. These methods are implemented sequentially and make up the life cycle of a servlet. Let's look at the phases that determine the life span of a servlet.

Life Cycle of a Servlet

Because a servlet is a Java class it needs to be executed in the Java Virtual Machine (JVM) by a *servlet engine*. A servlet engine loads a servlet for every request that is received from the client. Alternatively, a servlet can also be loaded when the Web server is started. Once loaded, a servlet remains in the server memory to handle all client requests. It is terminated either by explicit unloading or by a shutdown that is initiated when the Web server is stopped. The duration of servlet existence in the memory of the Web server does not need any extra coding and can be set as a part of the Web server's configuration.

Servlets that are loaded for every client request are called *temporary servlets*. Alternatively, servlets that are loaded when the Web server starts and retained until the Web server is shut down are called *permanent servlets*. Permanent servlets are installed on the Web server when the costs for the server startup, such as establishing connection with a database, are very high.

The life cycle of a servlet is made up of the following phases:

1. The instantiation phase, which creates an instance of the servlet.

2. The initialization phase, which involves calling the `init()` method.

3. The service phase, which begins after receipt of a client request and in turn calls the `service()` method.

4. The destroy phase, which involves calling the `destroy()` method to remove the servlet from the server memory.

5. The unavailable phase, which destroys the instance of the servlet.

Figure 3.3 depicts the various phases of the servlet life cycle.

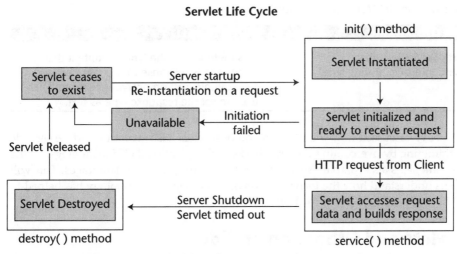

Servlet Life Cycle

Figure 3.3   Phases of the servlet life cycle.

A servlet is loaded only once in memory and is initialized in the init() method. After the servlet is initialized, it starts accepting requests from the client and processes them through the service() method until it is shut down by the destroy() method. The service() method is executed for every incoming request.

Table 3.2 describes a few methods that are used in creating a servlet.

Table 3.2   Servlet Methods

METHOD NAME	FUNCTIONALITY
Servlet.init(ServletConfig config) throws ServletException	This method contains the initialization code for the servlet and is invoked when the servlet is first loaded.
Servlet.service(ServletRequest, ServletResponse)	This method receives all requests from clients, identifies the type of the request, and dispatches them to the doGet() or doPost() methods for processing.
Servlet.destroy()	This method executes only once when the servlet is removed from server. The cleanup code for the servlet must be provided in this method.
ServletResponse.getWriter()	This method returns a reference to a PrintWriter object. The PrintWriter class is used to write formatted objects as a text-output stream to the client.

(continues)

Table 3.2 Servlet Methods *(Continued)*

METHOD NAME	FUNCTIONALITY
HttpServletResponse. setContentType(String type)	This method sets the type of content that is to be sent as response to the client browser. For example, setContentType("text/html") is used to set the response type as text.

We have discussed how the introduction of servlets has revolutionized server-side programming by overcoming the drawbacks of the traditional CGI technology. At the same time, let's also compare servlets with the existing scripting languages. This will help us understand how the incorporation of servlets in JSP technology has helped to add flexibility and efficiency to applications.

Servlets and Other Server-Side Scripting Technologies

Other server-side scripting technologies, such as Common Gateway Interface (CGI) scripts, JSP, and ASP, are alternatives to servlets. These technologies have their own advantages and disadvantages.

Servlets and CGI Scripts

We have already briefly discussed how servlets have helped overcome the drawbacks encountered in CGI programs. A CGI script is a program that is written in C, C++, or Perl and executed on a server. The disadvantages of using a CGI script are as follows:

- Whenever a CGI script is invoked, the server creates a separate process for it. The server has a limitation on the number of processes that can be created simultaneously. If the number of requests is too high, the server will not be able to accept the requests. In addition, creation of too many processes will bring down the efficiency of the server.

- The most popular platform for writing a CGI script is Perl. Even though Perl is a very powerful language for writing CGI applications, the server needs to load the Perl interpreter for each request that it receives. Therefore, for an incoming request, both the executable file of the CGI script and the Perl interpreter are loaded into memory, which brings down the efficiency of the server.

Unlike CGI scripts, the servlet initialization code is executed only once. In the case of servlets, a separate thread in the Web server handles each request. This helps to make the Web server more efficient by preventing the creation of unnecessary processes.

Servlets and Active Server Pages (ASP)

ASP is a server-side scripting language developed by Microsoft. ASP enables a developer to combine both HTML and a scripting language in the same Web page.

JavaScript and VBScript are two scripting languages supported by ASP. VBScript and JavaScript can also be used for server-side scripting by using the runat tag. A limitation of ASP is that it is not compatible with all the Web servers. The other Web servers need certain plug-ins to be installed to support ASP; however, adding plug-ins can decrease the system's performance.

This covers all the basic concepts required to understand the uses and functioning of servlets as an important component of a Web application. We now need to figure out the process of the deployment and execution of a servlet.

Creating a Servlet

Problem Statement

When the site for Banco de Glendanthi is online, it will constantly need modifications to the design and format of the pages in order to cope with customer feedback. In due time, with new policy introductions on the site, the bank will also need to estimate the popularity of the site. How can the bank staff, ignorant of application language and design, judge the popularity of the site?

Gwen, a senior supervisor in the loan department, is certain about the need to advertise updates on the bank's new loan policies on the Web site. She first needs to find out the popularity of the newly created Web site, especially during its initial period. To facilitate such an action, the project team has decided to use an already existing servlet code to keep track of the number of users visiting the bank Web site.

Let's look at the contents of the servlet application and the methodology used to execute a servlet.

> **NOTE** The focus of this problem statement is to clarify the functionality and robustness of a servlet application. Please keep in mind that the same technology can be applied by using the internal servlets of a JSP page. In that case, the servlet code written for the application will be internally generated during compilation by using certain JSP-specific components. The same will be apparent in subsequent chapters.

Task List

✔ **Identify the mechanism to record the number of hits on a Web site.**

✔ **Identify the classes to be used.**

✔ **Identify the methods to be used.**

✔ **Write the code for the servlet.**

✔ **Compile the servlet code.**

✔ **Deploy the servlet.**

✔ **Execute the servlet.**

Identify the Mechanism for Accepting and Displaying the Details

Whenever a user visits the bank Web site, the hit count must be incremented. The client browsers that are used to access the Web site run on different machines. If the hit count data is maintained on the client-side, it will be user specific. As a result, the client (or the browser) will not be able to keep track of the hit count data. This data has to be captured on the server-side. To add this type of functionality, you can develop an application by using the server-side scripting technology of servlets.

Identify the Classes to Be Used

A class named `hitcountServlet` that extends the `HTTPServlet` class needs to be coded. This servlet class will be used to keep track of the hit count.

An important set of methods in the HttpServlet class is the set that constitutes the `service()` method of the Servlet interface. The type of request (GET, POST, or HEAD) actually determines the method calls for the service phase of the servlet life cycle. As a result, each of these common request types calls the corresponding `service ()` method.

Identify the Methods to Be Used

The code to display the hit count for the JSP page will consist of the following methods:

- The `init()` method needs to be coded in the `hitcountServlet` class to initialize the hit counter to zero. This method is invoked automatically when the servlet is loaded in the memory. The servlet is loaded automatically either when the server is started or when it is installed manually using some administrative tools.

- The `doGet()` method needs to be coded to increment the hit counter whenever a client browser makes a request for the home page of the bank's Web site. The `doGet()` method includes two remarkable parameters: HttpServletRequest and HttpServletResponse. These objects provide access to all information about a request and control the response output sent to the client.

NOTE If a client does not explicitly specify the request type, then, by default, the `doGet()` method is invoked.

Write the Code for the Servlet

After establishing the classes, methods, and structure of the servlet code, let's now write the code that will display the hit count representing user visits to the Web page:

```
import javax.servlet.*;
import javax.servlet.http.*;
import java.io.*;
import java.util.*;
//hitcountServlet.java
public class hitcountServlet extends HttpServlet
{
/* Counter to keep track of the number of users visiting the Web site */
   static int count;
   public void init(ServletConfig config) throws ServletException
      {
      //The ServletConfig object must be passed to the super class
         super.init(config);
      }
/* When the user types URL of the banksite/hitcountServlet, the client
browser sends a request for the hitcountServlet page to the Bank server.
Because the client browser is requesting a page, the doGet() method of
hitcountServlet is invoked to process the request. This method returns
an html page to the client. */
   public void doGet(HttpServletRequest request, HttpServletResponse
response) throws ServletException, IOException
      {
         response.setContentType("text/html");
         PrintWriter out=response.getWriter();
         //increment counter
         count++;
         out.println("<html>");
         out.println("<head><title>BasicServlet</title></head>");
         out.println("<body>");
         out.println("You are user number    " + String.valueOf(count)
         + "  visting our Web site"+ "\n");
         out.println("</body></html>");
      }
//Used by the client browser to retrieve the servlet information
   public String getServletInfo()
      {
         return "BasicServlet Information";
      }
}
```

Compile the Servlet Code

The steps to compile the code are as follows:

1. Copy the code for the servlet into a text file and save it as hitcountservlet.java.

2. Compile the code by using the command `javac hitcountServlet.java` at the command prompt.

NOTE To compile the servlet, similar to the JSP technology, the PATH and the CLASSPATH variables need to be set by invoking the following commands at the command prompt. The PATH variable must be set to the folder where the Java compiler is present. The CLASSPATH variable must be set to the folder where all the system class files are present. If you change the name of the JDK folder, ensure that the same name is specified in the PATH and CLASSPATH variables.

```
set path=.;<System Drive>:<root directory>\<JDK Folder>\bin;<System
Drive>:<root directory>\<Java Enterprise Edition Folder>\bin
set classpath=.;<system Drive>:<root directory>\<JDK Folder>
\lib;<System Drive>:<root directory>\<Java Enterprise Edition
Folder>\lib\j2ee.jar
```

If you are unable to compile the code, check whether the path and the classpath variables are set appropriately. In addition, before you compile the program, ensure that the current working directory specified in the command prompt is correct.

Deploy the Servlet

Most applications use an HTML page as a base to collect user data received along with the request. It is imperative to first deploy a servlet or an HTML page on the Web server, in order to make it accessible from a client. Accordingly, the servlet or HTML page could contain a link to another servlet or response data.

A servlet can be deployed in the following servers:

Java Web Server (JWS).   JWS is a Web server from Sun Microsystems that is developed based on servlet technology and can be used to deploy servlets.

JRun.   JRun is a Java application server that is a product of Live software. JRun provides a high-performance, scalable solution for creating and delivering enterprise applications. The other Web-side technologies that can be deployed in JRun are Java Server Pages and Enterprise JavaBeans.

Apache.   Apache is a Web server from an organization called Apache that can be used to deploy servlets. Features that have made Apache popular are its freely distributed code, its robustness, and the security that it offers.

Java 2 Enterprise Edition (J2EE) server.   Java 2 Enterprise Edition (J2EE) is a set of specifications that defines the standards for creating distributed, component-based Java applications. J2EE also specifies how these technologies can be integrated to provide a complete solution. It is also a standard architecture that defines a multitier programming model. The Java 2 SDK, Enterprise Edition (J2EE) server is a product from Sun Microsystems that is based on Java 2 Enterprise Edition (J2EE). The J2EE server is used to deploy servlets and JSP files and enables users to access the same by implementing appropriate security.

Deploying a Servlet in J2EE

On deploying a servlet in J2EE, an application file is created (by J2EE) that is called Enterprise Archive (EAR) file. The EAR file consists of servlets and JSP components that together form Web components. Web components, in turn, can be combined with HTML files to create a Web Archive (WAR) file, which is consecutively added to the EAR file.

Before you start the J2EE server, the following environment variables need to be set. The JAVA_HOME variable must be set to the folder in which JDK is installed, and J2EE_HOME must be set to the folder in which J2EE is installed.

```
set JAVA_HOME=<System Drive>:<root directory>\<JDK Folder>
set J2EE_HOME=<System Drive>:<root directory>\<Java Enterprise Edition
Folder>
```

You also need to ensure that the PATH and CLASSPATH variables are set (as mentioned in the preceding note).

The following steps must be followed to deploy a servlet in J2EE:

1. Type start j2ee -verbose to start the J2EE server.

NOTE To check whether the J2EE server is started properly, start the browser and type http://<host address>:8000. The J2EE server can be installed on a local or a remote computer. Type the address of the computer in which the J2EE server is running.

2. Type deploytool at the command prompt. The Application Deployment Tool Window appears.
3. Choose File, New Application. The New Application dialog box is displayed.
4. Click the Browse button to select the working directory. Another New Application dialog box appears. Select the working directory. Edit the File name text box to **hitcountear**.
5. Click the New Application button. Verify that the complete path appears in the Application File Name box and hitcountear appears as the Application Display Name.
6. Click OK. The New Application dialog box closes. Verify that hitcountear appears in the upper-left pane of the Application Deployment Tool window. Notice the change in the title bar of the window.
7. Choose File, New Web Component. The New Web Component Wizard—Introduction dialog box appears.
8. Click Next. The New Web Component Wizard—WAR File General Properties dialog box appears.
9. Click Add. The Add Files to .WAR—Add Content Files dialog box appears. In this dialog box, you need to select the root directory by clicking the Browse button and add the HTML files, if any.

NOTE As we do not need an HTML file to execute this servlet, the step to add content files, such as HTML, JSP, or GIF files, can be ignored. In addition, you need to ensure that the working directory must be selected before adding the content files, such as HTML or GIF files, and the class files, such as servlets or JSP beans. In the example, it is assumed that the working directory is D:\Servlets\prog1.

10. In the Add Files to .WAR—Add Content Files dialog box, click Next. Figure 3.4 displays the Add Files to .WAR—Add Class Files dialog box that appears. In this dialog box, you need to choose the root directory and add the class files.

NOTE The path that is shown in the screen captures might vary from the ones that you actually see, depending on the directory and the drive in which you are working.

11. Click the Browse button, and select the working directory from the Choose Root Directory dialog box.

12. Click the Choose Root Directory button. The Choose Root Directory dialog box closes. Verify that the complete path appears in the Root Directory box. You now need to add the class files. Figure 3.5 displays The Add Files to .WAR—Add Class files dialog box after the selection of the root directory.

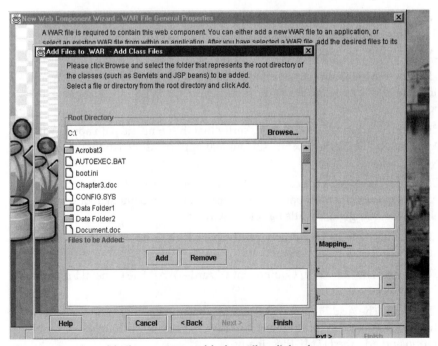

Figure 3.4   The Add Files to .WAR–Add Class Files dialog box.

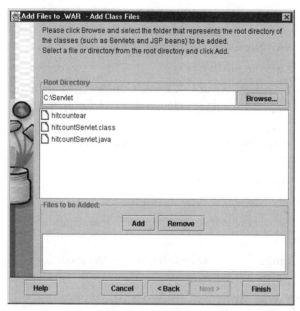

Figure 3.5   The dialog box after selecting the root directory.

13. Select **hitcountServlet.class**,and click the Add button. Notice that the file hitcountServlet.class appears in the lower text box. Figure 3.6 displays The Add Files to .WAR—Add Class files dialog box after the addition of the class file.

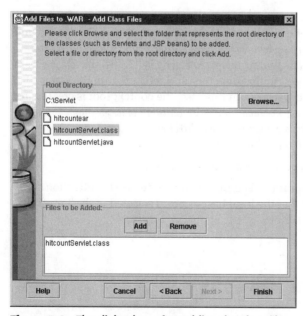

Figure 3.6   The dialog box after adding the class file.

14. Click the Finish button. The Add Files to .WAR—Add Class Files dialog box closes. Verify that hitcountServlet.class appears in the Contents area of the New Web Component Wizard—WAR File General Properties dialog box.

15. In the WAR Display Name box, type **hitcountwar**.

16. Click Next. The New Web Component Wizard—Choose Component Type dialog box appears. Verify that Servlet appears selected under Web Component Type.

17. Click Next. The New Web Component Wizard—Component General Properties dialog box appears.

18. From the Servlet Class list, select **hitcountServlet**.

19. In the Web Component Display Name box, type **hitcount**.

20. Click Next. The New Web Component Wizard—Component Initialization Parameters dialog box appears.

21. Click Next. The New Web Component Wizard—Component Aliases dialog box appears.

22. Click Add. In the Aliases box, type **hitcounter**. The servlet will be accessed by its alias name while being displayed in the browser.

NOTE The subsequent dialog boxes can be ignored at this time.

23. Click Finish. The Web component has been added. Verify that hitcountwar appears in the upper-left pane (just below hitcountear) of the Application Deployment Tool: hitcountear window.

24. Click the Web Context tab. You need to provide a context root name for the application. When a servlet is deployed, a folder is created with the same name as the context root name in *<system drive>:\<root directory>\ <Java Enterprise Edition Folder>\ public_html\<context root name>*. The WAR file, the .class files, and the HTML files are placed in this directory and fetched from the same directory while executing the servlet. In this case, the context root is created in *<system drive>:<root directoryt>\<Java Enterprise Edition Folder>\ public_html*, and the complete path is *<system drive>:<root directory>\ <Java Enterprise Edition Folder>\ public_html\hitcountwebcontext*.

25. In the Context Root box, type **hitcountwebcontext**.

26. Choose Tools, DeployApplication. The Deploy hitcountear—Introduction dialog box appears. Verify that the local host appears selected in the Target Server list.

NOTE If the J2EE server is deployed on a remote computer, you need to select the address of the remote computer as the Target Server.

27. Click Next. The Deploy hitcountear—.WAR Context Root dialog box appears.

28. Click Next. The Deploy hitcountear—Review dialog box appears.

29. Click Finish. The Deployment Progress dialog box appears.

NOTE You can also check the messages at the command prompt indicating successful completion of the task.

30. Click OK. The Deployment Progress dialog box closes. The application is now deployed. Verify that hitcountear appears in the Server Applications area.

Execute the Servlet

Open the browser window, and type **http://127.0.0.1:8000/hitcountwebcontext/ hitcounter** in the address bar to execute the servlet. Table 3.3 describes the components of the address.

In this problem statement, the servlet is accessed directly by typing the URL in the address box. When you execute the servlet for the first time, the servlet will be loaded into the memory and the hit count will be 1. Figure 3.7 illustrates the displayed output after execution of the servlet code for the first time.

Table 3.3 Components of the Servlet Address

COMPONENT	SPECIFIES
127.0.0.1	The address of the host, which is also known as the loop back address
8000	The port number through which the J2EE server accepts the client requests
hitcountwebcontext	The name of the Web context for this application name
hitcounter	The name of the alias that was specified in the deploy tool

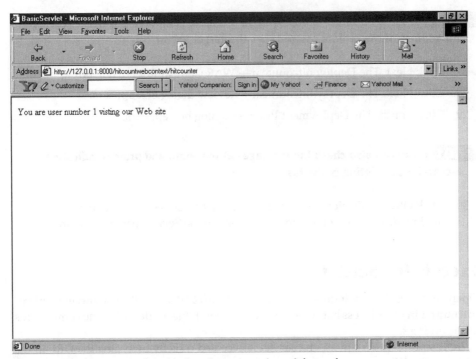

You are user number 1 visting our Web site

Figure 3.7   The output after the first-time execution of the code.

> **NOTE** A "Page not found" error encountered during the execution of the servlet denotes a nonassociation between the file and the alias name. To counter this error, you can do the following:
>
> 1. In the Application Deployment Tool dialog box, expand hitcounter to display its component files.
> 2. Select the Web component hitcount and click the Aliases tab, which is present in the right pane.
> 3. In the Aliases box, retype the alias name (hitcounter).
> 4. Redeploy the application. (Choose Tools, Update and Redeploy application.) Click OK once the application is redeployed.
> 5. Reexecute the servlet.

To pass a request to the servlet again, you need to refresh the document. After you refresh the document, the doGet() method of the servlet is invoked once again and the hit count is incremented by 1. Figure 3.8 illustrates the displayed output after the execution of the servlet code for the second time.

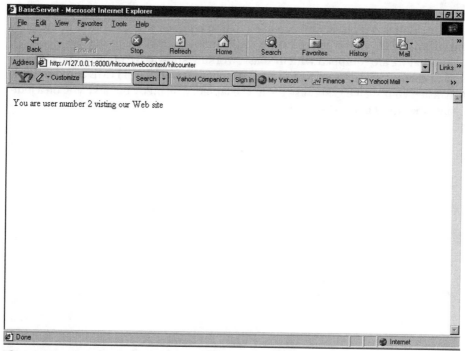

Figure 3.8 The output after the second-time execution of the code.

NOTE To shut down the J2EE server, type `j2ee -stop`.

Summary

Efficiency, portability, and ease of execution are a few of the features of Java servlets that have earned it an edge over the traditional CGI and other similar technologies. Servlet technology merges brilliantly into the request-response cycle model to add functionality and efficiency to Web applications.

In this chapter, we talked about both the architecture and life cycle of servlets. We discussed how a servlet, once invoked, goes through all the phases of its life cycle until it is explicitly eliminated. As a result, after a servlet is loaded, it remains in the server memory to process subsequent requests. You can actually verify this phenomenon. All you need to do is execute a servlet twice. The time required to display the resultant page the first time is longer than that for the second because during the second request, the servlet is already present in the server memory.

It is therefore not surprising that to add such extensibilities to applications, JSP pages are built based on servlet technology. After a JSP page is compiled, it internally generates a servlet, fitting perfectly into the JSP implementation framework.

Now that we are equipped with the basic working knowledge of JSP and servlets, in the next chapter we move on to creating JSP pages. Know basic HTML and core Java? Then fasten your seatbelts because the next chapters will, bit by bit, take you on a journey into the world of Java Server Pages.

Creating a JSP Page

OBJECTIVES:

In this chapter, you will learn to do the following:

- ✔ Identify the components of a JSP page by using the "Hello World" example
- ✔ Use comments in a JSP page
- ✔ Generate dynamic content by using JSP

Getting Started

The preceding chapters have highlighted the potential and popularity of JSP for developing Web applications. Such a wide acceptance can be attributed directly to JSP's ability to reuse existing software components. As a result, by using JSP technology, you can easily plug existing HTML pages and JavaBean components into a JSP page. Consider a situation where, as a part of a development team, you are assigned the task of creating an application for a music store. Because the header for a Web page plays an important role in projecting details about the contents of the application, the first task is to design the header for the application. In this case, it is not necessary for you to take a lot of effort in drawing the design for the header. You can save time by assigning the task to a Web designer. After the final draft for the header is formulated, you only need to plug in some components in the file by using JSP specific tags. As a result, without actually coding for the header, your application will include the header components. Doesn't that sound like a programmer's dream come true? Well, working with JSP is just that.

Before we delve into hard-core JSP programming, we will look at creating some basic JSP pages. In the course of creating these pages, we'll be able to identify and familiarize ourselves with the elements that represent a JSP page. This chapter will begin with a brief introduction to the components of JSP by using a simple "Hello World" example. In the next section, we will create a scenario-based JSP application to generate static content. The essence of JSP, however, is to promote dynamic content in Web applications. As a result, in the later sections of the chapter we will construct a JSP application to generate dynamic content.

Components of a JSP Page

We have already discussed, in detail, the technological background of JSP. Nonetheless, aided with the theoretical content of JSP, let's start creating some JSP pages. Before we create these pages, though, we need to understand the basic components that build a JSP page.

A JSP page is very similar to an HTML document except for the addition of some tags containing Java code. These tags, known as JSP tags, help to differentiate and segregate HTML- and JSP-specific components. Let's consider a simple JSP "Hello World" example code that will help us differentiate between these components in a JSP page. The example that follows will display the "Hello World" message on the screen:

```
<HTML>
<%--This is the HTML content--%>
<HEAD><TITLE>My first JSP Example</TITLE></HEAD>
<BODY>
<H1>My first JSP example</H1><HR>
   <%--This is the JSP content--%>
   <%="Hello World" %>
</BODY>
</HTML>
```

On close examination, you'll observe the use of two types of tags in the code example. These are the HTML tags enclosed within <-- --> and the JSP tags enclosed within <%-- --%>.

Therefore, you can categorize the contents of a JSP page as follows:

- HTML components consisting of HTML tags
- JSP components consisting of JSP tags

HTML Tags

The HTML content used in the preceding example is easily distinguishable by its placement within opening (<) and closing (>) tags. The HTML tags used in the "Hello World" example are as follows:

<HTML> This tag is an imperative beginning tag for every HTML document.

<HEAD><TITLE> This tag is used to display a heading for the output screen and is visible on the title bar.

<BODY> This tag is used for the body-specific HTML content. The body of an HTML document consists of numerous other tags, such as <P>, <TABLE>, and <FONT>.

<HR> This tag is placed within the BODY tag and is used to insert a horizontal line in output.

<H1> This tag is also placed within the BODY tag. It is used to display the first-level heading text.

Because most of you are conversant with basic HTML, you'll recollect that HTML tags, with the exception of empty tags such as <BR>, have ending tags, too. Nonetheless, an unchallenged fact remains that, equipped with basic HTML knowledge, almost all HTML tags are perceptible. Let's therefore proceed to identify and understand the other component of a JSP page.

JSP Tags

The JSP content can be easily distinguished by its placement within <% and %> tags. The statement <% ="Hello World" %> in the "Hello World" example is a JSP-specific tag. Table 4.1 is a quick reference to the various types of JSP tags and their functionality. We'll be using these tags across the chapters of the book.

Table 4.1 JSP Tags

JSP TAG	TAG NAME	USED TO
<%-- --%>	Comments	Describe the functionality of the code in the form of notes or remarks.
<%@ %>	Directives	Control the structure of the servlet and serve as mere messages for the JSP engine specifying actions for a particular JSP page.
<% %>	Scripting Elements	Encapsulate Java code snippets. These can be categorized as declarations, scriplets, and expressions.

(continues)

Table 4.1 JSP Tags *(Continued)*

JSP TAG	TAG NAME	USED TO
	Declarations	Define variables and methods. All declarative statements in a JSP page end with a semicolon, and the statements are enclosed within <%! %> tags.
	Scriplets	Specify Java code fragments, which are enclosed within <% %> tags.
	Expressions	Specify statements that are evaluated and displayed in the output. Enclosed within <%= %> tags.
<jsp: >	Actions	Insert a file, reuse beans, or forward the script control to another HTML.

After having distinguished between the types of tags in the "Hello World" example, let's now look at its screen output. Figure 4.1 represents the output of the "Hello World" example.

You'll notice that the output generated by the "Hello World" example is a message with static content and that you cannot see any changes in its output. As a result, the output will remain the same, regardless of the time when and location where you view it.

What we have discussed so far is just the tip of the iceberg. Continuing with the next task, let's now look at creating a static JSP page for the banking site.

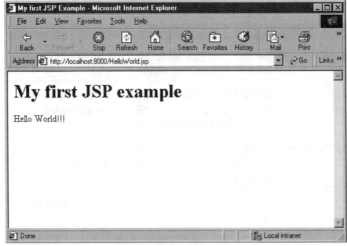

Figure 4.1 The "Hello World" example.

Generating Static Content by Using JSP

Problem Statement

As is customary, all good gestures in society are countered with an expression that demonstrates gratitude and acknowledges patronage. Therefore, it is evident that the site of Banco de Glendanthi will also contain a page acknowledging and thanking customer visits. As a part of the development team, you'll begin building the application by creating a simple JSP page with a thank you message.

Task List

✔ **Identify the basic HTML components.**

✔ **Identify the basic JSP components.**

✔ **Formulate the thank you statement for the JSP page.**

✔ **Write the code for the application.**

✔ **Execute the code.**

✔ **View the JSP page.**

Identify the Basic HTML Components of the Code

The HTML tags in the code will be these:

    <HTML>
    <HEAD>
    <TITLE>
    <BODY>

All these tags will also have their corresponding closing tags.

Identify the Basic JSP Components of the Code

The code is required to display a simple static message on the screen. As a result, you can easily map the JSP contents in accordance with those in the "Hello World" example, which was discussed earlier. Therefore, the JSP-specific components, as discussed earlier, will be in the form of comment entries and a JSP expression statement.

We have already looked at an example of JSP code to display static content. Now, let's explore the classification and categorization of the JSP tags. The JSP tags listed in Table 4.1 can also be broadly classified into the following two groups based on the time of their execution:

- Translation-time tags
- Request-time tags

You might recollect the two-phase compilation process of a JSP page. The first phase, or the translation phase, results in the automatic generation of a Java servlet while the second phase, or the request phase, results in the conversion of the servlet into an HTML page. As a result, the JSP tags of the preceding table can be categorized as translation-time and request-time tags based on the time of their execution. You can have the following groups of tags:

- Translation-time tags that include:

    Comments that are used to provide information about code snippets

    Directives that are used to convey overall information about a JSP page

- Request-time tags that include:

    Scripting elements such as scriplets, expressions, and declarations that consist of Java code snippets

- Actions that are used to influence the runtime behavior of a JSP.

Both translation-time and request-time tags will be dealt with in more detail in later chapters. In this chapter, we will discuss in detail the two types of comments used in almost every application.

Comments

For your current assignment, you need to create a static JSP page. You'll agree that the presence of remarks and observational lines in code can prove to be an advantage in identifying its exact purpose. These remarks indicate the logic and approach used during the formulation of the code. For example, consider what happens when a developer unexpectedly resigns in the middle of the project. The process of searching for and hiring a new employee is an ordeal by itself. Visualize the plight of the new developer. The work environment is new, and he or she faces the task of completing a half-finished job. Nevertheless, the predecessor's notes and remarks in the code can simplify the task of coding for the application. These remarks or comments can assist the new developer in grasping the exact status and intent of the developed code.

Comments in JSP are enclosed either within <%-- --%> tags or the regular HTML <!-- --> tags. Developers and programmers frequently use such comments to provide additional information about the various sections of the code. During compilation, when the JSP engine encounters such comments in a JSP page, it ignores them. As a result, the comment text is not included in the generated servlet and is not displayed in the output.

You can categorize comments as hidden or source comments based on their absence or presence in the source code. Hidden comments that are enclosed within the <%-- --%> tags do not show up in the HTML document displayed as a result of choosing the View, Source option of the browser. There might be situations, though, that require display of comments in the output HTML source code. At such times, developers use source comments or the regular HTML comment syntax enclosed within the <!-- --> tags. To understand the use of hidden and source comments, let's revisit our "Hello World" example. The code that we have used is given here:

```
<HTML>
<%--This is the HTML content--%>
<HEAD><TITLE>My first JSP Example</TITLE><HEAD>
<BODY>
<H1>My first JSP example</H1><HR>
   <%--This is the JSP content--%>
   <%="Hello World" %>
</BODY>
</HTML>
```

Because the comments used are of the hidden type (enclosed within `<%--  --%>` tags) the output of the HTML source code will not show the comment line entries. Figure 4.2 displays the output of an HTML source code with hidden comments.

Let's now change the hidden comments of the "Hello World" example to source comments. All we need to do is change the comment line tags from `<%--` and `--%>` to `<!--` and `-->`. The "Hello World" example code with source comments is given here:

```
<HTML>
<!--This is the HTML content-->
<HEAD><TITLE>My first JSP Example</TITLE></HEAD>
<H1>My first JSP example</H1>
<BODY>
   <!--This is the JSP content-->
   <%="Hello World!!!" %>
</BODY>
</HTML>
```

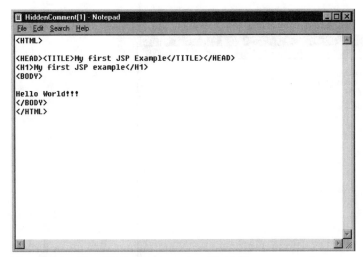

Figure 4.2 The HTML source code with hidden comments.

The comments used in the preceding example are source comments (enclosed within <!-- --> tags); hence the output of the HTML source code will show these comment line entries. Figure 4.3 displays the output of an HTML source code with source comments.

From the previous discussion, it is evident that comments are a boon for programmers and meaningless for readers. The choice of using either hidden or source comments is left to the author of the application. At the end of this discussion, let's finalize the choice of hidden comments for the JSP page.

Formulate the Acknowledgment Statement for the JSP Page

The acknowledgment statement for the page as forwarded by the bank's technical executive is as follows:

```
"Thank you for banking with Banco de Glendanthi"
```

Similar to its use in the "Hello World" example, this acknowledgment statement will also be displayed using the JSP expression statement. The code statement will read as follows:

```
<% out.println("Thank you for banking with Banco de Glendanthi "); %>
```

NOTE For the time being, let's use the JSP expression statement as it appears in the "Hello World" example. Please note that JSP expressions are discussed in detail in subsequent chapters.

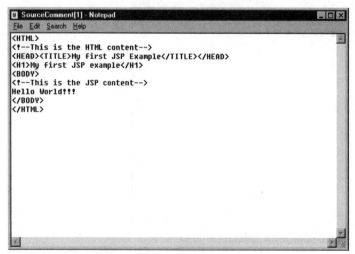

Figure 4.3 The HTML source code with source comments.

Write the Code for the Application

Taking a cue from the preceding discussions on the format and contents of acknowledgment page, the code will be as follows:

```
<HTML>
<HEAD><TITLE>Another static content example</TITLE></HEAD>
<BODY bgcolor="#FFEAFF" >
<H2> Concluded your session with us? </H2><HR>
    <% out.println("Thank you for banking with Banco de Glendanthi."); %>
</BODY>
</HTML>
```

Execute the Code

To implement or view the output of the acknowledgment page, you need to follow certain predefined steps, which include copying various files into their destination folders, initiating server startup, and, finally, running the code in the browser. Accordingly, to view the output of the page, simply follow these steps:

1. Copy the code for the page with the acknowledgment message into a text file and save it as Acknowledgment.jsp.

NOTE If you are using Notepad as the text editor, ensure that the file is not saved as Acknowledgment.jsp.txt. To save the file as a JSP file, after entering the name of the file in the File name text box, be sure to select All Files from the Save as type list.

2. Copy Acknowledgment.jsp in the public_html folder in the C:\j2sdkee1.2.1 directory.
3. Start the server by typing `start j2ee -verbose` at the command prompt.
4. Open the browser window and type `http://localhost:8000/Acknowledgment.jsp` in the address bar to execute the JSP code.

Table 4.2 describes the various components of the address.

Table 4.2 Components of the Address

COMPONENT	SPECIFIES
localhost	The address of the host on the local machine
8000	The port number through which the J2EE server accepts the requests
Acknowledgment.jsp	The name of the JSP file

View the JSP Page

Figure 4.4 represents the output of Acknowledgment.jsp.

That was fun and easy, wasn't it? An acknowledgment message flashed as a result of using HTML and JSP tags. You must have noticed that the output generated in the preceding code is a message; you cannot expect to see any changes in the output. As a result, the output will remain the same, regardless of the time and location where you view it. Such content that does not change in accordance with the change in time or other factors is known as static content.

Real-life application development is not limited to the incorporation of static content only. The contents of a Web page undergo changes almost every day. For example, the textual content in a news site such as those of CNN or *The Washington Post* will keep changing with changes in international events. Such content that keeps changing with changes in time and place is known as dynamic content.

At this moment, a question that will cross your mind is whether JSP can be used to code for dynamic content, too. The answer to this is yes! To reiterate this statement, let's build a simple dynamic page for the bank site.

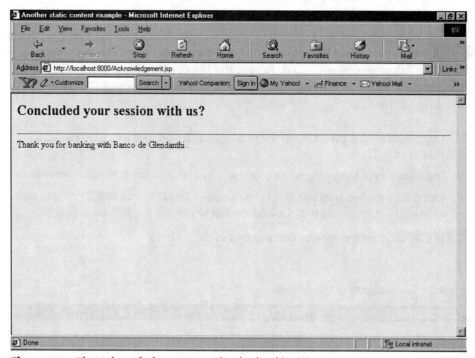

Figure 4.4   The Acknowledgment page for the banking site.

Generating Dynamic Content by Using JSP

Problem Statement

Another prevalent page displayed by most sites is the Welcome page. The technology team of Banco de Glendanthi has proposed the addition of a Welcome page as the first application page. According to the format of this page, a welcome message, along with the current date and time, is displayed in the browser window. Your task is to formulate the code to generate this output.

Task List

✔ **Identify the basic JSP components of the code.**

✔ **Write the code for the application.**

✔ **Execute the code.**

✔ **View the JSP page.**

Identify the Basic JSP Components of the Code

It is evident that the display of the current date and time requires the display of dynamic content. As a result, the content will keep changing at every instance of code execution. Other than textual changes to the message, the only addition to be made to this code to render it dynamic is the use of the Date() method or function. This Java function is used to extract and display the current date and time. The addition of the following line of code will ensure the display of the current date and time in the JSP page.

```
<%= new Date().toString() %>
```

Take note of the fact that this situation also makes use of the JSP expression statement to display the date and time.

Write the Code for the Application

Taking a cue from the preceding discussions on the format and contents of the welcome page, the code for the application will be as follows:

```
<HTML>
<%@ page import="java.util.*" %>
<%--This is the HTML content--%>
<HEAD><TITLE>A Dynamic Content example</TITLE></HEAD>
<BODY bgcolor="#FFEAFF">
```

```
<H1>Welcome to Banco de Glendanthi</H1><HR>
<H3>Today's date and time:</H3>
   <%--This is the JSP content that displays the server time by using
   the method Date()--%>
   <%= new Date().toString() %>
</BODY>
</HTML>
```

Execute the Code

To execute the code, do the following:

1. Copy the code for the page in a text file, and save it as Welcome.jsp.

2. Copy Welcome.jsp in the public_html folder in the C:\j2sdkee1.2.1 directory.

3. Start the server by typing `start j2ee -verbose` at the command prompt.

4. Open the Internet Explorer browser, and type the location of the .jsp file as `http://localhost:8000/ Welcome.jsp`.

View the JSP Page

Figure 4.5 represents the output of the Date-Time example.

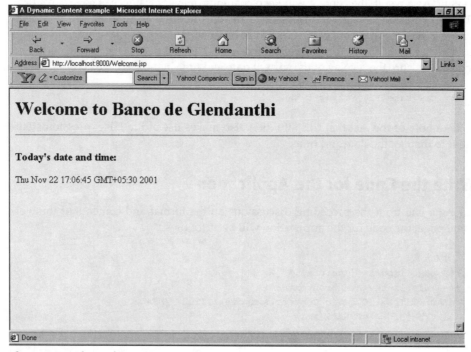

Figure 4.5   The welcome page for the banking site.

Summary

The HTML- and JSP-specific content in a JSP page is instantly recognizable due to its placement in explicit tags. Although until now we have created only simple JSPs, it is beyond doubt that knowledge of HTML provides the foundation for creating JSP pages.

In this chapter we've discussed the structure and components of a JSP. We learned that the structure of a JSP file is similar to that of an HTML file except for the use of some JSP-specific tags. We also discussed the categorization of JSP tags. Further, in this chapter, we distinguished the types and functionalities of the JSP comments, which are a type of translation-time tags.

To explain the importance of comments, we used the "Hello World" example to view how the insertion of hidden and source comments alters the output of the HTML source code. We also used the case study of Banco de Glendanthi and created two basic JSP pages to display both static and dynamic content. What is important to note is that by implementing the concepts covered in this chapter, you can easily begin developing JSP pages. This is simple because you already have a basic knowledge of HTML.

This is just the beginning; in the next chapter; we'll discuss the other translation-time tags or JSP directives. These directives are important building blocks of a JSP page because their inclusion affects the overall structure of the servlet that is generated at the end of the translation phase.

CHAPTER

5

Using JSP Directives and Action Elements

OBJECTIVES:

In this chapter, you will learn to do the following:

- ✓ Appreciate the use of directives in a JSP page
- ✓ Identify the types of directives
- ✓ Use JSP directives
- ✓ Appreciate the use of action elements in a JSP page
- ✓ Identify the types of standard actions
- ✓ Use JSP standard actions

Getting Started

In the last chapter, we created simple JSP pages to display messages with static and dynamic content. As a result, the content in the page was fairly easy to understand. The tasks, however, did not call for the use of special tags and were therefore not challenging. From this chapter begins the challenge to create JSP pages that use specific tags to generate static and dynamic content.

We have already discussed the use of translational tags, in the form of comments, to furnish information about the various sections of code; however, we still need to understand the use and importance of the other translational tags, known as JSP directives. In addition, in the course of our discussions in the preceding chapter, we also talked about JSP actions, which are request time tags, executed at the time of the client request. Although the JSP include action and the JSP include directive behave in a similar manner, they are executed during different phases of the compilation process. The perspective of their use is also very different. To bring out these differences, this chapter has been split into two sections, the JSP directives section and the JSP actions section.

The first section begins with a detailed discussion of the functioning of JSP directives. The later parts of this section discuss the three main directives to bring out their function as information providers for the JSP engine. The final parts of this section use a scenario-based example to show the effectiveness of the use of directives.

The second section begins with a discussion of the functioning of JSP actions. This is followed by a discussion, with examples, to identify the types of standard actions in JSP. Considering the similarity between the include directive and the include action, the later parts of this section compare the use and functioning of the two tags.

JSP Directives

The purpose of JSP directives is to serve JSP page-specific information to the JSP engine before compilation. The utility of such directives is very easily explained by the following example. Have you ever attended a technical seminar on the latest software technologies or a workshop on "healthy and positive living?" These seminars and workshops offer a platform for the presentation of new ideas that is also supported by practical sessions. The panels for such presentations consist of renowned experts, masters with expertise in the particular field of or subject. The sessions use informal discussions, slide shows, debates, and question-answer sessions to facilitate information exchange between the experts on the panel and the participants. Do these experts just walk into the venue and begin the sessions? The success of these seminars can be attributed to long and tedious hours of planning and preparation. As a result, what you experience as a participant is the outcome of excellent management. How is the session coordinated and organized to minimize the problem areas? The seminars owe their success to specific inputs in the form of number of participants, their profiles, session details, and other venue-specific information. Before the seminar starts, the organizers use these figures and statistics to schedule and manage the sessions. Similarly, in the case of a JSP page, before a page is compiled, prior information about its content helps the JSP engine prepare for the process of compilation and servlet generation.

The process of JSP compilation is engine-centric—that is, both the request and the response phases traverse through the JSP engine. It is therefore essential that the JSP engine is made aware of the status and content of a particular JSP before it begins the process of compilation. Because a JSP page consists of embedded Java code, it encapsulates various features and behaviors of Java-specific classes and methods. As a result, the information passed to the JSP engine prior to the generation of the servlet is used to set the values of global variables, methods, and class declarations of the page. It also contains explicit statements to determine the format type of the generated output. The statements that affect the overall structure of the generated servlet and provide the JSP engine with the global information about the JSP page are known as JSP directives. Let's look at the workings of a JSP directive by using an example from the online banking site.

Using JSP Directives

Problem Statement

A discussion with the client has resulted in a minor task addition to the almost complete login page. The CEO of Banco de Glendanthi has shown keen interest in the inclusion of the bank's name and logo in all the pages of the application. Owing to a last-minute crunch in the availability of a developer, your project manager has also assigned you the task of inserting the header elements into the login page. In addition, keeping the time constraints in mind, the team has unanimously decided to conduct the trial run for the task on the login page. Jonathan Nash, the Chief Graphic Visualizer for Graphical Arts, has already designed the header file (Header.html). The code for the header file is:

```
<html>
<head>
<title>Banco de Glendanthi</title>
</head>
<body bgcolor="#FFDFD7" text="#999966">
<p style="margin-top: 0; margin-bottom: 0"> <font size="7"
color="#0000FF"><img border="0" src="dd00448_1.gif">Banco de
Glendanthi</font></p>
<hr>
<hr>
</body>
</html>
```

Figure 5.1 displays the output of the header file.

Accordingly, in addition to designing the login page, your job now also involves adding the header elements to this page of the application.

Task List

✔ **Identify the data that needs to be accepted for the login screen.**

✔ **Design the user interface screen for the login page.**

✔ **Identify the JSP tag to add the bank's name and logo to the login page.**

✔ Write the HTML code for the login page.

✔ Add the tag-specific line of code to the login page code.

✔ Execute the code.

✔ Change the date and time of the schedule to verify that it has been updated in the JSP page.

✔ View the JSP page.

Identify the Data That Needs to Be Accepted for the Login Screen

Because the interface will accept inputs from the user, we will need to create controls to accept these inputs. HTML forms elements are used to create such controls. The next chapter is dedicated to the importance and working of HTML forms. As a result, we will use the form-specific tags to create the controls in the user interface. Let's list the inputs for this page that will be accepted from the user. The user interface for the login page screen will accept the following data:

- The login ID
- The password

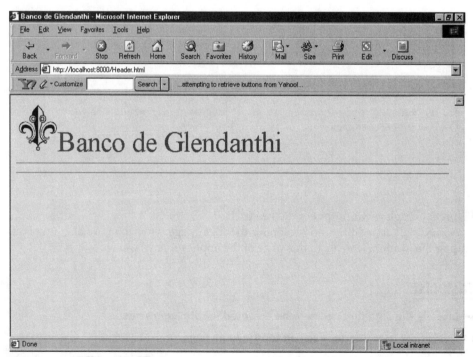

Figure 5.1   The header file.

Design the User Interface Screen for the Login Page

Once the elements for the page are decided, we need to map them to HTML tags that will help us in coding the page. Table 5.1 describes the HTML elements required for the login page screen.

NOTE HTML forms are discussed in detail in the next chapter. The user can specify the name for each of the inputs. As a result, you can also use `<input type'" text" name="name">` or `<input type'" text" name="Login">` to create the login and password controls.

After the formats for the interface elements of the login page have been finalized, let's determine the JSP tag that we will use to add the header elements to the login page.

Identify the JSP Tag to Add the Bank's Name and Logo to the Login Page

The following example shows the need for a JSP tag to identify inclusions of other files and elements in the page. Consider the situation where a JSP page needs to contain the integrated output of two or more files. In such a case would the JSP engine be expected to presume the addition of the individual file elements in the page output? No! The JSP engine will have to be specially notified about the inclusion of the additional file elements by specifying the names of the included files. As a result, when the page is compiled, the engine is able to relate to the file whose content will be subsequently added to the output of the JSP page. The JSP engine is provided with such notifications by using JSP directives in the application code. Directives serve as guides that are used by the JSP engine to handle the class and method declarations and the output content of a JSP page.

You might recollect that JSP tags are essentially enclosed within the `<%` and `%>` tags. Directives, however, are differentiated from other JSP tags by using `<%@` as the start tag. The syntax to represent a directive is as follows:

```
<%@ directivename (attribute="attribute value") %>
```

Table 5.1 The Form Elements of the Login Page

INPUT FIELD	HTML SPECIFICATIONS
Basic tags	`<HTML>, <HEAD>, <BODY> tags`

Background and font color tags	`< bgcolor="#FFDFD7">`
	`<font color="#0000FF" size="7"`
	`face="Arial" >`

Control for the login ID	`<INPUT type="text" name="T1">`
Control for the password	`<INPUT type="password" name="T2">`
Submit button	`<INPUT type="submit" name="B1">`

Attributes are used to specify and assign values for a directive. According to their functionality, JSP directives can be categorized as follows:

- The page directive
- The include directive
- The taglib directive

The directives and their attributes, if any, are discussed in the following sections.

The Page Directive

The page directive defines attributes that notify the JSP engine about the general settings of a JSP page. Table 5.2 describes the attributes that can be specified for a page directive.

Let's discuss each of these attributes in detail.

The contentType attribute

The contentType attribute of the page directive is used to set the Multipurpose Internal Mail Extension type (MIME type) for the response that is sent to the client. When configuring a Web server, you need to specify the formats or the file types of the Web sites, to be able to display their content in a specific format in the browser. These file types, or the MIME types, identify the type of content stored in the file to enable its retrieval by the Web server.

Table 5.2 The Attributes of the page Directive

ATTRIBUTE	SYNTAX
contentType	contentType="MIME type"
extends	extends="packagename.class"
errorPage	errorPage="URL"
isErrorPage	isErrorPage="true/false"
import	import="package list"
language	language="scripting language"
session	session="true/false"
isThreadSafe	isThreadSafe="true/false"
buffer	buffer="no specification/size of buffer in bytes"
Info	info="message specification"

The MIME type for an HTML document, which also is the default value of the contentType attribute, is text/html. Table 5.3 represents some MIME types that can be assigned to this attribute:

Let's look at an example that specifies the contentType for the generated response to be displayed as an Excel spreadsheet. For such code, all that you need to do is specify the contentType as application/vnd.ms-excel:

```
<%@ page contentType="application/vnd.ms-excel" %>
```

The extends Attribute

The extends attribute is used to specify the superclass of the servlet that is generated during the compilation of a JSP page. It is a good practice to be absolutely sure of the servlet's extended superclass name. Most of the time, the server extends custom superclasses for generated servlets. The extends attribute can be used in the following manner:

```
<%@ page extends="packagename.class" %>
```

The errorPage attribute

The errorPage attribute is used to specify the URL of the error page that will be used to handle unimpeded exceptions. The use of this attribute ensures that all exceptions that are thrown but not caught in the current page are automatically diverted to the specified error page. The errorPage attribute can be used in the following manner:

```
<%@ page errorPage="URL of the designated error page" %>
```

Table 5.3   Some Common MIME Types

MIME TYPE	FILE DESCRIPTION
text/html	An HTML file
text/plain	Plain text
image/tif	A TIFF image
video/mpeg	MPEG video clip
audio/midi	MIDI file
application/msword	A Microsoft Word document

The IsErrorPage attribute

The isErrorPage attribute is used to specify the availability of a JSP page as an error page for another JSP page. The isErrorPage attribute takes one of the following two values:

```
<%@ page isErrorPage="true" %> or <%@ page isErrorPage="false" %>
```

The default value for this attribute is false.

The import Attribute

In order to understand the use of the import attribute of the page directive, let's revisit the dynamic content code example from Chapter 4, "Creating a JSP Page." The code that we used for this example was this:

```
<html>
<%@ page import="java.util.*" %>
<%--This is the HTML content--%>
<head><title>A Dynamic Content example</title></head>
<body>
<h1>A simple JSP example to generate dynamic content</H1><HR
<h3> This is a code to display the current date and time</H3>
    <%--This is the JSP content that displays the server time by
    using the method Now()--%>
    <%= new Date().toString() %>
</body>
</html>
```

If you read through this example code, you'll come across the following line of code with the import attribute of the page directive:

```
<%@ page import="java.util.*" %>
```

Because the output of this particular code requires the use of the Date() constructor defined in the Date class contained in the Java utility package (Java.util), you'll need to import this package. If you don't, the execution of the code will display a server error reading "Unable to compile class for .... class Date() not found."

There is no specification that limits the use of more than one page attribute per JSP. As a result, you can add multiple page attributes to a JSP page. The example that follows consists of both the language and the import attributes:

```
<%@ page language="java" import=" import javax.swing.*; java.rmi.*;
java.awt.event.*; java.awt.*" %>
```

Nonetheless, with the exception of the import directive, a JSP page cannot specify multiple occurrences of the same page attribute in a single JSP page. The import attribute can be used to specify multiple occurrences in the following manner:

```
<%@ page import=" import javax.swing.*; java.rmi.*; java.sql.*;
java.awt.*" %>
```

The language Attribute

The language attribute is used to specify the scripting language that will be used when compiling the JSP. This attribute is not used much because the only language currently available for JSP is Java. The language attribute can be used in the following manner:

```
<%@ page language="Java" %>
```

The session Attribute

The session attribute is used to specify the availability of session data for the particular JSP. The session attribute takes one of the following two values:

```
<%@ page session="true" %> or <%@ page session="false" %>
```

Session here refers to an HTTP session that commences and ends with the beginning and end of a request-response cycle. As a result, all the variables and methods defined during a session are available to a JSP page by using certain session objects. The chapter on implicit objects discusses these session objects in detail. The default value for the session attribute is true.

The isThreadSafe Attribute

The isThreadSafe attribute is used to specify if the current page can service multiple requests at a time. Normally, servlets service multiple requests by using multiple threads for each of the requests, which simultaneously access the service() method of the same servlet instance. As a result, a servlet is thread safe only if it synchronizes access to its field data such that reordering of the thread execution does not result in the formation of inconsistent values. For example, it does not make much difference if, in a freak case, two users accessing a servlet end up with the same hit count. If such a case is repeated in the case of auto-generated login IDs (provided for the first time by an ISP), though, the consequences could be catastrophic. The isThreadSafe attribute takes one of the following two values:

```
<%@ page isThreadSafe="true" %> or <%@ page isThreadSafe ="false" %>
```

The latter specification indicates that the code is not thread safe. As a result, the generated servlet uses the SingleThreadModel interface that prevents simultaneous access to the same instance of the servlet.

The buffer Attribute

The buffer attribute is used to set the size of the buffer for the out object of the JspWriter() method. Once the buffer size is set, the document content is not sent to the client but is buffered until the number of document bytes equals the buffer size. For example, if the buffer size of a document is set to 48KB, the content of the document is sent to the client only after 48KB of content is accumulated or if the page is completed.

The buffer attribute takes one of the following two values:

```
<%@ page buffer="none" %> or <%@ page buffer ="size in kb" %>
```

The info Attribute

The info attribute is used to define a string, which can be retrieved from a servlet by using the getServletInfo() method. The info attribute can be used in the following manner:

```
<%@ page info="string specification" %>
```

Let's now understand the use and functioning of the include directive.

The Include Directive

The include directive is used to append static and dynamic content from another JSP at translation time. As the translational phase of the compilation is responsible for the generation of the servlet, the presence of the include directive directs the JSP engine to open the file included and add its content directly into the generated servlet. As a result, there is no need for the servlet to open and execute the included file each time it runs, which increases the speed of servlet generation.

The include directive uses the file attribute to specify the names of the files whose content needs to be inserted at the time of the compilation. This specification is in the form of the relative URL of the JSP or HTML files. An added advantage of using the include directive is that it can also be used to insert a part of the code that is common to multiple pages to avoid using a bean for each code instance separately.

Consider the following example of a file, first.jsp, that uses the include directive to add the content of another file, second.jsp. As a result, on compilation, first.jsp will also contain the output of second.jsp. The following example is the code for first.jsp:

```
<html>
<head><title> An Include example</title></head>
<body>
<h2>This is the content of first.jsp</h2><hr>
<%="Hello, welcome to the world of Java Server Pages!!!" %>
<%@ include file="second.jsp" %>
</body>
</html>
```

The following example contains the code for second.jsp:

```
<html>
<head><title> An Include example</title></head>
<body>
<h2>This is the content of second.jsp</h2><hr>
<%= "Hope you're having fun learning JSP" %>
</body>
</html>
```

Figure 5.2 displays the output of the preceding code.

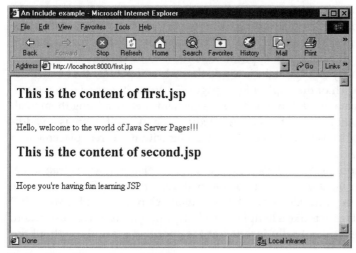

Figure 5.2   The output of first.jsp.

The third type of directive that we will discuss is the `taglib` directive.

The taglib Directive

The `taglib` directive is used to specify the inclusion of custom tags in a JSP. It is used to identify the tag library containing the defined custom tags. The custom tags of the tag library in JSP provide a mechanism that the programmer can use to encapsulate complex recurring code or tasks. Once encapsulated, these can then be reused in a simpler form. A tag library consists of a collection of functionally related, user-defined XML tags called custom tags.

The following example is the syntax to represent a `taglib` directive:

```
<% @taglib uri="taglib-examples" prefix="example" %>
```

The two attributes for the `taglib` directive are URI (Uniform Resource Identifier) and the prefix that are used to specify a unique identifier and a reference name for the particular tag library. The Uniform Resource Identifier (URI) can be defined as a union of the Universal Resource Name (URN) and the Uniform Resource Locator (URL). The URN is used to specify the Web placement of an object. The URL is used to specify strings such as http and ftp that are passed to the browser to locate an object on the Web.

When the JSP engine encounters insertion of the `taglib` directive, it uses the URI to locate the descriptor file for the particular library.

NOTE Customs tags are discussed in detail in the Chapter 15, "Developing Custom Tags."

We now need to conclude on the specific directive that is to be used to execute the task for the bank's Web site. Before inserting the respective JSP tag into the code of the login page, it is imperative to understand the two approaches favored in adding the header elements to all pages of an application.

The first approach that you might take is to add the code snippets for the header elements individually to each of the application's pages. To do so, it is crucial to remember the individual formats for each of the header's elements before adding them to all the pages of the application. Other than being a tedious job by itself, there is an additional burden of having to use the correct element along with its correct placement in all the application pages.

The other, simpler approach involves the use of a mechanism known as *templating*. Templating in JSP can be used to enhance the features of an application. This is achieved by the use of tags, which encapsulate common behaviors. The HTML or JSP file consisting of these tags acts like a template or a blueprint. As a result, on execution, contents of the tag are automatically inserted at the specified place through all the pages of the application.

NOTE It is noteworthy to remember that an approach such as templating can be implemented only through the static pages of the application.

By now, you'll be able to comprehend that the header elements of the application are static components and that the inclusion of these elements is a redundant task. To facilitate inclusion of these static elements you can write a header file and save it as either an HTML file or a JSP page. In addition, the repetitive task of including the header elements in all the pages of the application can be simplified by using the templating approach. As a result, all you need to do is encapsulate the contents of the header file into a tag and insert the tag in all the pages of the application. When the JSP engine encounters this tag in the page, it is directed to append the header elements to the content of the primary file. This task is easily performed by using the `include` directive.

The preceding discussion to identify the tag to include the header elements in the login page can be summarized as follows:

- The login page to be used is Login.jsp.
- The header file to be used is Header.html.

The `include` directive will be inserted in Login.jsp in order to add the elements of the header file to the login page.

Write the HTML Code for the Login Page

Once the decision about the use of the relevant tag and files is complete, first write the code for the user interface:

```
<html>
<head>
<title>Login Id</title>
</head>
```

```
<body bgcolor="#FFDFD7">
<form method="POST" action="Validate.jsp">
   <p><font color="#0000FF" size="4" face="Arial">
   Login Id</font>:::::::::::::::::::
   <input type="text" name="T1" size="20"></p>
   <p><font color="#0000FF" size="4" face="Arial">
   Password</font>::::::::::::::
   <input type="text" name="T2" size="20">
           
           
   </p>
   <p>  
           
        </p>
   <p>  
            
            
            
   <input type="submit" value="Submit" name="B1">
        
   <input type="reset" value="Clear" name="B2"></p>
</form>
</body>
</html>
```

Add the Tag-Specific Line of Code to the Login Page Code

We will now add the `include` directive to the HTML code, so that the header elements are inserted in the login page. The line of code specifying the inclusion of the directive is as follows:

```
<%@ include file="Header.html" %>
```

The HTML code with the include directive is this:

```
<html>
<head>
<title>Login Id</title>
</head>
<body bgcolor="#FFDFD7">
<%--The include directive is used here to add the elements of the file
Header.html to the login page--%>
<%@ include file="Header.html" %>
<form method="POST" action="Validate.jsp">
   <p><font color="#0000FF" size="4" face="Arial">
   Login Id</font>:::::::::::::::::::
   <input type="text" name="login" size="20"></p>
   <p><font color="#0000FF" size="4" face="Arial">
   Password</font>::::::::::::::
```

```
    <input type="text" name="pwd" size="20">
             
           
    </p>
    <p>  
           
       </p>
    <p>          
              
             
    <input type="submit" value="Submit" name="B1">
      
    <input type="reset" value="Clear" name="B2"></p>
 </form>
 </body>
 </html>
```

Execute the Code

In order to execute the code to view the output of the login page along with the header file elements, you need to follow certain predefined steps. These steps include copying the various files into their destination folders, initiating the server startup, and finally running the code in the browser. To view the output of the login page, simply follow these steps:

1. Copy the code for the login page with the include directive into a text file and save it as LoginHdr.jsp.

> **NOTE** If you are using Notepad as the text editor ensure that the file is not saved as LoginHdr.jsp.txt. To save the file as a JSP file, after entering the name of the file in the File name text box, be sure to select All Files from the Save as type list.

2. Copy LoginHdr.jsp, hdr.html, and the graphic file for the bank's logo, dd00448_1.wmf, into the public_html folder in C:\j2sdkee1.2.1 directory.

3. Start the server by typing start j2ee -verbose at the command prompt.

4. Open the Internet Explorer browser and type the location of the .jsp file as http://localhost:8000/ LoginHdr.jsp.

View the JSP Page

Figure 5.3 displays the output of the login page before the inclusion of the header elements.

What you see as the output will fill your heart with a sense of achievement. You have successfully added the content of Header.html to that of LoginHdr.jsp.

Figure 5.4 displays the output of the final login page.

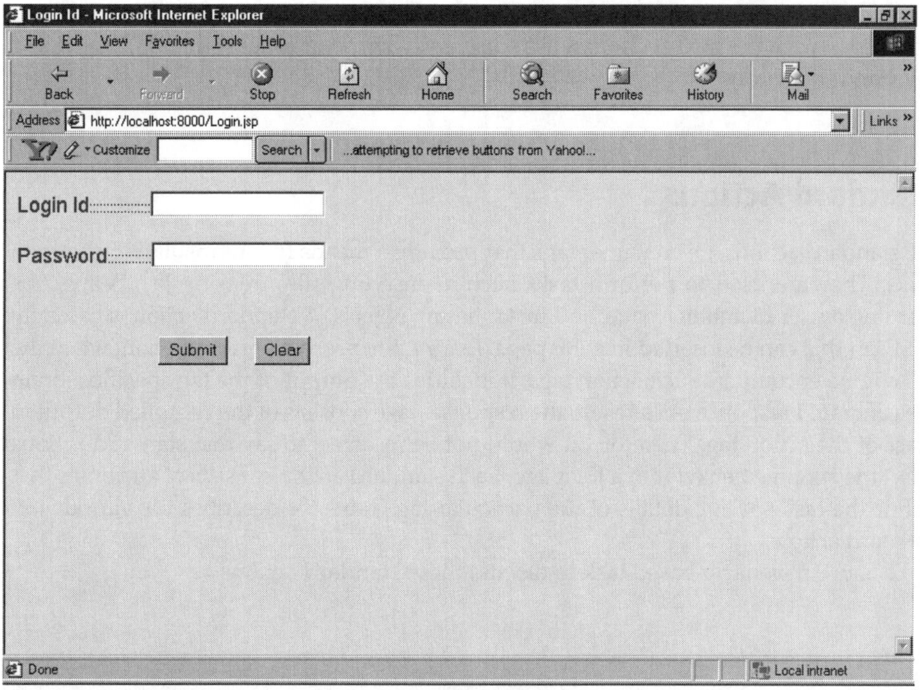

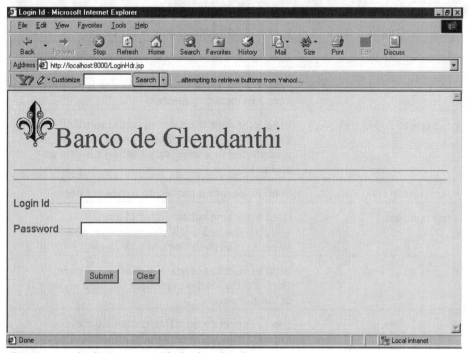

Figure 5.3   The login page without the header elements.

Figure 5.4   The login page with the header elements.

We have completed discussing the two types of translational tags in a JSP page. Let's now begin with the next section, which discusses a type of request time JSP tag called JSP standard actions.

Standard Actions

JSP standard actions are container tags that provide a means for encapsulating common tasks. They are used to perform tasks such as inserting files, reusing JavaBeans, forwarding a user to another page, and instantiating objects. A standard action is basically a JSP tag that can be inserted in a JSP page. During the process of compilation, when the JSP engine encounters such action tags, it includes the output of the tag specification in the generated response. As a result, the response page consists of the compiled output in place of the action tag. Therefore, it would not be incorrect to say that standard actions affect the runtime behavior of a JSP page. Each standard action consists of attributes that define the task-specific details of the particular tag. Table 5.4 describes the various JSP standard actions.

Let's use a scenario-based task to discuss these standard actions.

Table 5.4   The JSP Standard Actions

JSP ACTION	USAGE
`<jsp:useBean>`	Used to find and load an existing bean.
`<jsp:setProperty>`	Used to set the property of the specified bean. To set the value of the bean property, either an explicit value is specified or the value is obtained from a request parameter.
`<jsp:getProperty>`	Used to retrieve the property of the specified bean and direct it as output. The retrieved value is converted to a string value before it is sent as an output.
`<jsp:forward>`	Used to forward a request to a different page.
`<jsp:param>`	Used to include subattributes of the `<jsp:forward>`, `<jsp:include>`, and `<jsp:plugin>` actions.
`<jsp:include>`	Used to insert a file into a particular JSP page. The file inclusion takes place at the time of request of the JSP page.
`<jsp:plugin>`	Used to generate an HTML containing client-browser-dependent constructs.

Using JSP Standard Actions

Problem Statement

Banco de Glendanthi has proposed setting up a customer grievance forum that will meet once a month, depending on the availability of the executives concerned. The date and time for these meetings will be posted on their site from time to time.

You have been asked to choose a means to include the schedule for these meetings on the login page of the bank's site. The code for the file containing the meeting schedule is as follows:

```
<html>
<head>
<body>
<h3> If you have any complaints, be at the next meeting of the customer
grievance cell</h3>
<h4> The next meeting is scheduled on Saturday, 25th, January, 2002 at
10:30</h4>
</body>
<html>
```

Figure 5.5 displays the output of the schedule file.

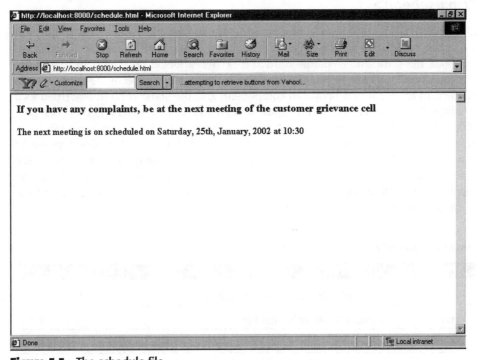

Figure 5.5 The schedule file.

Task List

✔ **Identify the mechanism to be used.**

✔ **Identify the JSP tag to add the content of the schedule to the login page.**

✔ **Add the tag-specific line of code to the login page code.**

✔ **Execute the code.**

✔ **View the JSP page.**

Identify the Mechanism to Be Used

From the preceding discussion, you'll immediately deduce that in order to achieve the required output, it is best to use the `include` directive. Bear in mind that the schedule will change constantly and will have to be updated on the site. Because the `include` directive helps in including only static content, we need to explore other JSP tags to carry out this task. The idea is to use a tag that can automatically update the change in schedule at run time. It is evident that we will use a request time tag to perform this task. JSP standard actions are request time tags that execute at run time and therefore continuously update the modifications in the associated files. Let's look at the various JSP actions in order to choose the one that can update the schedule on the bank site.

<jsp:usebean>

Chapter 9, "JSP and JavaBeans," discusses the use and function of the `usebean` action tag. In this section, we will discuss this tag in brief. As we have said before, JSP aims to segregate the static and dynamic content in a Web application. The principle of the `usebean` tag is to facilitate this segregation. The dynamic content of the application is bundled in the form of a JavaBean component, and the static content is written as a separate HTML file. How are the outputs of the two files displayed together? Is it possible to encapsulate the entire bean component through a relevant tag into a JSP page, by use of a single statement similar to the `include` directive? Picture this, if possible: A single tag inclusion will append the output of the bean component as a part of the generated response. Isn't it awesome! The `<jsp:usebean>` represents an entire JavaBean packed into a single tag declaration. Table 5.5 describes the attributes of the `<jsp:usebean>` action.

Table 5.5 Attributes of the `usebean` Action

ATTRIBUTE	USED TO...
id	Uniquely identify the instance of the bean
class	Specify the bean's class file
scope	Specify the life of the bean in terms of a page, session, or application
beanName	Specify a referential name for the bean

<jsp:setProperty>

This standard tag is used along with the `<jsp:usebean>` action to set the value of a bean property. Table 5.6 describes the attributes of the `<jsp:setProperty>` action.

<jsp:getProperty>

This standard action is paired with the `setProperty` action along with the `usebean` action. It is used to access the bean properties that are set by the `<jsp:setproperty>` action. Table 5.7 describes the attributes of the `<jsp:getProperty>` action.

> **NOTE** Both the `<jsp:setProperty>` and `<jsp:getProperty>` tags are used in conjunction with the `<jsp:usebean>` tag. Chapter 9 discusses the `<usebean>` action in detail. As a result, we will not discuss these actions in this chapter.
>
> **The** `<jsp:forward>`, `<jsp:include>`, `<jsp:param>`, **and** `<jsp:plugin>` tags are discussed in detail in this chapter.

<jsp:forward>

This standard action forwards a request from a JSP to another JSP page, a servlet, or a static resource. This action takes place at run time and leads to the termination of the current page. The `<jsp:forward>` action is primarily used along with conditional statements. The `<jsp:forward>` action uses the page attribute to specify the relative URL of the target file or resource.

The syntax of the `<jsp:forward>` action is as follows:

```
<jsp:forward page="URL specification" />
```

To understand the working of this action, let's consider a simple example. Consider the following instructions left at the reception of a computer service center. The instructions are as follows:

- If Ben returns by 13:00 hours, he should service Mr. O'Connor's computer.
- Else if Ben returns by 15:00 hours, he should service Mr. Holden's printer.

Table 5.6 Attributes of the `setProperty` Action

ATTRIBUTE	USED TO SPECIFY...
name	A name for the bean
property	The property for which values are to be set
value	The value for the bean property
param	The name of the request parameter to be used to set the value of the bean property

Table 5.7   Attributes of the `getProperty` Action

ATTRIBUTE	USED TO SPECIFY...
name	A name for the bean
property	The property from which values are to be retrieved

When we map these instructions to the `<jsp:forward>` action, we can understand that the request for service is forwarded to either Mr. O'Connor or Mr. Holden, depending on the time Ben reaches the office.

Let's look at another example of the use of the `<jsp:forward>` action. Consider the case of an organization, say Technospan Synergies Inc. All organizational and employee-related information is displayed online by using the intranet. The employees are segregated into three grades, managers (M), executives (E), and supervisors (S). We will use the `<jsp:forward>` action to determine the grade of an employee in order to display the incentive structure update for the corresponding grade. The code for this example can be written as follows:

```
<html>
<head><title>A <jsp:forward> action example</title></head>
<body>
<%
if ((request.getparameter("Grade")).equals("M")) {
%>
    <jsp:forward page="Managers.jsp" />
<% } else { %>
<% if ((request.getparameter("Grade")).equals("E")) {
%>
    <jsp:forward page="Executives.jsp" />
<% } else { %>
<% if ((request.getparameter("Grade")).equals("S")) {
%>
    <jsp:forward page="Supervisors.jsp" />
<%} %>
<% }%>
</body>
</html>
```

NOTE The preceding example uses request parameters to extract the values of the employee inputs in the form of their grades. In addition, the writing structure of the "if" statement within the scriplets may seem complex. All these concepts are covered in detail in the subsequent chapters. As for now, it is important to understand the use of the `<jsp:forward>` action.

Based on the grade specified by the user in the HTML interface, the request is forwarded to specific pages that display the grade-related incentives.

<jsp:param>

This standard action provides reference parameters in the form of subattributes along with the `<jsp:forward>`, `<jsp:include>`, and `<jsp:plugin>` actions. Table 5.8 describes the attributes of the `<jsp:param>` action.

The syntax for the `<jsp:param>` action is as follows:

```
<jsp:param name="parameter name" value="paramater value" />
```

To understand the use of the `<jsp:param>` action, consider the following example. A few kids residing on a common block have hosted a Web site for their group that actively volunteers hours at local orphanages and other NGOs (Non-Government Organizations). The site provides services such as a discussion forum for group members and chatting services. The site has a secret common password that allows members to log on. Let's use the request parameters to check the password of the logged user. If the user provides the correct password, the `forward` action is used to forward the page control to LatestEvents.jsp. Else, the user is forwarded to a general site with a few games and a message encouraging him or her to join the group. The code for this example is as follows:

```
<html>
<head><title>A <jsp:param> action with a <jsp:forward> action
example</title></head>
<body>
<%
if ((request.getparameter("password")).equals("buzkids")) {
%>
<jsp:forward page="LatestEvents.jsp">
<jsp:param="user" value="member" />
</jsp:forward>
<%
}
else {
%>
<jsp:forward page="Games.jsp">
<jsp:param="user" value="nonmember" />
</jsp:forward>
<%
}
%>
</body>
</html>
```

Table 5.8   Attributes of the `param` Action

ATTRIBUTE	USED TO SPECIFY...
name	A name for the parameter
value	A value for the named parameter

<jsp:include>

This standard action is used to include a static or dynamic file in a JSP page. The file inclusion occurs during the request time phase of the compilation process. Table 5.9 describes the attributes of the `<jsp:include>` action.

The syntax for the `<jsp:include>` action is as follows:

```
<jsp:include page="URL specification" />
```

From the preceding syntax, you'll observe that there is a lot of similarity in the function and declaration of the `include` directive and the `<jsp:include>` action. Although they appear similar, their executional results are different. To highlight the difference in the output by the use of the `include` directive and action, let's consider the following example of St. Peter's Convent's Web site. The forum posts updates on the meetings held in the school on a daily basis. We will use both the `include` directive and action with a dynamic and static resource to show the difference in their outputs. The static resource will be in the form of the information regarding a parents-teachers meeting in the following week. The dynamic resource will be in the form of the current date and time. Let's look at the code for this example:

```
<html>
<head><title>The include directive and action</title></head>
<body>
<h3>This example brings out the difference between the include directive
and the include action</h3><hr>
<h3>The output of the include directive</h3>
<%@ include file="time.jsp" %><hr>
<%@ include file="meeting.html" %><hr>
<h3>The output of the include action</h3>
<jsp:include page="time.jsp" flush="true" />
<jsp:include page="meeting.html" flush="true" />
</body>
</html>
```

Table 5.9   Attributes of the `include` Action

ATTRIBUTE	USED TO SPECIFY...
Page	The relative URL of the page to be included.
Flush	If the buffer has to be flushed. A mandatory Boolean attribute has to be included when declaring the include action.

The code for time.jsp is as follows:

```
<html>
<%@ page import="java.util.*" %>
<%--This is the HTML content--%>
<head><title>The dynamic resource</title></head>
<body>
<%= new Date().toString() %>
</body>
</html>
```

The code for meeting.html is as follows:

```
<html>
<head><title>The static resource</title></head>
<body>
<h4>The slots for the parents-teachers meeting for Vth grade </h4><hr>
<table border="1" width="47%">
  <tr>
    <td width="32%">Time slot</td>
    <td width="68%">Roll nos</td>
  </tr>
  <tr>
    <td width="32%">9:30-10:30</td>
    <td width="68%">1-10</td>
  </tr>
  <tr>
    <td width="32%">10:30-11:30</td>
    <td width="68%">11-20</td>
  </tr>
</table>
</body>
</html>
```

Figure 5.6 displays the output of the include directive.

The output of the include directive

Fri Dec 07 16:16:54 GMT+05:30 2001

The slots for the parents-teachers meet for Vth grade

Time slot	Roll nos
9:30-10:30	1-10
10:30-11:30	11-20

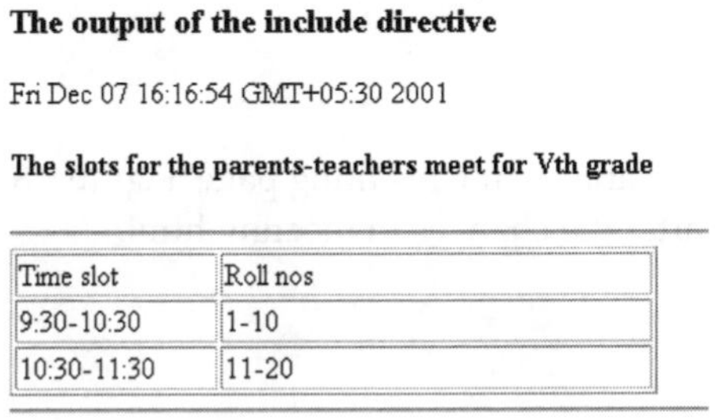

Figure 5.6 Output of the include directive.

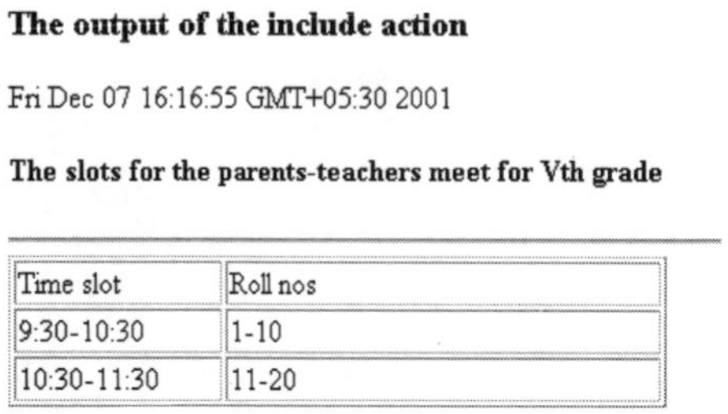

The output of the include action

Fri Dec 07 16:16:55 GMT+05:30 2001

The slots for the parents-teachers meet for Vth grade

Time slot	Roll nos
9:30-10:30	1-10
10:30-11:30	11-20

Figure 5.7 Output of the `include` action.

Figure 5.7 displays the output of the `include` action.

To understand the difference in the outputs, let's now change the static content of the file. Feedback from the parents has requested an increase in the time slots for the parents-teachers meeting. As a result, the code for meeting.html, after changes, is as follows:

```
<html>
<head><title>The static resource</title></head>
<body>
<h4>The slots for the parents-teachers meeting for Vth grade </h4><hr>
<table border="1" width="47%">
  <tr>
    <td width="32%">Time slot</td>
    <td width="68%">Roll nos</td>
  </tr>
  <tr>
    <td width="32%">9:30-11:00</td>
    <td width="68%">1-10</td>
  </tr>
  <tr>
    <td width="32%">10:30-12:00</td>
    <td width="68%">11-20</td>
  </tr>
</table>
</body>
</html>
```

Let's request this page again and observe the change in the resulting page. Figure 5.8 displays the output of the `include` directive after the changes in meeting.html.

The output of the include directive

Fri Dec 07 16:25:21 GMT+05:30 2001

The slots for the parents-teachers meet for Vth grade

Time slot	Roll nos
9:30-10:30	1-10
10:30-11:30	11-20

Figure 5.8 Output of the include directive after changes.

Figure 5.9 displays the output of the include action after the changes in meeting.
html.

What do you see? Is there a difference in the outputs generated by the include
directive and the include action? It is evident from the figures that the change in the
slot timings is updated in the content generated by the include action; however, the
output generated by the include directive still displays the old slot timings. What
does this mean? It means that the include directive does not update changes made to
a static resource. The include action, however, updates all the changes made to the
static resource because the parent page with the include directive remains unaltered
and is not recompiled. On the other hand, the output of the parent page with the
include action changes since it is recompiled. As a result, although the inclusions by
the include action are refreshed at each request, the inclusions by the include directive do not change.

The output of the include action

Fri Dec 07 16:25:21 GMT+05:30 2001

The slots for the parents-teachers meet for Vth grade

Time slot	Roll nos
9:30-11:00	1-10
10:30-12:00	11-20

Figure 5.9 Output of the include action after changes.

<jsp:plugin>

This standard action is used to generate browser-specific HTML tags by downloading Java plug-in software, which in turn executes an applet or a JavaBean component. As a result, the <jsp:plugin> tag is replaced by either the <object> or <embed> tag that facilitates the display of the embedded component. Table 5.10 describes the attributes of the <jsp:plugin> action.

The syntax for the <jsp:plugin> action is as follows:

```
<jsp:plugin type="Type of plugin" code="classfile" codebase="URL" />
```

Let's use the <jsp:plugin> action to embed an applet in a JSP page. Consider the example of an online library that provides facilities for the issue and delivery of books to members free of cost. To improve customer interactions, the site has a page assigned to accept feedback from customers regarding the book collection and services offered by the library. Let's use the <jsp:plugin> action to embed an HTML text area in the JSP page to accept these comments. The code for the Java file that will create the text area for this example will be as follows:

```java
import java.awt.*;
import java.awt.event.*;
import java.applet.*;
import javax.swing.*;
public class libApplet extends JApplet {
    boolean isStandalone = false;
    TextArea Txt = new TextArea();
    GridLayout gl =new GridLayout(1,2);
    public String getParameter(String k, String d){
        return (isStandalone ? System.getProperty(k, d): (getParameter (k)
!= null ? getParameter (k) : d));
    }
        public libApplet() {
    }
public void init() {
    try {
        Txt.setText(" ");
        this.setSize(new Dimension(400, 300));
        this.getContentPane().setLayout (gl);
        this.getContentPane().add(Txt, null);
    }
    catch (Exception ee) {
        ee.printStackTrace();
    }
}
public String getAppletInfo() {
```

```
   return " Information about Applet";
}
public String getParameterinfo() {
   return null;
}
static {
   try {
UIManager.setLookAndFeel(UIManager.getSystemLookAndFeelClassName());
}
catch (Exception ee) {}
}
}
```

The code for the supporting JSP will be as follows:

```
<html>
<head> <title>A plugin action example</title></head>
<body>
   <h3>Welcome to BookWorm library services</h3>
   <h4>Please add your notes or comments In the text area below</h4>
   <table>
   <tr><td>
   <jsp:plugin type="applet" code="libApplet.class"
codebase="/j2sdkee1.2.1/lib/classes" width="400" height="350">
   </jsp:plugin>
   </td></tr>
   </table>
</body>
</html>
```

NOTE Before executing this code, compile the .java file, and place the .class file in the C:\j2sdkee1.2.1\lib\classes folder.

In addition, when you execute the preceding code, you are prompted to install and run Java Plug-in 1.2.2 from the Sun Microsystems site. You can add notes into the text area only on completion of the installation.

Table 5.10 Attributes of the `plugin` Action

ATTRIBUTE	USED TO SPECIFY...
type	The type of included plug-in—for example, a Java applet
code	The name of the executable class of the Java plug-in
codebase	The relative path of the placement of the code attribute

Identify the JSP Tag to Add the Content of the Schedule to the Login Page

The examples in the preceding code have highlighted the use and importance of each of the standard actions. Summarizing the discussion to identify the tag that you'll use for including the schedule in the login page, you'll agree on the following points:

- The <jsp:include> action will be used to add the content of the schedule file to that of the login page.
- The login page to be used is Login.jsp.
- The schedule file to be used is Header.html.

Add the Tag-Specific Line of Code to the Login Page Code

Once the decision about the use of the relevant tag and files is complete, we can proceed to add the tag-specific line of code to that of Login.jsp. The code for Login.jsp with the include action is as follows:

```
<html>
<head>
<title>Login Id</title>
</head>
<body bgcolor="#FFDFD7">
<%--The include directive is used here to add the elements of the file
Header.html to the login page--%>
<%@ include file="Header.html" %>
<%--The include action is used here to add the details of the meeting
schedule of the file Schedule.html to the login page--%>
<jsp: include page="Schedule.html" flush="true" />
<form method="POST" action="validate.jsp">
<P>
<font color="#0000FF" face="Arial">
Login Id:::::::::::::::::</font>
<%--The input element to accept the login Id--%>
<INPUT type="text" name="T1" size="20">
</P>
<P><FONT color="#0000FF" face="Arial">
Password:::::::::::::::</FONT>
<%--The input element to accept the password--%>
<INPUT type="text" name="T2" size="20">
        
        
</P>
<P>
         
     
```

```
</P>
<P>
         
         
         
         
  
```

Execute the Code

To view the output of the login page, simply follow these steps:

1. Locate the file LoginHdr.jsp that we had saved at the end of the earlier task, and add the JSP include action-specific lines of code to it. Save the file as LoginHdrSchedule.jsp.

2. Copy LoginHdr.jsp, hdr.html, Schedule.html, and the graphic file for the bank's logo, dd00448_1.wmf, into the public_html folder in the C:\j2sdkee1.2.1 directory.

3. Start the server by typing `start j2ee -verbose` at the command prompt.

4. Open the Internet Explorer browser, and type the location of the .jsp file as `http://localhost:8000/ LoginHdrSchedule.jsp`.

View the JSP Page

Figure 5.10 displays the output of the login page after the inclusion of the schedule.

Change the Date and Time of the Schedule to Verify It Has Been Updated in the JSP Page

Both the `include` directive and the `include` action are used to add the content of other files to a JSP page. The `include` directive adds only static content to a JSP page. The `include` action, on the other hand, adds the content to the JSP page and updates the content with the corresponding changes made to the source file. Let's check this functionality of the `include` action by changing the date and time of the scheduled meeting in the source file. Make the following changes in Schedule.html:

1. Open the file Schedule.html from C:\j2sdkee1.2.1\public_html, and change the date and time of the meeting to:

   Saturday, 1st February, 2002

2. Reexecute LoginHdrSchedule.jsp.

Figure 5.11 displays the updated schedule added to the content of LoginHdr.jsp, the login page before the inclusion of the header elements.

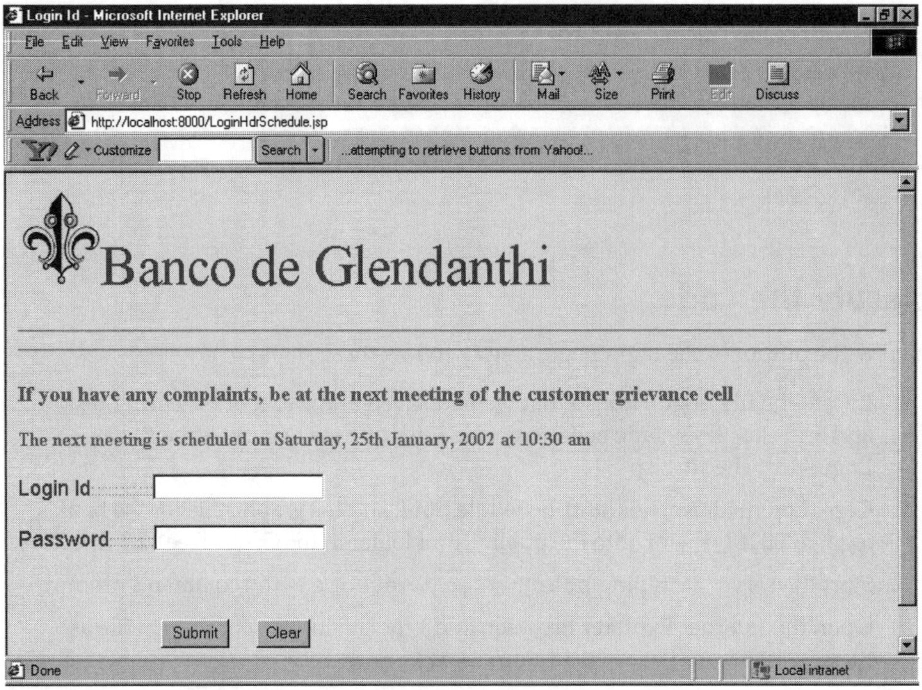

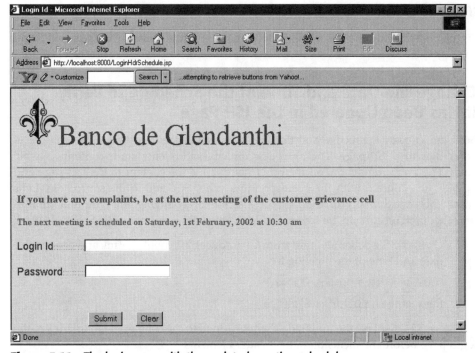

Figure 5.10   The login page with the meeting schedule.

Figure 5.11   The login page with the updated meeting schedule.

A feeling of exhilaration must have filled your hearts at the end of this task. In the course of this chapter we have covered directives and actions and seen outputs of quite a few examples. Nonetheless, this is still the beginning—what lies in store is much more that what we have accomplished until now.

Summary

A programmer's job requires coding for content that may be repetitive. With the introduction of JSP, the tedious and monotonous task of rewriting codes was encapsulated in tags. These tags facilitated the display of elements common to all pages of the application.

In this chapter, we have discussed two such tags that encapsulate recurring elements of a JSP page. These tags, called JSP directives and JSP actions, primarily bundle code segments into tags. As a result, a repetitive code can be added to a JSP page, by simply specifying the corresponding tag. We also discussed the difference between the `include` action and directive with an example.

The tasks for the bank site used both the `include` directive and `include` action to add static and dynamic content to the application pages. The login page that was used for these tasks consisted of text boxes to accept inputs from the user. Because these boxes or controls form an integral part of any user interface, in the next chapter we will discuss these controls in detail.

CHAPTER

6

Working with HTML Forms

OBJECTIVES:

In this chapter, you will learn to do the following:

- ✓ **Identify the role of form data**
- ✓ **Identify the various elements of an HTML form**
- ✓ **Identify the mechanism used for the transfer of form data**
- ✓ **Create an HTML form**
- ✓ **Validate the data in an HTML form**

Getting Started

In the last chapter, we used JSP directives and standard actions to incorporate both static and dynamic content in an application. Do these elements build only a JSP application? The execution of an interactive application is not complete without inputs from the user. These inputs help in the exchange of information between the client and the server and facilitate dynamic interactions. During a stock-trading transaction, user inputs help the server to identify the user and transfer the specified shares to his or her account. To facilitate these interactions, the inputs from the user need to be collected at the client side and subsequently forwarded to the server for necessary validation and processing.

All JSP elements facilitate the display of content, either directly or indirectly; however, they do not collect user-specific inputs that are important for server-side processing. The following example highlights the importance of collecting user-specific inputs. Have you ever gone shopping during the peak of the Christmas shopping fervor? The sound and noise in the stores during holiday time make it difficult to carry on a conversation. It comes as no surprise that you end up buying the wrong sizes as a result of the noisy, crowded environment and the miscommunication between you and the sales staff. Of course, in situations like this, you do have the option of exchanging the garment for one that is the right size. Would you make such mistakes when shopping online? The purpose of shopping from home is defeated if you still have to visit the shop to exchange a faulty or inappropriate item purchased from an online shopping mall. You'll surely not appreciate it if a page is incorrectly displayed or wrong items are billed to your credit card during an online shopping spree. Unless the user input is erroneous, miscommunication and slips of this type on the Web are not acceptable. The user expects the output to match his or her input when shopping online.

As part of Web interaction, collecting specific data from the user in order to deliver information that is specific and relevant to the input is important. Accordingly, applications require a medium to accept inputs from the user. This medium should facilitate access to the output that is specific to the input.

As regular users of the Internet, you must have used user interfaces that specify formats for input in the form of text boxes, buttons, and lists. For example, during a visit to an online bookstore, you are expected to log on by using a specific name and password. Subsequently, you also need to specify your purchase details and the mode of payment, check or credit card. The data for all these inputs is collected by controls created in an HTML document. These controls function as input collectors and transfer the collected data to the server. The document that is used to specify the design and layout of these controls is called an HTML form.

What are HTML forms, and how do they transmit data? The online banking site scenarios that we have chosen for the task-based sessions of these chapters need to accept inputs from the user. To accept these inputs, we will create controls in various formats to collect the user inputs. Because HTML forms primarily work as input collectors, this chapter will begin with a discussion of the structure and components of an HTML form. To help structure the design of the form, we will create a registration form to accept data from new customers who wish to open accounts with the bank. The final sections of the chapter will detail data transmission and validations before the commencement of processing at the server end.

HTML Forms

Filling out forms is a task related to everyday life in schools, offices, hospitals, and other institutions. New admission in a school? Fill out this form. Requisition for a particular book? We will mail it to you; please fill out this form. In the absence of forms, data cannot be collected for server-side processing. Therefore, Web interactions depend on HTML forms to collect user-specific data.

HTML forms are very similar to the paper forms described in the preceding examples. The only visible difference between a paper form and an HTML form is that an HTML form is an electronic document. It is an important component of a Web application because it accepts data from the user. Completed paper forms are processed after they reach specific departments. In a similar manner, HTML forms are submitted to the server for further processing.

To get an insight into the structure and components of an HTML form, let's create a form to accept the registration details of a new customer for the banking site.

Creating an HTML Form

Problem Statement

Banco de Glendanthi, by virtue of its prompt services and customer care, is a respected name in the banking sector today. With the hosting of its online banking services, new customers register and open accounts online every day. A customer only needs to fill out the online registration form. If all criteria essential for having an account with the bank are met, the bank's administrator processes the form, and the customer is given an account with the bank.

Let's design the registration form that will accept all customer details. The primary coding language for the static content of a Web application is HTML. Therefore, this will be an HTML form.

Task List

☑ **Identify the components of the user interface.**

☑ **Identify HTML form elements for the user interface.**

☑ **Identify the mechanism for the transfer of data using forms.**

☑ **Write the code for the HTML form.**

☑ **View the HTML form.**

☑ **Validate the form data values.**

☑ **Write the code to validate the user input.**

☑ **Submit the form to validate the data in the form.**

Identify the Components for the User Interface

The form has to be designed as a user interface to gather information about the customer. After the form is filled out and has been validated at the client end and the server end for correct format entries, it is transferred to the bank's database. In order to collect user-specific information, the form should contain the following categories of input and controls:

- Personal details
- The username that can be split into three parts for the title, the first name, and the last name
- The address consisting of the street, apartment or suite number, city, state, and zip
- The social security number to ensure that the account holder is a legal taxpayer
- The home phone number
- The email ID
- Financial details
- The annual income of the customer
- The source of income
- Account details
- The type of account desired

Identify the HTML Form Elements for the User Interface

Now that you understand the basic concepts of HTML, you'll be able to infer that the structure and design of the registration form will contain all basic HTML tags. Correspondingly, the following elements will be part of the HTML form. Table 6.1 describes the HTML tags used for the design of the form.

Although Table 6.1 provides a quick reference to the tags in the form, it does appear rather complex. We need to understand the various form- and input-specific tags of the HTML form. Let's now examine each of the form-specific tags in detail.

Table 6.1 The HTML Tags of the User Interface

INPUT	TAG TO BE USED
Basic tags	`<HTML>`, `<HEAD>`, `<BODY>` **tags**
Background and font color formats	`<bg color>` **and** `<font color>` **tags**
Bank's name and logo	The graphic file, `<img>` **tag, and name of the bank enclosed within the** `<p>` **tags**
Text boxes and other controls for user inputs	Form-specific tags
Submit button to submit the form data	Form-specific tags

An HTML form basically consists of the following tags:

The form tag. This tag defines the form and consists of various input elements.

The input tag. This tag consists of various elements such as text boxes and buttons in the form.

The select tag. This tag consists of various elements that are used to display options in the form of lists in the form.

The Form Tag

Just as the <html> tag defines the HTML document, the <form> tag defines a form. It creates an area for the display of the various controls to accept user input. The input and select elements of the <form> tag are used to create these controls.

Other than accepting user inputs, an HTML form also transfers the input data to the server side. The transferred data is appended to or contained in the request and interpreted on the server side. As a result, the <form> tag uses the following attributes to specify the type of request method, the URL of the target page or the server-side script, and the submission and acceptance criteria for the input data:

- The method attribute
- The action attribute
- The OnSubmit and OnReset attributes

It is obvious that the information specified by the attributes of the <form> tag specify the general transmission details of the form data. Let's examine these attributes to understand their role in the transmission of form data.

The method Attribute

The method attribute determines the type of request method to be used to transfer the form data. If the GET method is used, the data is appended to the URL and sent to the server. If the method specified is POST, then a new line is added to the body of the request to send the form data. The default method adopted to transmit the form data is the GET method. The syntax for using the method attribute is as follows:

```
<form method="GET/POST">
......</form>
```

Both the GET method and the POST method have their own advantages and disadvantages. The GET method is simpler to operate because it accepts the URL along with the appended data; however, this method is not suitable for sending huge volumes of data because some browsers restrict the size of the URL. In addition, the URL, along with the appended data, is visible in the address bar or the status bar of the browser. Therefore, this method is not suitable for sending confidential data. On the other hand, the POST method is used to transmit unlimited volumes of data. In addition, because the URL is not displayed in the address bar during data transmission, this method is preferred for sending confidential data.

The action Attribute

The `action` attribute is used to specify the URL of the page or the server-side that is the target for the data transmitted by the form. The action attribute of the form tag generally contains a URL to a server-side script that is invoked when the submit button is pressed and that initiates the processing of the form data. The syntax for using the `action` attribute is as follows:

```
<form method="GET/POST" action="URL of the processing page">
......</form>
```

For example, consider the case for an online technical help site for a hardware vendor. Headway Peripherals has an online technical help site where customers can log on to report their hardware problems. An HTML form is used to collect information about the hardware-related problem. Validation of registered users is based on the email address stored in the company's database. The structure for registering the complaint is as follows:

- After entering the email address and the details of the hardware problem, the user submits the complaint form.
- The form data is sent to a JSP page for validating the email.
- If the email address entered by the user matches the email address in the database, a confirmation message along with the date of service is sent back to the user's email address.

Let's consider the use of the form element along with the `method` and the `action` attribute to specify the lines of code for logging a service request at the Headway Peripheral's site. The following is the code snippet for posting the data to hdwaysupport.jsp:

```
<form action="hdwaysupport.jsp" action="GET/POST">
</form>
```

NOTE The preceding code example is just a part of the code in an HTML form. Remember that there will be various other elements between the `<form>` and `</form>` tags to specify the controls of the form.

The OnSubmit and OnReset Attributes

The `OnSubmit` and `OnReset` attributes are used to ensure that the user input follows a specified format, failing which the form is not submitted. Using these attributes, a JavaScript code is invoked after the user clicks the submit or reset button in the HTML form. The JavaScript code subsequently validates the format of the user input, which decides whether the form should be submitted. The syntax for using the `action` attribute is as follows:

```
<form method="GET/POST" action="URL of the processing page"
onSubmit/OnReset="Name of the JavaScript method that will validate the
```

```
content in the form controls">
......</form>
```

After the form is designed and its code is formulated, the form is presented to the user for input. Obviously, on completion, the user is expected to submit the form. What happens next? How is the input from the user transmitted to the server side? How is the data from the form extracted for further processing? To find answers to these questions, let's look at the mechanism of data transmission in HTML forms.

The Mechanism for Transfer of Data Using Forms

We have already discussed that interactions between the user computer or browser and the server take place through the request-response cycle. As a result, the data collected through the form travels to the server as a part of the request-response cycle. This cycle is initiated when the user specifies the URL of the requested page in the address bar of the browser. For example, the URL http://www.Technovarsity.com requests the home page of the online university site hosted by Ace Educational Services. Nevertheless, how is the user-specific information, such as the student login name and password or the choice of course, transmitted to the server? Curious? Let's look at how data is transmitted through forms.

An HTML form, as we have discussed, uses simple controls to accept data from the user and transfer it to the server. These controls are identified by a name and hold a value that is specified by the user. All the controls or elements of the form are collectively associated with the URL of the requested file. As a result, when the user submits the form, request methods such as POST or GET are used to transmit the values of the user input. Based on the type of request, the names and values of the elements of the form are collected into a string and then designated to the URL in the following two ways:

If the request uses the GET method. The string containing the names and values of the controls is directly appended to the end of the URL in the form of a query string. The query string is appended after the ? symbol of the URL. The values of the form data in the query string are separated by ampersands (&). Let's assume that the user input for the first name and the last name in the registration form for the Technovarsity site is Catherine and Jones, respectively. If the GET method is used to transmit this data to the server, these values will be attached to the end of the URL string in the following manner:

```
http://www.technovarsity.com?firstname=Catherine&lastname=Jones
```

If the request uses the POST method. The string containing the names and values of the controls is contained in a separate line within the body of the request. Such a method of data transmission is not displayed with the URL. As a result, it is a preferred means of transmitting confidential data.

The POST and GET methods inform the server about request- and data-related information. What about user-specific information? How does an HTML form collect user-specific data? It is easy to visualize text boxes in a form to accept the user input. What about the tags that are used to specify the various formats for the inputs? Do forms allow data input in formats other than text boxes and buttons? Yes, they do! You can add various types of controls such as text fields, text areas, check boxes, radio buttons, combo boxes, and list boxes. As discussed earlier, all these controls are created by using the input and select elements of the <form> tag. Let's examine each of these form elements before we write the code for the HTML form.

The input Element

The input element that is represented by the <input> tag is an empty tag. As a result, unlike the <form> tag, the input tag has only a start tag and does not require an end tag. The <input> tag accepts data in the form of controls and can be of the following four types: text controls, push buttons, radio buttons, and check boxes. Each of these controls has attributes that specify the type, name, and value of the control. Table 6.2 describes these attributes in detail.

An HTML form can include three types of controls that are created by using the <input> tag:

Text controls.   These controls accept textual content in the form of single- or multiple-line entries.

Push buttons.   These controls are displayed in the form of buttons that are clicked to submit or reset forms.

Radio buttons and check boxes.   These controls are used to display a predetermined set of options in the form of radio buttons and check boxes.

We will use simple examples to build a form to accept user input. Although these examples may seem disconnected, the aim is to understand the use of the controls created by the input and select elements. Let's examine each of these controls to understand their display format by using simple examples.

Text Controls

Text controls accept input in the form of text. According to the format of data input, text controls can be of the following three types: text fields, password fields, and text areas. Let's examine how these three specifications define varied formats for the user input.

Text fields accept input in the form of single-line textual entries. Table 6.3 describes the attributes of the <input> tag to create a text field.

Table 6.2 The Attributes of the input Element

ATTRIBUTE	USED TO SPECIFY...
type	The type of input object that is being used. This attribute determines the kind of control that will be used to accept the user input.
name	The name of the input object that identifies the control in the form.
value	The value that is drawn from the content accepted in the control.

Table 6.3 The Attributes of a Text Field

ATTRIBUTE	SPECIFIES...	EXAMPLE
type	The type of control to be created. The type attribute for a text field is text.	`<input type="text">`
name	The name for the input object.	`<input type="text" name="T1">`
value	If supplied, specifies the initial content in the control. If not supplied, the current contents of the control are posted along with the form submission.	`<input type="text" name="T1" value="Catherine">`

For example, the following code, for an e-greeting site, specifies two text controls to accept the login name and the last name of the user.

```
<html>
<head><title>A simple form</title>
<body>
<h3>An HTML form with text fields</h3>
<form method="POST" action="hdwaysupport.jsp">
Enter your first name:::::::::
<input type="text" name="T1" value="Joe"></br>
Enter your last name:::::::::
<input type="text" name="T2" value="Barns">
</form>
<body>
<html>
```

In the preceding example, the value attribute is used to display the initial values for the first and last name; however, the use of this attribute is optional because the data transmitted consists of the current content of the control. Figure 6.1 displays the output of this form.

NOTE You can save these files as .html files and view them from the local drive by using Internet Explorer.

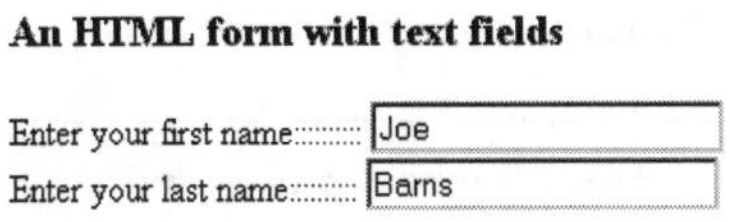

An HTML form with text fields

Enter your first name:········ | Joe |
Enter your last name:········ | Barns |

Figure 6.1 A form example with text fields.

Each day we use email services to read and send mails. Accordingly, we log in by specifying the user ID and the password. Have you noticed the difference in the display of the text in the ID and password boxes? The text entered in the ID box is displayed in the same form that it is entered; the text entered in the password box is displayed as asterisks. How does the text input change to asterisks? Because of its frequent use in displaying passwords, this type of text control is called the password field. Moreover, the task of changing the display format is not complex. All you need to do for the asterisks to display is change the type attribute from text to password. In addition, the value attribute is not specified to maintain the confidentiality of the user input. Table 6.4 describes the attributes of the <input> tag to create a password field.

The following code illustrates the use of the password field to accept the user input in the form of asterisks:

```
<html>
<head><title>A simple form</title>
<body>
<h3>An HTML form with text and password fields</h3>
<form method="POST" action="hdwaysupport.jsp">
Enter your first name:::::::::::
<input type="text" name="T1"></br>
Enter your last name:::::::::::
<input type="text" name="T2">
Enter your password::::::::::
<input type="password" name="T3">
Re-enter your password::::::::::
<input type="password" name="T4">
</form>
<body>
<html>
```

Figure 6.2 displays the output of the preceding code.

Often, user input can be in the form of multiline text. For example, a medical record at a hospital that requires information about allergies can run to more than one line of text. How do you accept entries that can run to multiple lines of text? The solution is to use the text area field. This type of text control does not use the value attribute. Instead, it specifies the length and width of the text area in the form of rows and columns. Table 6.5 describes the attributes of the <input> tag to create a text area field.

Table 6.4   The Attributes of the Password Field

ATTRIBUTE	SPECIFIES...	EXAMPLE
type	The type attribute for a password field is password.	`<input type="password">`
name	The name for the input object.	`<input type="password" name="T2">`

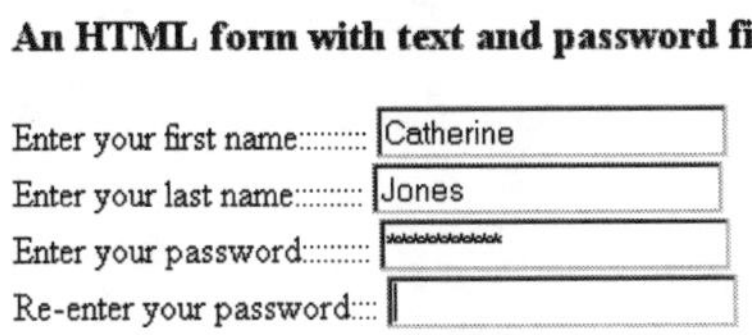

An HTML form with text and password fields

Enter your first name:·········· | Catherine |
Enter your last name:·········· | Jones |
Enter your password:·········· | ✲✲✲✲✲✲✲✲✲ |
Re-enter your password:···· | |

Figure 6.2 A form example with a password field.

The following code uses the text area field to accept user input in the form of a personalized message to be sent with an online e-greeting card:

```
<html>
<head><title>A simple form</title>
<body>
<h3>An HTML form with a text area</h3>
<form method="POST" action="hdwaysupport.jsp">
<h5> Would you like to add a personalized message with your choice of
greeting?</h5>
<textarea name="txt1" rows=10 cols=30>
</textarea>
</form>
</body>
</html>
```

Figure 6.3 displays the output of the preceding code.

Table 6.5 The Attributes of a Text Area

ATTRIBUTE	SPECIFIES	EXAMPLE
type	The type attribute for a text field is textarea.	`<input type="textarea">`
name	The name for the input object.	`<input type="textarea" name="TXT1">`
rows	The height of the text area.	`<input type="textarea" name="TXT1" rows="5">`
cols	The width of the text area.	`<input type="textarea" name="TXT1" rows="5" cols="25">`

An HTML form with a text area

Would you like to add a personalized message with your choice of greeting?

Figure 6.3 A form example with a text area.

An inevitable action that follows user input to the form controls is the submission of the form for further processing and output generation. What types of form elements are used to submit a form? HTML forms use buttons to submit forms. Let's examine the various types of buttons that can be added to an HTML form.

Push Buttons

The action of submitting and clearing or resetting a form is achieved with the help of push buttons. An HTML form contains two types of buttons, the submit button and the reset button. Both these tags are also elements of the `<input>` tag.

When clicked, the submit button automatically submits the data held in the form to the server for further processing. Like all the other input elements, the submit button also takes on a type, name, and value as attributes. The `type` is specified as submit because the type of control display is a submit button. The `name` attribute provides the identification for the button, while the `value` attribute, which is user defined, functions as a label and is displayed on the button. If the user does not specify the `value` attribute, the label attached to the button reads as "Submit Query." Table 6.6 describes the attributes of the `<input>` tag to create a submit button.

Figure 6.4 displays the submit button created by the following line of code:

```
<input type="submit" name="B1"  value="Send the query">
```

Table 6.6 The Attributes of a Submit Button

ATTRIBUTE	SPECIFIES...	EXAMPLE
type	The type attribute for a submit button is submit.	`<input type="submit">`
name	The name for the button.	`<input type="submit" name="B1">`
value	If supplied, is displayed on the button; else the default value of Submit Query is used.	`<input type="submit" name="B1" value= "Calculate">`

Send the query

Figure 6.4 A submit button.

Let's now add a submit button to the preceding code for the e-greeting. The code with a submit button will read as follows:

```
<html>
<head><title>A simple form</title>
<body>
<h3>An HTML form with a text area</h3>
<form method="POST" action="hdwaysupport.jsp">
<h5> Would you like to add a personalized message with your choice of
greeting?</h5>
<textarea name="txt1" rows=10 cols=30>
</textarea></br></br>
<input type="submit" name="B1"  value="Mail the e-Card">
</form>
</body>
</html>
```

Figure 6.5 displays the output of this code.

In addition to submitting the form, a user can also clear the values of a form or set them to their original default values. The only difference between the code for the submit button and the reset button is the specification for the `type` attribute. In the case of the submit button, the type specification is submit; the type specification for the reset button is reset. In addition, the `name` attribute for the reset button is not specified because this control only clears the form contents and does not require a reference during data transmission.

Table 6.7 describes the attributes of the `<input>` tag to create a reset button.

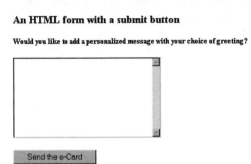

An HTML form with a submit button

Would you like to add a personalized message with your choice of greeting?

Send the e-Card

Figure 6.5 A form with a submit button.

Table 6.7   The Attributes of a Reset Button

ATTRIBUTE	SPECIFIES...	EXAMPLE
type	The type attribute for a reset button is reset.	`<input type="reset">`
value	The value attribute for a reset button is reset. Other values such as clear are also used.	`<input value = Clear" >`

```
<html>
<head><title>A simple form</title>
<body>
<h3>An HTML form with a text area</h3>
<form method="POST" action="hdwaysupport.jsp">
<h5> Would you like to add a personalized message with your choice of
greeting?</h5>
<textarea name="txt1" rows=10 cols=30>
</textarea></br></br>
<input type="submit" name="B1"  value="Mail the e-Card">
<input type="reset" value="Clear">
</form>
</form>
</body>
</html>
```

Figure 6.6 displays the output of the preceding code with a reset button.

You'll observe that, after the input of data in the preceding form, clicking the reset button clears the contents of the text area. That's exactly what a reset button does.

From the previous discussions, it is evident that the design of a form can include text controls and push buttons for accepting text entries from the user and submitting them for processing. A form need not require only text inputs or the submit/reset buttons. What about inputs that need to be based on certain selections? For example, at a shopping site, displaying the group of options for the mode of purchase as radio buttons and check boxes is preferred. Let's discuss the HTML tags used to create these controls.

An HTML form with a submit and reset button

Would you like to add a personalized message to your choice of greeting?

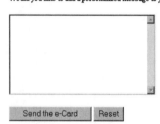

Figure 6.6   A form with a reset button.

Radio Buttons and Check Boxes

Both radio buttons and check boxes offer a set of predefined choices for the user. The difference between the two lies in the style used to display the chosen option.

Radio buttons are circular buttons that display a shaded spot ( ) when selected. They are grouped to ensure that one button is selected at a time. Like all other input tag elements, radio buttons also have the type, name, and value attributes. The type attribute is always "radio" and because the buttons form a group, they are all assigned a common name attribute. The value attribute takes different values for different options. Table 6.8 describes the attributes of the <input> tag to create a radio button.

When a radio button is selected, the value of the selected option is submitted along with the form. Let's add a group of radio buttons to the form for the e-greeting site. The user is presented with a choice of cards to send to friends and relatives. Let's now write the code to add the radio buttons for the different types of cards available for selection. The choices will be sorry cards, get well soon cards, anniversary cards, or birthday cards. The code for the insertion of radio buttons will be as follows:

```
<html>
<head><title>A simple form</title>
<body>
<h3>An HTML form with radio buttons</h3>
<form method="POST" action="hdwaysupport.jsp">
<h5> Choose the type of card that you would you like to send?</h5>
<input type="radio" name="card" value="sorry">Sorry Cards
<input type="radio" name="card" value="GWS">Get Well Soon Cards
<input type="radio" name="card" value="anniv">Anniversary Cards
<input type="radio" name="card" value="bday">Birthday Cards
</form>
</body>
</html>
```

Figure 6.7 displays the output of the preceding code.

Table 6.8 The Attributes of a Radio Button

ATTRIBUTE	SPECIFIES...	EXAMPLE
type	The type attribute for a text field is radio.	`<input type="radio">`
name	The name for the button that is common to the group of radio buttons.	`<input type="radio" name="RD1">`
value	The value of the button that is transmitted during form submission. This attribute is followed by a specification for text display alongside the radio button.	`<input type="radio" name="RD1" value= "Amex">Amex Card`

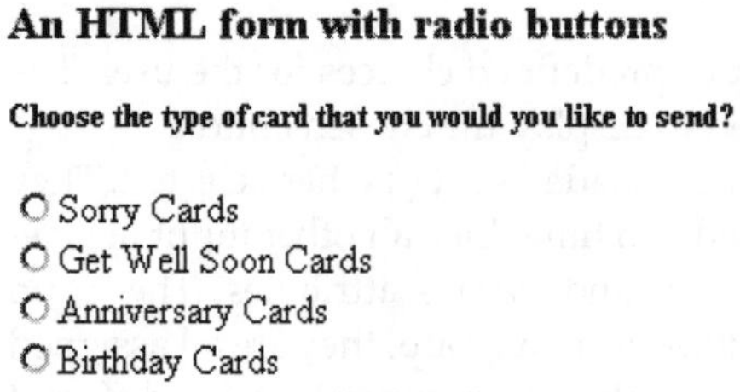

An HTML form with radio buttons

Choose the type of card that you would you like to send?

○ Sorry Cards
○ Get Well Soon Cards
○ Anniversary Cards
○ Birthday Cards

Figure 6.7   A form with radio buttons.

Check boxes, unlike radio buttons, are displayed as squares that present a tick mark (x) when selected. Unlike radio buttons, check boxes need to be singularly selected (checked) and deselected (unchecked) for a given set of choices. The `type` attribute for a check box takes the value as "checkbox." The `value` attribute is not specified for check boxes; however, you can specify the check or uncheck state of a particular check box by using the attribute `checked`. Table 6.9 describes the attributes of the `<input>` tag to create a check box.

Let's add check boxes to the code for the personalized message that is accepted in a text area. The check boxes will provide options to choose for a preview of the card before it is sent to the destination email address. The code for this example will be as follows:

```
<html>
<head><title>A simple form</title>
<body>
<h3>An HTML form with a text area, submit button, and check box</h3>
<form method="POST" action="hdwaysupport.jsp">
<h5> Would you like to add a personalized message with your choice of
greeting?</h5>
<textarea name="txt1" rows=10 cols=30>
</textarea></br></br>
<input type="checkbox" name="C1" Checked>Send card after a preview
<input type="checkbox" name="C2">Send card without preview</br></br>
<input type="submit" name="B1"  value="Mail the e-Card">
</form>
</body>
</html>
```

Table 6.9   The Attributes of a Check Box

ATTRIBUTE	SPECIFIES...	EXAMPLE
type	The type attribute for a text field is checkbox.	`<input type="checkbox">`
name	The name for the check box.	`<input type="checkbox" name="CB1">`

ATTRIBUTE	SPECIFIES...	EXAMPLE

checked	If a check box is to be checked by default when it is displayed. This attribute is followed by a specification for text display alongside the check box.	`<input type="checkbox"`
		`name="CB1" checked">`
		`Send a reminder`

Figure 6.8 displays the output of the preceding code.

So far, we have discussed the controls of the `input` element. Instead of displaying text boxes and options in the form of buttons or check boxes, you can also use lists to display the options. Let's discuss the attributes of the `select` element that are used to create these controls in the form of lists.

The select element

The `select` element that is represented by the `<select>` tag is a container tag. As a result, like the `<form>` tag, it has a start tag and an end tag. Based on whether the choice is singular or multiple, lists can be displayed as combo boxes or list boxes. Each of these controls has attributes that specify their name and the option value, which is derived from the control content.

Combo Boxes

The `select` element or the `<select>` tag is a container tag that requires a `name` attribute to identify the combo or list box. The choices for selection are specified by the use of the option entries that are embedded between the `<select>` tag and the `</select>` tag. The syntax to create a combo box is as follows:

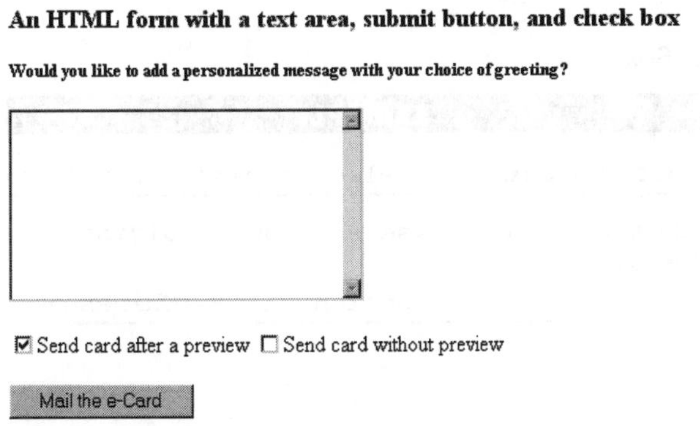

An HTML form with a text area, submit button, and check box

Would you like to add a personalized message with your choice of greeting?

☑ Send card after a preview ☐ Send card without preview

Mail the e-Card

Figure 6.8   A form with check boxes.

```
<select name="    ">
<option selected value="    ">Display name of option
<option selected value="    ">Display name of option
</select>
```

Table 6.10 describes the attributes of the <input> tag to create a list box.

Let's now create a combo box to list a few cuisines from which the user can select. The code to create this combo box is as follows:

```
<html>
<head><title>A simple form</title>
<body>
<h3>An HTML form with a combo box</h3>
<form method="POST" action="hdwaysupport.jsp">
<h5> Choose your favorite cuisine</h5>
<select name="cuisine">
<option selected value="C">Chinese
<option value="T">Taiwanese
<option value="M">Mexican
<option value="L">Lebanese
</select>
</form>
</body>
</html>
```

Figure 6.9 displays the output of the preceding code in the form of a combo box.

Figure 6.9 represents the combo box in its initial stage, where it displays only the option that is specified with the selected attribute. Figure 6.10 displays the combo box that is activated after the user clicks it.

The inclusion of the size attribute of the <select> tag decides if the display of the list will be as a combo or a list box. Table 6.11 describes the attributes of the <input> tag to create a combo box.

Table 6.10 The Attributes of a List Box

ATTRIBUTE	SPECIFIES...	EXAMPLE
name	The name for the combo box.	`<select name="cuisine">`
value	The various options that form the entries of the list.	`<select name="cuisine">`
		`<option value="Chinese>`

ATTRIBUTE	SPECIFIES...	EXAMPLE

selected	That the option appears as a default selection.	`<select name="cuisine">`
		
		`<option selected value="Taiwanese>`

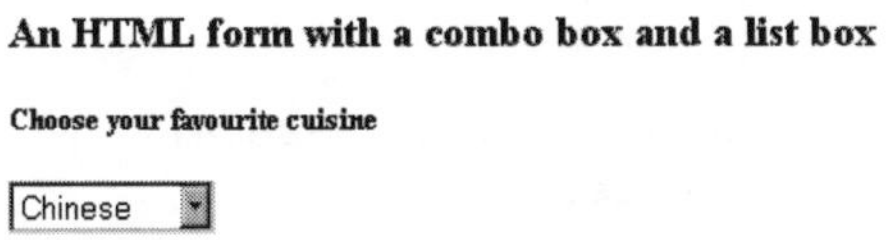

An HTML form with a combo box and a list box

Choose your favourite cuisine

Figure 6.9   A form with a combo box.

An HTML form with a cc

Choose your favourite cuisine

Chinese
Chinese
Taiwanese
Mexican
Lebanese

Figure 6.10   A form with all the listed options in the combo box.

Table 6.11   The Attributes of a Combo Box

ATTRIBUTE	SPECIFIES...	EXAMPLE
name	The name for the combo box.	`<select name="sports">`

value	The various options that form the entries of the list.	`<select name="sports">`
		
		`<option value="Tennis>`

(continues)

Table 6.11 The Attributes of a Combo Box *(Continued)*

ATTRIBUTE	SPECIFIES...	EXAMPLE
selected	That the option appears as a default selection.	`<select name="sports">`
		`<option value="Tennis" selected>`
size	The number of visible rows in the list box	`<select name="sports" size="3">`
		`<option value="Tennis" selected>`
		`<option value="Baseball" selected>`
		`<option value="Basketball" selected>`

To understand this principle, consider the code in the preceding example. To convert the combo box to a list box, all you need to do is add the following line to the `<select>` tag:

```
<select name="cuisine" size="4">
```

As a result, this code will be changed as follows:

```
<html>
<head><title>A simple form</title>
<body>
<h3>An HTML form with a combo box</h3>
<form method="POST" action="hdwaysupport.jsp">
<h5> Choose your favorite cuisine</h5>
<select name="cuisine" size="4">
<option selected value="C">Chinese
<option value="T">Taiwanese
<option value="M">Mexican
<option value="L">Lebanese
</select>
</form>
</body>
</html>
```

What of the output? How does it change? Figure 6.11 represents the change of the combo box into a list box by the addition of the `size` attribute.

An HTML form with a combo box and a list box

Choose your favourite cuisine

Figure 6.11   A form with a list box.

Similarly, all that you need to do to facilitate a multiple selection is to add the attribute `multiple` to the `<select>` tag; however, multiple selections are accepted in list boxes only. As a result, if the `multiple` attribute is added to the `<select>` tag in the preceding code for the combo box, it will be changed to a list box and accept multiple entries. The preceding code will then change as follows:

```
<html>
<head><title>A simple form</title>
<body>
<h3>An HTML form with a combo box</h3>
<form method="POST" action="hdwaysupport.jsp">
<h5> Choose your favorite cuisine</h5>
<select name="cuisine" multiple>
<option selected value="C">Chinese
<option value="T">Taiwanese
<option value="M">Mexican
<option value="L">Lebanese
</select>
</form>
</body>
</html>
```

Figure 6.12 shows the output of the combo box code with the `multiple` attribute.

Well, that completes our discussion of the various types of controls that can be added to an HTML form. We can now formulate the use of specific HTML tags and elements for the display of the various controls of the registration page. Table 6.12 describes the tags and elements for the controls of the page.

An HTML form with a combo box and a list box

Choose your favourite cuisine

Figure 6.12   A form that accepts multiple entries.

Table 6.12 The Controls of the Registration Form

INPUT	TYPE OF CONTROL	TAG TO BE USED
Title	Radio button	`<input type = "radio"name=" " value=" ">Display name`
First name	Text field	`<input type="text" name=" ">`
Last name	Text field	`<input type="text" name=" ">`
Home address, apt/suite#, city, state, zip	Separate text fields for each of the entries	`<input type="text" name=" ">`
Social security number	Three text fields	`<input type="text" name=" ">`
Home phone number	Three text fields	`<input type="text" name=" ">`
Annual income		`<input type="text" name=" ">`

Source of Income, account type	Combo boxes with appropriate options	`<select name=" ">`
		 `,option selected value=" ">Display name`
		 `</select>`

Reset and submit buttons	Push buttons	`<input type="button" name=" " value="Submit Form">` `<input type="reset" name=" " value="Reset">`

This completes the formulation of the structure and design of the registration form. Before we write the code for the form, let's decide on the mode of data transmission of the form.

Identify the Mechanism for Transfer of Data

We will use the POST method to submit the data in the registration form because it includes confidential customer details. In addition, let's specify the name of the target page as Validate.jsp, a JSP file, which will validate the data at the server side. As a result, the form-specific attributes for the <form> tag are as follows:

```
<form action="validate.jsp" action="POST">
```

Write the Code for the HTML Form

Now that we have concluded the choice of elements and the design of the user interface, let's write the code for the HTML form:

```
<html>

<head>

<title>Banco de Glendanthi</title>
</head>

<body bgcolor="#FFDFD7">

<form method="POST" action="Validate.jsp">
<p><font size="7" color="#0000FF">
<img border="0" src="dd00448_1.gif" >
Banco de Glendanthi</font></p>
    <hr>
    <p><font face="Arial" size="4" color="#FF6699">
    Registration   form for new account </font></p>
<hr>
<p><font color="#CC0099">
Please tell us about yourself:</font></p>
<p><font size="4"><font color="#0000FF">
Title (Optional)</font></font>::::::::::::::::
<font size="4"><font color="#0000FF">Mr</font>
<input type="radio" value="V1" checked name="R1">
<font color="#0000FF">Mrs</font>
<input type="radio" name="R1" value="V2">
<font color="#0000FF">Ms</font>
<input type="radio" name="R1" value="V3">
<font color="#0000FF">Dr</font>
<input type="radio" name="R1" value="V4"></font></p>
<p><font color="#0000FF" size="4">
First Name</font>::::::::::::::::::::::::::
<input type="text" name="T1" size="30"></p>
<p><font color="#0000FF" size="4">
Last Name:</font>:::::::::::::::::::::::
<input type="text" name="T2" size="30"></p>
<p><font color="#0000FF" size="4">
Social security #</font>:::::::::
<input type="text" name="T9" size="5">-
<input type="text" name="T10" size="8">-
<input type="text" name="T11" size="5"></p>
```

```
<p><font color="#0000FF" size="4">
Home Address</font>::::::::::::
<input type="text" name="T3" size="20"><font color="#0000FF"
size="4">Apt/Suite#</font>
<input type="text" name="T12" size="20"></p>
<p><font color="#0000FF" size="4">
City</font>::::::::::::::::::::::::::::::::::::::::
<input type="text" name="T13" size="20"><font color="#0000FF" size="4">
State</font>::::::
<input type="text" name="T14" size="14">
<font color="#0000FF" size="4">
Zip</font>:::::
<input type="text" name="T15" size="11"></p>
<p><font color="#0000FF" size="4">
Home</font>
<font color="#0000FF" size="4" face="Arial">
</font><font color="#0000FF" size="4">
Phone</font><font color="#0000FF" size="4" face="Arial">
</font>.::::::::::::::
<input type="text" name="T16" size="5">-
<input type="text" name="T17" size="8">-
<input type="text" name="T18" size="5"></p>
<p><font color="#0000FF" size="4">
Email</font><font color="#0000FF" size="4" face="Arial">
</font><font color="#0000FF" size="4">
Id</font>:::::::::::::::::::::::::::
<input type="text" name="T6" size="20">
<input type="text" name="T7" size="20"></p>
<p><font color="#CC0099">
Please provide us with your
financial information:</font></p>
<hr>
<p><font color="#0000FF" size="4">
Annual</font><font color="#0000FF" size="4" face="Arial">
</font><font color="#0000FF" size="4">
Income</font>::::::::::::
<input type="text" name="T5" size="20"></p>
<p><font color="#0000FF" size="4">
Source of Income</font>::::<select size="1" name="D2">
  <option selected>Business</option>
  <option>Service</option>
  <option>Agriculture</option>
  <option>Other sources</option>
```

```
</select></p>
<p><font color="#CC0099">Please tell us about the account
set up:</font></p>
<hr>
<p><font color="#0000FF" size="4">
Account</font><font color="#0000FF" size="4" face="Arial">
</font><font color="#0000FF" size="4"> Type</font>::::::::::::<select
size="1" name="D1">
  <option selected>Savings account</option>
  <option>Loan account</option>
  <option>Fixed deposits</option>
  <option>Recurring deposits</option>
</select></p>
  <p> </p>
  <p>  

            
            
       
  <input type="submit" value="Submit Form" name="B1">   <input
type="reset" value="Reset" name="B2"></p>
</form>
<p> </p>
</form>
</body>
</html>
```

View the HTML Form

To view the registration page follow the steps listed in the *Execute the Code* section of Chapter 5, "Using JSP Directives and Action Elements."

NOTE Although this code is HTML code, we will execute it on the J2EE server to clarify the subsequent concepts of data retrieval through forms.

Figure 6.13 shows the registration page as displayed in the browser window.

The next step after viewing the registration page is to validate the entry before submitting the form. Let's look at the methods used to validate data entry at the client side before submitting the form.

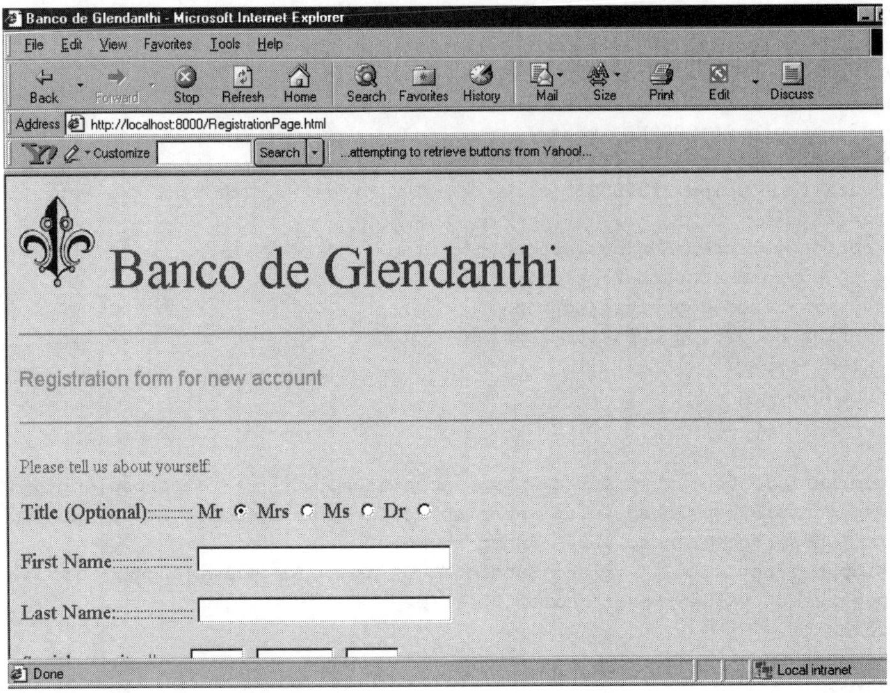

Figure 6.13 The registration page.

Validate the Form Data Values

The validation of data on the client side can be done by using JavaScript buttons. Only those browsers that support JavaScript accept these buttons. A JavaScript button creates a button that is very similar to an HTML button. The only difference is that when clicked, this button invokes a JavaScript code to validate the user entry. The attributes associated with the JavaScript code are OnClick, OnBlur, and OnFocus. The syntax for inclusion of such a button is as follows:

```
<input type="button" name="   " value="   " onClick="JavaScript method
name"
```

To understand such client-side validations, let's first create a simple HTML form to accept the login ID and password from the user. We can write the HTML code as follows:

```
<HTML>
<HEAD><TITLE>A sample HTML form</TITLE>
<BODY bgcolor="#FFDFD7">
<H1 Align="center">
<Font color="blue">Login check with JavaScript</Font> </H1><BR><BR>
       
```

```
        
     
<Font color="green"><B>Please login</B> </Font><BR><BR>
Login        
<INPUT Type="text" Name="Login" Value=""><BR>
Password  <INPUT Type="password" Name="pass" Value=""><BR><BR><BR>
            
        
<INPUT Type="button" Name="cmdSubmit" onclick="checkValues()"
Value="Submit" >
</BODY>
</HTML>
```

The validation to be performed after the submission of this form is to verify that entries for the login ID and password are not left blank. The JavaScript code to perform such a validation is as follows:

```
<SCRIPT language="JavaScript">
function checkValues()
{
var logName;
var logNameLength;
var password;
var passwordLength;
logName=Login.value;
logNameLength=logName.length;
while(logNameLength==0)
{
logName=prompt("Enter your Login Id","");
Login.value=logName;
logNameLength=logName.length;
}
password=pass.value;
passwordLength=password.length;
while(passwordLength==0)
{
password=prompt("Enter your Password","");
pass.value=password;
passwordLength=password.length;
}
}
</script>
```

Write the HTML Code to Validate User Input

NOTE The validation of user input uses the login page of Banco de Glendanthi before the addition of the header elements.

We will use the login page to validate its contents before data submission. The validation will use a JavaScript code to check that the text field for the login ID and password is not left blank. As a result, we need to attach a JavaScript code to the HTML form that will ensure that the user enters values in the form controls before clicking the submit button. The JavaScript code will check for null values in the controls and display a message box prompting the user to enter a value for the login and password. The HTML code for the validation will be as follows:

```
<HTML>
<HEAD>
<TITLE> A simple HTML page </TITLE>
<SCRIPT language="JavaScript">
function checkValues()
{
var logName;
var logNameLength;
var password;
var passwordLength;
logName=txtVisitorName.value;
logNameLength=logName.length;
while(logNameLength==0)
{
logName=prompt("Enter your Login Id","");
txtVisitorName.value=logName;
logNameLength=logName.length;
}
password=passVisitor.value;
passwordLength=password.length;
while(passwordLength==0)
{
password=prompt("Enter your Password","");
passVisitor.value=password;
passwordLength=password.length;
}
}
</script>
</HEAD>
<BODY bgcolor="#FFDFD7">
<H1 Align="center"><Font color="blue">Banco de Glendanthi</Font>
</H1><BR><BR>
           
        
<Font color="green"><B>Please login</B> </Font><BR><BR>
Login        
<INPUT Type="text" Name="txtVisitorName" Value=""><BR>
Password  <INPUT Type="password" Name="passVisitor"
Value=""><BR><BR><BR>
            
        
<INPUT Type="button" Name="cmdSubmit" onclick="checkValues()" Value="Submit" >
</BODY>
</HTML>
```

Figure 6.14   The JavaScript message box.

Submit the Form to Validate the Data in the Form

To validate the data at the client end you need to follow these steps:

1. Copy the code for the validation, and save the file as Login.html.
2. Open Login.html in Internet Explorer.
3. Click the submit button without entering the values for the login and the password.

When the form is displayed on the browser, skip entering a value in the first-name control of the form. When you have filled in the values for all the other controls of the form, click the submit button. A message box appears informing you that you have not entered a value for the first name. This validation is performed by the JavaScript code that is invoked by clicking the submit button. Figure 6.14 displays the JavaScript message box in the form that ensures entry in the text boxes of the form.

Summary

An interaction between the client and server ensures that results correspond to the user inputs. The HTML form controls help to collect inputs at the client end and transfer them after preliminary client-side validation to the server end for further processing.

In this chapter, we discussed the importance of forms and form controls as collectors of user-specific inputs. We further identified the various types of controls that can be included in an HTML form. To facilitate the opening of new accounts at the bank's Web site, we created a registration page to accept details from the user. The working of an HTML form does not end with the collection of user inputs. Forms also help to validate data at the client end before its submission. As a result, we used a JavaScript code to validate that the fields of the login page are duly filled out before form submission.

In this chapter, we discussed how the form data is transferred to the server side; however, we still need to understand the retrieval of the form data at the server end. In the next chapter, we will discuss implicit objects that can be used to retrieve the values of the form data. These implicit objects are predefined and use methods like `getParameter()` retrieve values from HTML forms. These objects do not require any coding because they are automatically available for use in JSP.

Implicit Objects

OBJECTIVES:

In this chapter, you will learn to do the following:

✔ Appreciate the role of implicit objects in a JSP page

✔ Identify the various implicit objects in JSP

✔ Understand the scope of implicit objects

✔ Use implicit objects

✔ Validate the data in a form

Getting Started

Web interactions involve an exchange of data and information between the client and server in the form of the request-response cycle. We have already discussed the role of forms and form data in such interactions. Forms aid in collection of data from the user in a predetermined format. Subsequently, once the task of data collection is completed, the data is forwarded or submitted to the server for further transactions. The submitted data contains information that can be extracted and stored before initiating such server-side transactions. How is this information extracted, and where is it stored?

Consider a very simple example to explain the need for the availability of information regarding the transmitted data. Traditionally, postal services were used to deliver mail and packages across continents. The introduction of email services provided a fast and simple way to transfer documents and mail. We still rely on the postal and courier services, though, to send parcels and packages across countries. The process is rather simple. You either drop off the parcel at the postal or courier office or have the courier pick up the parcel from your home. Once dispatched, how does the parcel reach its intended destination? Delivery staff operating mobile vans ensure that the right package reaches the right destination. What if a parcel is lost in transit? How do you find its exact location? The delivery staff and organizational documents are objects that help obtain parcel-specific information. Similarly, if we map this example to data transmission between the client and server, it is evident that these transmissions also need to use certain resources to store such data-specific information. A JSP page uses implicit objects that contain information about the transmitted data.

Interactions between the client and the server should be such that a specific and proper communication helps formulate a clear-cut understanding of the targeted task. As a result, implicit objects play a key role in facilitating the availability of information specific to the transactions incurred as a result of the request-response cycle. We begin this chapter with a discussion of the role of implicit objects. Next, we look at the various kinds of implicit objects by using simple code examples. Each implicit object is defined by a scope that determines the span or extent of its functioning. The next section defines the scope of implicit objects in a JSP page. In the final sections of the chapter, we use a scenario-based example to demonstrate the use and function of implicit objects in a JSP page.

Implicit Objects

In Chapter 3, "Servlet Basics," we discussed the various HTTP-specific servlet classes and interfaces that use methods to store the values specific to the request, response, and servlet configuration. As a result, the following information is available for data manipulation and processing:

- At the server end, the methods and objects of the HttpServletRequest interface are used to extract the request values.

- At the client end, the methods and objects of the HttpServletResponse interface are used to send the response to the client in the form of an HTML page.

- The methods of the Servlet interface are used to obtain servlet-specific information in terms of their configuration values.

In the case of JSP, some predefined objects perform the functions mentioned previously. These objects, rightfully called implicit objects, are predefined objects and therefore need not be declared explicitly. When the JSP engine encounters these objects, the engine treats them as explicit objects and parses and places them in the generated servlet.

Although the functioning of these objects is well defined, let's use a scenario-based example to understand each of the implicit objects in detail.

Using JSP Implicit Objects

Problem Statement

After a successful logon, a user visiting the Banco de Glendanthi site is greeted with the welcome page containing elements to perform various bank-related transactions. To give the page a more personalized look, the project team has decided to add the name of the user to the welcome message. The source of this name is the login ID that the user inputs as a registered user of the bank site.

You have been assigned the task of coding the content of the HTML page. The code to add the name of the user already exists and can be added to the page later. The HTML page will contain elements to perform the following tasks:

- Deposit money
- Withdraw money
- Transfer money
- View the balance amount
- Return to the home page

Because the page is still under construction, validating the login ID and password will be done later. In addition, the links to the transaction pages are yet to be coded. Currently, all that you have to do is write the code to display the personalized message along with the HTML components of the page.

Task List

✔ **Identify the components of the welcome page.**

✔ **Identify the HTML form elements.**

✔ **Identify the JSP elements for creating the personalized message.**

✔ **Write the code for the HTML form.**

✔ **Add the tag-specific code to the login page.**

✔ **Execute the code.**

✔ **View the JSP page.**

Identify the Components of the Welcome Page

The page displayed on successful logon will lead the customer to task-specific pages of the application. In addition to the usual page contents, such as the name and logo, the page also has to display a personalized message. This message will include the name of the user that has to be extracted from the login page. The user interface for this page will contain the following components:

- The name and logo of the bank.

- The personalized welcome message.

- The transaction-specific icons for depositing, withdrawing, and transferring money. The page can also contain icons to display the current balance and take the user back to the home page, if so desired.

- The buttons corresponding to the tasks that will function as transferring controls to display relevant pages of the application.

Once the design and components of the welcome page have been formulated, we will map the individual components to HTML-specific tags and elements.

Identify the HTML Form Elements

Once the components for the page are decided, we need to map them to HTML-specific tags that will help us code the page. Table 7.1 describes the HTML elements required for the page.

The principal task in the preceding assignment is to add the login ID of the user as part of the welcome message. How can you extract the value of the login ID from the user input and subsequently add it to the welcome message? To answer this question, let's first list the events that take place after the user clicks the submit button on the login page.

Events occur as a part of the request and data transmission process. The source of the login ID is an HTML form that tenders the data with the click of the submit button. To understand the transmission of data before the display of the transaction page, let's summarize the events following the request for validation of the data:

- The user enters the login ID and password and clicks the submit button.

- The values of the login and password are transmitted along with the URL of the requested page by using the GET/POST method.

- The values of the login ID and password are validated by comparing them with those held in the bank's database.

- On successful login, the transaction page is displayed along with the personalized message.

- The choice of buttons leads the user to other transaction-specific pages of the application.

Table 7.1   The HTML Elements of the Page

INPUT FIELD	HTML SPECIFICATIONS
Basic HTML tags	`<HTML>`, `<HEAD>`, `<BODY>` **tags**
Background and font color formats	`< bgcolor="#FFDFD7">`, `<font size="7" color="#0000FF">`, **and** `< font face="Arial" >` **tags**

INPUT FIELD	HTML SPECIFICATIONS
Personalized welcome message	JSP-specific objects to extract user's login ID
Password	`<INPUT type="password" name="T2">`
Submit button	`<INPUT type="submit" name="B1">`

Although the flow of the data is easy to grasp, after its explicit listing, what about the value of the login ID? How will it be extracted and displayed? Let's look at the methods used to extract and display the value of the login ID.

Identify the JSP Elements for Creating the Personalized Message

It is important to understand that to display the login name as a part of the welcome message, its value needs to be extracted and stored in a variable. The method used for displaying messages has already been covered in the preceding chapters. Let's begin by recognizing how the login ID value will be displayed.

From the examples in the preceding chapters, you'll recognize the use of the expression statements to display the extracted value of the login ID in the welcome message. If you are not able to relate to the use of these statements, it is because we have yet to discuss these statements in detail. Chapter 8, "Using Scripting Elements," discusses expressions in detail. Remember the "Hello World" example and the `<% ="Hello World" %>` statement? We'll use the extracted login ID with the welcome message in the same way. The welcome message can be written in plain HTML as follows:

```
<html>
<head><title>Displaying a personalized message</title></head>
<body>
<p> Welcome, <%= extracted value of the login Id %>
</body>
</html>
```

Of course, we still need to understand the mechanism used to extract the value of the login ID from the requested URL. The mechanism uses certain predefined JSP objects called implicit objects to extract the value of the login ID from the requested URL. What are these implicit objects, and what do they do?

Implicit objects in JSP are based on the servlet API and are implemented from servlet classes and interfaces. They are available automatically and can be accessed by using standard objects. As a result, they can be used without having to write any extra lines of code. Table 7.2 describes some of the implicit objects.

Table 7.2   Some JSP Implicit Objects

IMPLICIT OBJECT	DESCRIPTION
request	Represents a `request` object of HttpServletRequest. It is used to retrieve data submitted along with a request. An example of the `request` object's method is `request.getParameter()`.
response	Represents a `response` object of HttpServletResponse that is used to write a HTML output onto the browser using methods such as `response.getWriter()`.
pageContext	Represents an object of `javax.servlet.jsp.PageContext`. It serves as a single point of access for multiple page attributes that can be used to store shared data.
session	Represents a `session` object of HttpSession that is used to store objects between client requests.
application	Represents an `application` object of javax.servlet.ServletContext.
out	Represents a reference to a JspWriter of javax.servlet.jsp.JspWriter. It is used to write to the output stream and subsequently sent back to the user/client.
config	Represents a `config` object of javax.servlet.Servletconfig.
page	Represents the current instance of the JSP page that is, in turn, used to refer to the current instance of the generated servlet.

All these objects are used in JSP expressions and scriplets. As a result, you'll find them within the <% and %> tags or <% = %> tags. The syntax for using these implicit objects is similar to that used for Java object referencing:

```
Object.methodName (parameterName if used):
```

Let's now look at each of these implicit objects in detail.

The request object

This object provides access to information about the request that is sent from the browser. As a result, it contains details about the browser, the client computer, requested page, and accepted response formats. The request object implements methods of the `javax.servlet.http.HttpServletRequest` interface to retrieve browser-, computer-, request-, and response-specific information. Table 7.3 lists some methods that can be used with the `request` object.

Table 7.3   Methods of the `request` Object

METHOD	USED TO ACCESS INFORMATION ABOUT	DATA TYPE RETURNED
`getserverName()`	The name of the computer, on which the server is running	String
`getQueryString()`	The string in the URL, which is placed after the question mark (?) symbol	String
`getMethod()`	The method used to make the request, which is `GET`, `POST`, `TRACE`, `HEAD`, `PUT`, and `DELETE`	String
`getserverPort()`	The listening port for the server	String
`getParameter()`	The value of the named parameter or attribute	String

The following code example uses the request methods to access information about the server name:

```
<html>
<body>
<h4> An example of the request object that extracts the server name</h4>
<%= request.getServerName() %>
</body>
</html>
```

A very common method of the request object that is frequently used in JSPs is the `getParameter()` method. For example, let's use the `request.getParameter()` method to retrieve the value of the name input in the following page. The code to accept the user name is as follows:

```
<html>
<body>
<h3> Using the getParameter() method</h3>
<form action="answer.jsp" method="POST">
Your first name:::::::
<input type="text" name="fname">
Your last name:::::::
<input type="text" name="lname">
<input type="submit" >
</form>
</body>
</html>
```

To view the output, we have to create a JSP page that will extract the value input in the first-name text box. As a result, we'll use the `request.getParameter()` method to retrieve this value. The code for answer.jsp is as follows:

```
<html>
<body>
<h3> The page with the retrieved values of the HTML page</h3>
<%
//Retrieving the value of the user's first name
out.println("The first name in the text box was:" +
request.getParameter("fname"));
%>
<br>
<%
out.println("The last name in the text box was:" +
request.getParameter("lname"));

%>

</body>
</html>
```

NOTE Keep in mind that the data type of return values of all the request objects is String. As a result, when retrieving numeric values with the `getParameter()` method, you'll need to convert the data type of the returned numeric value to a string.

We now have an HTML page to accept input and a JSP page to extract a value from the HTML control and display it in the JSP. Well, what are we waiting for? Let's execute this code to check if the request object retrieves the value input in the first-name box. To check the correctness of the value extracted by the request object, let's input the first name as Marty and the last name as Brogcen. Figure 7.1 displays the HTML interface with the user inputs.

When you click the Submit Query button, a page with the retrieved values of the first name and the last name is displayed. Figure 7.2 displays the page with the retrieved values.

Fascinating, isn't it? That's just the first of the listed implicit objects. Let's move on to response objects to understand the functioning of this implicit object.

The response Object

The `response` object facilitates manipulation of the requested data in order to generate the response that is sent back to the client. A universal use of the `response` object is to write the HTML output back to the browser as a response. This is achieved by the use of the `out` object, discussed later. Table 7.4 lists some methods that can be used with the `response` object.

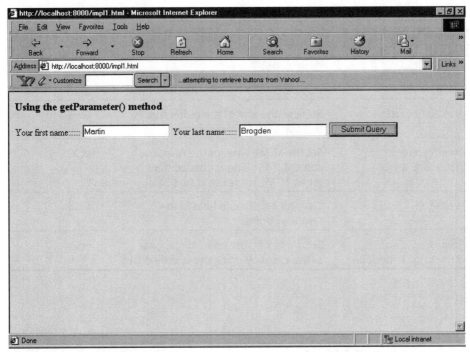

Figure 7.1   The HTML interface.

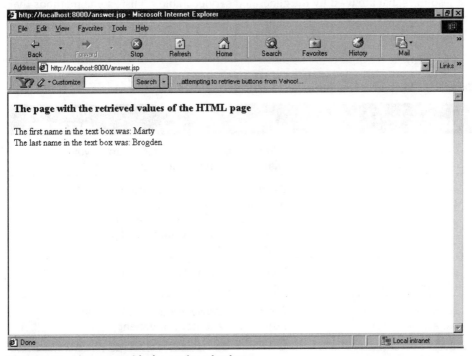

Figure 7.2   The page with the retrieved values.

Table 7.4 Methods of the `response` Object

METHOD	USED TO ...	DATA TYPE RETURNED
`setBufferSize (int size)`	Set the buffer size for the generated response.	void
`getBufferSize()`	Retrieve the size of the buffer that is actually used for the response.	void
`setContentType (String type)`	Set the MIME type for the response content. The value for the content type for an HTML response is text/html.	void
`reset()`	Clear all data that is held in the response buffer.	void
`sendRedirect (String location)`	Send a temporary redirect response to the client by using the specified URL.	void

The pageContext Object

This object is used to access other page attributes and implicit objects. It manages all the resources that are used by the generated servlet. Table 7.5 lists some methods that can be used with the `pageContext` object.

Table 7.5 Methods of the `pageContext` Object

METHOD	USED TO ...	DATA TYPE RETURNED
`setAttribute(String name, Object attribute)`	Add the object to the pageContext within the scope of the page.	void
`getAttribute (String name)`	Get the object that is associated with the name within the scope of the page. If the value returned is null, then it means that the object does not exist.	Object
`removeAttribute (String name)`	Remove the named object from the specified scope.	void
`forward(String relative URL)`	Redirect the servlet request and response to another component within the same application.	void

Table 7.6 Methods of the `session` Object

METHOD	USED TO ...	DATA TYPE RETURNED
`getCreationTime()`	The system time specifying the time of the initiation of the session.	long
`getLastAccessedTime()`	The time the session was last accessed. In other words, the last time a request was sent by a client for the particular session.	long
`getMaxInactiveInterval()`	The maximum time of inactivity of the session (in seconds) when it is open for client requests.	int
`getId()`	The value of the unique ID assigned to the particular session.	String

The session Object

The `session` object is used to represent sessions that are created for a requesting client. A session is created automatically at the initiation of the client/server interaction after a request. As a result, the `session` object is available throughout the session unless explicitly set to false. Table 7.6 lists some methods that can be used with the `session` object.

The application Object

The `application` object represents the attributes of the entire application. As a result, all pages of the application can access it as long as the JSP engine is running. Because the application object holds information specific to an application, it also defines the application's environment. The methods of the application object are similar to those of the `PageContext` object. The only notable difference is the scope of the object, which in this case is the application scope.

The out Object

The `out` object symbolizes a reference to the JspWriter. It is used to write into the output stream that is sent back to the client. The most frequent use of the `out` object is in conjunction with the `println()` method, which displays the output at the client end. In the course of the examples seen so far, we have already used the `out` object. Nevertheless, let's look at a simple example that uses the `out` object. The members of the Firebrand club, a local soccer club, wish to display a victory message after their glorious win over the Riverside club. The following code example displays the victory message:

```
<html>
<body>
<h3> <center>Using the out object to print a message</center></h3>
<%
out.println("<center><b>Three Cheers for the FIREBRANDS!</b></center>");
%>
<br>
<%
out.println("<center><b>HIP HIP HURRAY!</b></center>");
%>
</body>
</html>
```

Figure 7.3 displays the output of the preceding code.

The config Object

The `config` object is generated by the servlet engine and contains information about the servlet configuration. As a result, it defines the context of the generated servlet within which it will run. Table 7.7 lists some methods that can be used with the `config` object.

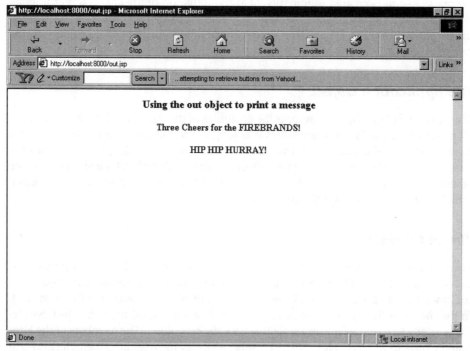

Figure 7.3 Using the out object to print a message.

Table 7.7 Methods of the `config` Object

METHOD	USED TO ...	DATA TYPE RETURNED
`getServletContext (String name)`	The ServletContext of the operating servlet.	An object that implements the ServletContext interface
`getInitParameter (String name)`	If the parameter specified by the name exists, it is returned in the form of a string. If not, the return value is null.	String
`getInitParameterNames()`	An enumeration of all the names of a particular set of parameters.	An object that implements the Enumeration interface

The page Object

This is the object of the current instance of a servlet or JSP. The use of the page object is very similar to that of the `this` object in Java, which references the current instance of the generated servlet.

While we are discussing implicit objects, it is important to understand the scope of objects. The scope of an object defines the duration and source of the availability of a particular object. As a result, be it an object in any form, an implicit object, or a Java object, it is crucial to define the scope of the object. JSP scopes are derived from the contexts. All JSP resources are enclosed within an invisible container. They interact with the environment by using interfaces provided by the context. For example, a servlet executing in a context is aware of its server information from the methods of the `ServletContext`. Similarly, the server is able to communicate with the servlet through the context. As a result, the context defines the scope for the exchange of information between the servlet and the server. JSP objects are defined within the following four scopes:

The page scope.   Objects defined within the page scope are available as long as the page responds to a current request. References to such objects are released in two situations. The first is after the response is sent back to the client, and the second is when forwarding the request to another resource. Objects within the page scope are defined for each client request to a page. Such objects are stored in the `pageContext` object. The default scope of the `<jsp:usebean>` action objects is page.

The request scope.   Objects defined within the request scope are available as long as the `HTTPRequest` object exists. References to such objects are released after the processing of the request is completed. In case the request is forwarded to another resource, within the same run time, the scope is still retained. Objects within the request scope are defined and destroyed at each request. Such objects are stored in the request object.

The session scope.   Objects defined within the session scope are available to the pages that process requests in the same session as that in which the page was created. Objects within the session scope are defined for each client and are available as long as the client session is valid. Such objects are stored in the session object.

The application scope.   Objects defined within the session scope are available to the pages that process requests in the same application as that in which the page was created. Objects within the application scope are not limited to individual clients but are accessed by all clients. Such objects are stored in the application object.

Now that we are well informed about the various implicit objects and their scope, let's decide on the object to be used for the assignment. You'll recollect that the value of the user input or the login ID needs to be extracted and displayed in the welcome message. Summarizing the discussions so far, it is evident that the value of the login ID will be extracted by using the `request.getParameter()` method. As a result, the line of code for this extraction will be this:

```
<% =request.getParameter(name of the text box) %>
```

The code for the welcome message can be written as follows:

```
<html>
<head><title>Displaying a personalized message</title></head>
<body>
<p> Welcome, <%= request.getParameter(login) %>
</body>
</html>
```

Let's now add all the other HTML components and write the code for the page.

Write the Code to Display the Personalized Message

The code for the page will be as follows:

```
<html>
<head>
<title>Banco de Glendanthi</title>
</head>

<body bgcolor="#FFDFD7>

<p><font face="Arial" size="6" color="#0000CC">
<img border="0" src="dd00448_1.gif" >
Banco de Glendanthi</font></p>

<hr>

<p><font face="Arial" color="#0000CC" size="5">
```

```
Welcome, <%= request.getParameter("login") %>;
</font></p>

<hr>

<p>Tells what you would like to do
(Click icon-specific button to view the page)?</p>

<p>           &nb
sp;           
</p>

<p>     
<img border="0" src="bs00508_1.gif" >
       
<img border="0" src="bd06517_1.gif" >
       
<img border="0" src="bd07153_1.gif" >
       
<img border="0" src="bs02064_1.gif" >
       
<img border="0" src="sy01265_1.gif" ></p>

<p>      </p>

<form method="POST" >
 <p>     
<input type="button" value="Deposit " name="B3">
            
  
  <input type="button" value="Withdraw " name="B4">
          
  <input type="button" value="Transfer " name="B5">
            
 
  <input type="button" value="Balance "
name="B6">          &n
bsp;  
  <input type="button" value=" Home" name="B7"></p>

</form>

<p>           &nb
sp;           
</p>

<p>  Not banking with us as yet? To
open a new account, click <a href="http://registration.jsp">HERE</a></p>
</body>

</html>
```

Execute the Code

To view the output of the transaction page with the personalized message, simply follow these steps:

1. Locate the file LoginHdr.jsp that we saved at the end of the earlier task.

2. Copy LoginHdr.jsp, WelcmPg.jsp, the graphic file for the bank's logo, and other button-related icons into the public_html folder in C:\j2sdkee1.2.1 directory.

3. Start the server by typing `start j2ee -verbose` at the command prompt.

4. Open the Internet Explorer browser, and type the location of the .jsp file as http://localhost:8000/ LoginHdr.jsp.

5. In the Login ID box, type TracieK.

6. In the password box, type password.

7. Submit the form.

View The JSP Page

Figure 7.4 displays the output of the login page with the personalized message.

We are gradually progressing toward building up the application for the Banco de Glendanthi site by using JSP-specific tags. The change in the login page with the addition of the personalized message is another feather added to the cap. As the excitement grows, we move on to thicker terrains of JSP programming. Let's further strengthen our concepts of implicit objects by using JSP implicit objects in another scenario-based example. Because all the concepts have already been discussed in the previous sections, this will be a straightforward application page creation.

Figure 7.4   The login page with the personalized message.

Using the JSP out Object

Problem Statement

The technical division of Banco de Glendanthi is preparing itself for the launch of the online banking site. To create awareness among its patrons, the team has already begun promotional activities. Banners and posters within the bank premises demonstrate the excitement and increased expectations from this launch. The youngest member of the technical team, Neil, has come up with the idea of holding promotional customer meetings within the bank's premises to help add value to the project in the construction stage.

The purpose of these meetings is to introduce regular customers of the bank to the design and features of the application and collate the customer's perspective and expectations from the online site. As a result, the final design of the application will ensure that the site is comprehensive and customer oriented.

The senior manager of the bank's administration is totally taken in by the idea and, after discussion with top executives, has decided to host informal customer meetings to look for value additions to the site based on customer feedback. These meetings have been scheduled for the third Saturday of the month and will be held in shifts, for two hours each in the morning, afternoon, and evening.

You have been assigned the task for creating a JSP page to display an interface listing the days and time slots for the informal customer meetings. On submission of the form, a page will display the choice with an acknowledgment message.

Task List

✔ **Identify the components of the HTML page.**

✔ **Identify the HTML form elements.**

✔ **Identify the JSP elements to be included in the acknowledgment page.**

✔ **Write the code for the HTML form.**

✔ **Write the code for the JSP page.**

✔ **Execute the code.**

✔ **View the JSP page.**

Identify the Components of the HTML Page

The HTML page has to display value-added services options. The user interface for this page will contain the following components:

- The name and logo of the bank
- The list displaying the options
- A button to submit or reset the form

Table 7.8 The HTML Elements of the Page

INPUT FIELD	HTML SPECIFICATIONS
Basic HTML tags	`<HTML>`, `<HEAD>`, `<BODY>` **tags**
Background and font color formats	`< bgcolor=" #FFDFD7">`, `<font size="7" color="#0000FF">`, **and** `< font face="Arial" >` **tags**
Form element with action page name	`<FORM method="POST" action= "Informal-Meet.jsp">`
Buttons to display the list of options for the additional services	`<INPUT type="radio" name="slot" value="Morning">`
	`<INPUT type="radio" name="slot" value="Afternoon">`
	`<INPUT type="radio" name="slot" value="Evening">`
Submit and reset buttons	`<INPUT type="submit" name="B1" value="Submit Form">`
	`<INPUT type="reset" name="B2" value="Clear Form">`

Identify the HTML Form Elements

Once the design and components of the page have been formulated, let's map them to HTML-specific tags and elements. Table 7.8 describes the HTML elements required for the page.

Identify the JSP Elements to Be Included in the Acknowledgment Page

To register for the informal customer meetings, users are presented with a list of options in order to select a slot for the meeting scheduled for the morning, afternoon, and evening. After submission of the form, the user's choice has to be extracted and displayed with an acknowledgment message. As a result, the following JSP-specific elements will be used in InformalMeet.jsp:

■ The getParameter method of the request object will be used to extract the value of the user's choice.

■ The out object will use the println() method to display the choice.

The code snippet for displaying the user's choice will be as follows:

```
<%
//Getting the user's choice from the request
out.println("<b>You have chosen the following slot: " +
```

```
request.getParameter("slot") + "</b>");
%>
```

Let's now add all the other HTML components and write the code for the page.

Write the Code for the HTML Form

The code for the page will be as follows:

```
<html>

<head>
<title>Banco de Glendanthi</title>
</head>

<body bgcolor="#FFDFD7">

<p><font face="Arial" size="6" color="#0000CC">
<img border="0" src="dd00448_1.gif" >
Banco de Glendanthi</font></p>

<hr>

<p><font face="Arial" color="#0000CC" size="5">
Want to attend our informal customers meet? </font></p>

<hr>

<p">We at Banco de Glendanthi value your inputs. You are invited to
attend an informal customers meeting for personal feedback about our Web
site.
</p>

<p">Please choose the time slots that suits you: 
</p>

<form method="POST" action="InformalMeet.jsp">

  <p>   
<input type="radio" value="Morning" checked name="slot"> 
  MORNING
            
           
  <input type="radio" name="slot" value="Afternoon"> 
  AFTERNOON
            
            
      
  <input type="radio" name="slot" value="Evening"> 
  EVENING</p>
  <p> </p>
  <p> </p>
```

```
<p>           &nb
sp;           &nb
sp;           &nb
sp;           &nb
sp;        
<input type="submit" value="Send Form"
name="B1">    
  <input type="reset" value="Clear Form" name="B2"></p>
</form>
<p>          
</p>
<p>  </p>
</body>
</html>
```

Write the Code for the JSP Page

The code for the JSP page to generate the personalized message is as follows:

```
<html>
<head><title>Customer meeting schedule request</title></head>
<body>
<h3> Customer Informal Meeting Request Received</h3><hr>
<h4>Thank you for your request, which has been recorded</h4>

<%
//Gettingg the user's choice from the request
out.println("<b>You have chosen the following slot: " +
request.getParameter("slot") + "</b>");
%>
<hr><h4>The exact time and venue will be mailed to you at the specified
email address </h4>
</body>
</html>
```

Execute the Code

To view the output of the transaction page with the personalized message, simply follow these steps:

1. Copy the code for the HTML and JSP files, and save them as InformalMeet.html and InformalMeet.jsp, respectively.

2. Copy InformalMeet.html, InformalMeet.jsp, and the graphic file for the bank's logo in to the public_html folder in C:\j2sdkee1.2.1 directory.

3. Start the server by typing `start j2ee -verbose` at the command prompt.

4. Open the Internet Explorer browser, and type the location file as `http://localhost:8000/ InformalMeet.html`.

Figure 7.5 displays the output of the HTML page with the options.

5. Select the Afternoon slot.

6. Submit the form.

View the JSP Page

The JSP page is displayed with the acknowledgment message along with the chosen option. Figure 7.6 displays the output of the JSP page with the acknowledgment message.

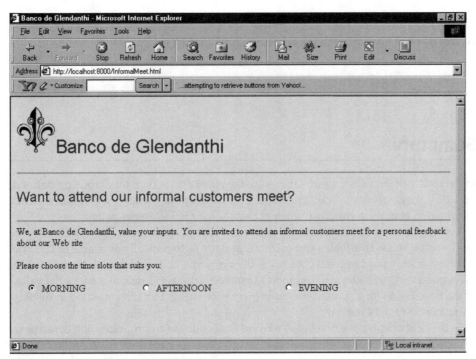

Figure 7.5 The HTML page with the options.

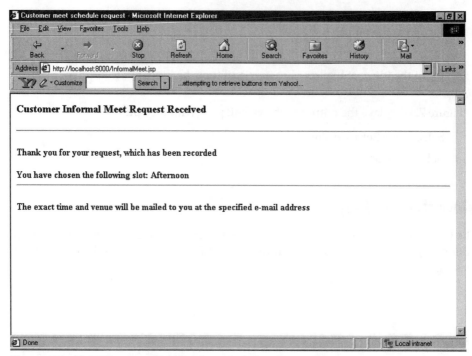

Figure 7.6 The JSP page with the acknowledgment message.

Summary

In the course of the exchange of data across the client and server, numerous predefined variables work as agents carrying request- and response-related information. This information is in the form of parameters that define the JSP environment.

In this chapter, we discussed those agents called implicit objects. The implicit objects work with standard variables and methods and are automatically available in JSP. The most commonly used implicit objects are the `request` and `out` objects. We have used the request `GetParameter()` method in our scenario-based task to retrieve the value of the user login. We also used the `out` object with the `println()` method to display an acknowledgment message.

In the next chapter, we will begin writing Java codes with programming constructs. Although these concepts relate to basic Java, a recap is necessary to strengthen base-level knowledge of the conditionals and loops. JSP retains the structure of these constructs. The only difference between the Java constructs and the JSP constructs is that the latter are encapsulated in special tags called scripting elements.

CHAPTER

8

Using Scripting Elements

OBJECTIVES:

In this chapter, you will learn to do the following:

- ✔ Appreciate the need for scripting elements in JSP
- ✔ Identify the types of scripting elements
- ✔ Use declarations
- ✔ Declare variables and methods
- ✔ Use scriptlets
- ✔ Use conditional constructs in scriptlets
- ✔ Use expressions
- ✔ Use scripting elements to create a table directly in a JSP
- ✔ Use scripting elements to create a transaction page

Getting Started

The contents of a Java Server Page can be categorized as static or dynamic. Static content is written using regular HTML, and dynamic content is generated by the Java servlet using the JSP tags. You may wonder how a JSP engine identifies the part of the page it needs to convert into dynamic content while generating the Java servlet. How are the contents of a page segregated to distinguish their placement? The segregation of content is provided by enclosing the dynamic content within special tags that start with <% and end with %>. These JSP-specific tags enclose the Java code that is manipulated to generate the dynamic content.

Consider the "Hello World" example again. You'll recollect the use of the <%= Hello World %> statement to display the "Hello World" message on the screen. Let's revisit this code example to understand how the JSP engine deals with the content within the HTML and JSP tags:

```
<HTML>
<%--This is the HTML content--%>
<HEAD><TITLE>My first JSP Example</TITLE><HEAD>
<BODY>
<H1>My first JSP example</H1><HR>
<%--This is the JSP content--%>
<%="Hello World" %>
</BODY>
</HTML>
```

When this page is compiled, the HTML content, identified by the HTML tags, is first generated. When the engine encounters the <% tag, the engine understands that it has to place dynamically generated content in the page. That is exactly what it does! After this is done, the "Hello World" message is displayed on the screen.

The JSP-specific tags used in the preceding "Hello World" example are called scripting elements, which help separate the static and dynamic content in a JSP page. JSP is an extension of both servlet and Java technology. As a result, instead of using other special-purpose languages, the dynamic content is generated by using the familiar Java and servlet programming constructs. The fact remains, though, that while Java programming is actually used in JSP application codes, the implementation of servlet programming is automatically incorporated by the generated servlet.

This chapter begins with an introduction to scripting elements, followed by a detailed discussion of the different types of scripting elements. The final sections of the chapter use the online banking site example to create a page for transferring money to a specified account.

Scripting Elements

Scripting elements encapsulate the Java code within the <% and %> tags that can be directly placed in an HTML page. The encapsulated code becomes part of the generated servlet. Scripting elements are of the following three types:

Declarations. Declarations are enclosed within the `<%!` and `%>` tags. They are used to define the variables and methods of the Java code.

Scriptlets. Scriptlets are enclosed within the `<%` and `%>` tags. They contain blocks of Java code and include JavaBeans, declarations, and expressions.

Expressions. Expressions are enclosed within the `<% =` and `%>` tags. They are used to directly display the evaluated output in the resultant page.

Using JSP Scripting Elements

Problem Statement

Financial dealings form the backbone of all the transactions that take place at a banking site. Accordingly, the site for Banco de Glendanthi facilitates deposits, withdrawals, and transfer of money. You have been assigned the task of developing a JSP page for the transfer of money to an account specified by the user.

Putting aside issues such as application integration and the mode of transfer, let's develop this page that will accept the account details and the transfer amount. After completing the transaction, a summarized report detailing the various transactional attributes and the balance in the user's account is displayed on the screen.

Task List

✔ **Identify the components of the page.**

✔ **Identify the elements of the HTML file.**

✔ **Identify the elements of the JSP page.**

✔ **Write the code for the HTML file.**

✔ **Write the code for the JSP page.**

✔ **Execute the code.**

✔ **View the JSP page.**

Identify the Components of the Page

The contents of the page are of the following two types:

Static content. This includes all the components of the user interface, which will accept inputs from the user. This includes the account details for transfer and the transfer amount.

Dynamic content. This includes the balance calculated at the end of the transaction. In addition, all the attributes of the transaction in the form of the user input have to be displayed with the balance amount.

NOTE It is important to understand that the page for the transaction is currently in a nonintegrated form. The idea is to understand and appreciate the use of JSP scripting elements to generate the dynamic content in the form of the balance.

The structure of the page illustrates that the static and dynamic content can be placed in different files. The static content can be placed in an HTML file while the dynamic content can be placed in a JSP page. Let's look at the individual components of each file.

Identify the Elements of the HTML File

The HTML file will contain elements to create the controls and textual contents of the interface. In addition, form elements will be used to accept user details in the form of the account number of the transferee, the bank name and address, and the amount to be transferred. The action attribute of the form element will ensure the exchange of form data between the two files. After specifying the transfer details, when the user clicks the submit button, the contents of the HTML controls are transferred to the JSP page. After calculating the balance amount, the summarized report is displayed on the screen. Table 8.1 describes the individual elements of the HTML file.

Table 8.1   The Elements of the HTML User Interface

INPUT	TAG TO BE USED
Basic HTML tags	`<HTML>`, `<HEAD>`, `<BODY>` **tags**
Background and font color formats	`<bg color>` **and** `<font color>` **tags**
Name and logo of the bank	The graphic file, `<img>` tag, and name of the bank enclosed within the `<p>` tags
Form element with the action and method attributes	`<form method="POST" action="Transfer.jsp">`
Text boxes and other controls to accept the account and transfer amount details	`<INPUT type="text" name="amount">` `<INPUT type="text"name="account">` `<INPUT type="text" name="name">` `<INPUT type="text"name="address">`
Submit button to submit the form data to the JSP page	`<INPUT type="submit" name="B1" value="Go!">`

Let's move on to the elements of the JSP file.

Identify the Elements of the JSP Page

The JSP page primarily enables the calculation of the balance amount after the transfer. It will include elements to perform the following tasks:

- Extract the value of the transfer amount to subtract it from the opening balance amount in the user's account.

- Check if the amount to be transferred is more than the opening balance. If so, the message "Insufficient balance" will be displayed on the screen.

- If the transfer amount is available in the user's account, the balance will be displayed in the form of a summarized report with the other input values.

From the preceding list and on the basis of the type of generated content, you'll infer that scripting elements will be used in the JSP page. These elements will be used to compare the transfer and opening balance amounts to decide if the transaction will take place. In addition, these elements will be used to calculate the balance amount at the end of the transaction. Scripting elements form an integral part of the JSP page. Therefore, let's discuss them in detail.

The scripting elements of a JSP page can be categorized as declarations, scriptlets, and expressions. Let's look at each one in detail.

Declarations

The basic programming language in JSP is Java. Java supports variables of different data types. A variable is a stored value that changes in the course of program execution. The change in the value of a variable is mostly attributed to the manipulations and calculations that ultimately generate the dynamic content.

Declarations are used to define the variables and methods of the Java code in a JSP page. When you declare a variable or a method, you assign it a name and a value. The process of initially assigning a value to a variable is called initialization. You'll recall that the request, response, and out objects of the preceding chapter were predefined and did not require declarations. As a result, they were aptly called implicit objects. Because the variables and methods in a JSP page need to be explicitly declared at the beginning of the code, they are also called explicit objects. Like all variables and methods in Java, declarations also need to be initialized. A declaration in a JSP page is initialized along with the initialization of the page.

Declarations statements are enclosed within the <%! and %> tags and are always terminated with the semi-colon. The following syntax is used to declare a variable number in JSP by using a declaration:

```
<%! int number = 0 %>;
```

Although the preceding declaration assigns an initial value to the variable, the following declaration statements are also valid:

```
<%! String name;
int number;
%>
```

Similarly, the following syntax is used to declare a method in JSP:

```
<%! public int add(int num1, int num2) { return num1+num2; }
```

Let's now look at an example that uses declarations:

```
<html>
<body>
<h3>Using declarations</h3>
<%!int   num1 = 3;
int num2 = 5;
%>
<p> The value of the first number is: <%= num1%>
<p> The value of the second number is: <%= num2%>
<p> The sum of the two numbers is: <%= num1+num2 %><p>
</body>
</html>
```

NOTE The subsequent examples use the expression statement defined within the <%= and %> tags to display the output. Although expressions are dealt with in detail in the later sections, they have been used in the earlier chapters.

In the preceding example, a declaration is used to assign values to two variables, num1 and num2. The two numbers are then displayed one after the other, followed by the sum. Figure 8.1 displays the output of the preceding code.

After the variables and methods are defined, they can be used in coding statements or constructs to add programming functionalities to an application. In JSP, these statements are used in the form of blocks of Java code, which are enclosed within special tags called scriptlets. Let's now look at JSP scriptlets.

Scriptlets

Scriptlets are blocks of Java code that are enclosed within the <% and %> tags. They are executed at request time and generate dynamic content. Because scriptlets contain blocks of Java code, let's briefly recap a few basic concepts of Java. The discussions in this chapter introduce Java at a very basic level. The subsequent chapters, however, require coding for JavaBean components that calls for a good, if not experienced, hand in Java programming. Nevertheless, there is no end to how much you can learn in Java. JSP was developed primarily as a transition for programmers in Java. The contents of this chapter will refresh programming constructs that are frequently used in JSP applications.

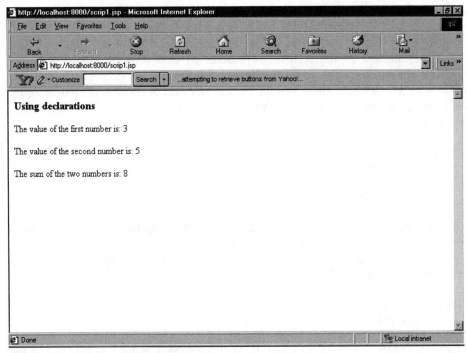

Figure 8.1   Using a declaration.

The blocks of Java code in a JSP page mostly use control structures such as conditional expressions and loops to control the flow of a program. Let's examine each of these concepts one by one.

Conditional expressions, as the name suggests, are Java statements that yield results on the basis of the evaluation of certain expressions. Consider the following example. For months, you have wanted to buy an antique piece of furniture for your living room. The piece is expensive, but beautiful enough for you to save to buy it. You visit the bank to check the balance amount to find out how much you need to save to buy the piece. How is your decision to purchase the antique piece of furniture related to the balance amount in your bank? It is simple. If the balance amount is equal to the cost of the antique piece, you buy it. Otherwise, you wait until you save the required amount.

You have used a simple conditional expression to make a decision to purchase the antique piece. You would write the conditional expression in the following way:

```
if (balance equals cost of antique)
you buy it
else
you wait until next month
```

Java statements use the same principle in conditional evaluations. The if...else construct is used to symbolize conditional expressions. These expressions consist of two statements, and the evaluation of the first determines the course of action. In the preceding example, if the first statement evaluates to true or if the bank balance equals the price of the antique piece, you'll be able to buy it. Alternatively, if the first statement evaluates to false, which implies that the bank balance is not equal to price of antique, you'll have to postpone the purchase. You can compare two numbers by using conditional expressions in the following way:

```
if (num1 > num2)
    System.out.println("num1 is greater than num2");
else
    System.out.println("num2 is greater than num1");
```

Another type of control structure used in Java is the loop that is used to replicate actions. Consider the following example. Your colleague Jane is on leave. In her absence, you are assigned her task of filing. How would your boss explain the situation to you? He would use the following statement to express himself:

```
while(Jane is on leave)
you do her filings
```

Java statements use the while loop to replicate actions as long as the evaluatory statements continue to be true. For example, the while loop can be used to increment the value of a variable in the following way:

```
int num1 = 0;
while(num1 <=10) {
    System.out.println(The value of the number Is:" +num1);
    Num1 = num1 + 1;
}
```

Another loop construct that can be used to replicate actions is the for loop. Consider the following example. The customer relations manager in your organization is available at the home office for customer feedback between the seventh and the tenth of every month. This statement can also be expressed in the following way:

```
for(date between 7-10)
Customer relations manager is at HO
```

Java statements use the for loop to create a variable, initialize it, and perform repetitive actions until the variable reaches a predetermined value. For example, the for loop can be used to display a name five times in the following way:

```
String name = "Jane";
for(int count=0; count<=5; count++) {
    System.out.println("My name Is " + name);
}
```

Let's now look at an example of a scriptlet that accepts a name from the user and displays it with a message. An HTML interface is used to accept the name from the user. In addition, instead of directly displaying the name and the message, the name is retrieved using the request object and stored in a variable. The variable is subsequently displayed using the expression statement. Observe the use of declaration, request object, and variable.

The code for the HTML interface is as follows:

```
<html>
<body>
<h3> The user interface</h3>
<form method =POST action="name.jsp">
<input type="text" name="name">
<input type="submit" name="Go!">
</form>
</body>
</html>
```

The code for the JSP page is as follows:

```
<html>
<body>
<h3>Using declarations and scriplets</h3>
<%! String name=" ";%>
<%
name= request.getParameter ("name");
out.println (" Hello" + name);
%>
</body>
</html>
```

The use of scriptlets in JSP begins with the use of control structures. Scriptlets encapsulate Java control structures in the form of conditionals and loops. Let's look at the syntax of each of these structures in a JSP page.

The function and syntax for writing the `if` construct remain the same as those discussed earlier. The only addition is the inclusion of scriptlet-specific tags before and after the construct. For example, the following code accepts the marks for four subjects and calculates their average. In addition, the average is graded and displayed with an appropriate message. An HTML page is used to accept the marks from the user. The input is forwarded to a JSP page that calculates and displays the average score. The code for the HTML page is as follows:

```
<html>
<body>
<h3>Using scriplets</h3>
<form method="POST" action="Grade.jsp">
English::::::<Input type="text" name="Eng" value="0">
French::::::<Input type="text" name="French" value="0">
```

```
Maths:::::<Input type="text" name="Maths" value="0">
Science:::::<Input type="text" name="Science" value="0">
<Input type="submit" name="Submit">
</form>
</body>
</html>
```

The code for the JSP page is as follows:

```
<html>
<body>
<h3>Using declarations and scriptlets</h3>
<%! String eng =" ";
String maths =" ";
String french =" ";
String science =" ";
int average =" ";
%>
<%
eng = request.getParameter ("Eng");
french = request.getParameter ("French");
maths = request.getParameter ("Maths");
science = request.getParameter ("Science");
out.println (" Hello" + name);
%>
<%
average = (Integer.parseInt(eng)+Integer.parseInt(maths)+
Integer.parseInt(science)+Integer.parseInt(french))/4
%>
<%
If ( average > 80 ) { %>
<p> excellent, your grade Is A</p>
<% } else { %>
<% If ( average > 60 && < 80 ) { %>
<p> Good, your grade Is B</p>
<% } else { %>
<% If ( average > 40 && < 60 ) { %>
<p> Fair, your grade Is C</p>
<% } else { %>
<% If ( average < 40 ) { %>
<p> You need to work harder</p>
<% } %>
<% } %>
</body>
</html>
```

The for and while loops are also used in a JSP page to perform repetitive tasks. The following example uses the for loop to display the product of two numbers. The HTML interface accepts two numbers from the user and displays their product. The code for the HTML page is as follows:

```
<html>
<head></head>
<body>
<h3> Multiplication </h3>
<form method="post" action="multiplication.jsp">
First Number::::<input type="text" name="a1" size="30">
Second Number::::<input type="text" name="a2" size="30">
<input type="submit" value="Product">
</form>
</body>
</html>
```

The code for the JSP page is as follows:

```
<%@ page import="java.util.*" %>
<%@ page  language="java" %>
<html>
<head></head>
<body>
<%!
int i=0;
int j=0;
int z=0;
int prod=0;
%>
<%
i=Integer.parseInt(request.getParameter("a1"));
j=Integer.parseInt(request.getParameter("a2"));
for (z=1 ; z<=j ;z++)
{
prod=i * z;
}
%>
<p> The product of the two numbers is:  <%=prod %> </p>
</body>
</html>
```

Figure 8.2 displays the output of the preceding code.

The preceding discussions have highlighted the use of declarations and scriplets in a JSP page. The use of these tags clearly distinguishes the content within them. In fact, each of the scripting elements contains Java components in a specific form. The declarations contain the definitions of the variables and methods of the application. The scriplets contain executable statements in Java that also use control structures. After execution, the scriplets generate content that needs to be displayed. Expressions are used in JSP to display the output on the browser screen.

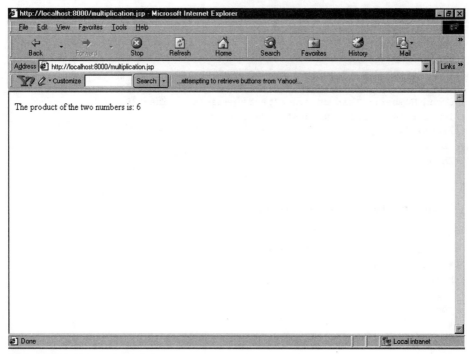

Figure 8.2 Using a scriptlet.

Expressions

An expression returns the evaluated value of a Java expression back to the client. As a result, the output is directly placed in the JSP page. Expression statements are enclosed within the <%= and the %> tags. The syntax to use expressions, in JSP is this:

```
<%= new Date().toString() %>
```

The preceding expression statement displays the current date and time on the screen. The evaluation of expressions takes place at run time. During this time, the expression is evaluated, converted to a string and then inserted in the page.

At the end of the discussion of the various scripting elements, you'll be able to infer that the generation of dynamic content requires the use of all these elements. Let's now tabulate the various elements of the JSP page for the bank site that will display the balance and other transactional details. To further strengthen your knowledge of HTML concepts, let's display the summary report of the transaction in the form of a table. Table 8.2 describes the individual elements of the JSP page.

Table 8.2 The Elements of the JSP Page

INPUT	TAG TO BE USED
Basic HTML tags	`<HTML>`, `<HEAD>`, `<BODY>` **tags**
Background color for the page	`<bg color>` **and** `<font color>` **tags**
Table elements to display the various transactional parameters	`<table>`, `<tr>`, `<td>` **tags**
Scripting elements to enclose the Java code.	`<@!` `%>` **to declare variables** `<%` `%>` **to contain the constructs and** **Java statements** `<%+` `%>`

In order to calculate the balance amount in the account, the value of the transfer amount has to first be extracted from the particular form control by using the `request.getParameter()` method. It is important to understand that this method accepts string values only. Because monetary calculations involve numeric variables, the variable has to be converted to a string value. This conversion is done using Java's `Integer.parseInt()` method. Let's now formulate the contents of various scripting elements.

The declaration statement will define the variables for the transfer amount and the details of the account number, bank name, and address. The declaration will therefore contain the following statements:

```
<%!int o_bal = 3800;
int c_bal = 0;
int w_amt = 0;
%>
```

NOTE With online banking sites, the calculation made after the transfer extracts the opening balance of the account from the database. The opening balance has been given an initial value of $3800.

Table 8.3 describes the various Java statements that will be used in the scriplets to calculate the balance amount.

Table 8.3   Java Statements Used in the Scriplet to Calculate Balance Amount

INPUT	JAVA STATEMENT
Extract the value of the transfer amount	`w_amt = Integer.parseInt(request. getParameter ("amount"));`

Evaluate if the transfer amount is more than the opening balance	`if  (w_amt > o_bal) { %>`
	`<%`
	`out.println( "<b> Insufficient Balance </b>" ); %>`

If transfer amount is less than the opening balance, calculate the difference	`<% } else {` `c_bal = o_bal-w_amt;`

Display the account detail	`Request.getParameter(Integer. parseInt("account")`
	
	`Request.getParameter(Integer. parseInt("amount")`
	
	`Request.getParameter("name")`

Write the Code for the HTML File

The code for the user interface is as follows:

```html
<html>

<head>
<title>Banco de Glendanthi</title>
</head>

<body bgcolor="#FFDFD7">

<p><font size="7" color="#0000FF"><img border="0"
src="dd00448_1.gif">Banco
de Glendanthi</font></p>
<hr>
<p><font face="Arial" size="4" color="#FF6699">Transfer
form  </font></p>

<form method="POST" action="Balance.jsp">
<p><font color="#0000FF" size="4">Transfer
amount</font>::::::::::::::::::::::::::<input type="text" name="amount"
size="15"></p>
```

```
<p><font color="#0000FF" size="4">Account
number:</font>::::::::::::::::::::::<input type="text" name="account"
size="20"></p>

<p><font color="#0000FF" size="4">Name of
bank:</font>:::::::::::::::::::::::::::::<input type="text" name="name"
size="20"></p>
<p><font color="#0000FF"
size="4">Address</font>:::::::::::::::::::::::::::::::::::::::::::::<inpu
t type="text" name="address" size="20"></p>
<p>  
            
            
    
            
  <input type="submit" value="Transfer"
name="B1">          &n
bsp;
<input type="submit" value="Clear" name="B1"></p>
<p> </p>

</form>
</body>

</html>
```

Write the Code for the JSP Page

The code for the JSP page is as follows:

```
<html>

<head>
<title>Banco de Glendanthi</title>
</head>
<body bgcolor="#FFDFD7">
<p><font face="Arial" color="#0000CC" size="4"></font></p>

<%!int o_bal = 3800;
int c_bal = 0;
int w_amt = 0;
%>
<%
w_amt = Integer.parseInt(request.getParameter ("amount"));
if  (w_amt > o_bal) { %>
```

```
<%
out.println( "<b> Insufficient Balance </b>" ); %>
<% } else {
c_bal = o_bal-w_amt;
//out.println ("<b> The balance In you're account Is: " + c_bal +
"</b>");
}
%>

<h3> A summary of the last transaction from your account</h3>
<table border="1" width="100%">
  <tr>
    <td width="50%">Transferee's account number</td>
    <td width="50%"><%= Integer.parseInt(request.getParameter
("account")) %></td>
  </tr>
  <tr>
    <td width="50%">Transferee's bank name</td>
    <td width="50%"><%= request.getParameter("name") %></td>
  </tr>
  <tr>
    <td width="50%">Transferred amount</td>
    <td width="50%"><%= Integer.parseInt(request.getParameter
("amount")) %></td>
  </tr>
  <tr>
    <td width="50%">Balance in your account</td>
    <td width="50%"><%=c_bal %></td>
  </tr>
</table>
</body>
</html>
```

Execute the Code

To execute the code, do the following:

1. Save the the user interface as **Transfer.html**.
2. Save the JSP page as **Balance.jsp**.
3. Copy the two files in the public_html directory.
4. Start the server.
5. In the Internet Explorer address bar, type

   http://localhost:8000/Transfer.jsp.

6. Enter the following values in the transfer form:

    Transfer amount = 550

    Account number = 110907865

    Bank name = ABN Amro Bank

    Bank address = 10, Sunthorpe House, London

    Figure 8.3 displays the transfer form with the specified values.

7. Click Transfer.

View the JSP Page

Because the initial balance amount was $3,800, the balance amount after the transfer should be $3,250. Figure 8.4 displays the output of the JSP page.

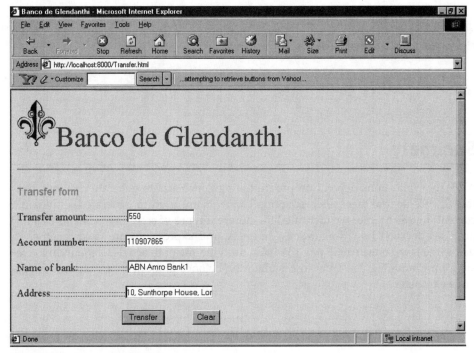

Figure 8.3   The transfer form.

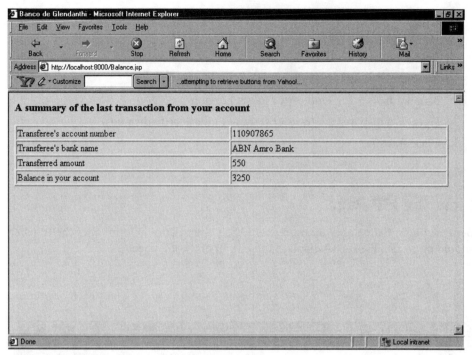

Figure 8.4   The summary report after the transfer.

Summary

All Web applications depend on programming constructs to generate dynamic content. In JSP, special tags called scripting elements are used to generate the dynamic content. In this chapter we identified the different types of scripting elements in a JSP page. We learned how declarations, scriplets, and expressions are used together to define the Java code in a JSP page. We also used the site of Banco de Glendanthi to create a programming construct to calculate the balance amount in an account after a money transfer.

CHAPTER

9

JSP and JavaBeans

OBJECTIVES:

In this chapter, you will learn to do the following:

   ↙ **Identify the features of a JavaBean**

   ↙ **Identify different property types**

   ↙ **Use JavaBeans in JSP**

   ↙ **Create a JSP page by using JavaBeans**

Getting Started

The concepts discussed in the previous chapters have used examples that helped strengthen your basic understanding of the components that can be used to build JSP pages. What we have discussed so far covers basic JSP syntax, constructs, and semantics. At this juncture, we need to recall that JSP technology primarily aims to segregate the work profiles of a Web designer and developer by the separation of dynamic and static content of an application. Therefore, the Web designer needs to concentrate on only the structure of the application in relation to its presentation components while the developer uses Java to write code for the application. This is also the fundamental difference between process-oriented programming and object-oriented programming. In process-oriented programming, you create software systems that work only with specific applications. In object-oriented programming, you create small software systems that can be plugged into any application. For example, the components of an old model of the Beetle car cannot be plugged into a Mercedes-Benz; however, a company may decide to manufacture a brake that can be plugged into any type of car.

Using the principles of object-oriented programming, JSP provides special tags that can be plugged into Java components such as JavaBeans. As a result, the encapsulated code can be reused and the developer is saved from the task of rewriting common Java code. The most commonly used approaches for encapsulations of this type involve using the useBean tag and the XML-based custom tag. The use of the useBean tag facilitates the placement of the Java code in a bean, which is then shared with other pages of the application. The custom tag also facilitates this type of encapsulation, except that the component used is in the form of a class file instead of bean component.

In this chapter, we will use JavaBeans as the pluggable components of a JSP page. It is obvious that for a task such as this, you need a basic understanding of a JavaBean. We will use JavaBean components primarily as pluggables, and therefore only a few concepts about JavaBeans will need to be summarized. For more details on JavaBeans, look up the documentation available at http://java.sun.com/beans/docs/. The later sections of this chapter discuss specific tags that facilitate the use of the JavaBean component in a JSP page. Toward the end of the chapter, we create a JSP page using a scenario-based example that will include a JavaBean component. Let's begin with a short recap of JavaBeans.

A Bean Component

A JavaBean, generally referred to as a bean component, follows the rules of object-oriented programming basics. The terms "object" and "component" need to be well defined and understood before we move on to discussing a bean. The basic difference between an object and a component is that objects cannot be plugged into other applications such as Word or Visual Basic.

You know that an object is a runtime instance of a class. For example, if you have created and distributed a chat application by using Java 1.1, the application can be executed on any target platform. A Visual Basic or Visual C programmer on the target platform, however, will not be able to extend the functionality of the chat application. As a result, the classes and objects created using Java 1.1 become unsuitable for reuse on the target platform. To make up for this shortcoming, component architecture support has been added to versions of Java starting with 1.2. We have already discussed the component architecture in brief in Chapter 1, "Introducing Web Development." Component architecture adds flexibility to applications with the use of individual components that can be plugged together. As a result, changes to the application require only component-based upgrading or change rather than a change in the total application. For example, the electronic circuit boards consist of numerous reusable components that are plugged together. Similarly, a car is not a single unit but is made up of numerous functional components that are put together. As a result, if one of the parts of the car fails to work, you can replace it with a part made from another manufacturer.

Similarly, a software component is a reusable object that can be plugged into any software application from different vendors. You can reuse or extend the functionality of a software component on the target application. Some of the plug-in software components that you can create are the spell-check utility, the calculator, the text editor, the find-and-replace utility, and more complex components such as the login validator and the balance sheet generator.

JavaBeans

A bean is a reusable and self-contained software component that can be manipulated in any Integrated Development Environment (IDE). Beans take advantage of all the security and platform-independent features of Java. Consider that you are using IBM Visual Age IDE to develop a chat application for your latest project. If you have already created a similar application in an earlier Java project, you might want to reuse the old code in your current project. Can you load the application in your earlier Java project onto the menu bar of the current IDE? Well, IBM Visual Age does not have a standardized way of recognizing the class files of your earlier application. Do you have to re-create all the class files of the chat application in IBM Visual Age IDE? The answer is no. All that you need to do is include a small piece of code in the chat application to convert it into a bean. Now your chat bean is ready to be loaded not only in IBM Visual Age IDE but also in other IDEs such as Bean Development Kit, Kawa, and Borland JBuilder.

Phases of a Bean

Like all natural processes, human life can be split into small comprehensible segments or phases. As a result, we can structure the life of man into phases such as infancy, childhood, and adolescence. Similarly, science and technology offer various resources that can be fragmented into phases to identify the exact status of the particular resource. For example, we have already discussed the different phases of a servlet in Chapter 3, "Servlet Basics." Even a task as simple as tea making can be segmented into phases based on the status of the task. Each ingredient used to make a cup of tea can be a component that is manufactured separately. For example, sugar is manufactured separately in a sugar factory and therefore can be considered a component. The process of gathering the various ingredients can be defined as the construction phase. The actual process of preparing the tea can be considered the building phase. Finally, the process of drinking tea can be considered as the execution phase.

A bean also exists in one of the following three phases: the construction phase, the building phase, or the execution phase. The construction phase involves creation of the bean and its user interface. A bean cannot exist by itself. To expose its functionality, a bean must be placed in another element of a running application, which is called as a container. A container can be either a frame window or a Web page. The building environment involves placing a bean in the target container. When the container application is executed, a bean enters the execution phase.

For example, consider the chat bean, which exists in one of the following three phases:

- When you create a frame window for chatting, the chat bean is in the construction phase.

- The frame window can be placed either on an IBM Visual Age form or on an HTML form. You can change the background color of the frame window to match the background color of the form. In addition, you can change the company logo displayed on a label control in the chat frame window. The chat bean is in the building phase.

- When the VisualAge form is executed, the end user actually participates in the chatting session. The chat bean is in the execution phase.

Elements of a Bean

Each bean comprises three fundamental elements: properties, methods, and events. The bean uses these elements to interact with the container of the target application into which it is placed. The properties of a bean define its characteristics. The bean properties can be read and modified by using the setXXX() and the getXXX() methods. For example, consider that a separate chat window is displayed for each user with whom you are currently chatting. You want the list of users with whom you are chatting to be displayed in the IBM Visual Age IDE menu bar. To do this, the chat bean should expose its user list property to Visual Age IDE.

Component Specification of a Bean

A simple Java object develops into a bean when all its member data are private and are accessible only through the member functions of the class. As per the JavaBean Component Specification, a simple Java object must support the following five features to develop into a bean:

Properties.   The private member data of a bean. For example, the chat bean might have properties such as the background color of the chat window, the size of the chat window, company logo, and the font displayed in the chat window.

Customization.   The process of changing the properties of a bean during the building phase. A bean can allow a few or all its properties to be customized by the target application. For example, the chat bean might expose only the background color and company logo property. A bean can be customized by using either property editors or mutator or setter methods.

Persistence.   The process of saving the state of a bean to a disk or other storage device when its execution is terminated. As a result, a bean is reloaded with the same settings next time. For example, the state of the chat bean, such as the background color and the user with whom you had a chat the last time, can be saved to a file and then reloaded at the next chat session.

Communication.   Used to communicate with other beans and the target application with the help of the delegation event model. For example, to open a new chat window to chat with different users, a menu item has to be added to the IBM Visual Age IDE menu bar. This is achieved by using a chat bean to raise an event whenever a new instance of the bean is created. This event can be handled by IBM Visual Age IDE to add a menu item to its menu bar.

Introspection.   Used by a programmer to query the properties, methods, and events supported by a bean.

Table 9.1   Types of Beans

BEAN TYPE	DESCRIPTION
Control beans	Are graphical user interface beans. You can create a control bean by extending one of the Swing component classes. An animated button control is an example of a control bean.
Container beans	Are used to hold other Java beans. You can create a container bean by extending one of the Swing container classes. An Explorer window created by extending the JTree class is an example of a container bean.
Invisible runtime beans	Are invisible to the end user during the execution phase of the bean. Spell Checker is an example for this type of bean. A bean that provides connectivity to any kind of data source, such as a SQL Server database, an Excel worksheet, or a flat file, is also an example of an invisible runtime bean.

NOTE Property editors are similar to the Display Properties window of the Windows operating system. Accessor methods are the methods used by a bean to get the value of a property. Mutator methods are used to set the value of a property. For example, the chat bean might have a `getBackgroundColor()` accessor method and a `setBackgroundColor()` mutator method to retrieve and set the background color of the chat frame window.

Types of Beans

After discussing the component specification of a bean, let's examine the types of beans that can be created in Java. Table 9.1 provides a list of beans that you can create.

Each bean has associated properties that can be modified. For example, a bean can be used to create an image. The size property of the image could be associated with a color so that there is a change in its color when the size of the image is changed. As part of the recap session, let's create a bean component by using the bank scenario.

Handling Changes in the Bean Property

Problem Statement

A customer visiting the Banco de Glendanthi Web site is given the option of changing his or her account type at any time. When the account type is changed, a check has to made to see if the account type is valid. This check is done using another bean that contains a list of all valid account types.

To simplify the scenario, we will use the following types of accounts to check for the functionality of the bean:

- Business Checking Account
- Personal Checking Account
- Personal Savings Account
- Certificate of Deposit Account
- Mortgage Loan Products

Let's look at the code for the account holder and the account type beans to implement this functionality.

Task List

- ✔ **Identify the mechanism to be used to validate the change in the account type.**
- ✔ **Identify the classes and methods to be used.**
- ✔ **Write the code for the AccountHolder bean.**
- ✔ **Write the code for the listener bean.**
- ✔ **Add the bean to an application.**
- ✔ **Compile and execute the programs.**
- ✔ **Verify the execution of the program.**

Identify the Mechanism to Be Used to Validate the Change in the Account Type

The bean representing the information related to the customer must notify the bean that represents the account types each time the account type is changed. The account type bean should prevent any change from being made if the type of account specified is invalid. Therefore, the account type property of the account holder bean must be a constrained property.

Identify the Classes and Methods to Be Used

Two beans are required, one for accepting the account holder's login information and another for maintaining a list of valid account types and performing the validation. The classes and methods that are required to implement the constrained property are as follows:

- A bean class, AccountHolder, to represent the account holder's information, with the following two attributes:
  - The attribute name of String type
  - The attribute accountType of String type
- A bean class, AccountValidate, to represent the types of accounts.

Write the Code for the Bean

The code for the bean component is as follows:

```java
import java.awt.*;
import java.awt.event.*;
import java.io.Serializable;
import javax.swing.*;
import java.beans.*;
//AccountHolder.java
public class AccountHolder extends JPanel implements ActionListener
{

/* Create the User Interface for accepting the account holder name and
account type */

    JLabel lName,ltype;
    JTextField tName,ttype;
    JButton submit;
    private String accType=new String("");
    public boolean canUpdate=false;
    public AccountHolder()
    {
        lName=new JLabel("Account Holder Name:");
        tName=new JTextField(8);
        ltype=new JLabel("Account Type:");
        ttype=new JTextField(15);
        ttype.setText(accType);
        submit=new JButton("Modify Details");
        setLayout(new FlowLayout());
        add(lName);add(tName);
        add(ltype);add(ttype);
        submit.addActionListener(this);
        add(submit);
    }
    protected VetoableChangeSupport changes=new
                VetoableChangeSupport(this);

    //Track changes in the account type
    public void setAccType(String temp)
    {
        String old=new String();
        old=accType;
        try
        {
        changes.fireVetoableChange("AccountType",old,temp);
        }
        catch(PropertyVetoException e)
        {
            System.out.println(e);
        }
        if (canUpdate)
```

```
        {
            accType=temp;
            JOptionPane.showMessageDialog(this,new String("Valid Account
Type"));
                    canUpdate=false;
        }
        else
            JOptionPane.showMessageDialog(this,new String("Invalid Account
Type"));
    }
    public String getAccType()
    {
        return accType;
    }
    public void actionPerformed(ActionEvent evt)
    {
        Object obj=evt.getSource();
        if(obj==submit)
            setAccType(ttype.getText());
    }

/* The following method is used to register listeners that keep track of
changes in the account type of an account holder */

    public void addVetoableChangeListener(VetoableChangeListener l)
    {
        changes.addVetoableChangeListener(l);
    }
    public void removeVetoableChangeListener(
            VetoableChangeListener l)
    {
        changes.removeVetoableChangeListener(l);
    }
}
```

Write the Code for the Listener Bean

The code for the listener bean is as follows:

```
import java.awt.*;
import javax.swing.*;
import java.awt.event.*;
import java.beans.*;
import java.io.*;

//AccountValidation.java

public class AccountValidation implements VetoableChangeListener
{
/* This class maintains a list of valid account types. You can modify
the code to retrieve the valid account types from a database */
```

```
String[] validAccTypes={"Business Checking Account","Personal Checking
Account","Personal Savings Account","Certificate of Deposit
Account","Mortgage Loan Products"};
AccountHolder ahpanel=new AccountHolder();
public AccountValidation()
{
/* Register this class as a listener of changes in the account type of
an account holder */
ahpanel.addVetoableChangeListener(this);
}


/* The following method is invoked whenever the account type of an
account holder is changed. This method is invoked as a response to the
fireVetoableChange() method that is called in the AccountHolder class.
getNewValue() is a method of the PropertyChangeEvent class and is used
to obtain the new value that has been set currently to a property. */
    public void vetoableChange(PropertyChangeEvent pcevent)
    {
        String accType=(String)pcevent.getNewValue();
        for(int i=0;i<validAccTypes.length;i++)
        {
            if(accType.equals(validAccTypes[i]))
            {
                ahpanel.canUpdate=true;
                break;
            }
        }
    }
}
```

Add the Bean to an Application

The code to add the bean to an application is as follows:

```
import java.awt.*;
import javax.swing.*;
import java.awt.event.*;
import java.beans.*;
import java.io.*;

//AccountValidation.java

public class AccountValidation implements VetoableChangeListener
{
        // ---- Rest of the code ----
        AccountHolder ahpanel=new AccountHolder();
        static JFrame frameObj;
        public AccountValidation()
        {
        //Adding the user interface of the bean to the frame window
        frameObj.getContentPane().add(ahpanel);
        ahpanel.addVetoableChangeListener(this);
```

```
          }
        public static void main(String args[])
      {
      frameObj=new JFrame("Account Type Modification");
      new AccountValidation();
      frameObj.setSize(400,400);
      frameObj.setVisible(true);
      }
        // ---- Rest of the code ----
  }
```

Compile and Execute the Programs

Create a folder and save both programs in the same folder. Compile the programs by using the following command at the command prompt:

```
javac *.java
```

Because the AccountHolder bean has been implemented using a Java application, you use the following command to execute the program:

```
java AccountValidation
```

NOTE Before executing the program, remember to set the class path variable to include the directory into which you have copied the two Java files and compiled them.

After the execution of the code, a frame window is created in which the AccountHolder bean panel is displayed. Figure 9.1 displays the AccountHolder bean panel.

Verify the Execution of the Program

To verify the execution of the program and validate the account type accepted from the customer, do the following:

1. Enter the value of account holder name as **Catherine.**
2. Enter the value of account type as **Personal Checking Account**, click the Modify Details button, and check whether a message box showing "Valid Account Type" is displayed.

   Figure 9.2 displays the "Valid Account Type" message box.
3. Enter the value of account type as **Debit**, click the Modify Details button, and check whether a message box showing "Invalid Account Type" is displayed.

   Figure 9.3 displays the "Invalid Account Type" message box.

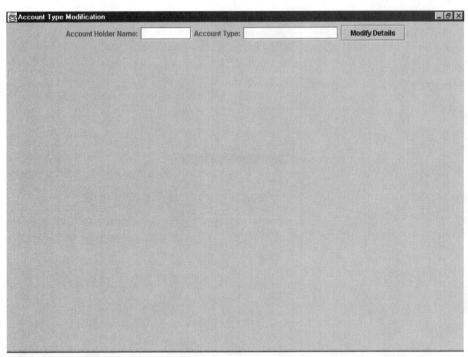

Figure 9.1   The `AccountHolder` bean panel.

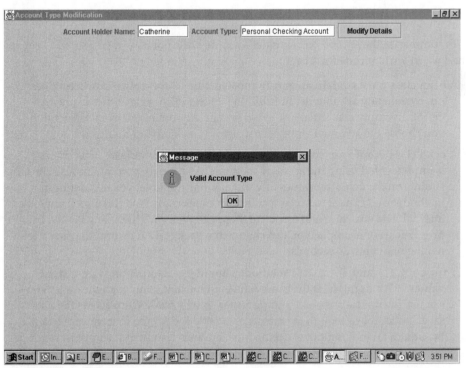

Figure 9.2   The "Valid Account Type" message box.

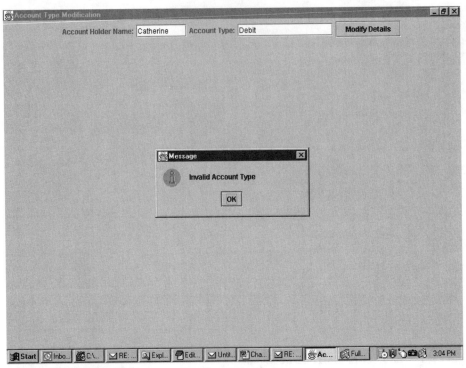

Figure 9.3   The "Invalid Account Type" message box.

To summarize the session on beans, let's list the basic points that you should keep in mind when writing code for a bean:

A bean class must contain an empty constructor.   An empty constructor does not contain any arguments. To fulfill this criterion, you can either explicitly define an empty constructor or avoid specifically defining any constructor. If you choose the latter, an empty constructor is created automatically.

A bean class should not contain any public fields or variables.   This criterion is implemented using the accessor methods. As a result, you can impose constraints on the accepted values of variables. For example, you can define a method, setSize(), to accept positive numbers only. You can also change the internal data structure and associate these changes with the change in the bean properties. For example, you can change the background color if the user does not log on within 30 seconds.

The getXXX() **and** setXXX() **methods should be used to access persistent values.**   For example. if the bean defines a constant value for a message, you can use the setMessage() and getMessage() methods to access the message. Notice that although the message variable is declared in lowercase letters, the setXX() and getXXX() method declarations are always in uppercase letters.

The use of beans in a JSP page emphasizes the fundamental principle of JSP, which is to separate programming from page authoring or designing. The programmer implements the business logic in the bean component by defining the properties that are applicable to the logic. Alternatively, the page designer uses the bean properties to access the values that are used in the pages of the application. As a result, the business logic is encapsulated in a Java object represented by the bean component, which is then instantiated and accessed from a JSP page. Although this mechanism does seem complex, it involves the use of three JSP standard actions already discussed in Chapter 5, "Using JSP Directives and Action Elements."

Let's now look at the implementation of beans in a JSP page. We begin with a detailed discussion on the JSP tags that are used to work with beans in a JSP page. In the final section of the chapter, we apply the concepts in a scenario-based example to create and implement beans in JSP.

Before we begin the discussion on the JSP tags used for the bean implementation, let's look at the output generated by the use of a bean in a JSP page. Figure 9.4 displays the output of a JSP page, in which a bean component is used to retrieve the "Hello World" message.

At the end of this chapter, we will have created a page for the bank application by using a bean component. In the course of defining tags for bean implementation, we will use the code of the "Hello World" message bean example.

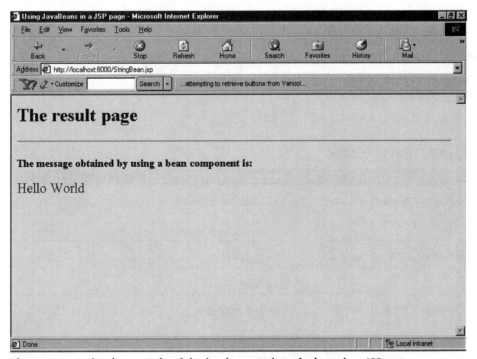

Figure 9.4 A simple example of the implementation of a bean in a JSP page.

A JSP Example Using JavaBeans

Problem Statement

A customer visiting Banco de Glendanthi to open a new account with the bank is presented with the option of opening various types of accounts. Table 9.2 describes the types of accounts at Banco de Glendanthi.

Each of these accounts requires specifications in terms of their opening amounts, rate of interest, or minimum balance amount. The design of this application will use an HTML page to accept input in the form of a specific type of account. Thereafter, a bean component will be used to retrieve the account-specific details from the HTML page request and display it on the result page. We will also use a JSP page to specify the details of the bean component.

Task List

☑ **Identify the mechanism for displaying account type details based on the user input.**

☑ **Identify the elements of the user interface screen.**

☑ **Identify the tags for the JSP page.**

☑ **Identify the components of the bean.**

☑ **Write the code for the HTML page.**

☑ **Write the code for the JSP page.**

☑ **Write the code for a bean.**

☑ **Compile the Java file.**

☑ **View the JSP page.**

Table 9.2   Types of Accounts

TYPE OF ACCOUNT	ACCOUNT CATEGORIES
Business Checking Accounts	Basic Business Checking
	Business Checking Biz+
Personal Checking Accounts	Basic Checking
	Checking Plus+
Personal Savings Accounts	Student Savings
	Passbook Savings
Certificate of Deposit Account	Certificates of Deposit
Mortgage Loan Products	Mortgage Loans

Identify the Mechanism for Displaying Account Type Details Based on the User Input

The application page accepts the customer's choice of account type and displays information regarding the account opening and minimum balance amounts for the specified account type. The code for this application can be split into three parts based on the presentation content and the dynamic business content. Considering the structure of the page, we can create an HTML page to design the components to accept the customer name and account type details. A bean component can be written to check the account type and display the relevant information. In addition, the application can include a result page containing the JSP-specific tags for the inclusion of the output of the bean component in a JSP page. It is evident that structurally, the application page clearly classifies the work profile of the page author or designer and the programmer. The designer can write the presentation logic in HTML while the programmer can concentrate on the business logic to validate the customer details by using the various elements of JSP.

Identify the Elements of the User Interface Screen

The user interface will consist of the following elements:

- A text box to accept the customer name
- A combo box to display the list of the various account types available at the bank site

Table 9.3 lists the HTML tags to be used for designing the user interface.

Table 9.3   The Elements of the User Interface

INPUT FIELD	SPECIFICATIONS
Bank's name and logo	`<%@include file="Header.html"%>`
Control to accept the customer name	`<input type="text">`

Combo-box to display the various account types	`<select size="1" name="account">`
	
	`<option selected>Personal Checking Account`
	`<option value=" Business Checking Account ">`
	`Business Checking Account`
	`......................................</select>`

Submit and reset buttons	`<input type="submit">`
	
	`<input type="reset">`

Identify the Tags for the JSP Page

The three JSP standard actions that we will define in the JSP page to enable the integration of a bean component with the JSP page are these:

<jsp:useBean>   This JSP action is used to locate and instantiate a bean component. A variable name (ID) is used to identify a bean.

<jsp:setProperty>   This JSP action is used with the `<jsp:useBean>` action to set the value of the bean property.

<jsp:getProperty>   This JSP action is also used with the `<jsp:useBean>` action to access the value of the bean property.

> **TIP** Have you received error messages when specifying firstfile.jsp as Firstfile.jsp in the address location bar of Internet Explorer? Did you observe and identify JSP as a case-sensitive language? If you have followed the naming conventions for the attributes and other JSP tags, you may not have encountered any problems so far. You do need to consider that, similar to all other JSP tags, the `<jsp:xxx>` tags are case-sensitive and should be written according to specifications. All these tags are container tags. Therefore, these tags should contain end tags. In addition, you can write the JSP actions in a JSP page in two ways. You can specify these tags either as `<jsp:xxx />` or `<jsp:xxx>` and `</jsp:xxx>`.

Let's examine the preceding JSP standard actions individually and look at their definitions in a JSP page.

The <jsp:useBean> Action

The `<jsp:useBean>` action is used to find and load an existing bean in a JSP page. The definition of this action associates the bean instance with a name and scope. The name for the bean component is defined by using a unique ID. Table 9.4 lists the attributes that can be specified for the `useBean` action.

Table 9.4   Attributes of the `useBean` Action

ATTRIBUTE	USED TO SPECIFY...
id	A variable or a unique name to identify the instance of the bean.
class	The class from which the bean object has to be implemented. The class specified should not be abstract but should be a public constructor without an argument.
scope	The life of the bean in terms of a page, session, application, or request. The default value of the scope attribute is page.

ATTRIBUTE	USED TO SPECIFY...
beanName	A referential name for the bean that can be used to initialize the `instantiate()` method of the `java.beans.Beans` class.
type	The data type of the variable used to identify the bean. The specified data type is not the same as that of the instantiated class of the bean. The fully qualified type name for the bean can either be the bean's superclass or an interface implemented by the bean's class. If undefined, the value of the `type` attribute is the same as that defined for the `class` attribute.

NOTE All the attribute names of the standard actions `<jsp:useBean>`, `<jsp:setProperty>`, and `<jsp:getProperty>` are case-sensitive and should conform to the naming conventions used for the scripting language, which is Java.

The syntax for using the `<jsp:useBean>` action is as follows:

```
<jsp:useBean id="name of the bean instance"
scope="page/session/application/request" class="package.class"
/>
```

How does the `<jsp:useBean>` tag locate a bean component? Well, the `<jsp:useBean>` tag follows these steps to instantiate the bean component:

1. The `id` and `scope` attributes are used to locate the specific bean.

2. After locating the bean, a reference to the bean is stored in a variable with the specified name or ID.

3. If the `type` attribute is specified, the located bean is assigned the specified data type.

4. If the `<jsp:useBean>` tag is unable to locate the specified bean, the tag uses the class attribute to instantiate the bean, and a reference to the bean is stored in a variable.

5. If the located bean contains a body or elements between the opening `<jsp:useBean>` and closing `</jsp:useBean>` tags, the body is processed.

The *<jsp:setProperty>* Action

The `<jsp:setProperty>` action is used to modify the property of a bean by using the `setXXX()` method. A bean property can be of the following types:

Bound properties.   Just as you are informed about a change in your friend's telephone number, beans need to inform other beans when their properties change.

For example, a timer might be created as a bean. An animation bean might use the timer bean to decide the duration for which the animation should play. When users change the play time property of the timer bean, the timer bean should notify the animation bean about the change. The properties of a bean that provide notification to other beans about changes in its value are called *bound properties*.

Constrained properties. Some properties of a bean might need to be prevented from being changed by another bean. Such properties that have to be stopped from being changed by another bean are called *constrained properties*. For example, a bean might be created to represent the screen coordinates. This bean can then be used to restrict an animation bean to play within valid coordinates. The screen coordinates bean should be informed of any change in the coordinates of the animation bean. The screen coordinates bean can then prevent the change of a coordinate in the animation bean if the new value is invalid. The constrained properties are very similar to bound properties.

Indexed properties. The properties of a bean that are indexed under a single name with each index being an integer value are called *indexed properties*. For instance, you might create a bean to represent an animation character. An animation is a series of images where each image represents a movement that is played in a sequence. The different image files will represent each movement of the animation. Therefore, the file property of an animation bean cannot have a single value. It can be represented in the form of an array. Each element of the array will represent a different filename.

To set the value of the bean property, either an explicit value is specified or the value is obtained from a `request` parameter. Corresponding to the specified request property value, the `setXXX()` method of the bean is called with the matching value. Table 9.5 lists the attributes that can be specified for the `setProperty` action.

The syntax for using the `<jsp:setProperty>` action is this:

```
<jsp:setProperty name="name of the bean instance" property="*/name of
the bean property" value="value assigned to the bean property" />
```

The properties of a bean can be set in several ways.

Table 9.5 Attributes of the `setProperty` Action

ATTRIBUTE	USED TO SPECIFY...
name	A name for the bean.
property	The property for which values are to be set. If set to `"*"` specifies that the `set` methods for all specified values should be called.
value	An explicit value for the bean property.
param	The name of the request parameter to be used to set the value of the bean property.

Using the request Object

The parameters of the `request` object can be used to set the bean properties at request time. For example, the following statement can be used to set all the properties of a bean named languageBean:

```
<jsp:setProperty name="languageBean property="*" />
```

Similarly, the following statement can be used to explicitly set a single property of a bean named languageBean:

```
<jsp:setProperty name="languageBean property="java" />
```

Using a String or an Expression

An evaluated value of `String` or `Expression` can also be used to set the value of a bean property. Such a property setting occurs at request time.

For example, the following statement uses `String` to set the property of a bean named messageBean:

```
<jsp:setProperty name="testBean property="message" value="Hello, this is
the message set by the set property of UseBean" />
```

Similarly, the following statement uses `Expression` to set the property of a bean named testBean:

```
<jsp:setProperty name="testBean property="message" value="<%=
request.getParameter("name") %>" />
```

The <jsp:getProperty> Action

The `<jsp:getProperty>` action is used to access the property of a bean. The `<jsp:getProperty>` action accesses the bean property and converts it to a `String`. The `String` is then printed as output in the result page. Table 9.6 lists the attributes that can be specified for the `setProperty` action.

Table 9.6   Attributes of the `getProperty` Action

ATTRIBUTE	USED TO SPECIFY...
name	A name for the bean.
property	The property for which values are to be set. If set to `"*"`, specifies that the `set` methods for all specified values should be called.

The syntax for using the `<jsp:getProperty>` action is this:

```
<jsp:getProperty name="name of the bean instance" property="*/name of
the bean property" />
```

You may recall that at the beginning of the chapter, we displayed the output of the implementation of a simple bean in a JSP page. After the preceding discussion on the various actions to be used to create a link between the JSP page and a Java file containing a bean component, let's understand the code for the previous example. The code for the JSP page is as follows:

```
<jsp:useBean id="stringBean" scope="page" class="StringBean">
<jsp:setProperty name="stringBean" property="message" value="Hello
World"/>
</jsp:useBean>

<html.
<head><title>Using JavaBeans in a JSP page</title></head>
<body bgcolor="#FFDFD7">
<h1>The result page</h1><hr>
<p><h3>The message obtained by using a bean component is:</h3>
<font size="5" color="#0000FF"><jsp:getProperty name="stringBean"
property="message" /></p>
</body>
</html>
```

Notice the use of the `<jsp:useBean>`, `<jsp:setProperty>`, and `<jsp:getProperty>` actions. The `<jsp:useBean>` action is used to define an instance of a bean of the class `StringBean` with a name or ID as `stringBean`. The `<jsp:setProperty>` action is used to get the value of the message "Hello World," which has to be displayed in the result page. In addition to the zero-argument constructor for StringBean, the code for the bean component will define the `setXXX()` and `getXXX()` methods for the message property. As a result, the code for the bean is as follows:

```
public class StringBean {
   private String message = "No message specified";
   public String getMessage() {
      return (message);
      }

   public void setMessage (String message) {
      this.message = message;
      }
   }
```

In the initial sections of the chapter, we saw the output of the preceding code after setting the value of the message as "Hello World." What are the changes in the output if the value of the message property is not set in the JSP page? Let's remove the `value` attribute of the `<jsp setProperty>` action and observe the changes in the output.

The only change in the JSP code is the removal of the `value` attribute, which now changes to this:

```
<jsp:useBean id="stringBean" scope="page" class="StringBean">
<jsp:setProperty name="stringBean" property="message" />
</jsp:useBean>
```

Figure 9.5 displays the output of the JSP page without a specified message.

Let's now define the structure for the HTML and JSP pages of the application that will accept the account type from a customer. From the preceding discussions, we can conclude the following about the codes for the bank application:

- An HTML file will accept the customer's choice of the account type.
- The form method transfers the control to a JSP page that will specify the bean component to be used to retrieve the account type details. In addition, the `setProperty` and `getProperty` actions will be used to set and retrieve the value for the `accountType` property.
- The bean component will check for the customer's choice of accout type and display the details about the corresponding account.

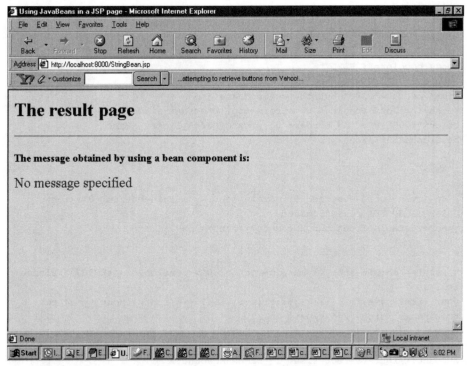

Figure 9.5   The earlier example without a message specification.

Identify the Components of a Bean

The main components of the bean code will include an empty constructor without an argument and the setXXX() and getXXX() methods corresponding to the bean properties specified in the JSP page. The output of the bank scenario will display the name of the customer, the choice of the type of account, and the details of the account in the resulting JSP page. Therefore, the code will consist of the following statements and methods:

- Variable declarations for the customer name, the account type, and account details.

- The setXXX() and getXXX() methods for the customer name, the account type, and account details.

- The if conditional statement to check for the customer's choice of account and the details of the account included as a string in the return statement.

Write the Code for the HTML Page

The code for the user interface to accept customer-specific inputs is as follows:

```
<html>

<head>

<title>The HTML page for the useBean example</title>
</head>

<body bgcolor="#FFDFD7">

<form method="POST" action="usebeancase.jsp">
<p style="word-spacing: 0; margin-top: 0"><font size="7"
color="#0000FF"><img border="0" src="dd00448_1.gif" >Banco
de Glendanthi</font></p>

  <hr>

  <p style="word-spacing: 0; margin-top: 0; margin-bottom: 0"><font
color="#0000FF" size="5">Need
  more details about our accounts?</font></p>
<hr>

<p style="margin-top: 0; margin-bottom: 0"><font color="#CC0099">Please
tell us
your first name:::::::::::::::::::::::::::::::</font><input type="text"
name="name" size="27"></p>

<p><font color="#CC0099">Please tell us about your choice of
account:</font><select size="1" name="account">
    <option value="Business Checking Account">Business Checking Account
```

```
  <option value="Personal Savings Account">Personal Savings Account
  <option value="Personal Checking Account">Personal Checking Account
 <option value="Certificate of Deposit Account">Certificate of Deposit
Account
  <option value="Mortgage Loan Products">Mortgage Loan Products
</select></p>

<p> </p>

  <p>  

            
            
       
  <input type="submit" value="Display Details" name="B1">  
  <input type="reset" value="Reset" name="B2"></p>
  </form>
  </body>
  </html>
```

Write the Code for the JSP Page

The code for the JSP page that will be used to load the bean component is as follows:

```
<jsp:useBean id="accountBean" scope="page" class="AccountBean">
<jsp:setProperty name="accountBean" property="*"/>
</jsp:useBean>

<html.
<head><title>The result page</title></head>
<body>
<h1>The result page</h1>
<p>Hello, <jsp:getProperty name="accountBean" property="name"/></p>
<p>Your choice of account is <jsp:getProperty name="accountBean"
property="account"/></p>
<p>Details about the account: </p>
<p><jsp:getProperty name="accountBean" property="details"/></p>
</body>
</html>
```

Write the Code for a Bean

The code for the bean component to check the account type specified by the customer
and display the account type-specific information is as follows:

```
public class AccountBean {
private String name;
private String account;
```

```java
private String  details;

public AccountBean() {}

public void setName(String name) {
this.name=name;
}
public String getName() {
return name;
}

public void setAccount(String account){
this.account=account;
}
public String getAccount() {
return account;
}
public void setDetails(String details) {
details=details;
}
public String getDetails() {
if (account.equals("Business Checking Account") ) {
return "Minimum balance " +
    "to open is $100 with a monthly maintainence charge of $10";
}else if (account.equals("Personal Savings Account") ) {
return "Minimum balance " +
    "to open is $5000 with a monthly maintainence charge of $100";
}else if (account.equals("Personal Checking Account") ) {
return "Minimum balance " +
    "to open is $100 with a monthly maintainence charge of $7";
} else if (account.equals("Certificate of Deposit Account") ) {
return "The certificate of posting account acrues interest of 1.98%" +
 "for a deposit of $500 for 91 days and 2.47% for 182 days";
}else if (account.equals("Mortgage Loan Products") ) {
return " For an auto loan upto $50,000 for a period of 12-36 months at
6.25% interest"
+ "For a home loan upto $350,000 for a period of 61-120 months at 7.25%
interest";
}else {
return "Sorry, never heard of " + account +  ".";
}
}
}
```

Compile the Java File

To compile the Java file you'll need to perform the following steps:

1. Copy the code for the bean component and save the file as AccountBean.java in the C:\j2sdkee1.2.1\lib\classes directory.

2. Compile the code for the bean and debug the same if necessary.

View the JSP Page

To view the JSP page, do the following:

1. Save the HTML file as usebean.html.

2. Save the JSP file as usebeancase.jsp.

3. Copy the HTML and JSP files in the C:/j2sdkee1.2.1/public_html directory.

4. Initiate the server startup and open usebean.html in the browser.

5. Enter the following values in each of the controls of the input page:

   First Name—Michelle

   Choice of account—Personal Savings Account

   Figure 9.6 displays the output of the HTML page.

6. Click the Display Details button.

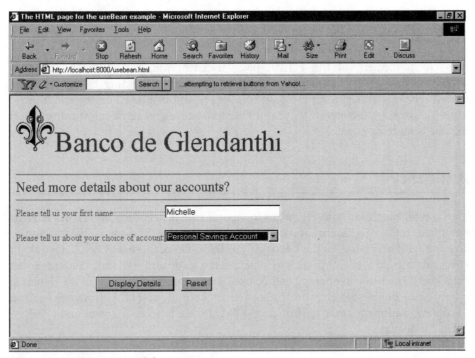

Figure 9.6 The output of the HTML page.

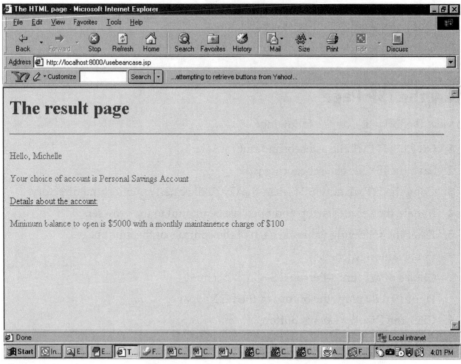

Figure 9.7   The output retrieved from the HTML and JSP page by using a bean component.

The form element of the HTML page transfers the control of the page to `usebeancase.jsp`. Subsequently, the information corresponding to the specified account type is retrieved from the bean component and displayed on the result page. Figure 9.7 displays the screen that represents the successful retrieval of information from the bean component.

Summary

Beans can be integrated with JSP pages to separate the Java code from HTML. All that is required in this mechanism of incorporating a bean in a JSP page is the addition of three standard action tags in the JSP page. The inclusion of these tags helps not only to retrieve data from a bean but also to separate the static and dynamic contents of an application. The bean component can be used to encapsulate one part of the dynamic content or the business logic in an application. In addition, an HTML form can be used to write dynamic pages that, in turn, access data from a bean component and generate results for display.

In this chapter, we briefly reviewed the basic structure and function of a bean. We also discussed the three actions that help embed a bean within a JSP page. The bank scenario was used to accept the customer's choice of account. The details of the account were retrieved from a bean and displayed in the result page. This type of approach separates logic from the presentation and makes a JSP page easier to be modified by a designer who is unskilled in Java programming.

In the next chapter, we move on to advanced concepts of JSP related to server-side transactions. The next few chapters promise more interactivity between the client side and the server side to perform transactions involving databases.

CHAPTER

10

Implementing JDBC Connectivity

OBJECTIVES:

In this chapter, you will learn to do the following:

- ✔ Identify the significance of databases
- ✔ Use JDBC to connect to a database
- ✔ Execute SQL statements
- ✔ Create a database table from a JSP page
- ✔ Insert records into a database table from a JSP page

Getting Started

In the previous chapters, we recapitulated the use of JSP in distancing programmers or developers from the intricacies of Web page designing. We have also discussed how JSP can be used to simplify the process of coding for applications. In Chapter 9, "JSP and JavaBeans," we saw how the inclusion of the useBean tag helped to encapsulate a bean component in an application. This technique saves time that is otherwise lost in rewriting the same parts of code.

In the examples that you have worked with so far, input was accepted and ouptut was displayed with the help of user-specific inputs. Transactions of this type do not require the use of stored data resources that can be accessed and manipulated to yield the required outputs. Stored data resources sounds like a complicated, unattainable, specialized feat, doesn't it? Take a breather because although the feature sounds very complicated, it actually provides users with the ability to create well-formatted and structured data repositories with common data accessibility and availability across networks. What we are talking about is database management!

Before you learn about database management, let's try to understand the term "database" with the help of an example. Kids Corner is a bookstore that specializes in all kinds of books for children aged 3 to 12 years. Donald, the proprietor of the store, has decided to expand by creating a Web site with library assistance. The idea is to make books readily available for reading at a nominal charge by facilitating online issue. In addition to the prospect of increasing sales and popularity, the concept of going online has Donald worried for other reasons. Currently, Donald and his assistant easily manage the small stock in the store; however, the thought of single-handedly managing the increase in the volume of sales and stock intimidates Donald. Donald's friend, Joe, a software engineer, suggests the use of a database to store all book-related information. The additional support provided by the database is the access to the stored information as and when required.

What we are talking about here is easy storage, access, and manipulation of large amounts of data. Addressing a situation similar to the one in the preceding example, this chapter will begin with an insight into the fundamentals of database management and connectivity. In the next section, you will learn to relate the basic concepts to access and manipulate databases in Java applications by using Java Database Connectivity (JDBC) and its two database access models. The chapter then discusses the various types of JDBC drivers needed to establish database connectivity. Finally, you learn about concepts such as the creation of a database table to store information and the use of query statements to access and manipulate data by using the Banco de Glendanthi application scenario.

Database Management and Connectivity

Databases provide a methodology to structure and organize large amounts of data in the form of either inventory details or customer information. A Database Management System (DBMS) presents the software mechanism to store, access, and retrieve the data in the database. MS-Access, MS-SQL, Oracle, Sybase, Informix, and Ingress are a few examples of the DBMS/RDBMSs available. Structured Query Language or SQL is the de-facto non-procedural language used to access and retrieve data from a relational database. In addition, the International Organization for Standardization (ISO) and American National Standards Institute (ANSI) have decided on a standardized query format to retrieve data from a database.

Introduction to SQL

Consider an example. Fun 'N Learn is a preparatory school where children of diverse nationalities speaking different languages are enrolled. Regardless of the difference in languages, how can Jane, the teacher, converse and communicate with all the children? How do these children share experiences and work together? The key to this is very simple. Communication and exchange of ideas are facilitated by the use of a common language, English. Thankfully, all the children speak English. Therefore, interaction and exchange of ideas is easy.

In the same way, a common language is needed for interaction with databases. You'll agree that in today's world, speed and effectiveness are the key factors that determine the success of technology. By integrating both these factors, databases provide data resources that can be accessed and modified using applications through multiple locations; however, such communication cannot be brought about by the use of vendor-specific languages. SQL provides for a methodology that has earned support from all database vendors with a few minor product-specific enhancements.

A database, as explained before, consists of data stored in tables. A table comprises rows and columns, where columns represent the attributes of the entity for which the data is to be represented, and rows represent data for each and every instance of an entity. Figure 10.1 portrays a row and column entry in a table. A single entry of this type is known as a record.

The rows of a table can be accessed and manipulated using SQL-specific commands that allow users to retrieve results from databases. Let's look at a few basic SQL commands and their uses. Table 10.1 tabulates each of these commands to demonstrate their implementations.

Let's now look at the implementations of the SQL commands with the help of examples.

Creating a Table

The CREATE TABLE command is used to create a table in a database. The following syntax illustrates the line of code for creating a table:

```
CREATE TABLE tableName (columnName1 datatype, columnName2 datatype...);
```

Consider the process of creating a table for a database of a bank. A user at the ATM of the bank uses the records of the database to validate the authenticity of the account ID and PIN number. The column fields for this table are cAccountId and cPin_no. The following code snippet shows the use of the CREATE TABLE command to create the Login table:

```
CREATE TABLE Login (cAccount_Id char(10), cPin_no char(10));
```

VendorID	VendorName	Address	Phone
SS0145	Earnest Software Solutions	20, Thomson Place, Boston MA 02210	1-800-648-7130

Figure 10.1 An example of a record in a table.

Table 10.1 The Basic SQL Commands

SQL COMMAND	USED TO...
CREATE TABLE	Create a table in a database
SELECT	Select records from a table
INSERT INTO	Insert new records in a table
UPDATE	Modify values in the records of a table
DELETE	Delete records from a table
DROP	Delete a table from a database

Viewing the Records of a Table

The SELECT command is used to retrieve and view the rows of a table in a database. The following syntax illustrates the line of code for viewing all the rows and columns of a table:

```
SELECT * from tableName;
```

The use of an asterisk specifies the retrieval of all rows and columns from a particular table. The WHERE clause is used with the selection criterion to specify selective retrieval of rows from a table. The syntax in such a case will be the following:

```
SELECT * from tableName WHERE selectionCriterion;
```

The following code snippet shows the use of the SELECT command for the retrieval of records for a customer named Garrett:

```
SELECT * from Registration WHERE firstName="Garrett";
```

Inserting Records in a Table

The INSERT INTO command is used to insert new records in a table. The following syntax illustrates the line of code for creating a table:

```
INSERT INTO tableName VALUES (columnValue1, columnValue2 ...);
```

It is important to maintain the sequence for the column values being inserted, which should be similar to the order of the column names specified during table creation. The following code snippet is used to insert the first name, last name, address, account type, and annual income of a customer in the registration table:

```
INSERT INTO Registration VALUES("Dunston", "Payne", "21, Sunley House,
Eastern Avenue", "Loan", 20000);
```

Modifying Records in a Table

The UPDATE command is used to modify the records in a table. The following syntax illustrates the line of code for creating a table:

```
UPDATE tableName SET columnName="newColumnValue";
```

The following code snippet is used to modify the last name of Betty from Smith to Charles after her marriage:

```
UPDATE Registration SET lastName="Charles" where first_name='Betty';
```

Deleting Records from a Table

The DELETE command is used to delete records from a table. The following syntax illustrates the SQL statement for deleting all the records of a table:

```
DELETE * from tableName;
```

Parallel to its usage with the SELECT command, the use of the asterisk specifies the deletion of all records from a particular table. The WHERE clause is used with the selection criterion to specify selective deletion of records from a table. The syntax in such a case will be the following:

```
DELETE * from tableName WHERE selectionCriterion;
```

The following code snippet shows the use of the DELETE command for the deletion of records for a customer named Jonathan:

```
DELETE * from Registration WHERE firstName="Jonathan";
```

Deleting a Table

The DROP TABLE command is used to delete a table from a database. The following syntax illustrates the SQL statement for deleting a table:

```
DROP TABLE tableName;
```

The following code snippet shows the use of the DROP TABLE command to delete the tempTransaction table:

```
DROP TABLE tempTransaction;
```

Before we move on, let's create a table for the database of a bank. The table, named Counter, consists of the details and financial status of the various ATM counters of the bank. Table 10.2 describes the structure of the table.

Table 10.2   Table Structure for the Counter Table

TABLE FIELD NAME	CONTAINS	FIELD DATA TYPE AND SIZE
cCounter_id	The ID of the ATM counter	char(10)
CAddress	The address of the ATM counter	char(50)
McashBalance	The available cash in the counter	Money
MminBalance	The minimum balance of cash to be maintained in the ATM counter	Money

Let's now write the code to create the table. The SQL statements of the code will be the following:

```
create table Counter
(
cCounter_id char(10) not null primary key,
cAddress char(50) not null,
mCashBalance money not null,
mMinBalance money not null
)
```

Similarly, the SQL statements to insert records into the table will be the following:

```
insert into Counter values('CT0001','Hummingway Street NY', 8000, 50000)
insert into Counter values('CT0002','Timothy Square NY', 9000, 50000)
insert into Counter values('CT0003','Sunley Estate CA', 15000, 70000)
insert into Counter values('CT0004','Bayer House LS', 50000, 50000)
insert into Counter values('CT0005','Mackinnon Street CA', 45000, 80000)
```

You have looked at the structure and method used to query a database. Before beginning any database transaction, it is imperative to establish a communication or interaction mode with the database. We are referring to a scenario wherein the database server and the application are running on different hosts across a network. To facilitate communication between a database and an application, the following information needs to be obtained:

- The type of RDBMS/DBMS used for database communication
- The location of the database
- The name of the database

During the process of database communication the preceding information restricts the use of a database. As a result, an application is able to interact with the specified type of database only. In such situations, Open Database Connectivity (ODBC) from Microsoft, a standard for database communications in applications, can be used to provide accessibility to a variety of databases.

Database Connectivity in Java

You can add programming features to applications to customize, add logic to, and enhance the functionality of applications. Similarly, using programming languages can increase the accessibility and quality of a database interaction. This is accomplished by the use of the Application Programming Interface (API), which consists of database-specific statements and functions provided by database vendors. Therefore, the introduction of ODBC API has resulted in the availability of a set of library routines or functions to provide access to multiple databases.

Because the programming language used in JSP is Java, let's now look at database access and manipulation in Java applications. In Java, the retrieval of data from a database is achieved using JDBC API. As a result, with the addition of JDBC, Java applications can communicate with a database by using SQL statements. The addition of JDBC also helps isolate Java programmers from database-specific details, such as the name of the database accessed and the tables and drivers used for access. Accordingly, Java programmers can concentrate on querying and retrieving data from the database by using SQL statements instead of focusing on the mode and method adopted for the communication.

How are the connectivity and interactivity of databases achieved in Java? Consider that you are presented a brand new car on your nineteenth birthday. Does the present alone actually symbolize the use of the car? In other words, of what use is the car standing at your doorstep without a driver to steer it to the specified destination? In the same way, you need a database driver to establish a link or act as an intermediary between the application and the database. The driver is also required because a database can understand only SQL statements, not Java language statements. Java applications cannot directly communicate with a database to submit and retrieve the results of queries. Therefore, an intermediary medium is required to translate Java statements to SQL statements.

When you initiate a database interaction in Java applications by using JDBC, it is necessary to address the following issues before considering and fulfilling the requirement for the intermediary component:

- Different kinds of databases, such as MS Access, SQL Server, Sybase, and Oracle, are available in the market. A Java application should be flexible enough to be able to communicate with any kind of database.

- In addition, a Java application should be database independent. This implies that an application that is written to communicate with one kind of DBMS, such as MS Access, should also be able to communicate with another kind of DBMS, such as SQL Server. In addition to a switch of this type, the database should be chosen without having to make any major modifications to the application.

In the JDBC model, JDBC API uses a JDBC driver, the intermediary component to tackle the previously mentioned concerns. The driver-mediated interaction between the application and the database can be summarized in the following steps:

- The Java applications invoke the methods of JDBC API, which, in turn, help convert the Java commands to generic SQL statements.

Figure 10.2 The JDBC architecture.

- Subsequently, the JDBC API submits the queries in the form of SQL statements to the JDBC driver to communicate with the database.

- The JDBC driver converts the queries to a form that the specific DBMS/RDBMS can understand.

- The result of the SQL queries is retrieved by the JDBC driver and converted into equivalent JDBC API classes and objects used by the application.

Assuming that the JDBC driver takes care of interactions with the database, any change made to the database does not affect the application. Figure 10.2 shows the components of the JDBC architecture.

The concepts covered so far explain JDBC architecture in relation to its components and their functionality. All these components collectively work toward providing access to a database. The access to the database can further be categorized into two access models based on the mode adopted for the database interactivity. Let's now look at the modes and types of access that can be used in JDBC architecture.

The JDBC Database Access Models

You know that the Java application, JDBC API, JDBC driver, and database functionally complement each other to enable access to the data stored in the database. The placement of individual components and modes of interactivity used to access the database form the base for the classification of a database into the following two types of access models:

- Two-tier database access model
- Three-tier database access model

The Two-Tier Database Access Model

In the two-tier database access model, which is a relatively simpler model, the Java application interacts directly with the database. The JDBC driver acts as a hub between the two and is responsible for sending the SQL commands to the database. The results of these commands are accepted and then sent to the application. This type of database access consists of two tiers. The first tier is formed by the application, and the JDBC driver and database form the second tier.

Figure 10.3 represents the two-tiered database model.

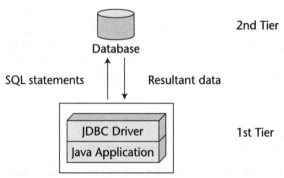

Figure 10.3   The two-tier database access model.

The Three-Tier Database Access Model

The three-tier database access model does not permit direct interaction between the application and the database. This model, in addition to the presence of the application, JDBC driver, and the database, also includes a middle tier represented by an application server. Therefore, the flow of commands is diverted through the middle tier before being sent to and from the database. As a result, the queries from the application are sent to the database through the middle tier. Subsequently, the resultant data is sent back to the application through the middle tier. Figure 10.4 represents the three-tier database model.

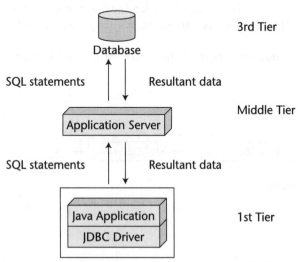

Figure 10.4   The three-tier database access model.

The importance of the JDBC driver as a mediating agent between the application and the database has been frequently implied in the concepts discussed so far. You may want to know about the functionality and methodology used by the JDBC drivers to acquire database connectivity for Java applications. Let's now look at the different types of drivers and understand their workings during a database interaction.

Types of JDBC Drivers

The JDBC drivers that are provided by the database vendor need to be installed, and the communicating application needs to contain certain statements to facilitate database interaction. The JDBC drivers used for such interactions can be categorized into the following four types:

Type 1.   The JDBC-ODBC bridge + ODBC driver.

Type 2.   The Part Native Part Java driver.

Type 3.   The JDBC-Net pure Java driver.

Type 4.   The Native protocol pure Java driver.

Let's now try to understand the various approaches used by applications when using each of these drivers in a database communication.

Type 1: JDBC-ODBC Bridge

As part of JDBC, Sun Microsystems has provided a driver to access ODBC data sources from JDBC. This driver, which provides a bridge between JDBC API and ODBC API, is appropriately called a *JDBC-ODBC bridge*. The JDBC-ODBC bridge interprets all JDBC API calls to the corresponding ODBC API calls that are subsequently passed on to the database or data source.

Figure 10.5 shows how an application can use the JDBC-ODBC bridge to communicate with a database.

Figure 10.5   Type 1 JDBC-ODBC bridge driver.

Figure 10.6 The type 2 part native-part Java driver.

Type 2: Part Native-Part Java Driver

The data access that uses type 2 drivers is a combination of that in Java applications and other vendor-specific native calls. The JDBC driver interprets all JDBC API calls to the corresponding vendor-specific API calls, which are subsequently passed on to the database or data source.

Figure 10.6 shows how an application can use the *part native-part Java JDBC driver* to communicate with a database.

Type 3: JDBC-Net Pure Java Driver

The data access that uses type 3 drivers is based on the three-tier database access model. It consists of a middle-tier comprising the server that facilitates connections between multiple Java applications and multiple database servers. The JDBC API calls are sent to the data source routed through the middleware server. The middle tier uses the services of another driver, such as the type 2 driver, to complete the request for the data from the data source.

Figure 10.7 shows how an application can use the *JDBC-Net pure Java driver* to communicate with a database.

Type 4: Native Protocol Pure Java Driver

A database access that uses this type of driver is a pure substitute for the type 2 drivers. The JDBC calls in this case are straight away converted to the database interface or its native protocol. As a result, the driver communicates directly with the database without any translations between the application and the database.

Figure 10.7 The type 3 JDBC-Net pure Java driver.

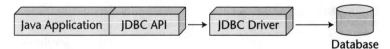

Figure 10.8   The type 4 pure Java driver.

Figure 10.8 shows how an application can use the *native protocol pure Java driver* to communicate with a database.

The concepts covered so far attempt to strengthen basics about databases, database connectivity in Java, and the drivers used to establish database connections. Let's now look at how the preceding concepts can be used to manipulate the data in a database.

Accessing a Database from a JSP Page

Problem Statement

The Web site of Banco de Glendanthi has provisions for new customers to open accounts online. Based on the minimum deposit required to open the accounts and the average daily balance, various types of accounts can be opened with the bank. Table 10.3 describes the types of accounts of Banco de Glendanthi.

Table 10.3   Types of Accounts

ACCOUNT TYPE	ACCOUNT CATEGORIES
Personal Checking Accounts	Basic Checking
	Checking Plus+
Business Checking Accounts	Basic Business Checking
	Business Checking Biz+
Personal Savings Accounts	Student Savings
	Money Market Plus
	Certificates of Deposit
	Club Account
	Passbook Savings
Commercial Savings	Glendanthi Biz
Commercial Loan Products	Commercial Loans
Consumer Loan Products	Consumer Loans
Mortgage Loan Products	Mortgage Loans

Customers need to register themselves by filling the online registration form. The administrator of the bank processes the request, and if all criteria essential for having an account with the bank are met, the customer is duly informed regarding the new account. The database is then updated with the new customer's details.

Your colleague Dave has designed the interface for the page that will be used to update the database with the accepted customer details. As a programmer you have been assigned the task of writing the code for the database interaction. After execution, the code will insert the customer details in the related database table. The prototype for this specific application also requires creating the registration table before inserting the records.

NOTE The format and appearance of the HTML forms for the application will change as the application progresses toward completion.

The following HTML code for the registration page accepts inputs for the processed customer registrations:

```
<html>

<head>

<title>Banco de Glendanthi</title>
</head>

<body bgcolor="#FFDFD7">

<form method="POST" action="InsertRec.jsp">
<p><font size="7" color="#0000FF"><img border="0" src="dd00448_1.gif"
>Banco
de Glendanthi</font></p>

  <hr>

  <p><font face="Arial" size="4" color="#FF6699">Registration
  form for new account </font></p>
<hr>
<p><font color="#CC0099">Please tell us about yourself:</font></p>
<p><font size="4"><font color="#0000FF">Title
(Optional)</font></font>::::::::::::::<font size="4">
<font color="#0000FF">Mr</font>
<input type="radio" value="V1" checked name="R1"> <font
color="#0000FF">Mrs</font>
<input type="radio" name="R1" value="V2"> <font
color="#0000FF">Ms</font>
<input type="radio" name="R1" value="V3">
<font color="#0000FF">Dr</font>
<input type="radio" name="R1" value="V4"></font></p>
<p><font color="#0000FF" size="4">First
Name</font>:::::::::::::::::::::::::
```

```
<input type="text" name="T1" size="30"></p>
<p><font color="#0000FF" size="4">Last
Name:</font>::::::::::::::::::::::::
<input type="text" name="T2" size="30"></p>
<p><font color="#0000FF" size="4">Social Security #</font>:::::::::
<input type="text" name="T3" size="30"></p>
<p><font color="#0000FF" size="4">Home
Address</font>::::::::::::::::::::::::::::::::::::::::::::::::::::::::::
:::::::::::::::::::::::::::::: </p>
<p>
<font color="#0000FF"
size="4">Apt/Suite#</font>:::::::::::::::::::::::::::
<input type="text" name="T4" size="30"></p>
<font color="#0000FF"
size="4">Street#</font>::::::::::::::::::::::::::::::::::
<input type="text" name="T5" size="30">
<p><font color="#0000FF"
size="4">City</font>:::::::::::::::::::::::::::::::::::::
<input type="text" name="T6" size="30"></p>
<p><font color="#0000FF" size="4">State</font>:::::::::::::::
<input type="text" name="T7" size="14"><font color="#0000FF"
size="4">Zip</font>:::::::::::::::::::::::
<input type="text" name="T8" size="13"></p>
<p><font color="#0000FF" size="4">Home</font><font color="#0000FF"
size="4" face="Arial">
</font><font color="#0000FF" size="4"> Phone</font>:::::::::::::::::::::
<input type="text" name="T9" size="30"></p>
<p><font color="#0000FF" size="4">Email</font><font color="#0000FF"
size="4" face="Arial">
</font><font color="#0000FF" size="4">
Id</font>:::::::::::::::::::::::::::::::::
<input type="text" name="T10" size="30"></p>
<p><font color="#CC0099">Please provide us with your
financial information:</font></p>
<hr>
<p><font color="#0000FF" size="4">Annual</font><font color="#0000FF"
size="4" face="Arial">
</font><font color="#0000FF" size="4"> Income</font>:::::::::::::
<input type="text" name="T11" size="20"></p>
<p><font color="#0000FF" size="4">Source of Income</font>:::::::::
<select size="1" name="D1">
  <option selected>Business</option>
  <option>Service</option>
  <option>Agriculture</option>
  <option>Other sources</option>
</select></p>
<p><font color="#CC0099">Please tell us about the account
set up:</font></p>
<hr>
```

```
<p><font color="#0000FF" size="4">Account</font><font color="#0000FF"
size="4" face="Arial">
</font><font color="#0000FF" size="4"> Type</font>::::::::::::::
<select size="1" name="D2">
  <option selected>Personal Checking Account</option>
  <option>Business Checking Account</option>
  <option>Personal Savings Account</option>
 <option>Commercial Savings Account</option>
 <option>Commercial Loan Products</option>
 <option>Consumer Loan Products</option>
 <option>Mortgage Loan Products</option>
</select></p>
  <p> </p>
  <p>  

            
            
       
  <input type="submit" value="Submit Form" name="B1">   <input
type="reset" value="Reset" name="B2"></p>
</form>
<p> </p>

</body>

</html>
```

Figure 10.9 displays the output of the registration page.

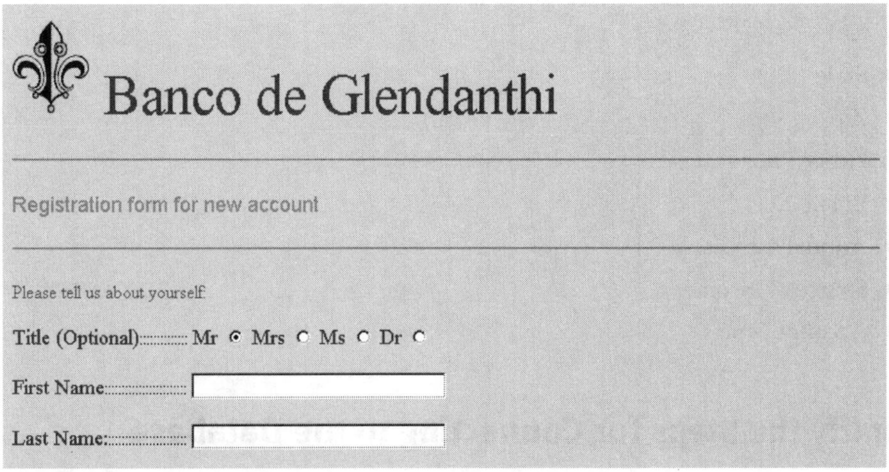

Figure 10.9 The registration page to input customer details.

Task List

✓ **Identify the elements of the input page.**

✓ **Identify the steps for connecting to the database.**

✓ **Identify the statements to create a table for the registration entries.**

✓ **Identify the SQL query for inserting the customer details.**

✓ **Write the code to create a table in the database.**

✓ **Write the code to insert the registration details in the table.**

✓ **Create a DSN for the database.**

✓ **Execute the code to create the table in the database.**

✓ **Execute the code to insert data into the table.**

✓ **Verify the data in the database.**

Identify the Elements of the Input Page

The page for entering accepted customer registrations will contain the following input elements:

- Title
- First Name
- Last Name
- Social Security Number
- Apt/Suite#
- Street#
- City
- State
- Zip
- Home Phone
- Email ID
- Annual Income
- Source of Income
- Account Type

Identify the Steps for Connecting to the Database

Before you begin to manipulate the data in the tables of the database, you first need to execute the following steps:

1. Load the driver. Because all interactions with a database are initiated using a specific driver, you need to identify the driver supplied by the vendor and load it.

2. Connect to the database. After loading the specific driver, you need to identify the database that will be queried and then connect to the specific database.

3. Query the database. After connecting to a database, you can submit and retrieve the results of the query by using the connection.

Loading the Driver

It is evident that the personal details of a customer have to be stored in the database of the bank. The database has been created using SQL Server, which is ODBC compliant. Therefore, the driver to be used for connecting to the database is the type 1 JDBC-ODBC bridge driver.

The initiation of a connection with the database is a process involving two steps, loading the driver and then making a connection. The process of loading the driver involves writing a one-line code. To load the database-specific driver, you need to call the forName() method of the class called Class. Accordingly, the following line of code will be used to load this driver:

```
Class.forName("sun.jdbc.odbc.JdbcOdbcDriver");
```

Connecting to the Database

After loading the driver, establish a connection to the database. The java.sql package contains classes and interfaces that help connect to a database, send SQL statements to the database, and process query results. The DriverManager class is used to obtain a connection and then query the database.

Using the DriverManager Class

The DriverManager class of the java.sql package initiates a direct connection to the database using the services of the driver loaded using the forName() method of the class Class. The Connection object is first created. The getConnection() method is then called from the DriverManager class. The getConnection() method attempts to locate the driver to be used to connect to the database. The following lines of code illustrate the sequence of statements used to establish a connection with the database:

```
Connection con = Drivermanager.getConnection("url, username, password")
```

The URL is represented by three parts, namely the protocol, the subprotocol, and the subname:

- The protocol used in the URL of a JDBC is always jdbc.

- The subprotocol is the name of the database connectivity mechanism. If the mechanism for retrieving the data is an ODBC-JDBC bridge, the subprotocol should be odbc.

- The subname or data source name (DSN) is used to identify the database. The DSN contains information about the location of the database server, the database name, the username, and the password to be used to connect to the database server.

NOTE The steps to create the DSN or ODBC driver for the database are covered in the later section.

The following methods and objects will be included in the code to connect to the database:

- The connection object
- The Class.forName() method
- The getconnection() method

Identify the Statements to Create a Table for the Registration Entries

After a connection between the application and the database is established, you use various SQL statements to send simple queries to the database. Before executing these queries, it is necessary to create the following objects of the getConnection class:

- The statement object
- The resultSet object
- The PreparedStatement object

Using the Statement Object

You can create the Statement object by using the createStatement() method of the connection interface. It returns an object that implements the Statement Interface. The following line of code can be used to illustrate the creation of the Statement object:

```
Statement stat = con.createStatement();
```

The statement object uses the following methods for querying the database:

- The execute() method is used to execute a SQL statement that may return multiple results.
- The executeQuery() method is used to execute a simple select query and return a ResultSet object.
- The executeUpdate() method is used to execute a SQL INSERT, UPDATE, or DELETE statement.

To understand the database connectivity mechanism covered so far, let's now write the code snippet to load the driver, establish a database connection, and use the statement object by using the following parameters:

DSN: MyDataSource

Username: sa

Password: No password

Table name: Counter

Query: Display all records from the table

The following code snippet illustrates the use of the executeQuery() method of the statement object and the other methods used to establish connectivity with a database by using the preceding parameters:

```
Class.forName ("sun.jdbc.odbc.JdbcOdbcdriver");
Connection con=DriverManager.getConnection("jdbc:odbc:MyDataSource",
"sa","");
Statement stat=con.createStatement();
stat.executeQuery("Select * from Counter");
```

Using the ResultSet Object

The methods of the ResultSet object can be used to access data from a table. Executing a SQL statement usually generates a ResultSet object. The ResultSet object maintains a cursor pointing to its current row of data. Initially, the cursor points to the first row. The next() method is used to move the cursor to the next row.

You can retrieve data from the ResultSet rows by calling the getXXX(int cn) method where XXX refers to a datatype of a column, such as String, Integer, and Float. cn is used to specify the column number in the result set. Table 10.4 represents the various options that you can use when calling the getXXX() method.

Table 10.4 ResultSet get() Methods

DATA TYPE	GET() METHOD USED
Boolean	getBoolean()
Date	getDate()
Integer	getInt()
Short	getShort()
Long	getLong()
Float	getFloat()
String	getString()
Double	getDouble()

The following piece of code illustrates the use of the getString() method of the resultSet object in the preceding code snippet:

```
Class.forName("sun.jdbc.odbc.JdbcOdbcDriver");
Connection con = DriverManager.getConnection("jdbc:odbc:
MyDataSource", "sa","");
Statement stat=con.createStatement();
ResultSet result=stat.executeQuery("Select * from Counter");
/* The next() method moves the cursor to beginning of the
next record. This method returns a false if cursor is
after the last record in the result set.*/
    while(result.next())
    {
        //Retrieves the second column from the result set
        System.out.println(result.getString(2));
    }
```

Using the PreparedStatement Object

The PreparedStatement object allows the execution of parameterized queries. For example, consider a situation where you need access to the records of a specific publisher. To display resultant records, you will need to use the publisher ID as the search criterion. This implies that you need to submit parameterized queries to the database at run time with an appropriate value in the where clause. The SQL statement for this query is the following:

```
Select * from publishers where pub_id = ?
```

In this type of case, to submit the parameterized query, the PreparedStatement object is created using the prepareStatement() method of the Connection object.

Using stat as the Connection object, the following line of code illustrates the use of PreparedStatement:

```
stat=con.prepareStatement("Select * from publishers where pub_id = ?");
```

NOTE The prepareStatement() method of the Connection object takes a SQL statement as a parameter. The SQL statement can contain placeholders (?) that can be replaced by INPUT parameters at run time.

Based on the preceding discussions, you create the registration table for the accepted customer entries containing their personal details. Table 10.5 represents the composition of the registration table.

Table 10.5   Elements of the Registration Page

TABLE FIELD NAME	CONTAINS	DATA TYPE
firstName	First name of the customer	VARCHAR(30)
lastName	Last name of the customer	VARCHAR(30)
socialsecurity	Social security number	VARCHAR(30)
apt	Apartment name and number	VARCHAR(30)
street	Street name	VARCHAR(30)
city	City	VARCHAR(20)
state	State	VARCHAR(20)
zip	Zip code	VARCHAR(10)
Homephone	Residential telephone number	VARCHAR(10)
emailed	Email ID	VARCHAR(20)
annualIncome	Annual income	VARCHAR(20)
source	Source of income	VARCHAR(30)
accType	Type of account to be opened	VARCHAR(30)

The statements to create the registration table are as follows:

```
//The create statement
Statement stat = con.createStatement();
    //The statement to create the registration table
    stat.executeUpdate("CREATE TABLE Registration" + "( firstName
VARCHAR(30), " + "lastName VARCHAR(30), " + " socialsecurity
VARCHAR(30), " + " apt VARCHAR(30), " + " street VARCHAR(30), " + " city
VARCHAR(20), " + " state VARCHAR(20), " + " zip VARCHAR(10), " + "
Homephone VARCHAR(10), " + " emailId VARCHAR(20), " + " annualIncome
VARCHAR(20), " + " source VARCHAR(30), " + " accType VARCHAR(30))");
```

Identify the SQL Query for Inserting Customer Details

The SQL query to be used to insert the customer details in the registration table is this:

```
insert into registration (firstName, lastName, socialsecurity, apt,
street, city, state, zip, Homephone, emailId, annualIncome, source,
accType) values (?, ?, ?, ?, ?, ?, ?, ?, ?, ?, ?, ?, ?)
```

The values for these fields will be collated at run time. Therefore, you will also need to add the `prepareStatement()` method with placeholders. The number of placeholders should be proportional to the number of columns to be updated with the customer details. The code for inserting data into the registration table is the following:

```
PreparedStatement st=con.prepareStatement("insert into registration
(firstName, lastName, socialsecurity, apt, street, city, state, zip,
Homephone, emailId, annualIncome, source, accType) values (?, ?, ?, ?,
?, ?, ?, ?, ?, ?, ?, ?, ?)");
```

Write the Code to Create a Table in the Database

The code to create the registration table is as follows:

```
<html>
<head><title>Creating a database table</title></head>
<body>
<%@ page language="java" import="java.sql.*" %>
<%
Connection con = null;
try {
    //Load the class file for the driver
    Class.forName("sun.jdbc.odbc.JdbcOdbcDriver");
    //Establish a connection with the oDBC datasource
    con = DriverManager.getConnection("jdbc:odbc:MyDataSource","sa", "");
    //The create statement
    Statement stat = con.createStatement();
    //The statement to create the registration table
    stat.executeUpdate("CREATE TABLE Registration" + "( firstName
VARCHAR(30), " + "lastName VARCHAR(30), " + " socialsecurity
VARCHAR(30), " + " apt VARCHAR(30), " + " street VARCHAR(30), " + " city
VARCHAR(20), " + " state VARCHAR(20), " + " zip VARCHAR(10), " + "
Homephone VARCHAR(10), " + " emailId VARCHAR(20), " + " annualIncome
VARCHAR(20), " + " source VARCHAR(30), " + " accType VARCHAR(30))");
    }
catch (SQLException se) {
    out.println (se.getMessage());
    }
catch(ClassNotFoundException ce) {
    out.println (ce.getMessage());
    }
catch (Exception ee){
    out.println (ee.getMessage());
    }
finally {
try {
    if (con != null) {
    // Close the connection
    con.close();
    }
```

```
    }
catch (SQLException se) {
    out.println (se.getMessage());
    }
}
out.println ("The Registration table has been created");

%>
</body>
</html>
```

Write the Code to Insert the Registration Details in the Table

The code to insert records in the registration table is as follows:

```
<html>
<head><title>Inserting records into a database table</title></head>
<body>
<%@ page language="java" import="java.sql.*" %>
<%
//Using the request object to extract input values of registration page
String fname = request.getParameter("T1");
String lname = request.getParameter("T2");
String socialsecurity = request.getParameter("T3");
String apt = request.getParameter("T4");
String street = request.getParameter("T5");
String city = request.getParameter("T6");
String state = request.getParameter("T7");
String zip = request.getParameter("T8");
String Homephone = request.getParameter("T9");
String email = request.getParameter("T10");
String Annualinc = request.getParameter("T11");
String Sourceinc = request.getParameter("D1");
String acctype = request.getParameter("D2");

Connection con = null;
try {
    //Load the class file for the driver
    Class.forName("sun.jdbc.odbc.JdbcOdbcDriver");
    //Establish a connection with the ODBC datasource
    con = DriverManager.getConnection("jdbc:odbc:MyDataSource","sa", "");
    //The prepared statement to insert values in the table at runtime
    PreparedStatement st=con.prepareStatement("insert into registration
(firstName, lastName, socialsecurity, apt, street, city, state, zip,
Homephone, emailId, annualIncome, source, accType) values (?, ?, ?, ?,
?, ?, ?, ?, ?, ?, ?, ?, ?)");
    //The statement to insert appropriate values into the registration
table
    st.setString(1, fname);
```

```
        st.setString(2, lname);
        st.setString(3, socialsecurity);
        st.setString(4, apt);
        st.setString(5, street);
        st.setString(6, city);
        st.setString(7, state);
        st.setString(8, zip);
        st.setString(9, Homephone);
        st.setString(10, email);
        st.setString(11, Annualinc);
        st.setString(12, Sourceinc);
        st.setString(13, acctype);
        st.executeUpdate();
    }
    finally {
    try {
        if (con != null) {
        // Close the connection
        con.close();
        }
    }
    catch (SQLException se) {
    out.println (se.getMessage());
    }
    }
    out.println ("Record inserted successfully");

%>
</body>
</html>
```

Create a DSN for the Database

To create a DSN to be used for connecting to the database, perform the following steps:

1. Choose Start, Settings, Control Panel to display the Control Panel window.

2. Double-click the ODBC Data Sources icon to open the ODBC Data Source Administrator dialog box. Figure 10.10 displays the Data Source Administrator dialog box.

3. Click Add to open the Create New Data Source dialog box.

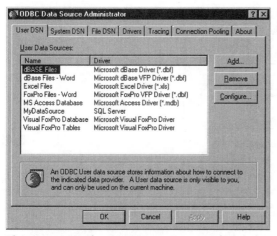

Figure 10.10 The ODBC Data Source Administrator dialog box.

4. From the displayed list of drivers, select SQL Server and then click Finish. Fig-
    ure 10.11 shows the Create a New Data Source to SQL Server dialog box that is
    displayed.

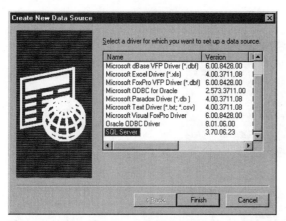

Figure 10.11 The Create New Data Source dialog box.

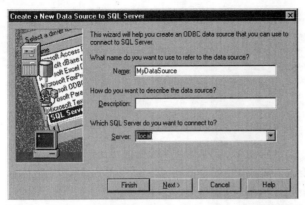

Figure 10.12   The Create a New Data Source to SQL Server dialog box.

5. In the Name text box, type **MyDataSource** as the name for the data source. From the displayed list of Servers, select the SQL Server to which you want to connect. Click the Next button. Figure 10.12 shows the Create a New Data Source to SQL Server dialog box that is displayed.

6. Select With SQL Server authentication by using a login ID and password entered by the user option. Then, specify the Login ID (**sa**) and Password (**leave it blank**) to be used to connect to the SQL Server and click Next. Figure 10.13 shows the Create a New Data Source to SQL Server dialog box that is displayed.

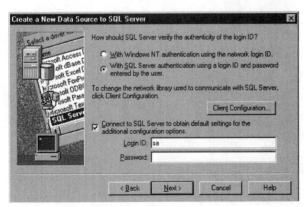

Figure 10.13   The Create a New Data Source to SQL Server dialog box after Step 6.

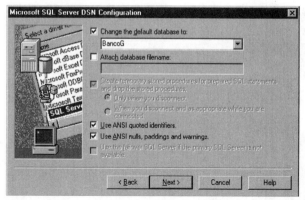

Figure 10.14   The Create a New Data Source to SQL Server dialog box after step 7.

7. Check the Change the default database to: option and select the BancoG data-base as the default database. Figure 10.14 shows the Create a New Data Source to SQL Server dialog box that is displayed.

8. Click Next. Figure 10.15 shows the Create a New Data Source to SQL Server dialog box that is subsequently displayed.

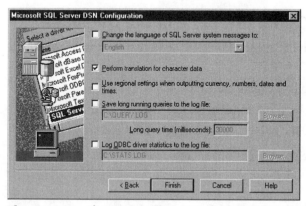

Figure 10.15   The Create a New Data Source to SQL Server dialog box.

Figure 10.16   The ODBC Microsoft SQL Server Setup dialog box.

9. Click Finish. The ODBC Microsoft SQL Server Setup dialog box is displayed as shown in Figure 10.16.

10. Click Test Data Source to check for proper connectivity and click OK.

11. Click OK to close the wizard.

12. Click OK to close the ODBC Data Source Administrator dialog box.

13. Close Control Panel.

Execute the Code to Create the Table in the Database

To implement or view the output of the code to create the Registration table, you need to execute the following predefined steps:

1. Save the file to create a table as **CreateTable.jsp**.

2. Copy this file into the public_html folder in the C:\j2sdkee1.2.1 directory.

3. Initiate the server startup, and open CreateTable.jsp in the browser.

Figure 10.17 displays the screen on which you see the successful creation of the table in the database.

Execute the Code to Insert Data in the Table

To implement or view the output of the code to create the Registration table, you need to execute the following predefined steps:

1. Save the file to insert data in the table as **InsertRec.jsp**.

2. Copy InsertRec.jsp, RegistrationPage.html, and the graphic file for the bank logo dd00448_1.wmf into the public_html folder in the C:\j2sdkee1.2.1 directory.

3. Initiate the server startup, and open RegistrationPage.html in the browser.

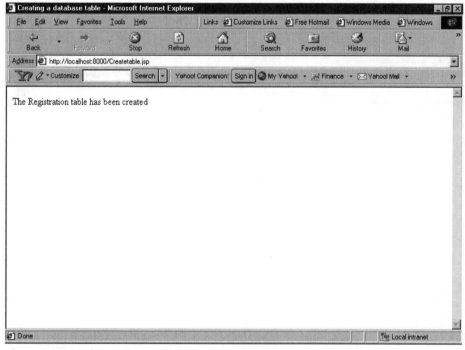

Figure 10.17   The screen message after creation of the table.

4.   Enter the following values in each control of the input page:

   First Name—Carol

   Last Name—Hutchinson

   Social Security Number—56432786

   Apt/Suite#—34, South Angel

   Street#—343

   City—Providence

   State—Rhode Island

   Zip—RI02918

   Home Phone—4018650300

   Email ID—carolh@usa.net.in

   Annual Income—90000

   Source of Income—Agriculture

   Account Type—Personal Savings Account

5.   Click the Submit Form button.

6.   Figure 10.18 displays the screen on which you can see the successful insertion of the customer details in the table.

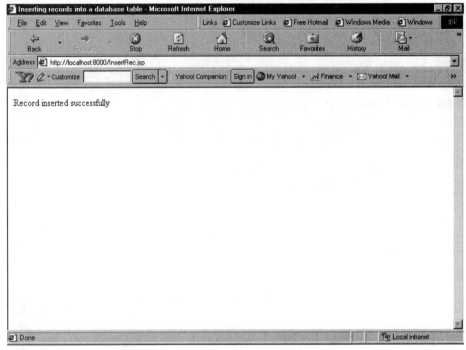

Figure 10.18   The screen message after insertion of data in the table.

Verify the Data in the Database

An interactive and graphical query viewer or SQL Server Query Analyzer is used to access the data of the tables in a database. After executing the preceding pieces of code, you can use the following steps to access the records of the registration table:

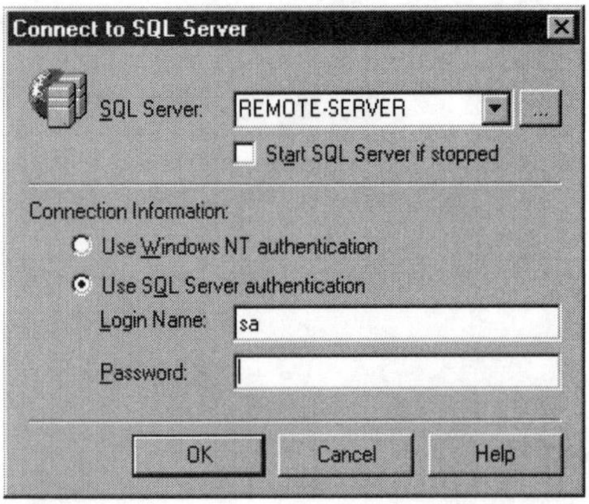

Figure 10.19   The Connect to SQL Query window.

1. Choose Start, Programs, Microsoft SQL Server 7.0, Query Analyzer to open the Connect to SQL server dialog box. Figure 10.19 displays the Connect to SQL server dialog box.

2. From the list of servers, select the SQL server and specify the login ID and the password in the respective text boxes.

3. Click OK to open the Query window in SQL Query Analyzer. Figure 10.20 displays SQL Query Analyzer with the Query window.

4. Click the Show Results pane button to display the Results pane. Figure 10.21 displays the Show Results pane button.

5. In the Query window, type the following SQL command:

   ```
   select * from registration
   ```

   Select the query statement and click the Execute Query button.

6. Compare and verify the field values in the table columns of the Query Analyzer Results section with the field values entered in the registration page. Figure 10.22 displays a section of output representing the successful insertion of records in the Registration table.

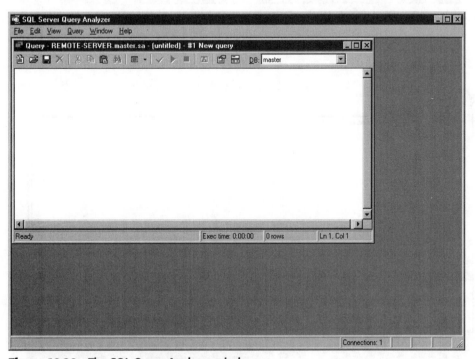

Figure 10.20   The SQL Query Analyzer window.

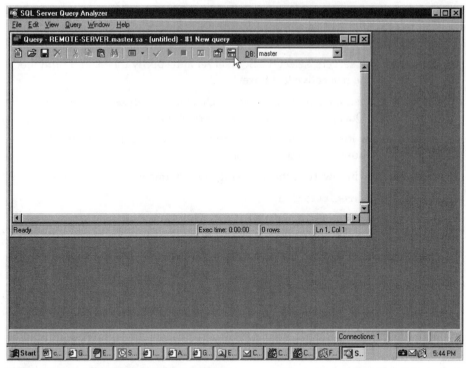

Figure 10.21   The Show Results pane button.

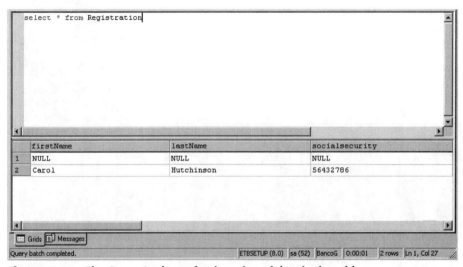

Figure 10.22   The Query Analyzer after insertion of data in the table.

Summary

In this chapter, we discussed the importance of databases as data resources and their structure and characteristics. You learned that by using a common interactive language, such as SQL, it is possible to query and retrieve records from a database. You also recognized that it is important to establish connectivity before you begin database interaction. In addition, these basic concepts were used to focus on database connectivity for Java applications. To understand the mode and criteria for such database interactions, we discussed the two access models and the various types of drivers used to establish database connectivity.

The registration page of Banco de Glendanthi's Web site was used to explain the process of database connectivity and interaction. The individual steps of the task list helped guide you in performing and understanding the methodology adopted to create tables and insert records in a database.

At the end of this chapter, you added a feather to your cap. Not only can you now develop basic JSP pages, you can add database functionality to these pages. As a result, what you are looking at is a method that facilitates structured and easy storage of data. After a database and its relevant tables are created, you can access and manipulate the data. Continuous progress and dynamism are the key factors that are used to describe Web pages. As you have seen, using JSP, you can continually add new features and functionalities to your application. In the next chapter, we'll discuss methods to enhance database interactions by using the connection pooling bean. We'll also make use of the useBean feature of JSP to perform database access and record retrieval.

CHAPTER

11

Building JDBC Applications

OBJECTIVES:

In this chapter, you will learn to do the following:

✔ **Initiate a database interaction by using JavaBeans**

✔ **Appreciate connection pooling**

✔ **Identify the classes of the connection pool**

✔ **Use the connection pool in JSP**

Getting Started

It is an accepted fact that databases provide large amounts of data for retrieval and manipulation. Therefore, it is not surprising that the Java platform uses the JDBC standard library to access relational databases. JDBC is an API that provides access to a database from a Java program. As an extension of the servlet technology, which is based on the Java platform, JSP has enhanced its functionality by incorporating database interactions in JSP applications.

The performance of a Web application is assessed in terms of the overhead used for processing a request and the time taken for generating the response. The overhead can be measured in terms of the use of resources and the load on network traffic. Because a Web application caters to requests from multiple clients, the efficiency of the application directly depends on its speed to serve the client requests by minimizing the use of available resources. You'll agree that the overhead incurred for memory allocation increases with the creation of a new object. Because the number of clients and requests is unpredictable in the case of Web applications, it is good practice to minimize the number of objects created in a Web application. In other words, client requests should be served by reusing objects from a pool.

In Chapter 10, "Implementing JDBC Connectivity," each request for a record or a piece of data from a database resulted in the opening of a new connection to the database. The fact remains that the process of opening a connection to a database is both lengthy and time-consuming. Therefore, the time taken for opening a connection is longer than that taken for querying a database. As a result, even a simple query for extracting a name from a database seems to take a long time. Under these circumstances, it is natural to think of a process to shorten the time taken to establish a database connection. After all, economizing by sharing resources is part and parcel of life. For example, in a professional environment, we often come across organizations that share resources such as printers, fax machines, and copiers.

This chapter discusses a mechanism called connection pooling, which can be used for managing and reusing objects to access a database. We'll begin with a brief discussion on the intent and purpose of creating a pool to open a connection with a database. In the later sections of the chapter, we discuss the class and method definitions that are required for the implementation of a connection pool. In the final section of this chapter, we create a pool connection to retrieve data from a table in a database.

You'll recall that in Chapter 9, "JSP and JavaBeans," we discussed the use of JSP-specific tags to embed a bean component in a JSP page. Chapter 10 discussed database interactions in JSP applications. Integrating the concepts of Chapter 9 and Chapter 10, before discussing connection pooling in JSP, we'll begin this chapter with a scenario-based example that uses a bean component to validate the user login by accessing the login table in the bank database.

Creating a JSP Page

Problem Statement

Because the site for Banco de Glendanthi is a banking site, it is natural that registered users or customers with valid accounts will visit the site to access account information or perform monetary transactions, such as deposits, withdrawals, and transfers. Before accessing account information or performing any monetary transaction, the account number of a customer and the password assigned to the account are validated. The validation process involves database interaction for checking the values of the account ID and the password of the login table and the values submitted by the customer.

Larry Myers, the project manager, has entrusted the development team with the task of creating an application to validate the account number and password of each customer before displaying the transaction page. To speed up the development cycle, the project team has been split in two. The first team has been assigned the task of coding for the static content of the application. This will involve designing the user interface.

The second team comprising Java professionals will be responsible for coding the dynamic content of the application.

Task List

✔ **Identify the files to be used for validating user input.**

✔ **Identify the various elements of the user interface.**

✔ **Identify the methods and classes of the bean component.**

✔ **Identify the elements of the JSP page for referencing the bean component.**

✔ **Write the Java code for the bean.**

✔ **Write the code for the JSP page with the bean reference.**

✔ **Compile the code for the bean component.**

✔ **View the JSP page.**

Identify the Various Files to Be Used for Validating User Input

Arnold, a member of the development team, has designed the application so that it consists of the following two parts:

- The first part contains the code to create controls for the user interface to accept the account ID and password of a customer.

- The second part contains the code to validate the authenticity of customers by mapping their details against those held in the supporting database. After validation, a message regarding acceptance or rejection of user input can be displayed.

Considering the structure of the page, a bean component (in Java) can be written for user validation and plugged into the JSP file. As a result, both a developer and a designer can work on the application independently. The designer can write the presentation logic in HTML while the developer or the programmer can concentrate on business logic to validate customer details by using the various elements of JSP. As a result, we'll create the following three files for validating user input:

- An HTML page to accept the account ID and password of a customer

- A bean component to validate customer input with the records of the database table

- A JSP page to accept the return value of validation and display the corresponding message

Identify the Elements of the User Interface

We have already created the login page in Chapter 6, "Working with HTML Forms." The components of the page for accepting customer input are these:

- The user interface accepts input from a customer regarding an account number and a password.

- Two text boxes will accept values for the account number and password of a customer. In addition, two buttons for submitting and clearing form contents will be added to the HTML page.

- The header consisting of the bank's name and logo will be added to the JSP page by using the `include` directive.

Table 11.1 lists the HTML and JSP tags to be used for the design of the user interface. Let's examine the code for the page that will be used to accept the account ID and password of a customer:

```html
<html>

<head><title>User validation</title></head>

<body bgcolor="#FFDFD7">

<%--The include directive is used here to add the elements of the file
Header.html to the login page--%>
<%@ include file="Header.html" %>
<form method="post" action="Usebean.jsp">
<table border="0" cellspacing="1" cellpadding="5">

<tr>
<td width="100" align="right">
<b><font color="blue">Account No</font></b>
</td>
<td align="left">
<input type="text" name="sAccountID" size="30"></td>
</tr>
```

Table 11.1   The HTML and JSP Tags of the User Interface

INPUT FIELD	SPECIFICATIONS
Bank's name and logo	Inserted by including an HTML file, Header.html
Account number	`<input type="text">`
Password	`<input type="text">` and `<input type="password">`
Submit and reset buttons	`<input type="submit" value="Validate" name="B1"`
	`<input type="reset" value="Clear" name="B2">>`

```
<tr>
<td width="100" align="right">
<b><font color="blue">Password</font></b></td>
<td align="left">
<input type="password" name="sPin" size="30"></td>
</tr>
<tr>
<td> width="100"   </td>
<td align="right"></td>
</tr>

<tr>
<td width="100">   </td>
<td align="left">
           
<center><input type="submit" value="Submit" ></center></td>

</tr>
</table>
</form>
</body>
</html>
```

Figure 11.1 displays the output of the preceding code for the login page.

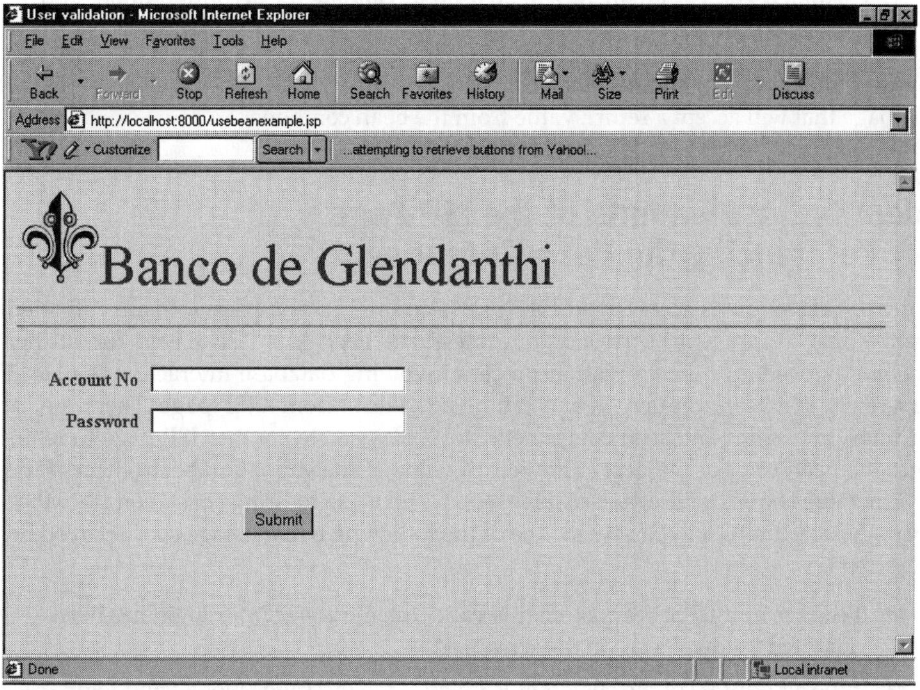

Figure 11.1   The login page.

A bean component will be used to validate the values of the account ID and password accepted from a customer. Let's identify the classes and methods of the bean.

Identify the Classes and Methods of the Bean Component

The bean component will consist of the following classes and methods:

- The properties defined for the bean in the JSP page are `accountID` and `password`. As a result, the bean component will define the `setXXX()` and `getXXX()` methods for each of these properties.

- Database connectivity will be established using the following statements in the `AccountValidate()` method:

```
Class.forName("sun.jdbc.odbc.JdbcOdbcDriver");
connect=DriverManager.getConnection("jdbc:odbc:MyDataSource","sa","");
String strQuery = "Select cPin_no from Login where
cAccount_id='"+sAccountID+"'";
state = connect.createStatement();
ResultSet result = state.executeQuery(strQuery);
ResultSet result = state.executeQuery(strQuery);
```

- In addition, the `while` statement will be used to extract the record in the login table, which has the account number and the password specified by a customer. The `if` statement will be used to validate the account number and the password.

After finalizing the contents of the bean component, let's identify the elements of the JSP page that will accept a return value from the bean component.

Identify the Elements of the JSP Page for Referencing the Bean Component

After the user input is accepted and the user's account ID and password are validated by the bean component, corresponding messages need to be displayed for further action. Java code for the validation process involving database interaction is placed separately in a bean component and can be referenced from a JSP page. Therefore, in addition to creating the bean component, we'll also create another JSP page to reference the bean component, accept the return value of the validation bean, check if the return value is true or false, and display a corresponding message. Based on the validity of the account ID and password, one of the following two messages is displayed on the screen:

- If the account ID of the customer is valid, the message "Your login has been validated" is displayed on the screen.

- If the account ID of the customer is invalid, the message "Not a valid login. Please register!" is displayed on the screen.

To reuse a bean, a reference to identify the bean component is added to the JSP page. The <jsp:useBean> action is used to create a reference to specify the inclusion of a predefined bean component in the JSP page. The code statement to specify the use of a bean in a JSP page is this:

```
<jsp:useBean id="BA" scope="application" class="BankAccount" />
```

In addition to the bean reference, the JSP page will also contain the Java code to accept and check the return value of the bean component. The Java code snippet for the previously mentioned task is this:

```
String sAccountID= BA.getsAccountID();
    String sPin = BA.getsPin();
    boolean validate = BA.AccountValidate();
    if(validate == true)
    {
        out.println("<h3>" + "Your login has been  validated" + "</h3>");
    }

    else
    {
        out.println("<h3>" + " Not a valid login, please register!" +
"</h3>");
```

The code for the JSP page will also contain the following elements:

- The page directive specifying import and language attributes.
- The useBean action to specify the use of a bean component.
- The setProperty action to specify values for the bean properties.
- The HttpServletRequest object to accept the values of the account number and password of a customer.

Write the Java Code for the Bean

The code for the bean component is as follows:

```
import java.io.*;
import java.sql.*;

public class BankAccount
{
    private String sAccountID=" ";
    private String sPin=" ";
    private boolean AccountValidate;
    Connection connect = null;
    Statement state = null;
    ResultSet result = null;
        public void setsAccountID(String sAccountID)
        {
```

```
                System.out.println("Inside setter method"+sAccountID);
                this.sAccountID=sAccountID;
        }
    public void setsPin(String sPin)
        {
            this.sPin=sPin;
        }
    public String getsAccountID()
        {
            return this.sAccountID;
        }
    public String getsPin()
        {
                return sPin;
        }
    public BankAccount() throws ClassNotFoundException
        {
            Class.forName("sun.jdbc.odbc.JdbcOdbcDriver");
        }


        public boolean AccountValidate()
        {
            boolean   validate=false;
            String sPinNo="";
            try{
                sAccountID=getsAccountID();
                sPin=getsPin();
                System.out.println("Inside VALIDATE method"+sAccountID);
connect=DriverManager.getConnection("jdbc:odbc:MyDataSource","sa","");
                String strQuery = "Select cPin_no from Login where
cAccount_id='"+sAccountID+"'" ;
                System.out.println("Query: "+strQuery);
                state = connect.createStatement();
                ResultSet result = state.executeQuery(strQuery);
                while(result.next())
                {
                    sPinNo = result.getString(1);
                    System.out.println("Inside Result method"+sPinNo+sPin);

                }
                sPinNo=sPinNo.trim();
                sPin=sPin.trim();
                if(sPinNo.equals(sPin))
                    {
                        validate = true;
                    }

            }
            catch(Exception e)
```

```
        {
            System.out.println("SQL Exception is caught.");
        }
        return validate;
    }
}
```

Write the Code for the JSP Page with the Bean Reference

The code for the JSP page with the bean reference is as follows:

```
<%@ page import="java.util.*" %>
<%@ page language = "java" %>
<jsp:useBean id="BA" scope="application" class="BankAccount" />
<jsp:setProperty name="BA" property="sAccountID" param="sAccountID" />
<jsp:setProperty name="BA" property="sPin" param="sPin" />
<html>
<head><title>RESULT PAGE</title></head>
<h2>The Result Page</h2><hr><hr>
<body bgcolor="#FFDFD7">
<%
    String sAccountID= BA.getsAccountID();
    String sPin = BA.getsPin();
    boolean validate = BA.AccountValidate();
    if(validate == true)
    {
        out.println("<h3>" + "Your login has been  validated" + "</h3>");
    }
    else
    {
        out.println("<h3>" + " Not a valid login, please register!" +
"</h3>");
    }

%>
</body>
</html>
```

Compile the Code for the Bean Component

To compile the Java file, do the following:

1. Save the bean component code as BankAccount.java.

2. Compile the Java code.

3. Copy the class file into C:\j2sdkee1.2.1\lib\Classes.

View the JSP Page

To be able to view the output of the JSP page, execute the following steps:

1. Save the JSP files defining the user interface and the `useBean` tag as **Usebeanexample.jsp**, and **Usebean.jsp**, respectively.

2. Save the JSP files under the public_html folder.

3. Start `j2ee` in verbose mode.

4. In the Internet Explorer Address bar, type the location of the JSP file as **http://localhost:8000/Usebeanexample.jsp** where the filename denotes the name of the JSP file.

5. Enter the following values in the text controls for account number and password:

    Account No.—AH0001

    Password—1001

Figure 11.2 displays the output that is displayed after a successful login.

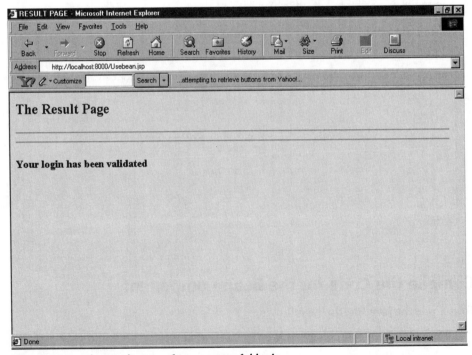

Figure 11.2 The result page after a successful login.

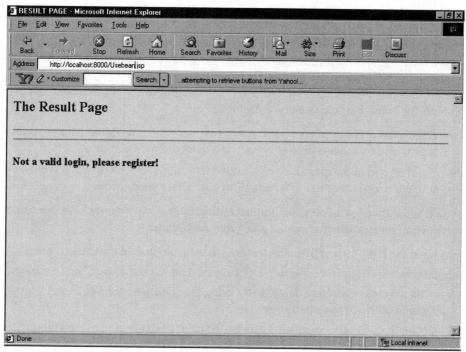

Figure 11.3   The result page after an unsuccessful login.

6. Enter the following values in the text controls for account number and password:

   Account No.—AH0001

   Password—abc0123

Figure 11.3 displays the output that is displayed after an unsuccessful login.

That was an appropriate and befitting use of a bean component that validates the customer account number and password. Such validations ensure that only valid users log on to the site and perform any banking transactions.

So far, all requests for a retrieval of data from the database used a new instance of the connection object. As discussed in the introductory paragraph of this chapter, the creation of new instances of an object is a very expensive operation.

Connection Pooling in JSP

Creating new `Connection` objects and keeping a connection in a session variable are far too expensive in terms of client connections to the database. As a result, controlling connections to a database instead of connecting to the database for each page is an inexpensive means of resource management in Web applications. Keeping this approach in mind, people often create pools for connections to a database. This facilitates sharing a set of connections among clients, and creating new connections for each request is not required. The use of a connection pool ensures that a client is able to access a database and retrieve results by reusing connection objects without having to open and close new connections to the database.

Before creating a connection pool for a server-side application providing access to a database, the following criteria need to be looked at:

- The design of the application should be Internet-centric so that database access is provided by the use of a set of common database user accounts.

- The duration of database access is limited to a single request. In other words, a single session serves a single request for a database connection.

You'll recall that in Chapter 10, "Implementing JDBC Connectivity," we discussed the following seven steps that are used to query a database:

1. Load the JDBC driver by using the forName() method of the class Class.
2. Specify the URL of a connection by using the static getConnection() method.
3. Obtain a connection to a database by using the static getConnection() method of the DriverManager class.
4. Create the Statement object by using the createStatement() method of the Connection interface.
5. Query the database by using the execute(), executeQuery(), or executeUpdate() method.
6. Process the results by using the methods of the ResultSet object.
7. Close the connection.

The process involved in creating a connection pool to access and retrieve data from a database consists of the following class definitions:

Database connection pool class.   A database connection pool class is used to obtain a connection from a pool, return the pool connection, and close all connections after releasing the resources at shutdown.

Manager class.   A manager class is used to register all available JDBC drivers, create a database connection pool object, map the connection pool names to the database connection pool instances, and keep track of the client connections in order to close connections at the end of the client's database interaction.

Displaying Records from the Database by Using Connection Pooling

Problem Statement

Cost-effective resource management determines the economics of a Web application. Most of the customer interactions on the bank's Web site will involve database connections for user validations, transaction updates, and report generations. As a result, it is not surprising that the management of Banco de Glendanthi will choose to economize the use of all available network resources in order to improve the performance of database interactions.

After evaluating various approaches to be used to better resource management, the technical team has decided to create connection pools for database interactions. According to the report submitted by the team, the following problems can be tackled by using a connection pool for database interactions:

- Minimize wait periods for establishing a connection with the database
- Minimize network overheads incurred for opening and closing a new connection for each request from a user
- Erase awkward situations where a validation method is unable to obtain a valid connection due to nonspecification of the number of connections allowed

Let's understand the approach and methodology adopted to add such functionality to the application.

Task List

✔ **Identify the elements of the JSP page.**

✔ **Identify the various Java files to be used for creating a connection pool.**

✔ **Write the Java code for the ConnectionPool class.**

✔ **Write the Java code for the DriverUtilities class.**

✔ **Write the Java code for the DatabaseUtilities class.**

✔ **Write the Java code for the DBResults class.**

✔ **Create a package for the Java files.**

✔ **Compile the Java files.**

✔ **View the JSP page.**

Identify the Elements of the JSP Page

In order to use connection pooling to retrieve records from a database table, the JSP page will contain both HTML- and JSP-specific tags. The HTML tags will be used to create a table to display the records retrieved from the registration table. On the other hand, the JSP tags will be used to encapsulate Java code snippets to obtain a connection from the pool and then retrieve records from a specified table of the database. The structure of the JSP page is such that it uses different Java classes for the various tasks associated with the creation of the pool and the retrieval of the records. Each of the Java files is referenced in the JSP page by using objects corresponding to class files.

Table 11.2 lists the HTML elements to be used to create the table.

Table 11.2 The Elements of the HTML Page

INPUT FIELD	SPECIFICATIONS
Bank's name and logo	`<%@include file="Header.html"%>`
Table to display the records retrieved from the registration table	`<table border=0 cellspacing=2 cellpadding= 5 width=400>`
	`<th><font size="4">First name</th>`
	`<th><font size="4">Last name</th>`
	`<th><font size="4">Registration Id</th>`

Identify the Various Java Files to Be Used for Creating a Connection Pool

The intent of JSP is to limit the use of Java code along with the code for the presentation content. As a result, a good practice for implementing business or dynamic functionality in a JSP page can be brought about by segregating the business-specific code in a Java file. The Java files can then be imported in a JSP page by using the `import` attribute of the page directive. In order to create a connection pool, we'll use the following Java files:

ConnectionPool.java. The `ConnectionPool` class will be used to assign advance connections for accessing the database, manage the available connections, allot new connections, wait for availability of connections, and close connections after the client completes the task.

DriverUtilities.java. The `DriverUtilities` class will be used to specify the name of the database driver and directly generate the URL of the database in an appropriate format. The separation of this class ensures that changes made for the use of specific drivers are easier to incorporate.

DatabaseUtilities.java. The `DatabaseUtilities` class will be used to execute a query, create a table in the database, retrieve and print all the rows of a table on the standard output, and print the results of a previous query on the standard output.

DBResults.java. The `DBResults.java` is an auxiliary class used to store and return the accumulated results in a specific format within an HTML table.

ServletUtilities.java. The ServletUtilities.java contains static methods that serve as time savers for frequently used code snippets.

Let's look at the class definitions for all these individual files.

ConnectionPool Class

The ConnectionPool class contains definitions for five methods to execute the following tasks:

- Assign advance connections
- Manage all available connections
- Assign new connections as and when required
- Wait for the availability of new connections
- Close connections

Let's look at each of these method definitions in detail.

Method to Assign Connections in Advance

The task for advance allocations of connections will be performed in the class constructor itself. Such an approach ensures that a number of connections are readily available even before specific requests from the user. As a result, the initial delay amounting to the wait period is eliminated. To ensure the preallocation of connections, it is important to initialize the servlet in advance and then build the connection pool from the init() method of the servlet. In addition, vectors can be used to store the values of both unavailable busy connections and available idle connections. The class definitions declare variables to store the value of the driver, URL, username, and password. This is followed by calling the getConnection() method of the DriverManager. The following code uses the getConnection() method to make a new connection:

```
availableConnections = new Vector(initialConnections);
busyConnections = new Vector();
for(int i=0; i<initialConnections; i++) {
availableConnections.addElement(makeNewConnection());
}
```

Method to Manage All Available Connections

As soon as a request for a connection is received, an available idle connection is assigned to fulfill the request. Subsequently, the connection is returned as an entry in the list of busy connections. The busy list of connections is also referenced to ensure that the assigned connection does not cross the limit of the total number of connections set previously. In addition, a check is made to ensure that connections are not closed or timed out. In case connections are unavailable due to instructions to the pool for closing connections, the connection is discarded and a new request is made. The following code performs these tasks:

```
public synchronized Connection getConnection()
throws SQLException {
    if (!availableConnections.isEmpty()) {
```

```
      Connection existingConnection =
        (Connection)availableConnections.lastElement();
      int lastIndex = availableConnections.size() - 1;
      availableConnections.removeElementAt(lastIndex);
      if (existingConnection.isClosed()) {
// To ensure availability of a freed-up a spot for anybody waiting
        notifyAll();
// To repeat process of request and check for available connections
        return(getConnection());
      } else {
        busyConnections.addElement(existingConnection);
        return(existingConnection);
      }
    }
```

Method to Assign New Connections As and When Required

A background thread is used to assign a new connection in situations where on request for a connection no idle connection is available and the connection limit is not reached. The wait() method is used to wait for the connection. The following three cases are checked, and the corresponding approach is used to assign a new connection:

- Maximum limit of set connections not reached due to which a connection is established in the background. This is followed by a wait period for availability of a new or released connection. The following code is used to check the limit of connections and make a background connection:

```
if ((totalConnections() < maxConnections) &&
!connectionPending) {
   makeBackgroundConnection();
}
```

- If the maximum limit of set connections is reached, the value of the waitIfBusy flag is false, and then a SQL exception is raised. The following code is used if the value of waitIfBusy flag is false:

```
else if (!waitIfBusy) {
   throw new SQLException("Connection limit reached");
   }
```

- If the maximum limit of set connections is reached, the value of the waitIfBusy flag is true, and the wait() method is invoked till the next connection is available. The following code is used if the value of waitIfBusy flag is true:

```
// Wait for a new connection to be established irrespective of the
fact that you either called makeBackgroundConnection() or areusing an
existing connection after it is freed up.
   try {
   wait();
   } catch(InterruptedException ie) {}
   // Someone freed up a connection, so try again.
```

```
        return(getConnection());
    }
     }
```

In cases where no connection is available in the foreground, it makes no sense to wait for a connection to free up. A thread can be started in the background to initiate a connection and then wait for the release or availability of a new connection. The following code is used to start a background process for establishing a connection:

```
private void makeBackgroundConnection() {
    connectionPending = true;
    try {
      Thread connectThread = new Thread(this);
      connectThread.start();
    } catch(OutOfMemoryError oome) {
      // Give up on new connection
```

Wait for the Availability of New Connections

In case there are no available connections or if the number of connections used crosses the previously set limit of connections, then the wait() method is used once again to wait for the availability of a connection. The following code is used to wait for the availability of a connection:

```
try {
   wait();
   } catch(InterruptedException ie) {}
   // Someone freed up a connection, so try again.
   return(getConnection());
```

Close Connections

Connections do not always need to be closed explicitly, but they are also closed during the process of garbage collection. The following code can be used for a more explicit control over the process of connection closing:

```
public synchronized void closeAllConnections() {
    closeConnections(availableConnections);
    availableConnections = new Vector();
    closeConnections(busyConnections);
    busyConnections = new Vector();
  }
```

DriverUtilities Class

Keep in mind that the versatility of an application is decided by its portability across all platforms. Because different databases are used for access and retrieval of data, a good code is a general-purpose code that supports driver specifications for databases such as Oracle, Sybase, and SQL. The `DriverUtilities` class file is used as a utility class for building JDBC connections in Oracle, Sybase, and SQL. The use of a general-purpose code with various driver specifications minimizes the time and effort that is otherwise required to make changes to the code with the corresponding change in the driver. The vendor for the driver is checked first, and the URL for the same is then specified. For example, the following line of code is used to check and specify the URL for an Oracle database:

```
public static String makeURL(String host, String dbName,
                                 int vendor) {
    if (vendor == ORACLE) {
      return("jdbc:oracle:thin:@" + host + ":1521:" + dbName);
    }
```

Similarly, drivers for Sybase and SQL can be checked and the corresponding specifications for the URL can then be added to the code.

DatabaseUtilities Class

After a connection is established, the query is executed in order to retrieve the result set containing the database records. The `DatabaseUtilities` class is used to implement the following four static methods to perform the query-related tasks:

- `createTable()` method to create a table in the database
- `getQueryResults()` method to query and retrieve records from the database
- `printTable()` method to retrieve and print all rows of a database table
- `printTableData()` method to retrieve and print the results of a previous query

Let's look at the functioning of each of these methods in detail.

Create a Database Table

The `createTable()` method is used to specify the table name, column format, and row values for creating a new table in the database. Prior to creating the table, a database connection is established and the corresponding statements for CREATE TABLE and INSERT ROWS are generated. If a table with the specified name already exists, the table is dropped and a new table is then created. The code for `DatabaseUtilities()` contains two versions for creating a table, one with a new connection and the other by using an existing connection. The following code can be used to create a table by using a new connection:

```
public static Connection createTable(String driver,
String url,String username,String password,String tableName,
String tableFormat,String[] tableRows,boolean close) {
    try {
      Class.forName(driver);
      Connection connection =
```

```
        DriverManager.getConnection(url, username, password);
      return(createTable(connection, username, password,
                         tableName, tableFormat,
                         tableRows, close));
    } catch(ClassNotFoundException cnfe) {
      System.err.println("Error loading driver: " + cnfe);
      return(null);
    } catch(SQLException sqle) {
      System.err.println("Error connecting: " + sqle);
      return(null);
    }
  }
```

The following code can be used to create a table by using a new connection:

```
public static Connection createTable(Connection connection,
String username,String password,String tableName,
String tableFormat,String[] tableRows,boolean close) {
    try {

      Statement statement = connection.createStatement();
      // Drop previous table if it exists, but don't get
      // error if it doesn't. Thus the separate try/catch here.
      try {
        statement.execute("DROP TABLE " + tableName);
      } catch(SQLException sqle) {}
      String createCommand =
        "CREATE TABLE " + tableName + " " + tableFormat;
      statement.execute(createCommand);
      String insertPrefix =
        "INSERT INTO " + tableName + " VALUES";
      for(int i=0; i<tableRows.length; i++) {
        statement.execute(insertPrefix + tableRows[i]);
      }
      if (close) {
        connection.close();
        return(null);
      } else {
        return(connection);
      }
    } catch(SQLException sqle) {
      System.err.println("Error creating table: " + sqle);
      return(null);
    }
  }
```

Execute a Query

The getQueryResults() method is used to retrieve records from a table. This method puts the retrieved rows as a String in the DatabaseResults object. Similar to the createTable() method, the code for DatabaseUtilities() contains two versions for retrieving records from a table, one with a new connection and the other by using an existing connection. The following code can be used to retrieve values from a table by using a new connection:

```
public static DBResults getQueryResults(String driver,
String url,String username,String password,
String query,boolean close) {
    try {
      Class.forName(driver);
      Connection connection =
        DriverManager.getConnection(url, username, password);
      return(getQueryResults(connection, query, close));
    } catch(ClassNotFoundException cnfe) {
      System.err.println("Error loading driver: " + cnfe);
      return(null);
    } catch(SQLException sqle) {
      System.err.println("Error connecting: " + sqle);
      return(null);
    }
}
```

The following code can be used to retrieve values from a table by using an existing connection:

```
public static DBResults getQueryResults(Connection connection,
String query,boolean close) {
    try {
      DatabaseMetaData dbMetaData = connection.getMetaData();
      String productName =
        dbMetaData.getDatabaseProductName();
      String productVersion =
        dbMetaData.getDatabaseProductVersion();
      Statement statement = connection.createStatement();
      ResultSet resultSet = statement.executeQuery(query);
      ResultSetMetaData resultsMetaData =
        resultSet.getMetaData();
      int columnCount = resultsMetaData.getColumnCount();
      String[] columnNames = new String[columnCount];
      // Column index starts at 1 (a la SQL) not 0 (a la Java).
      for(int i=1; i<columnCount+1; i++) {
        columnNames[i-1] =
          resultsMetaData.getColumnName(i).trim();
      }
      DBResults dbResults =
        new DBResults(connection, productName, productVersion,
                      columnCount, columnNames);
      while(resultSet.next()) {
        String[] row = new String[columnCount];
        // Again, ResultSet index starts at 1, not 0.
        for(int i=1; i<columnCount+1; i++) {
```

```
        String entry = resultSet.getString(i);
        if (entry != null) {
          entry = entry.trim();
        }
        row[i-1] = entry;
      }
      dbResults.addRow(row);
    }
    if (close) {
      connection.close();
    }
    return(dbResults);
  } catch(SQLException sqle) {
    System.err.println("Error connecting: " + sqle);
    return(null);
  }
}
```

Retrieve and Print All Rows of a Table

The printTable() method is used to print all the rows and column of a specified table on the standard output. The name of the specified table is used to create a query in the form of the following select statement:

```
"Select * from specifiedTableName"
```

The following code can be used to print the resultant rows and columns retrieved after execution of the preceding select statement:

```
public static void printTable(String driver,
                              String url,
                              String username,
                              String password,
                              String tableName,
                              int entryWidth,
                              boolean close) {
  String query = "SELECT * FROM " + tableName;
  DBResults results =
    getQueryResults(driver, url, username,
                    password, query, close);
  printTableData(tableName, results, entryWidth, true);
}
/** Prints out all entries in a table. Each entry will
 *  be printed in a column that is entryWidth characters
 *  wide, so be sure to provide a value at least as big
 *  as the widest result.
 */

public static void printTable(Connection connection,
                              String tableName,
                              int entryWidth,
```

```
                                          boolean close) {
        String query = "SELECT * FROM " + tableName;
        DBResults results =
          getQueryResults(connection, query, close);
        printTableData(tableName, results, entryWidth, true);
    }
```

Retrieve and Print the Results of a Previous Query

An object of DBResults is used in the printTableData() method to store the results of a previous query. The results are then printed on the standard output. The following code can be used to store and print the values of a previous query on the standard output. The printTableData() method is also used as the underlying method for the prinTable() method.

DBResults Class

The DBResults class is used as the auxiliary class for the code of the main class represented by the DatabaseUtilities() to store the results that are accumulated at the end of the query execution. The stored results are returned in the following two forms:

- The getRow() method is used to return the results in the form of an array of strings.

- The toHTMLTable() method is used to wrap the results inside an HTML table.

The following lines of code can be used to return the results by using the getRow() method:

```
public String[] getRow(int index) {
    return((String[])queryResults.elementAt(index));
  }
```

The following lines of code can be used to return the results by using the toHTMLTable() method:

```
public String toHTMLTable(String headingColor) {
    StringBuffer buffer =
      new StringBuffer("<TABLE BORDER=1>\n");
    if (headingColor != null) {
      buffer.append("  <TR BGCOLOR=\"" + headingColor +
                    "\">\n    ");
    } else {
      buffer.append("  <TR>\n    ");
    }
    for(int col=0; col<getColumnCount(); col++) {
      buffer.append("<TH>" + columnNames[col]);
    }
    for(int row=0; row<getRowCount(); row++) {
      buffer.append("\n  <TR>\n    ");
```

```
    String[] rowData = getRow(row);
    for(int col=0; col<getColumnCount(); col++) {
      buffer.append("<TD>" + rowData[col]);
    }
  }
  buffer.append("\n</TABLE>");
  return(buffer.toString());
}
```

Identify the Tags for the JSP Page

The JSP page will contain class definitions to perform the following tasks:

- The associated support files **DBResults.java** and **ConnectionPool.java** will be imported using the `import` attribute.

  ```
  <%@ page import="DBResults" %>
  <%@ page import="ConnectionPool" %>
  ```

- The `java.io.*`, `javax.servlet.*`, `java.sql.*` packages will also need to be imported.

  ```
  <%@ page import="java.io.*" %>
  <%@ page import="javax.servlet.*" %>
  <%@ page import="java.sql.*" %>
  ```

- The `usebean` tag will be used to reference the Java files for establishing a connection with a database and creating the query statement.

  ```
  <jsp:useBean id="third" class="DBResults" scope="session" />
  <jsp:useBean id="connectionPool" class="ConnectionPool"
  scope="session" />
  ```

- The specifications for the driver and the name of the database will be added to the JSP page.

  ```
  String driver = DriverUtilities.getDriver(vendor);
      String host = "testing-d185";
      String dbName = "Test";
      String url = DriverUtilities.makeURL(host, dbName, vendor);
      String username = "scott";
      String password = "tiger";
  ```

NOTE Because the codes for the associated files are very extensive, please refer to the explanations in the previous sections. You can also find clues in the comments inserted between the code sections.

Write the Java Code for the ConnectionPool Class

The code creating a pool of connections is as follows:

```java
//package coreservlets;

import java.sql.*;
import java.util.*;

/** A class for preallocating, recycling, and managing
 *  JDBC connections. Taken from Core Servlets and JavaServer Pages
 * from Prentice Hall and Sun Microsystems Press, *
 http://www.coreservlets.com/. ; may be freely used or copied.
 *  <P>
 *  */

public class ConnectionPool implements Runnable {
  private String driver, url, username, password;
  private int maxConnections;
  private boolean waitIfBusy;
  private Vector availableConnections, busyConnections;
  private boolean connectionPending = false;

public ConnectionPool()
{}
  public ConnectionPool(String driver, String url,
                        String username, String password,
                        int initialConnections,
                        int maxConnections,
                        boolean waitIfBusy)
      throws SQLException {
    this.driver = driver;
    this.url = url;
    this.username = username;
    this.password = password;
    this.maxConnections = maxConnections;
    this.waitIfBusy = waitIfBusy;
    if (initialConnections > maxConnections) {
      initialConnections = maxConnections;
    }
    availableConnections = new Vector(initialConnections);
    busyConnections = new Vector();
    for(int i=0; i<initialConnections; i++) {
      availableConnections.addElement(makeNewConnection());
    }
  }
}

  public synchronized Connection getConnection()
      throws SQLException {
    if (!availableConnections.isEmpty()) {
      Connection existingConnection =
        (Connection)availableConnections.lastElement();
      int lastIndex = availableConnections.size() - 1;
      availableConnections.removeElementAt(lastIndex);
      // If connection on available list is closed (e.g.,
      // it timed out), then remove it from available list
```

```
      // and repeat the process of obtaining a connection.
      // Also wake up threads that were waiting for a
      // connection because maxConnection limit was reached.
      if (existingConnection.isClosed()) {
        notifyAll(); // Freed up a spot for anybody waiting
        return(getConnection());
      } else {
        busyConnections.addElement(existingConnection);
        return(existingConnection);
      }
    } else {

      // Three possible cases:
      // 1) You haven't reached maxConnections limit. So
      //    establish one in the background if there isn't
      //    already one pending, then wait for
      //    the next available connection (whether or not
      //    it was the newly established one).
      // 2) You reached maxConnections limit and waitIfBusy
      //    flag is false. Throw SQLException in such a case.
      // 3) You reached maxConnections limit and waitIfBusy
      //    flag is true. Then do the same thing as in second
      //    part of step 1: wait for next available connection.
      if ((totalConnections() < maxConnections) &&
          !connectionPending) {
        makeBackgroundConnection();
      } else if (!waitIfBusy) {
        throw new SQLException("Connection limit reached");
      }
      // Wait for a new connection to be established
      // (if you called makeBackgroundConnection) or for
      // an existing connection to be freed up.
      try {
        wait();
      } catch(InterruptedException ie) {}
      // Someone freed up a connection, so try again.
      return(getConnection());
    }
  }

  // You can't just make a new connection in the foreground
  // when none is available because this can take several
  // seconds with a slow network connection. Instead,
  // start a thread that establishes a new connection,
  // then wait. You get woken up either when the new connection
  // is established or if someone finishes with an existing
  // connection.

  private void makeBackgroundConnection() {
    connectionPending = true;
    try {
      Thread connectThread = new Thread(this);
```

```
      connectThread.start();
    } catch(OutOfMemoryError oome) {
      // Give up on new connection
    }
  }

  public void run() {
    try {
      Connection connection = makeNewConnection();
      synchronized(this) {
        availableConnections.addElement(connection);
        connectionPending = false;
        notifyAll();
      }
    } catch(Exception e) { // SQLException or OutOfMemory
      // Give up on new connection and wait for existing one
      // to free up.
    }
  }

  // This explicitly makes a new connection. Called in
  // the foreground when initializing the ConnectionPool,
  // and called in the background when running.

  private Connection makeNewConnection()
      throws SQLException {
    try {
      // Load database driver if not already loaded
      Class.forName(driver);
      // Establish network connection to database
      Connection connection =
        DriverManager.getConnection(url, username, password);
      return(connection);
    } catch(ClassNotFoundException cnfe) {
      // Simplify try/catch blocks of people using this by
      // throwing only one exception type.
      throw new SQLException("Can't find class for driver: " +
                             driver);
    }
  }

  public synchronized void free(Connection connection) {
    busyConnections.removeElement(connection);
    availableConnections.addElement(connection);
    // Wake up threads that are waiting for a connection
    notifyAll();
  }

  public synchronized int totalConnections() {
    return(availableConnections.size() +
           busyConnections.size());
  }
```

```
/** Close all the connections. Use with caution:
 *  be sure no connections are in use before
 *  calling. Note that you are not <I>required</I> to
 *  call this when done with a ConnectionPool, since
 *  connections are guaranteed to be closed when
 *  garbage collected. But this method gives more control
 *  regarding when the connections are closed.
 */

public synchronized void closeAllConnections() {
  closeConnections(availableConnections);
  availableConnections = new Vector();
  closeConnections(busyConnections);
  busyConnections = new Vector();
}

private void closeConnections(Vector connections) {
  try {
    for(int i=0; i<connections.size(); i++) {
      Connection connection =
        (Connection)connections.elementAt(i);
      if (!connection.isClosed()) {
        connection.close();
      }
    }
  } catch(SQLException sqle) {
    // Ignore errors; garbage collect anyhow
  }
}

public synchronized String toString() {
  String info =
    "ConnectionPool(" + url + "," + username + ")" +
    ", available=" + availableConnections.size() +
    ", busy=" + busyConnections.size() +
    ", max=" + maxConnections;
  return(info);
}
}
```

Write the Java Code for the DriverUtilities Class

The code for specifying the URL of the database drivers is as follows:

```
//package coreservlets;

/** Some simple utilities for building Oracle and Sybase
 *  JDBC connections. This is <I>not</I> general-purpose
 *  code -- it is specific to my local setup. Taken from Core Servlets
```

```
 * and JavaServer Pages
 * from Prentice Hall and Sun Microsystems Press,
 * http://www.coreservlets.com/. ; may be freely used or copied.
 *   <P>
 *    */

public class DriverUtilities {
  public static final int ORACLE = 1;
  public static final int SYBASE = 2;
  //public static final int SQLSERVER= 3;
  public static final int UNKNOWN = -1;

  /** Build a URL in the format needed by the
   *  Oracle and Sybase drivers I am using.
   */

  public static String makeURL(String host, String dbName,
                               int vendor) {
    if (vendor == ORACLE) {
      return("jdbc:oracle:thin:@" + host + ":1521:" + dbName);
    } else if (vendor == SYBASE) {
      return("jdbc:sybase:Tds:" + host  + ":1521" +
             "?SERVICENAME=" + dbName);
    }
    //this is for SQLSERVER
    /*else if (vendor ==SQLSERVER) {
       // the following String is to be checked with SQLSERVER document
       return("<String for SQL driver>" + host  + ":1521" +
              "?SERVICENAME=" + dbName);
       */
    else {
      return(null);
    }
  }

  /** Get the fully qualified name of a driver. */

  public static String getDriver(int vendor) {
    if (vendor == ORACLE) {
      return("oracle.jdbc.driver.OracleDriver");
    } else if (vendor == SYBASE) {
      return("com.sybase.jdbc.SybDriver");
    }
    // to be included for SQLSERVER

    /*
    else if(vendor == SQLSERVER)
      {
        return("<driver class name for sql server >");
      }
    */
    else {
```

```
      return(null);
    }
  }

  /** Map name to int value. */
  public static int getVendor(String vendorName) {
    if (vendorName.equalsIgnoreCase("oracle")) {
      return(ORACLE);
    } else if (vendorName.equalsIgnoreCase("sybase")) {
      return(SYBASE);
    }
        // to be included for SQLSERVER

    /*
        else if (vendorName.equalsIgnoreCase("sqlserver")) {
        return(SQLSERVER);
        */
    else {
      return(UNKNOWN);
    }
  }
}
```

Write the Java Code for the DatabaseUtilities Class

The code for querying the database is as follows:

```
//package coreservlets;

import java.sql.*;

/** Taken from Core Servlets and JavaServer Pages
 * from Prentice Hall and Sun Microsystems Press,
 *    http://www.coreservlets.com/. ; may be freely used or copied.
 *    Three database utilities:<BR>
 *    1) getQueryResults. Connects to a database, executes
 *        a query, retrieves all the rows as arrays
 *        of strings, and puts them inside a DBResults
 *        object. Also places the database product name,
 *        database version, and the names of all the columns
 *        into the DBResults object. This has two versions:
 *        one that makes a new connection and another that
 *        uses an existing connection. <P>
 *    2) createTable. Given a table name, a string denoting
 *        the column formats, and an array of strings denoting
 *        the row values, this method connects to a database,
 *        removes any existing versions of the designated
 *        table, issues a CREATE TABLE command with the
 *        designated format, then sends a series of INSERT INTO
 *        commands for each of the rows. Again, there are
```

```
 *      two versions: one that makes a new connection and
 *      another that uses an existing connection. <P>
 *   3) printTable. Given a table name, this connects to
 *      the specified database, retrieves all the rows,
 *      and prints them on the standard output.
 *  <P>
 *   */

public class DatabaseUtilities {

  /** Connect to database, execute specified query,
   *  and accumulate results into DBRresults object.
   *  If the database connection is left open (use the
   *  close argument to specify), you can retrieve the
   *  connection with DBResults.getConnection.
   */

  public static DBResults getQueryResults(String driver,
                                          String url,
                                          String username,
                                          String password,
                                          String query,
                                          boolean close) {
    try {
      Class.forName(driver);
      Connection connection =
        DriverManager.getConnection(url, username, password);
      return(getQueryResults(connection, query, close));
    } catch(ClassNotFoundException cnfe) {
      System.err.println("Error loading driver: " + cnfe);
      return(null);
    } catch(SQLException sqle) {
      System.err.println("Error connecting: " + sqle);
      return(null);
    }
  }

  /** Retrieves results as in previous method but uses
   *  an existing connection instead of opening a new one.
   */

  public static DBResults getQueryResults(Connection connection,
                                          String query,
                                          boolean close) {
    try {
      DatabaseMetaData dbMetaData = connection.getMetaData();
      String productName =
        dbMetaData.getDatabaseProductName();
      String productVersion =
        dbMetaData.getDatabaseProductVersion();
      Statement statement = connection.createStatement();
      ResultSet resultSet = statement.executeQuery(query);
```

```
    ResultSetMetaData resultsMetaData =
      resultSet.getMetaData();
    int columnCount = resultsMetaData.getColumnCount();
    String[] columnNames = new String[columnCount];
    // Column index starts at 1 (a la SQL) not 0 (a la Java).
    for(int i=1; i<columnCount+1; i++) {
      columnNames[i-1] =
        resultsMetaData.getColumnName(i).trim();
    }
    DBResults dbResults =
      new DBResults(connection, productName, productVersion,
                    columnCount, columnNames);
    while(resultSet.next()) {
      String[] row = new String[columnCount];
      // Again, ResultSet index starts at 1, not 0.
      for(int i=1; i<columnCount+1; i++) {
        String entry = resultSet.getString(i);
        if (entry != null) {
          entry = entry.trim();
        }
        row[i-1] = entry;
      }
      dbResults.addRow(row);
    }
    if (close) {
      connection.close();
    }
    return(dbResults);
  } catch(SQLException sqle) {
    System.err.println("Error connecting: " + sqle);
    return(null);
  }
}
/** Build a table with the specified format and rows. */

public static Connection createTable(String driver,
                                     String url,
                                     String username,
                                     String password,
                                     String tableName,
                                     String tableFormat,
                                     String[] tableRows,
                                     boolean close) {
  try {
    Class.forName(driver);
    Connection connection =
      DriverManager.getConnection(url, username, password);
    return(createTable(connection, username, password,
                       tableName, tableFormat,
                       tableRows, close));
  } catch(ClassNotFoundException cnfe) {
    System.err.println("Error loading driver: " + cnfe);
```

```
        return(null);
      } catch(SQLException sqle) {
        System.err.println("Error connecting: " + sqle);
        return(null);
      }
    }

    /** Like the previous method, but uses existing connection. */

    public static Connection createTable(Connection connection,
                                         String username,
                                         String password,
                                         String tableName,
                                         String tableFormat,
                                         String[] tableRows,
                                         boolean close) {
      try {

        Statement statement = connection.createStatement();
        // Drop previous table if it exists, but don't get
        // error if it doesn't. Thus the separate try/catch here.
        try {
          statement.execute("DROP TABLE " + tableName);
        } catch(SQLException sqle) {}
        String createCommand =
          "CREATE TABLE " + tableName + " " + tableFormat;
        statement.execute(createCommand);
        String insertPrefix =
          "INSERT INTO " + tableName + " VALUES";
        for(int i=0; i<tableRows.length; i++) {
          statement.execute(insertPrefix + tableRows[i]);
        }
        if (close) {
          connection.close();
          return(null);
        } else {
          return(connection);
        }
      } catch(SQLException sqle) {
        System.err.println("Error creating table: " + sqle);
        return(null);
      }
    }

    public static void printTable(String driver,
                                  String url,
                                  String username,
                                  String password,
                                  String tableName,
                                  int entryWidth,
                                  boolean close) {
      String query = "SELECT * FROM " + tableName;
      DBResults results =
```

```
          getQueryResults(driver, url, username,
                          password, query, close);
     printTableData(tableName, results, entryWidth, true);
   }
   /** Prints out all entries in a table. Each entry will
    *  be printed in a column that is entryWidth characters
    *  wide, so be sure to provide a value at least as big
    *  as the widest result.
    */
   public static void printTable(Connection connection,
                                 String tableName,
                                 int entryWidth,
                                 boolean close) {
     String query = "SELECT * FROM " + tableName;
     DBResults results =
       getQueryResults(connection, query, close);
     printTableData(tableName, results, entryWidth, true);
 }

 public static void printTableData(String tableName,
                                   DBResults results,
                                   int entryWidth,
                                   boolean printMetaData) {
     if (results == null) {
       return;
     }
     if (printMetaData) {
       System.out.println("Database: " +
                          results.getProductName());
       System.out.println("Version: " +
                          results.getProductVersion());
       System.out.println();
     }
     System.out.println(tableName + ":");
     String underline =
       padString("", tableName.length()+1, "=");
     System.out.println(underline);
     int columnCount = results.getColumnCount();
     String separator =
       makeSeparator(entryWidth, columnCount);
     System.out.println(separator);
     String row = makeRow(results.getColumnNames(), entryWidth);
     System.out.println(row);
     System.out.println(separator);
     int rowCount = results.getRowCount();
     for(int i=0; i<rowCount; i++) {
       row = makeRow(results.getRow(i), entryWidth);
       System.out.println(row);
     }
     System.out.println(separator);
   }
```

```java
// A String of the form "| xxx | xxx | xxx |"

private static String makeRow(String[] entries,
                              int entryWidth) {
  String row = "|";
  for(int i=0; i<entries.length; i++) {
    row = row + padString(entries[i], entryWidth, " ");
    row = row + " |";
  }
  return(row);
}


// A String of the form "+------+------+------+"

private static String makeSeparator(int entryWidth,
                                    int columnCount) {
  String entry = padString("", entryWidth+1, "-");
  String separator = "+";
  for(int i=0; i<columnCount; i++) {
    separator = separator + entry + "+";
  }
  return(separator);
}
private static String padString(String orig, int size,
                                String padChar) {
  if (orig == null) {
    orig = "<null>";
  }
  // Use StringBuffer, not just repeated String concatenation
  // to avoid creating too many temporary Strings.
  StringBuffer buffer = new StringBuffer("");
  int extraChars = size - orig.length();
  for(int i=0; i<extraChars; i++) {
    buffer.append(padChar);
  }
  buffer.append(orig);
  return(buffer.toString());
}
}
```

Write the Java Code for the DBResults Class

The code for storing the retrieved values from the database is as follows:

```java
//package coreservlets;

import java.sql.*;
import java.util.*;

/** V Taken from Core Servlets and JavaServer Pages
 * from Prentice Hall and Sun Microsystems Press,
```

```
 *     http://www.coreservlets.com/. ; may be freely used or copied.
 *     Class to store completed results of a JDBC Query.
 *   Differs from a ResultSet in several ways:
 *   <UL>
 *     <LI>ResultSet doesn't necessarily have all the data;
 *         reconnection to database occurs as you ask for
 *         later rows.
 *     <LI>This class stores results as strings, in arrays.
 *     <LI>This class includes DatabaseMetaData (database product
 *         name and version) and ResultSetMetaData
 *         (the column names).
 *     <LI>This class has a toHTMLTable method that turns
 *         the results into a long string corresponding to
 *         an HTML table.
 *   </UL>
 *   <P>
 *   */

public class DBResults {
  private Connection connection;
  private String productName;
  private String productVersion;
  private int columnCount;
  private String[] columnNames;
  private Vector queryResults;
  String[] rowData;

  public DBResults()
  {
  }

public DBResults(Connection connection,
                 String productName,
                 String productVersion,
                 int columnCount,
                 String[] columnNames) {
    this.connection = connection;
    this.productName = productName;
    this.productVersion = productVersion;
    this.columnCount = columnCount;
    this.columnNames = columnNames;
    rowData = new String[columnCount];
    queryResults = new Vector();
  }

  public Connection getConnection() {
return(connection);
  }
public String getProductName() {
    return(productName);
  }
```

```java
public String getProductVersion() {
  return(productVersion);
}
public int getColumnCount() {
  return(columnCount);
}

public String[] getColumnNames() {
  return(columnNames);
}

public int getRowCount() {
  return(queryResults.size());
}

public String[] getRow(int index) {
  return((String[])queryResults.elementAt(index));
}

public void addRow(String[] row) {
  queryResults.addElement(row);
}

/** Output the results as an HTML table, with
 *  the column names as headings and the rest of
 *  the results filling regular data cells.
 */

public String toHTMLTable(String headingColor) {
  StringBuffer buffer =
    new StringBuffer("<TABLE BORDER=1>\n");
  if (headingColor != null) {
    buffer.append("  <TR BGCOLOR=\"" + headingColor +
                  "\">\n    ");
  } else {
    buffer.append("  <TR>\n    ");
  }
  for(int col=0; col<getColumnCount(); col++) {
    buffer.append("<TH>" + columnNames[col]);
  }
  for(int row=0; row<getRowCount(); row++) {
    buffer.append("\n  <TR>\n    ");
    String[] rowData = getRow(row);
    for(int col=0; col<getColumnCount(); col++) {
      buffer.append("<TD>" + rowData[col]);
    }
  }
  buffer.append("\n</TABLE>");
  return(buffer.toString());
}
}
```

Write the Code for the Servlet Utilities

```java
//package coreservlets;

import javax.servlet.*;
import javax.servlet.http.*;

/** Some simple time savers. Note that most are static methods.
 *  Taken from Core Servlets and JavaServer Pages
 * from Prentice Hall and Sun Microsystems Press,
 *  http://www.coreservlets.com/. ; may be freely used or copied.<P>
 * */

public class ServletUtilities {
  public static final String DOCTYPE =
    "<!DOCTYPE HTML PUBLIC \"-//W3C//DTD HTML 4.0 " +
    "Transitional//EN\">";
  public static String headWithTitle(String title) {
    return(DOCTYPE + "\n" +
           "<HTML>\n" +
           "<HEAD><TITLE>" + title + "</TITLE></HEAD>\n");
  }
  /** Read a parameter with the specified name, convert it
   *  to an int, and return it. Return the designated default
   *  value if the parameter doesn't exist or if it is an
   *  illegal integer format.
   */

  public static int getIntParameter(HttpServletRequest request,
                                    String paramName,
                                    int defaultValue) {
    String paramString = request.getParameter(paramName);
    int paramValue;
    try {
      paramValue = Integer.parseInt(paramString);
    } catch(NumberFormatException nfe) { // null or bad format
      paramValue = defaultValue;
    }
    return(paramValue);
  }

  /** Given an array of Cookies, a name, and a default value,
   *  this method tries to find the value of the cookie with
   *  the given name. If there is no cookie matching the name
   *  in the array, then the default value is returned instead.
   */

  public static String getCookieValue(Cookie[] cookies,
                                      String cookieName,
                                      String defaultValue) {
    if (cookies != null) {
```

```
      for(int i=0; i<cookies.length; i++) {
        Cookie cookie = cookies[i];
        if (cookieName.equals(cookie.getName()))
          return(cookie.getValue());
      }
    }
    return(defaultValue);
  }

  /** Given an array of cookies and a name, this method tries
   *  to find and return the cookie from the array that has
   *  the given name. If there is no cookie matching the name
   *  in the array, null is returned.
   */

  public static Cookie getCookie(Cookie[] cookies,
                                 String cookieName) {
    if (cookies != null) {
      for(int i=0; i<cookies.length; i++) {
        Cookie cookie = cookies[i];
        if (cookieName.equals(cookie.getName()))
          return(cookie);
      }
    }
    return(null);
  }

  /** Given a string, this method replaces all occurrences of
   *  '<' with '&lt;', all occurrences of '>' with
   *  '&gt;', and (to handle cases that occur inside attribute
   *  values), all occurrences of double quotes with
   *  '&quot;' and all occurrences of '&' with '&amp;'.
   *  Without such filtering, an arbitrary string
   *  could not safely be inserted in a Web page.
   */

  public static String filter(String input) {
    StringBuffer filtered = new StringBuffer(input.length());
    char c;
    for(int i=0; i<input.length(); i++) {
      c = input.charAt(i);
      if (c == '<') {
        filtered.append("&lt;");
      } else if (c == '>') {
        filtered.append("&gt;");
      } else if (c == '"') {
        filtered.append("&quot;");
      } else if (c == '&') {
        filtered.append("&amp;");
      } else {
        filtered.append(c);
      }
    }
```

```
        return(filtered.toString());
    }
}
```

Write the Code for the JSP Page

The code for the JSP page is as follows:

```
<%@ page import="DBResults" %>

<%@ page import="ConnectionPool" %>

<%@ page import="java.io.*" %>
<%@ page import="javax.servlet.*" %>
<%@ page import="java.sql.*" %>

<jsp:useBean id="third" class="DBResults" scope="session" />

<jsp:useBean id="connectionPool" class="ConnectionPool" scope="session"
/>
<%

   int vendor = DriverUtilities.ORACLE;
       String driver = DriverUtilities.getDriver(vendor);
       String host = "testing-d185";
       String dbName = "Test";
       String url = DriverUtilities.makeURL(host, dbName, vendor);
       String username = "scott";
       String password = "tiger";

         connectionPool =
           new ConnectionPool(driver, url, username, password,
                          2,
                             10,
                             true);
  String table;
       String query =
         "SELECT cFirst_name, cLast_name " +
         " FROM Final_Registration WHERE cRegistration_id = 103";
       Connection connection = connectionPool.getConnection();
       DBResults results =
DatabaseUtilities.getQueryResults(connection,     query, false);
       connectionPool.free(connection);
       table = results.toHTMLTable("#FFDFD7");
 //    response.setContentType("text/html");
 //    response.setHeader("Pragma", "no-cache");
 //    response.setHeader("Cache-Control", "no-cache");
     //PrintWriter out = response.getWriter();
     String title = "Connection Pool Test";
     out.println(ServletUtilities.headWithTitle(title) +
                 "<BODY BGCOLOR=\" #FFDFD7\">\n" +
```

```
                          "<CENTER>\n" +
                          table + "\n" +
                          "</CENTER>\n</BODY></HTML>");
    %>

          <%

      /*public void init() {
        // int vendor = DriverUtilities.SYBASE;
         int vendor = DriverUtilities.ORACLE;
         String driver = DriverUtilities.getDriver(vendor);
         String host = "testing-d185";
         String dbName = "Test";
         String url = DriverUtilities.makeURL(host, dbName, vendor);
         String username = "scott";
         String password = "tiger";
           connectionPool =
             new ConnectionPool(driver, url, username, password,
                                   initialConnections(),
                                   maxConnections(),
                                   true);
       }
     */
     %>

     </body>
     </html>
```

Compile the Java Files

A single project for developing a particular Web application consists of multiple programmers each assigned the task of writing the code for a section of the project. Therefore, it is likely that two programmers working on different sections of the project might use the same filenaming convention to identify the files they develop. In such a case, how can we differentiate the files and associate them with a particular section of the application?

Packaging files is a prevalent practice among programmers to avoid name conflicts for various files used in the same project. The use of packages changes the process of compilation and invocation of the particular file. You'll recall that all through the previous chapter, the Java files used were placed under the C:\j2sdkee1.2.1\lib\classes directory, which is the default path for placement of the class files. If packages are used for separate placement of Java files, then the server needs to be informed about the shift in the path settings of the class files. The following steps are used to package files:

- Create a folder with an appropriate name to identify the contained files. For example, in order to store all four Java files for this task, we'll use a package named connection. All the Java files can be moved to this folder and then compiled. Alternately, the Java files can be stored elsewhere and only the class files obtained after compilation can be moved to the connection folder.

- The following line is inserted at the beginning of each file in the package. For example, the first line in ConnectionPool.java will be:

```
package connection;
```

You can compile packaged files by setting the CLASSPATH variable to include the path of the folder containing the files of the package. For example, to include a pointer to a folder named Pool under C:\j2sdkee1.2.1, add the following path to the CLASSPATH variable:

```
C:/j2sdkee1.2.1\Pool;
```

To compile the files for the Banco de Glendanthi application, do the following:

1. Place ConnectionPool.java, DriverUtilities.java, DatabaseUtilities.java, and DBResults.java in a separate folder named connection.

2. Compile the files by typing the following command at the DOS prompt:

```
javac *.java
```

3. Add the path of the folder containing the class files to the CLASSPATH variable.

View the JSP Page

To view the JSP page, do the following:

1. Save the JSP file as **ConnectionPool.jsp**.
2. Copy the JSP file under the public_html directory.
3. Initiate the server startup and open **ConnectionPool.jsp** in the browser.

NOTE We are using an Oracle database for retrieving the results of the query. The code for driver specification is a general-purpose code. As a result, you can add the name of the SQL driver URL as url=jdbc:odbc:dsnname and the driver name as driver=sub.jdbc.odbc.Jdbcodbcdriver.

Summary

A Web application services requests from multiple clients. With the increase in the number of clients, the importance of serving clients effectively also increases. The economics of resource management is the primary factor taken into consideration when judging the efficiency and effectiveness of an application. Maximum reuse of objects is one of the techniques used for serving clients effectively. The process of creating a new object for each request adds to resource overhead in terms of memory allocation, initialization, and constant tracking of the objects for garbage collection. Therefore, it is advisable to maximize reuse of objects in an application to eliminate the need to create a new object for each request. Interactions over the Web involve frequent and repeated requests for stored records of the database. In this chapter, we have discussed how connection pooling is used to do away with the practice of creating new objects for the retrieval of data from the database. At the end of this chapter, you'll be able to create applications for database interactions by using a pool of connections.

We have not encountered any inaccuracies in the applications developed so far. All the applications codes were compiled to ensure that they executed without any errors. As programmers, though, you need to be aware of the methods implemented to track and debug errors in JSP. The next chapter discusses the various approaches for handling errors in JSP.

CHAPTER 12

Handling Errors

OBJECTIVES:

In this chapter, you will learn to do the following:

- ✔ Identify the steps to handle errors
- ✔ Create an error page for an application
- ✔ Generate a customized error message

Getting Started

The preceding chapters helped you create data-driven and nondata-driven applications in JSP. The applications that you created varied in complexity by degrees. A common aspect of all these applications is that you were able to execute them successfully and produce the desired output.

That you were able to execute your application implies that you did not commit any programming or logical errors; however, users might interact with your application in more than one way. For example, users may type "sixteen" as their age instead of "16." In this case, though the user is correct in specifying the age, your application might not produce the intended result if it expects an Integer data type. Alternatively, your application might stop responding. Similarly, if you need to access data from a database and the database is not accessible, your application might terminate.

To avoid termination of your program as a result of such errors, you need to make your application robust. You can make your application robust by implementing an error-handling mechanism that handles runtime errors. An error-handling mechanism not only prevents runtime errors, but also informs the user that an error has occurred and offers the user another alternative. For example, if a JSP page is missing from the Web application, you can inform a user about the missing page and allow the user to send an email about the missing page to a system administrator. Doesn't that sound interesting? Well, it is! In this chapter, we explore the capabilities of JSP that help implement error handling. We also add error pages to an application for implementing an error-handling code. We take the online portal of Banco de Glendanthi to new heights by examining how incorrect data formats can cause application errors and how the error-handling code takes care of such errors.

Handling Errors in JSP

There is more than one way to handle errors. For example, to ensure that a user has input complete information, you may want to check all the fields in a form when a user clicks the submit button. We've already discussed this method of ensuring inputs from the user in a text control, in Chapter 6, "Working with HTML Forms."

Another method, and definitely a more efficient one, is to implement error handling the way it is done in this chapter. The error-handling method described in this chapter pertains to handling exceptions. Each time your application encounters an error it throws an exception. An exception is any abnormal condition in a program, such as the presence of a `String` data type instead of an `Integer` as we described earlier. When your application throws an exception, it checks for an exception handler that may be defined for the exception. If the application finds an exception handler, it executes the code in the exception handler. Alternatively, when an application does not find an exception handler it terminates abnormally.

To handle exceptions, follow the three simple steps listed here:

1. Create an error page for your application.

2. Include the `errorPage` directive on the page for which you want to handle exceptions.

3. Use the `try` and `catch` blocks to label code that is likely to cause errors in the code.

The last step in the preceding list is optional; however, if you use `try` and `catch` blocks in your application, you can obtain clues on errors in your application and display customized messages to the user accordingly. Let's look at error pages and how to utilize them in an application by using an example from the Banco de Glendanthi application.

Creating an Error Page

Problem Statement

Before customers engage in any financial transaction, it is important for them to have an accurate estimate of returns on their investment in a specified time span. Banco de Glendanthi has been providing this type of service to its customers ever since it was established. The bank now wants to provide the same service to its online customers.

As part of the development team, you're required to create a JSP application that can provide an accurate estimate of returns on an investment in the specified period of time. You're also entrusted with the task of ensuring that the application does not terminate abruptly if it encounters an error because of incorrect data supplied by customers or any other anomalies.

Task List

✔ **Design the user interface to accept information from customers.**

✔ **Identify the structure of an error page.**

✔ **Identify the tag to link an error page to a JSP page.**

✔ **Identify the components of the JSP page to calculate the return on investments.**

✔ **Write the code for the user interface.**

✔ **Write the code for the JSP page to calculate the return on investments.**

✔ **Write the code to display error messages**

✔ **View the JSP page.**

Design the User Interface to Accept Information from Customers

You need to display an HTML page that allows a user to provide the following information:

■ Total investment that the user wishes to make

■ Rate of interest currently offered by the bank

Table 12.1 lists the HTML tags to be used for the design of the user interface.

Table 12.1 The Elements of the User Interface

INPUT FIELD	SPECIFICATIONS
Bank's name and logo	`<%@include file="Header.html"%>`
Control to accept customer name	`<input type="text">`
Submit button	`<input type="submit">`

You'll notice that we are accepting the rate of interest from the customer—the customer might want to check out the gain on an investment at different interest rates, which might be applicable to different periods or schemes of investment.

The format of the application for Banco de Glendanthi uses a standard appearance for all its Web pages. Each Web page includes the bank logo and name on top and a link to the copyright page at the bottom. To facilitate standardization across Web pages developed by different development teams, the bank logo and name are included in the Header.html file and the link to the copyright page is included in the Copyright.html page.

A form is rendered on the Default.jsp page that allows a user to specify the investment and rate of interest by using the `<form>` and `<input>` HTML tags. You must be familiar with these tags because they have been used several times in the preceding chapters.

Identify the Structure of an Error Page

An error page is a page that can be invoked each time your application throws an exception. You might have come across Web sites that provide a single logon page that is invoked when an unauthenticated user requests a Web page that requires authentication. The mechanism of an error page is similar. Each time your application encounters an error, the control passes to the error page, which implements the required logic to handle the error and prevents the application from terminating.

An error page is similar to any other JSP page, except that the error page specifies an `isErrorPage=true` statement in the `page` directive. Therefore, the page directive in an error page can be specified as follows:

```
<%@ page isErrorPage="True" %>
```

After you specify this directive, you can use the `exception` object to display information about an error. The `exception` object is an instance of either the `java.lang.Throwable` class or its subclasses that obtain information about an exception. The `java.lang.Throwable` class includes the following subclasses:

java.lang.Exception. The `java.lang.Exception` class specifies the exceptions that can occur on a JSP page.

java.lang.Error. The `java.lang.Error` class specifies errors that might occur on a JSP page. The errors specified by the `java.lang.Error` class should not be confused with the exceptions described in the `java.lang.Exception` class. That's because the `java.lang.Error` class describes those errors from which your Web application might not be able to recover, such as errors pertaining to inadequate memory.

After instantiating the `exception` object, you can display information about the exception, such as the exception name and the stack trace when the exception was caused. We'll use the `exception` object later in this chapter. But before we do that, let's examine the role of the `errorPage` directive.

Identify the Tag to Link an Error Page to a JSP Page

An `errorPage` directive is used for linking a JSP page to an error page. When an exception occurs on a JSP page, the JSP engine examines the error page associated with the JSP page by using the `errorPage` directive and transfers control to that page.

You can declare an error page by using the following syntax:

```
<%@ page errorPage="ExceptionHandler.jsp" %>
```

In the preceding code, the `errorPage` directive specifies ExceptionHandler.jsp as the error page for the JSP page. After you specify this statement in your JSP page, all errors and exceptions are directed to the ExceptionHandler.jsp page.

Identify the Components of the JSP Page to Calculate the Returns on Investments

After writing the code for the Default.jsp page, your task is to write the code for computing the interest on the investment at the specified interest rate. We'll use the CalcInterest.jsp page to write the code for computing the interest.

On the CalcInterest.jsp page, the first step is to include the `errorPage` statement in the page directive by specifying the following code:

```
<%@ page errorPage="ExceptionHandler.jsp" %>
```

The Web application should display the interest on an investment for the next 25 years. Therefore, to make the coding easy and the form visually appealing, you should display data in a tabular format. To create a table and its header rows, you can specify the following HTML code:

```
<body bgcolor="#FFDFD7">
<HR>
<p align="center"><b><i><font face="Century Gothic">Estimated Capital
Growth in 25
Years</font></i></b></p>
```

```
<BR>
<p> <font face="Bookman Old Style" size="4"> Amount invested: US $
<%=request.getParameter("Amount")%></p>
<p> <font face="Bookman Old Style" size="4"> Rate of interest:
<%=request.getParameter("Rate")%> %</p>
<TABLE border="2" width=100%>
<TR>
<TD><font face="Bookman Old Style">Year</font></TD>
<TD><font face="Bookman Old Style">Amount (US $)</font></TD>
</TR>
```

Notice that before beginning the table with the <TABLE> tag, we have displayed the amount invested and the rate of interest that the user had specified on the Default.jsp page. We retrieved these details from the request string.

After creating the table and rendering the header row, you use the amount invested and rate of interest per annum to compute the capital at the end of each year for the next 25 years. The logic to compute the capital is specified here:

1. Obtain the amount invested and rate of interest from the request string.
2. Convert the request string to the integer format.
3. Divide the interest rate by 100 and multiply the result with the amount invested to obtain the capital at the end of the first year.
4. Display the result on the JSP page.
5. Repeat Steps 3 and 4 to obtain successive capitals for the next 25 years and display the result on the JSP page.

The following code uses this logic to display the growth of investment for the next 25 years:

```
<%
double Investment = 0;
Investment=Integer.parseInt(request.getParameter("Amount"));
int Year=2001;
double Rate = 0;
Rate=Integer.parseInt(request.getParameter("Rate"));
int Counter=1;
while (Counter<26)
{
Year=Year + 1;
Investment=Investment + (Investment * (Rate*.01));
%>
<TR>
<TD><font face="Bookman Old Style"><%=Year%></font></TD>
<TD><font face="Bookman Old Style"><%=Investment%></font></TD>
</TR>
<%
Counter = Counter+1;
}
%>
</TABLE>
```

In the preceding code, notice that we have assumed 2001 as the base year and displayed the growth of investment for the next 25 years, until 2026.

Write the Code for the User Interface

As is evident from the description of the application, the first JSP page involves the use of HTML tags to display a form to users. The code for the first JSP page, Default.jsp, is given here:

```
<html>
<%@include file="Header.html"%>
<body bgcolor="#FFDFD7">
<p align="center"><b><i><font face="Century Gothic">Estimated Capital
Growth in 25
Years</font></i></b></p>
<form method="POST" action="CalcInterest.jsp">
<p>Specify the sum that you want to invest: <input type="text"
name="Amount" size="20">US
$ at <input type="text" name="Rate" size="20"> %</p>
  <p>  
nbsp;          &
nbsp;          &
nbsp;          &
nbsp;          &
nbsp;          &
nbsp;          &
nbsp;   
  <input type="submit" value="Submit"></p>
</form>
<p> </p>
<HR>
<%@include file="Copyright.html"%>
</body>
</html>
```

Write the Code for the JSP Page to Calculate the Returns on Investments

The complete code of the CalcInterest.jsp page, after adding references for the Header.html and Copyright.html pages, is given here:

```
<%@ page errorPage="ExceptionHandler.jsp" %>
<html>
<%@include file="Header.html"%>
<body bgcolor="#FFDFD7">
<HR>
<p align="center"><b><i><font face="Century Gothic">Estimated Capital
```

```
Growth in 25
Years</font></i></b></p>
<BR>
<p> <font face="Bookman Old Style" size="4"> Amount invested: US $
<%=request.getParameter("Amount")%></p>
<p> <font face="Bookman Old Style" size="4"> Rate of interest:
<%=request.getParameter("Rate")%> %</p>

<TABLE border="2" width=100%>
<TR>
<TD><font face="Bookman Old Style">Year</font></TD>
<TD><font face="Bookman Old Style">Amount (US $)</font></TD>
</TR>
<%
double Investment = 0;
Investment=Integer.parseInt(request.getParameter("Amount"));
int Year=2001;
double Rate = 0;
Rate=Integer.parseInt(request.getParameter("Rate"));
int Counter=1;
while (Counter<26)
{
Year=Year + 1;
Investment=Investment + (Investment * (Rate*.01));
%>
<TR>
<TD><font face="Bookman Old Style"><%=Year%></font></TD>
<TD><font face="Bookman Old Style"><%=Investment%></font></TD>
</TR>
<%
Counter = Counter+1;
}
%>
</TABLE>
<HR>
<%@include file="Copyright.html"%>
</body>
```

For the code for the CalcInterest.jsp page, you'll specify ExceptionHandler.jsp as the error handler for all exceptions generated on the CalcInterest.jsp page. Let's now code the functionality of the ExceptionHandler.jsp page that notifies the user in case of any error and provides a link to the Default.jsp page of the Web application.

Write the Code to Display the Error Messages

We have already discussed the implementation of error pages earlier in this chapter. An error page begins with the `isErrorPage="True"` statement in the `page` directive. The complete page directive for the CalcInterest.jsp page is given here:

```
<%@ page errorPage="ExceptionHandler.jsp" %>
```

The next significant method used by the error-handler page is the toString method of the exception object. This method returns a string value that specifies the description of the error or exception. The complete code of the ExceptionHandler.jsp page is given here:

```
<%@ page isErrorPage="True" %>
<html>
<%@include file="Header.html"%>
<body bgcolor="#FFDFD7">
<HR>
<p> <font face="Bookman Old Style" color="red">There was an error in
processing your request:</font></p>
<p> <font face="Bookman Old Style"
color="red"><B><%=exception.toString()%></B></font></p>
<p><font face="Bookman Old Style" color="red"><a href="Default.jsp">Try
Again</a></font></p>
<HR>
<%@include file="Copyright.html"%>
</body>
</html>
```

View the JSP Page

To view the JSP page, do the following:

1. Save the user interface file as Default.jsp.

2. Save the JSP file as CalcInterest.jsp.

3. Save the error page as ExceptionHandler.jsp

4. Copy all three JSP files in the C:/j2sdkee1.2.1/public_html directory.

5. Initiate the server startup and open Default.jsp in the browser.

   Figure 12.1 shows the output of the Default.jsp page of the application in which we have specified the preceding code.

6. Specify the amount invested and rate of interest as 80000 and 10, respectively.

7. Click the submit button.

   Figure 12.2 displays the computed interest applicable on the specified investment.

The preceding code enables you to display a description of any error that might occur on a JSP page. For example, if the customer specifies US $80,000 as the investment amount instead of 8,000 (the code application prefixes US $ to the value automatically; therefore, the user should not specify the same), the code displays a description of the error as shown in Figure 12.3.

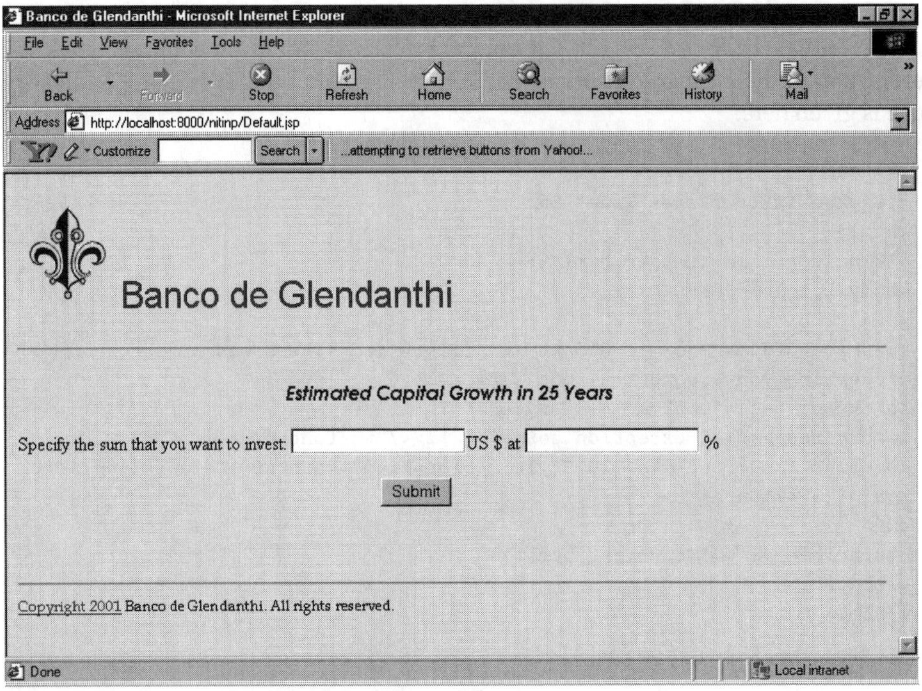

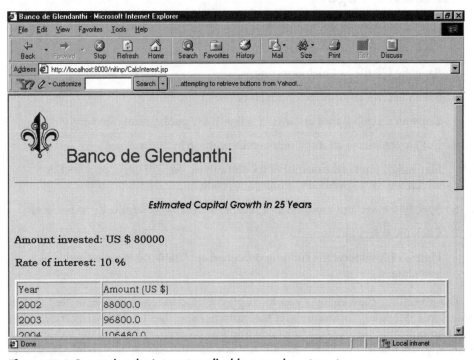

Figure 12.1 The startup page of the application.

Figure 12.2 Computing the Interest applicable on an investment.

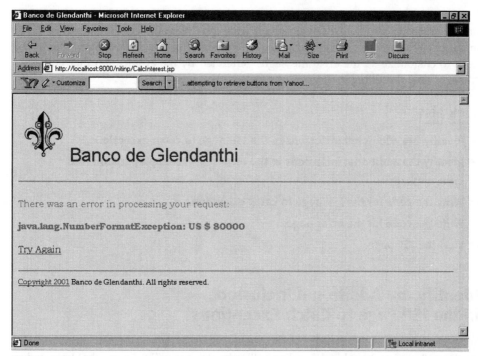

Figure 12.3   An error message appears if the user does not specify the correct values.

In Figure 12.3, notice the link Try Again to the Default.jsp page. Therefore, the application does not terminate but allows the user to display the Default.jsp page again and specify valid values for the investment and the rate of interest.

What you just saw was an important aspect of error handling in JSP. The next question that comes to mind is whether JSP can help provide a detailed description of the cause of an error. As a result, even a nontechnical person without any programming experience, such as some of your customers, can interpret the error message. That's our next destination! Let's customize the error page to provide a detailed description of the error.

Generating Customized Error Messages

Problem Statement

The development team has been successful in creating the application for estimating returns on an investment; however, the application has one drawback. Customers cannot easily interpret the error messages generated by the application. With the increasing user friendliness of Web applications, it has become essential to make the online portal of Banco de Glendanthi as user-friendly as possible.

One step toward improving user interaction with the online portal is the customization of error messages. The development team is required to customize all the error messages generated by the application. As a member of the development team, you need to customize all the error messages generated by the application that you have created in the preceding section.

Task List

✔ **Identify the additional inclusions in the JSP page to catch exceptions.**

✔ **Identify the additional inclusions in the error page to display customized error messages.**

✔ **Write the code for the JSP page to catch exceptions.**

✔ **Write the code for the error page.**

✔ **View the JSP page.**

Identify the Additional Inclusions in the JSP Page to Catch Exceptions

To catch exceptions, use the `try` and `catch` blocks. We've already discussed the implementation of these blocks earlier in the chapter; we will now use that knowledge here. You can save on the development effort by reutilizing a coded application. You will find it easier to modify the application that you've created for your first assignment in this chapter. Let's see how we can utilize the existing application.

The Default.jsp page, which displays text boxes for accepting the amount invested and the rate of interest, remains the same. The next page, CalcInterest.jsp, needs modification. You need to determine the code of the CalcInterest.jsp file that is likely to cause errors and include the code in the `try` block. For the programming logic that you have implemented in the CalcInterest.jsp file, only the code in which you are converting the `string` data type to `int` is likely to cause errors if the user has not specified the information in the correct format. You should enclose the susceptible code in the `try` block, as we do in the code that follows:

```
try
{
Investment=Integer.parseInt(request.getParameter("Amount"));
Rate=Integer.parseInt(request.getParameter("Rate"));
}
```

If an exception occurs while parsing the `string` data type to `int`, the JSP page will throw a `NumberFormatException` exception. A `catch` block, which immediately follows the `try` block, catches this exception. The syntax of the `catch` block is given here:

```
catch (NumberFormatException e) {
throw new JspException ("Please enter a valid integer value!");
}
```

In the preceding code, the catch block catches the NumberFormatException exception and throws a new exception that is instantiated from the JspException class. A NumberFormatException occurs when a value is expected in the integer format but is not supplied correctly. Because you have defined no exception handler for the new exception generated in the catch block, the control of the Web application passes to the ExceptionHandler.jsp page, whose implementation we will discuss in the next section.

Identify the Additional Inclusions in the Error Page to Display Customized Error Messages

In the last stages of optimizing the application, you'll code the ExceptionHandler.jsp page, which is not very different from the corresponding page that you created in the previous section. On the ExceptionHandler.jsp page, we use the getMessage() method of the exception object. The getMessage() method retrieves the error message associated with an exception. This error message, in our case, is the message that we have specified in the catch block of the CalcInterest.jsp page.

Write the Code for the JSP Page to Catch Exceptions

Before we delve into that, here is the complete code for the CalcInterest.jsp file:

```
<%@ page errorPage="ExceptionHandler.jsp" %>
<html>
<%@include file="Header.html"%>
<body bgcolor="#FFDFD7">
<HR>
<p align="center"><b><i><font face="Century Gothic">Estimated Capital
Growth in 25
Years</font></i></b></p>
<BR>
<p> <font face="Bookman Old Style" size="4"> Amount invested: US $
<%=request.getParameter("Amount")%></p>
<p> <font face="Bookman Old Style" size="4"> Rate of interest:
<%=request.getParameter("Rate")%> %</p>

<TABLE border="2" width=100%>
<TR>
<TD><font face="Bookman Old Style">Year</font></TD>
<TD><font face="Bookman Old Style">Amount (US $)</font></TD>
</TR>
<%
double Investment = 0;
int Year=2001;
double Rate = 0;
try
{
Investment=Integer.parseInt(request.getParameter("Amount"));
```

```
Rate=Integer.parseInt(request.getParameter("Rate"));
}
catch (NumberFormatException e) {
throw new JspException ("Please enter a valid integer value!");
}
int Counter=1;
while (Counter<26)
{
Year=Year + 1;
Investment=Investment + (Investment * (Rate*.01));
%>
<TR>
<TD><font face="Bookman Old Style"><%=Year%></font></TD>
<TD><font face="Bookman Old Style"><%=Investment%></font></TD>
</TR>
<%
Counter = Counter+1;
}
%>
</TABLE>
<form method="POST" action="Default.jsp">
<% Counter=1;
while (Counter<30)
{
Counter=Counter+1;
%>
 
<%
}
%>
<input type="Submit" value="OK">
</form>
<HR>
<%@include file="Copyright.html"%>
</body>
```

Write the Code for the Error Page

The complete code of the ExceptionHandler.jsp page is given here:

```
<%@ page isErrorPage="True" %>
<html>
<%@include file="Header.html"%>
<body bgcolor="#FFDFD7">
<HR>
<p> <font face="Bookman Old Style" color="red">There was an error in
processing your request:</font></p>
<p> <font face="Bookman Old Style"
color="red"><B><%=exception.getMessage()%></B></font></p>
<p><font face="Bookman Old Style" color="red"><a href="Default.jsp">Try
```

```
Again</a></font></p>
<HR>
<%@include file="Copyright.html"%>
</body>
</html>
```

View the JSP Page

To view the JSP page, do the following:

1. Copy the updated code of CalcInterest.jsp.

2. Copy the updated code of ExceptionHandler.jsp.

3. Copy all three JSP files including Default.jsp in the C:/j2sdkee1.2.1/public_html directory.

4. Initiate the server startup and open Default.jsp in the browser.

5. Specify the amount invested as $80,000.

When you click the submit button, you will notice that the error message, on specifying invalid data, is customized, as shown in Figure 12.4. Compare Figure 12.4 with Figure 12.3 to appreciate the difference in output from that of the previous application.

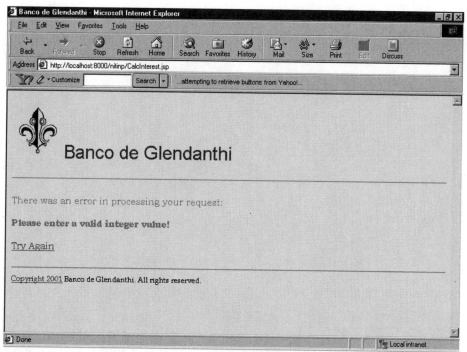

Figure 12.4 A customized error message appears on using the `try` and `catch` blocks.

NOTE Depending on the machine settings and the path settings, the message may differ from that displayed in Figure 12.4.

Summary

Error handling is an important feature of any application. To ensure that your code performs as expected, you can utilize the error-handling capabilities of JSP.

Error handling can be categorized into two broad tasks, ensuring that a user has specified complete information and handling unexpected anomalies encountered by an application. While the former can be achieved easily by programming logic alone, the latter involves the use of specialized features of JSP, namely error pages and the try and catch blocks.

Error pages are JSP pages that are invoked when an application encounters unexpected errors. An error page is declared using the isErrorPage="True" statement in the page directive. You also need to associate an error page with a JSP page by using the @errorPage directive.

The try and catch blocks are used to demarcate code that is susceptible to errors. When a statement in the try block generates an error, the control passes to the catch block, which implements the necessary error-handling routine to recover from the error.

CHAPTER 13

JSP Sessions

OBJECTIVES:

In this chapter, you will learn to do the following:

✔ Identify the mechanisms that are used for session tracking in JSP

✔ Use cookies for session tracking

✔ Use session objects for session tracking

✔ Use URL rewriting for session tracking

Getting Started

We already covered the basics of Servlet API in Chapter 3, "Servlet Basics." The function of a servlet is to receive requests, along with parameters, and process the requests to generate an appropriate response. Because the compilation of a JSP page automatically generates a servlet, serving of requests with appropriate responses is a built-in function of a JSP page. A JSP page, however, does not use a single servlet to generate responses. Each request for a JSP page is associated with a servlet. As a result, a typical Web application uses multiple servlets to cater to client requests; however, the request-response cycle uses the HTTP protocol, which is a stateless protocol. A stateless protocol does not maintain contextual information regarding a particular client request. In other words, at the end of the cycle for a particular request, the Web server is unable to maintain information regarding the request. As a result, each transaction, corresponding to a request-response cycle, is independent with no connections to previous transactions.

Although such an approach speeds up the request-response cycle, it also shows drawbacks in maintaining contextual information of previous transactions. The need to store contextual information is easily explained by the following example. An avid book reader always remembers the name of his or her favorite author. Similarly, you always store information regarding discount sales and other good bargain offers at the local shopping outlets. The storing of contextual information regarding the discount sales enables you to visit the shops and utilize the discounts for shopping at reduced rates.

The implementation of session tracking uses the servlet context that consists of the Web application and the Web container. The container is a nonstandard interface that is used to define the nature and structure of the run time and to provide access to APIs for services such as transaction processing and database access. The approaches to session tracking use cookies, hidden form fields, and URL rewriting to keep track of user information in HTTP transactions. This chapter will discuss all three implementations in detail. We'll use a scenario-based example to bring out the differences in the implementation of session tracking by the use of cookies, hidden fields, and URL rewriting.

The Session Tracking API

The Session Application Programming Interface (Session API) uses session-tracking mechanisms to overcome the statelessness of an HTTP transaction and enable storage of contextual information regarding client requests. Due to session tracking, each user can be individually identified, and all information regarding the particular user transaction can be stored and retrieved. As a result, in spite of multiple request and response handling, the server is able to uniquely identify each user. This approach has worked wonders for sites that provide online shopping facilities for transactions. Have you ever wondered how the server keeps track of the items added to the shopping cart? For example, while you keep adding items to the shopping cart, the server is able to retrieve information regarding items that were previously present in the cart. The bill for the shopping includes all the items added to the cart.

We have used the term "stateless" to define the HTTP protocol used in the request-response transaction. The implementation of session tracking indirectly adds state to the HTTP session. Before proceeding, let's first understand the meaning of the terms "sessions," "stateless protocol," and "stateful protocol."

A session is the period of time defined between requests from the same user. Alternately, a session defines the transaction of a single user. In a stateless protocol, a client requests a resource that is served by the response. At the end of such a transaction, the server fails to retrieve any information regarding the client. As a result, a request from the same client is always treated as a fresh request. Contrary to a stateless protocol, a stateful protocol can serve responses for current requests that can be also based on the results of previous requests. A stateful protocol is typically used to serve multiple requests that are sent across a single network connection and are suitable for long business transactions.

The need for stateful protocol can be explained by using the example of an online bank, such as Banco de Glendanthi. After you have logged on, do you need to specify your ID or password and have it validated when accessing various pages of the application? No! Your ID or password is validated once, and the server is able to subsequently serve all your requests till the termination of the session (until you log out or sign out of the session). As a result, a single business transaction can consist of multiple requests for pages displaying balances and mini statements, as well as requisitions for new checkbooks. For such a banking transaction, a stateless protocol would require that you provide your credentials (ID and password) with every request. In other words, each business transaction would serve only a single request.

You can also map the use of the stateful protocol when shopping online. In a situation such as this, after adding the items to the cart, when you move on to the page requesting your payment specifications, the server is able to retain and recollect the items of the cart in order to generate the billing amount. Have you ever thought about how the server is able to calculate the billing amount based on the previous request (addition of items to the shopping cart)? Well, session tracking is used to add a stateful functionality to the otherwise stateless protocol used for the shopping transaction. How can you track sessions in a JSP page so that the server is able to retain contextual information regarding previous requests? The following approaches are used to implement session tracking in JSP:

- Using cookies
- Using hidden fields
- Using URL rewriting

Beginning with cookies, we'll look at each of the approaches for session tracking in detail. Cookies are bits of session-related information sent by a Web server to a browser. The browser stores the cookie on the client computer in the form of a name-value pair that can be extracted during subsequent visits to the same site.

Using Cookies for Session Tracking

Problem Statement

Almost all Web sites display information regarding the number of hits to a Web site. This information, popularly known as the hit count, is displayed in various formats. Some of the most prevalent methods used to display the hit count contain a generalized format depicting a numeric count equivalent to the total number of hits. The other, which is a personalized format, contains the date of the user's current visit or dates of current and previous visits to a particular Web site.

In keeping with the trends, it is natural that the development team assigned the task of creating the site for Banco de Glendanthi will use a mechanism to display the hit counts on the home page. The development team has decided to display a personalized hit count displaying the date and time of last access. The hit count will be displayed on the home page that is currently under construction. To demonstrate the effect and use of session tracking, we'll use the semi-constructed page to display the chosen format of the hit count. Let's look at the approach and methodology adopted to add such functionality to the application.

Task List

✔ Identify the elements of the home page.

✔ Identify the JSP tags to be included in order to display the hit count.

✔ Write the code for the JSP page.

✔ View the JSP page.

Identify the Elements of the Home Page

The hit count will be displayed on the home page. As a result, the Java code for adding the personalized hit count containing the last accessed date will be included in the home page. The home page is still under construction and does not contain all links to the other pages of the application. We will use the semi-constructed home page to check the functionality of the hit count. The user interface will consist of the following elements:

- The header elements consisting of the bank name and logo

- A brief write-up introducing the bank and its activities

- The copyright statement, which is a common inclusion for any Web site

The code for the home page is as follows:

```html
<html>

<head>

<title>Banco de Glendanthi</title>
</head>

<body bgcolor="#FFDFD7">
<table border="0" cellpadding="3" cellspacing="0" width="661"
height="540">
  <tr>
    <td align="center" width="1" height="57"></td>
    <td align="right" valign="top" width="216" height="57"></td>
    <td align="center" width="422" height="57"><font
size="1"><em><strong></strong></em></font><font color="#0000FF"
size="7">Banco
de Glendanthi</font><hr><hr></td>
  </tr>
  <tr>
    <td align="center" width="1" nowrap height="1"></td>
    <td align="right" valign="top" width="216" nowrap height="1"><font
size="2"></font></td>
    <td align="center" width="422" nowrap height="1"><font
size="1"><em><strong></strong></em></font></td>
  </tr>
  <tr>
    <td align="center" width="1" height="527"></td>
    <td align="right" valign="top" width="216" height="527">
```

```
        <p align="left">Banco de Glendanthi was
        established in 1975 with headquarters in New York. Today, under the
        chairmanship of Marty Bates, the bank has spread across the world
        and has
        its regional headquarters at London, Paris, Istanbul, Cairo, Kuala
        Lumpur,
        and Singapore. Broadly, the bank specializes in the following
        three activities -
        regular deposits, loans, and credit. Customers can open different
        types of
        accounts, such as personal accounts, commercial accounts, and
        certificates of deposit accounts with the bank. Any person can
        avail of the loan facility by registering
        with the bank, provided certain prerequisites are fulfilled. A
        customer
        can choose from the commercial loan, consumer loan, or mortgage
        loan schemes. The bank also offers a credit card facility and has
        ATM (Any Time Money) centers in most of
        its business branches.
        <p> </td>
    <td align="center" width="422" height="527"><img border="0"
src="C:/j2sdkee1.2.1/public_html/7044.jpg" width="387" height="294"><br>
        <br>
    </td>
  </tr>
  <td height="1" width="1">
</table>

</body>

</html>
```

Figure 13.1 displays the output of the home page in its current state.

Figure 13.1 The Banco de Glendanthi home page.

Identify the JSP Tags to Be Included in Order to Display the Personalized Hit Count

The cookies are stored on the client computer and are managed by the browser. When the client sends a request to the server for a site visited previously, the server accesses these cookies to retrieve the site-related information. In the case of a request from a JSP page, the same methodology is applied to retrieve information regarding repeated requests for the same page. As a result, cookies can be used in the following cases:

User identification.   Cookies provide a link for identifying users on subsequent visits to a Web site. Such a methodology is best explained using the example of an online store. Taking into account the fact that the HTTP connection is closed at the end of adding an item to the shopping cart, how is the server able to identify the user during subsequent item selections? The Web server stores cookies on a client computer by requesting the client computer to create a cookie. The cookie is sent back to the Web server in the form of HTTP headers when a client sends a request to the server.

Username and password specifications.   Cookies can be used as an alternative to store user identification rather than specifying the username and password during subsequent visits to a Web site. In such a case, after a user registers for the Web site, a cookie is created with a unique ID associated with that specific user. Thereafter, on subsequent visits to the site, the user ID is used to identify the registered user without needing the username and password specifications; however, such a methodology is used only for low-security sites.

Web page customizations.   Cookies can store user-specified formats that are used to change the appearance of the Web pages according to the user's preference. The changed format of the pages is retained and can be retrieved during subsequent visits to the site.

The number of cookies and amount of information that can be stored on a computer can be limited to save hard disk space. In addition to limiting the amount of information stored by a cookie, you can also specify the time interval for retaining a cookie on a computer.

The Web server references cookies as an instance of the `javax.servlet.http` `Cookie` class. Both the response and request objects in a JSP page can instantiate and use the `javax.servlet.http.Cookie` class. Table 13.1 lists the various methods of the `Cookie` class.

In addition to the methods of the `Cookie` class, the `addCookie()` method of the response implicit object is used to send a cookie to the browser. To use the `add-Cookie()` method, you need to specify an instance of the `Cookie` class as a parameter to the method. If a cookie is already stored on the client computer, the stored cookie is updated with the information that is sent with the new cookie. If there is no cookie on the client computer, the `addCookie()` method creates and stores a new cookie on the client computer.

NOTE The implicit object response is an instance of the javax.servlet.http. HttpServletResponse class.

Table 13.1 The Methods of the `Cookie` Class

METHOD NAME	USED TO...
`String getName()`	Identify the name that has been assigned to the cookie. The `getName()` method returns a `String` value to the calling function
`Void setComment(String)`	Describe the purpose of a cookie. You need to specify a `String` that describes the purpose of a cookie as a parameter to this method.
`String getComment()`	Access a comment that describes the purpose of the cookie. This method returns a `String` to the calling function.
`void setDomain(String)`	Specify the domain in which the cookie should be present. You need to specify the domain name as a parameter to this method.
`void setMaxAge(int)`	Set the time period of a cookie. You need to pass an `integer` value as the parameter to this method. The `integer` value represents the time period of the cookie in seconds.
`void setPath(String)`	Specify the path on the Web server. This path is used to send the cookie to the Web server from the client. You need to pass a `String` value as the parameter to this method. The `String` value represents the path of the Web server.
`String getPath()`	Return the path of the Web server that receives the cookie from the client. The method returns a `String` value.
`void setSecure(boolean)`	Specify whether the cookie is sent over a secure protocol such as HTTPS or SSL. The method accepts a Boolean value, True or False, as a parameter
`boolean getSecure()`	Identify whether the cookie is sent over a secure protocol. If the cookie is sent over a secure protocol, the Boolean value True is returned; otherwise, False is returned.
`void setValue(String)`	Assign a new value to the cookie. The `String` parameter that is passed to the method specifies the new value of the cookie.
`String getValue()`	Retrieve the value of the cookie.
`void setVersion(int)`	Set the version of the protocol with which the cookie is compiled.
`int getVersion()`	Retrieve the version of the protocol with which the cookie is compiled. The `getVersion()` method returns an integer value.

The JSP page at the server end can access the cookies stored on the client computer by using the getCookie() method of the request implicit object. The getCookie() method returns an array of instances of the Cookie class.

NOTE The implicit object request is an instance of the javax.servlet.http. HttpServletRequest class.

Let's look at an example that retrieves the number and details of the cookies:

```
<HTML>
<HEAD>

<TITLE>
A cookie example
</TITLE>
</HEAD>

<BODY BGCOLOR="#FFDFD7">
<% // Set up initial variables
Integer integer = Integer.valueOf("1");
%>

<H2><center>A cookie example</center></H2><HR>
<%
if (request.getParameter("CookieValue") != null)
  {
    integer = Integer.valueOf(request.getParameter("CookieValue"));
    Cookie cookie = new Cookie("Cookie-#" +
request.getParameter("CookieValue"), "User Define Cookie");
    cookie.setMaxAge(-1);
    response.addCookie(cookie);
  }
%>
<INPUT size="10" type="hidden" name="CookieValue"
value="<%=integer.intValue() + 1%>">
<INPUT size="50" type="hidden" name="PrevSession"
value="<%=session.getId()%>">
</FORM>
<BR>

<% // Enumerate and display cookies
Cookie[] cookies = request.getCookies();
out.println("<H3>" + "<center>"  + " Cookies  currently available: " +
cookies.length + "</center></H3>");
  if ( cookies != null && cookies.length > 0 )
    {
      out.println("<H3>" + "<center>"  + " Cookies that are currently
available: </center></H3>");
      out.println("<center><TABLE  Border=\"2\" WIDTH=\"65%\"
```

```
></center>");
    for ( int i=0; i<cookies.length; i++ )
      {
        out.println("<tr><td>" + cookies[i].getName() + "</td><td>" +
cookies[i].getValue() +
        "</td></tr>");
      }
    out.println("</table><BR><BR>");
  }
%>

</BODY>
</HTML>
```

Figure 13.2 displays the details of the available cookies.

Let's identify the JSP elements to be included in the code to add a personalized hit count displaying the date and time of last access. The JSP elements in the code will consist of the following methods and statements:

- The Date() method will be used to retrieve the stored value of the user's last date of visit to the Web site. In addition, the date of last visit will be displayed in a specific format. As a result, we need to import two packages, java.text.DateFormat and java.util.Date.

- The server will use the request object to retrieve all the cookies stored on the local machine, which is used to access the Banco de Glendanthi Web site.

- The cookie storing the date of access will be searched by using the iterative statement. If a cookie with the specific name (MyCookie) is found, the cookie value will be displayed in the form of the last date of access. If not found, a cookie will be created and assigned an initial value of the current date and time.

- When creating a new cookie, the methods used will be these:

  - new Cookie("MyCookie", newValue) to create a new instance of a cookie

  - setMaxAge() to set the age of the cookie, in seconds

  - setPath() to specify the path that is used by the client to return the cookie

  - response.addCookie() to add the cookie to the response object and send it back to the browser.

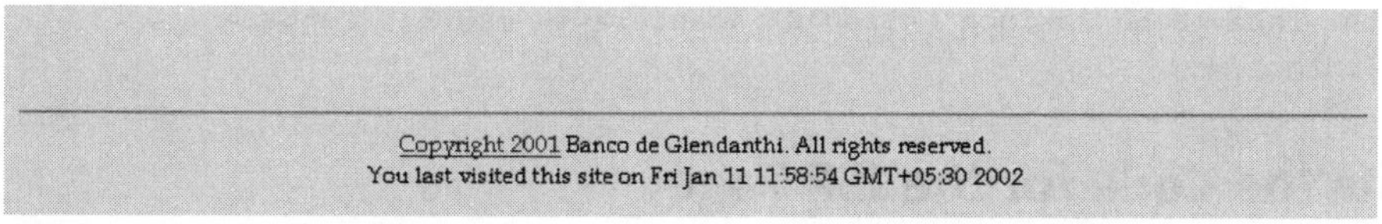

Copyright 2001 Banco de Glendanthi. All rights reserved.
You last visited this site on Fri Jan 11 11:58:54 GMT+05:30 2002

Figure 13.2 The cookies example.

The code containing the JSP elements is as follows:

```
<%@ page language="java" import="java.text.DateFormat, java.util.Date" %>

<%
  boolean found = false;
  Cookie info = null;
  String msg = "This is the first time you've visited this page.";

  // Get all the cookies that came with the request
  Cookie[] cookies = request.getCookies();
  for(int i = 0; i < cookies.length; i++) {
    info = cookies[i];
    if (info.getName().equals("MyCookie")) {
      found = true;
      break;
    }
  }

  String newValue = "" + System.currentTimeMillis();

  if (!found) {
    // Create a new cookie and set its age.
    info = new Cookie("MyCookie", newValue );
    info.setMaxAge(60*1);
    info.setPath("/");

    response.addCookie(info);
  } else{
    long conv = new Long(info.getValue()).longValue();
    msg = "You last visited this site on " + new Date(conv);
    // Set the new value of the cookie, and add it to the response
    info.setValue(newValue);
    // keep the cookie for 1 month.
    info.setMaxAge(10*24*60*60);

    // Set the path so that the cookie is available everywhere on the
server
    info.setPath("/");
    response.addCookie(info);
  }
%>
<hr><center><%--The include directive is used here to add the elements
of the file Header.html to the login page--%>
<%@ include file="Copyright.html" %></center>
<!--<font color="#0000FF">-->
<font face="Book Antiqua" size="2"><center><%= msg %></center>
</font>
```

Write the Code for the JSP Page

The code for the JSP page containing both the HTML and JSP elements is as follows:

```
<html>

<head>
<meta http-equiv="Content-Type" content="text/html; charset=windows-
1252">
<meta http-equiv="Content-Language" content="en-us">
<meta name="GENERATOR" content="Microsoft FrontPage 4.0">
<meta name="ProgId" content="FrontPage.Editor.Document">
<title>Banco de Glendanthi</title>
</head>

<body bgcolor="#FFDFD7">
<table border="0" cellpadding="3" cellspacing="0" width="661"
height="540">
  <tr>
    <td align="center" width="1" height="57"></td>
    <td align="right" valign="top" width="216" height="57"></td>
    <td align="center" width="422" height="57"><font
size="1"><em><strong></strong></em></font><font color="#0000FF"
size="7">Banco
de Glendanthi</font></td>
  </tr>
  <tr>
    <td align="center" width="1" nowrap height="1"></td>
    <td align="right" valign="top" width="216" nowrap height="1"><font
size="2"></font></td>
    <td align="center" width="422" nowrap height="1"><font
size="1"><em><strong></strong></em></font></td>
  </tr>
  <tr>
    <td align="center" width="1" height="527"></td>
    <td align="right" valign="top" width="216" height="527">
      <p align="left">Banco de Glendanthi was
      established in 1975 with headquarters in New York. Today, under the
      chairmanship of Marty Bates, the bank has spread across the world
      and has
      its regional headquarters in London, Paris, Istanbul, Cairo, Kuala
      Lampur,
      and Singapore. Broadly, the bank specializes in the following
      three activities:
      regular deposits, ss, and credit. Customers can open different
      types of
      accounts, such as current account, savings accounts, and credit
      accounts,
      with the bank. Any person can avail of the loan facility by
      registering
      with the bank, provided certain prerequisites are fulfilled. A
      customer
      can choose from the personal loan, car loan, housing loan, or
      business
```

```
      loan schemes. The bank also offers a credit card facility and has
      ATM (Any Time Money) centers in most of
      its business branches.
         <p> </td>
     <td align="center" width="422" height="527"><br>
         <img border="0" src="file:///C:/j2sdkee1.2.1/public_html/7044.jpg"
width="387" height="294">
       </td>
   </tr>
   <td height="1" width="1">
</table>
   <%@ page language="java" import="java.text.DateFormat, java.util.Date"
%>

<%
  boolean found = false;
  Cookie info = null;
  String msg = "This is the first time you've visited this page.";
  // Get all the cookies that came with the request
  Cookie[] cookies = request.getCookies();
  for(int i = 0; i < cookies.length; i++) {
    info = cookies[i];
    if (info.getName().equals("MyCookie")) {
      found = true;
      break;
    }
  }

  String newValue = "" + System.currentTimeMillis();

  if (!found) {
    // Create a new cookie and set its age.
    info = new Cookie("MyCookie", newValue );
    info.setMaxAge(60*1);
    info.setPath("/");

    response.addCookie(info);
  } else{
    long conv = new Long(info.getValue()).longValue();
    msg = "You last visited this site on " + new Date(conv);

    // Set the new value of the cookie, and add it to the response
    info.setValue(newValue);
   // keep the cookie for 1 month.
   info.setMaxAge(10*24*60*60);

    // Set the path so that the cookie is available everywhere on the
server
    info.setPath("/");
    response.addCookie(info);
  }
```

```
%>
<hr><center><%--The include directive is used here to add the elements
of the file Header.html to the login page--%>
<%@ include file="Copyright.html" %></center>
<!--<font color="#0000FF">-->
<font face="Book Antiqua" size="2"><center><%= msg %></center>
</font>
  </body>

</html>
```

View the JSP Page

To view the JSP page, do the following:

1. Save the JSP file as **cookie.jsp**.

2. Copy the JSP file in the **C:/j2sdkee1.2.1/public_html** directory.

3. Initiate the server startup in verbose mode.

4. In the Internet Explorer address, type the location of the JSP file as **http://localhost:8000/filename.jsp** where the filename denotes the name of the JSP file.

5. Compare and verify the screen display. Figure 13.3 displays the section of the home page containing the hit count that is retrieved by using a cookie.

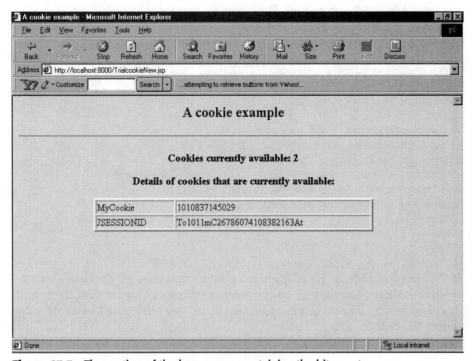

Figure 13.3 The section of the home page containing the hit count.

NOTE The preceding figure displaying the home page may vary because the hit count generated by using cookies is dynamic content, changing with each access to the home page.

Cookies are used to provide a user with session-related information that can consist of anything ranging from login information to number of hits for a page. Despite all the misleading information associated with cookies, the fact remains that cookies do not pose any security threats simply due to their mode of creation: Ccookies are not implemented, interpreted, or executed in any way, but created and stored on the client computer. As a result, they do not harbor or bring virus attacks on computers. In addition, the control level for storing cookies is 20 per site, 300 cookies in total that on average allocates about 4KB of memory space to each cookie on the client computer. As a result, inappropriate use of cookies is controlled. That cookies store user-related information could pose serious privacy threats, which are disliked by many Net surfers. For example, we would not want search results for job sites to display banner ads specifying user information regarding previous visits to the site. Therefore, users often prefer to disable cookies to override their privacy concerns.

Let's discuss another way to track sessions—using hidden form fields.

Session Tracking by Using Hidden Form Fields

Hidden fields are form elements that are primarily used to store unchanging names and values. As a result, the names and values of a hidden field are passed on to the server irrespective of the user input. The syntax for using a hidden field is this:

```
<input type="hidden" name="..........." value="...........">
```

For example, consider the following HTML code:

```
<html>
<body>
<h3>A simple hidden field example</h3>
<form method="post" action="Result.jsp">
<p>Product name? <input type="text" name="name">
<p>Number of Items ordered? <input type="text" name="num">
<p><input type="hidden" name="discount" value="25%">
<input type="submit" name="Submit Query">
</form>
</body>
</html>
```

In the preceding code, an HTML page accepts user input for a product and the number of items ordered. Although the page contains a text control for discount, the output of this page does not create a graphical element in the browser. Figure 13.4 displays the output of this code.

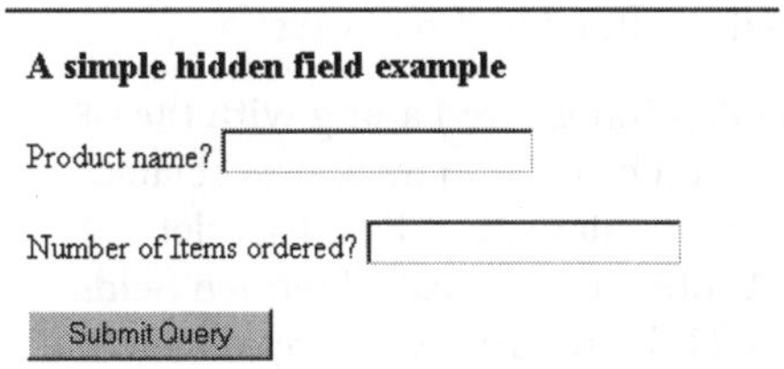

A simple hidden field example

Product name? [   ]

Number of Items ordered? [   ]

[Submit Query]

Figure 13.4 The output of the HTML page with a hidden field.

On submission of the form, the name and value of the hidden field are added to the form data and can be retrieved using JSP-specific tags. A user can view the hidden fields on a JSP page by right-clicking the document area of the Web browser and then selecting the View Source command. The code for the JSP page that displays the values of the form data is this:

```
<html>
<body>
<h3>Retrieving values from hidden.html</h3>
<%
String Pname = request.getParameter("name");
String Pnumber = request.getParameter("num");
String itemDiscount = request.getParameter("discount");
%>

<p>The name that you entered was: <%= Pname %>
<p>The product specified was: <%= Pnumber %>
<p>Thediscount offer specified using the hidden field: <%= itemDiscount
%>
</body>
</html>
```

Figure 13.5 displays the output of this code.

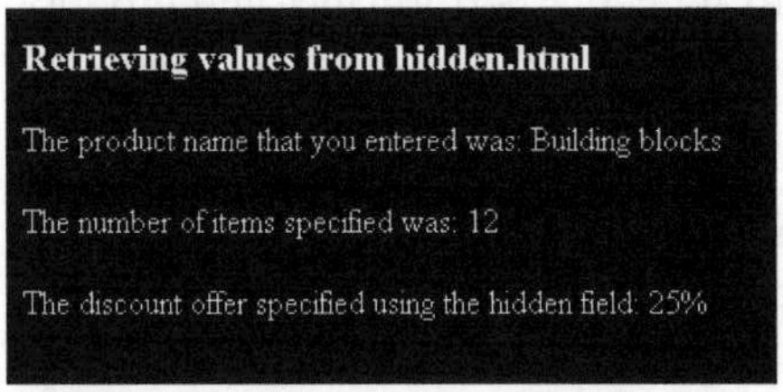

Retrieving values from hidden.html

The product name that you entered was: Building blocks

The number of items specified was: 12

The discount offer specified using the hidden field: 25%

Figure 13.5 The output of the JSP page containing the value of the hidden field.

Hidden fields are used for session tracking in the following three ways:

The name and value attached to a hidden field is transferred along with the GET **or** POST **method.** As a result, hidden fields can be used to track user-related information while the user moves around a particular site. JSP and servlet developers do not rely on this approach but substitute the use of hidden fields for session tracking by using session objects. Hidden form fields implement session tracking at a relatively low level.

A predefined output can be supplied by using a hidden form field particularly in situations where different static HTML pages are used as a source of information for the same application on the server. For example, commissions payable for promoting a particular site can use a hidden field to provide the referral ID of the promoter. As a result, a form displaying the shopping catalog can also contain a hidden field with the ID of the promoter to keep track of the number of visitors accessing a site.

Referential information of dynamically generated pages can be stored in hidden fields. For example, an online store can use a hidden field in the order confirmation form to contain the product ID of the order. As a result, the form contains contextual information about the product ID that is static as compared to the other elements that the user can change before final submission.

A third approach that is used to track sessions is using session objects. A session object is an implicit object that stores the information for only the current interaction with the user. The session object is an instance of the HttpSession interface and is available to all JSP pages.

Using a Session Object for Session Tracking

Problem Statement

An employee of Banco de Glendanthi, like most professionals, has multiple duties to be undertaken each day. As a result, it is not surprising that tasks are often left undone or not prioritized according to their importance. A prevalent practice among executives is the use of a to-do list to keep track of day-to-day activities.

As a part of professional facilities designed to aid better performance and productivity, the project development team has been asked to provide an online to-do list for the bank personnel. The proposed online list will be a part of the in-house application accessible only to the bank personnel. The application will enable documentation of daily activities along with a time schedule. The design drawn up by the team is such that tasks can be added to the list and deleted as they are completed. The provision of the to-do list will therefore help an executive keep track of day-to-day tasks. In addition, the entries for the tasks should be retained even after the page is refreshed so that the details are not lost. Let's understand the approach and methodology adopted to add such functionality to the application.

Task List

✔ **Identify the HTML elements of the page.**

✔ **Identify the JSP tags to be included in order to display the hit count.**

✔ **Write the code for the JSP page.**

✔ **View the JSP page.**

Identify the HTML Elements of the Page

The user interface will consist of the following elements:

- The header elements, consisting of the bank name and logo
- A table to display the tasks that are added to the list
- Text controls to accept the task details and their corresponding time slots
- HTML buttons to add and delete tasks from the list

Table 13.2 lists the HTML tags to be used for designing the user interface.

Table 13.2 The Elements of the User Interface

INPUT FIELD	SPECIFICATIONS
Bank's name and logo	`<%@include file="Header.html"%>`
Table to display added tasks	`<table border=0 cellspacing=2 cellpadding=5 width=400>`
	`<th><font  size="4">Task to do</th>`
	`<th><font  size="4">Time</th>`
Controls to accept the task details and time slots	`<input type="text">`
HTML buttons to add and delete tasks	`<input type="submit" value=" Add to List " name="AddValue">`
	`<input type="submit" value="Delete from List" name="DeleteValue">`

The code for the HTML page is as follows:

```html
<!doctype html public "-//w3c/dtd HTML 4.0//en">
<html>
<head>
<title>Session Servlet</title>
</head>

<body bgcolor="#FFDFD7">

<font  size="4">
<p><b>In-house to-do list for executives</b></font></p>

<center>
<table border=1 cellspacing=2 cellpadding=5 width=400 >
<th colspan=2><font  size="4">Entries for the to-do list<br>
</th>
<tr>
<td><B><font  size="4">Task</B></td>
<td><B><font  size="4">Time</B></td>
</tr>

</table>
</center>
<p>

<form method="post" name="SessionServlet" action="Sessions3.jsp">

<center>
<table border=0 cellspacing=2 cellpadding=5 width=400>
<th><font  size="4">Task to do</th>
<th><font  size="4">Time</th>
<tr>

<td><input type="text" name="NameField"></td>
<td><input type="text" name="ValueField"></td>
</tr>
<tr>
<td colspan=2 align=center><input type="submit" value=" Add to List "
name="AddValue"></td>
</tr>
<tr>
<td colspan=2 align=center><input type="submit" value="Delete from List"
name="DeleteValue"></td>
</tr>
</table>
```

```
</center>

</form>

</body>
</html>
```

Figure 13.6 displays the output of the home page in its current state.

Identify the JSP Tags to Be Included in Order to Display the Entries for the List

When a user interacts with a JSP page, a unique session ID is assigned to the user. The session object and session ID are stored as a cookie on the client computer. When a user navigates from one page to another, the server stores and retrieves the data related to the user interaction on previous pages from the session object. The methods of the `HttpSession` interface are used to store and retrieve data from the session object. Table 13.3 lists the methods of the `HttpSession` interface.

You can access the value stored in the session object by using the `getSession()` method of the `HttpServletRequest` interface. The `HttpServletRequest` interface contains methods to access the session information from session objects. Table 13.4 lists the methods of the `HttpServletRequest` interface.

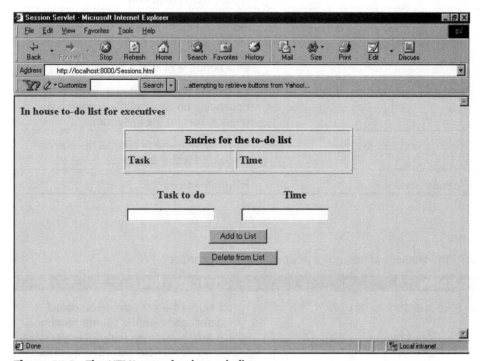

Figure 13.6 The HTML page for the to-do list.

Table 13.3 The Methods of the `HttpSession` Interface

METHOD NAME	USED TO...
`Object getAttribute()`	Return the object bound to the string in the parameter.
`void setAttribute()`	Bind the object in the parameter to the string that is specified in the parameter.
`void removeAttribute()`	Unbind the object in the parameter to the string that is specified in the parameter.
`Enumeration getAttributeNames()`	Return the names of all attributes in the session.
`long getCreationTime()`	Return the time when the session was created. The time value is returned in milliseconds from January 1, 1970.
`long getLastAccessedTime()`	Return the time when the session was last accessed. The time value is returned in milliseconds from January 1, 1970.
`int getMaxInactiveInterval()`	Retrieve the maximum time for which a session can remain active when there is no user intervention. After the time period is over, the session ends.
`void setMaxInactiveInterval()`	Specify the maximum time for which a session can remain active when there is no user interaction. After the maximum time period is over, the session ends.
`boolean isNew()`	Return the Boolean value, True or False, depending on whether the session has been started for the first time.
`void invalidate()`	End a session and unbind all the objects associated with a session.
`String getId()`	Return the session ID.

Table 13.4 The Methods of the `HttpServletRequest` Interface

METHOD NAME	DESCRIPTION
`HttpSession getSession()`	Returns the `HttpSession` object associated with the current session. A new session is created if any session does not already exist. The method returns an object of `HttpSession` class.

METHOD NAME	DESCRIPTION
`HttpSession getSession(boolean)`	Returns the `HttpSession` object associated with the current session. A new session is created if any session does not already exist; however, a session is created only if `TRUE` is passed as a parameter to the method. The method returns an object of `HttpSession` class.
`String getRequestSessionId()`	Returns the session ID of the current session. The return type of `getRequestSessionId()` is `String`.
`boolean isRequestedSession-IdValid()`	Identifies whether the session ID is still valid. If the session ID is valid, `True` value is returned; otherwise, `False` is returned.
`boolean isRequestedSessionId-FromCookie()`	Identifies if the session ID came from a cookie. The method returns `True` value if the session ID comes from a cookie; otherwise, `False` is returned.
`boolean isRequestedSession-IdFromURL()`	Identifies if the session ID came from an encoded URL. The method returns `True` value if the session ID comes from an encoded URL; otherwise, `False` is returned.

Let's look at an example of session tracking by using session objects:

```
<!--SessionName.jsp-->
<body>
<form method="post" action="SaveName.jsp">
Your name please?
<input type="text" name="user">
Your mail-id please?
<input type="text" name="mail">
Your mode of payment:</b>
<b>Credit
Card</b></font>
<input type="radio" value="Credit Card" checked
name="ModeOfPayment">  <font size="3"><b>Payment
on Delivery</b></font>
<input type="radio" value="Payment on Delivery" name="ModeOfPayment">
</p>
<p align="left"><font color="#cc3300" size="3"><b>
If mode of payment selected is
Credit Card, please provide details about card Type:</b></font></p>
<p align="left"><b><font size="3"><b>Master
Card</b></font> <input type="radio" value="Master Card" name="CardType">
```

```html
<font size="3"><b>Visa
Card</b></font>  <input type="radio" value="Visa Card"
name="CardType"></p>
<p align="left"><b><font size="3"><b>Not Applicable</b></font> <input
type="radio" value="Not applicable" name="CardType">
<p><input type="submit"></p>
</form>
</body>
</html>

<!--SaveName.jsp-->
<html>
<body>
<%
String name = request.getParameter("user");
String mailid = request.getParameter("mail");
String mode = request.getParameter("ModeOfPayment");
String card = request.getParameter("CardType");
session.setAttribute("yourName", name);
session.setAttribute("yourMail", mailid);
session.setAttribute("yourModeOfPayment", mode);
session.setAttribute("yourCardType",card);
%>
<a href="NextPage.jsp">View next page</a>
</body>
</html>

<!--NextPage.jsp-->
<html>
<body>
Hi ! <%= session.getAttribute("yourName") %>
<br>
Your mail id is:  <%= session.getAttribute("yourMail") %>
<br>
Your mode of payment is:  <%= session.getAttribute("yourModeOfPayment")
%>
<br>
Your card type is:  <%= session.getAttribute("yourCardType") %>
</body>
</html>
```

The code containing the JSP elements is as follows:

```jsp
<%--The include directive is used here to add the elements of the file
Header.html to the login page--%>
<%@ include file="Header.html" %>
<p><b>In house to-do list for executives</b></font></p>
<%!
  HttpSession session;
%>

<%
  session = request.getSession(true);
```

```
  if (request.getParameter("AddValue") != null) {
    session.putValue( request.getParameter("NameField"),
                      request.getParameter("ValueField"));
  } else if (request.getParameter("DeleteValue") != null) {
    session.removeValue(request.getParameter("NameField"));
  }

%>
<%
  String[] sessionNames = session.getValueNames();
  if (sessionNames != null) {
    for (int index = 0; index < sessionNames.length; index++) {
%>

<tr>
<td><%= sessionNames[index] %></td>
<td><%= session.getValue(sessionNames[index]) %></td>
</tr>

<%
    }
  }
%>
```

Write the Code for the JSP Page

The code for the user interface to accept customer-specific inputs is as follows:

```
<!doctype html public "-//w3c/dtd HTML 4.0//en">
<html>
<head>
<title>Session Example</title>
</head>

<body bgcolor="#FFDFD7">

<%--The include directive is used here to add the elements of the file
Header.html to the login page--%>
<%@ include file="Header.html" %>
<font color="#0033CC" size="4">
<p><b>In-house to-do list for executives</b></font></p>

<%!
  HttpSession session;
%>

<%
  session = request.getSession(true);

  if (request.getParameter("AddValue") != null) {
    session.putValue( request.getParameter("NameField"),
                      request.getParameter("ValueField"));
```

```
      } else if (request.getParameter("DeleteValue") != null) {
        session.removeValue(request.getParameter("NameField"));
      }

%>
<center>
<table border=1 cellspacing=2 cellpadding=5 width=400 >
<th colspan=2><font color="#0033CC" size="4">Entries for the to-do
list<br>

</th>
<tr>
<td><B><font color="#0033CC" size="4">Task</B></td>
<td><B><font color="#0033CC" size="4">Time</B></td>
</tr>

<%
  String[] sessionNames = session.getValueNames();
  if (sessionNames != null) {
    for (int index = 0; index < sessionNames.length; index++) {
%>

<tr><font color="#0033CC" size="4">
<td><font color="#0033CC" size="4"><%= sessionNames[index] %></td>
<td><font color="#0033CC" size="4"><%=
session.getValue(sessionNames[index]) %></td>
</tr>

<%
    }
  }
%>

</table>
</center>
<p>

<form method="post" name="SessionServlet" action="Sessions3.jsp">
<center>
<table border=0 cellspacing=2 cellpadding=5 width=400>
<th><font color="#0033CC" size="4">Task to do</th>
<th><font color="#0033CC" size="4">Time</th>
<tr>
<td><input type="text" name="NameField"></td>
<td><input type="text" name="ValueField"></td>
</tr>

<tr>
<td colspan=2 align=center><input type="submit" value=" Add to List "
name="AddValue"></td>
</tr>
<tr>
```

```
<td colspan=2 align=center><input type="submit" value="Delete from List"
name="DeleteValue"></td>
</tr>
</table>
</center>

</form>

</body>
</html>
```

View the JSP Page

To view the JSP page, do the following:

1. Save the JSP file as **Sessions.jsp**.

2. Copy the JSP file in the **C:/j2sdkee1.2.1/public_html** directory.

3. Initiate the server startup in verbose mode.

4. In the Internet Explorer address, type the location of the JSP file as **http://localhost:8000/filename.jsp** where the filename denotes the name of the JSP file.

5. Add and delete values in the two text controls to specify professional engagements for the day. Note the subsequent addition and deletion of the tasks from the session.

Figure 13.7 displays the sample output of the page after addition of some tasks. Figure 13.8 displays the sample output of the page after the deletion of a task.

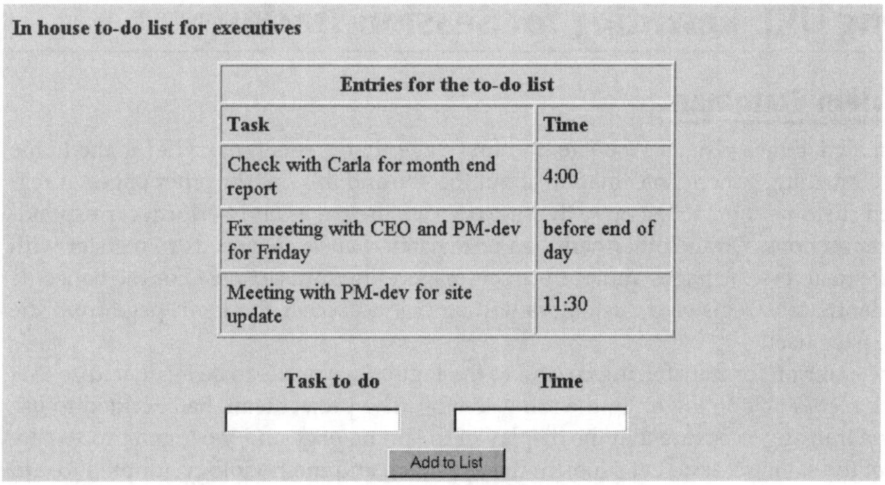

In house to-do list for executives

Entries for the to-do list	
Task	**Time**
Check with Carla for month end report	4:00
Fix meeting with CEO and PM-dev for Friday	before end of day
Meeting with PM-dev for site update	11:30

Task to do   **Time**

[   ]   [   ]

[Add to List]

Figure 13.7 The sample screen output after the addition of tasks.

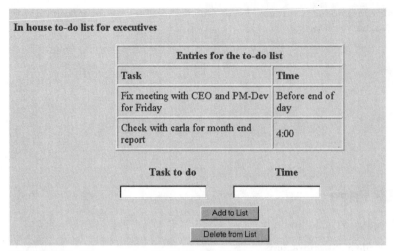

Figure 13.8 The screen output after the deletion of a task.

For a login page, the values of the form controls are lost after a page is refreshed. For the preceding task, though, you'll observe that the values for the tasks are retained even after the page is refreshed. The values of the form controls are stored in session objects and so are automatically retrieved for a session, lost only after the browser is closed.

A third approach used to track sessions is using URL rewriting. In URL rewriting, information about a session is appended to the end of the URL of the JSP page. You can modify a URL to store the session ID and other session-related information.

Using URL Rewriting for Session Tracking

Problem Statement

When a customer visits a Web site, the first page that greets him or her is the home page containing generic information about the site and links to the other pages. A registered customer opts to log on to the site to access the pages and perform corresponding transactions. On the other hand, an unregistered customer needs to register with the site to access the pages and perform corresponding transactions. For the Banco de Glendanthi site, registered customers will be able to access the login page from the home page itself.

The criterion for transferring control to the login page needs to be evaluated so that a customer is able to log on in the same session. The project team has decided to use session tracking to ensure that the display of the home page and the logon process are part of the same session. Let's look at the approach and methodology adopted to add such functionality to the application.

Task List

✔ **Identify the HTML elements of the page.**

✔ **Identify the JSP tags to be included to ensure that the customer is able to log on in a single session.**

✔ **Write the code for the JSP page.**

✔ **View the JSP page.**

Identify the HTML Elements of the Page

The home page will be used to add a link to the login page so that a registered user is able to log on. Because we have already discussed the elements of the page earlier, let's simply revisit the HTML code for the home page.

The code for the home page is as follows:

```
<html>

<head>

<title>Banco de Glendanthi</title>
</head>
<body bgcolor="#FFDFD7">
<table border="0" cellpadding="3" cellspacing="0" width="661"
height="540">
  <tr>
    <td align="center" width="1" height="57"></td>
    <td align="right" valign="top" width="216" height="57"></td>
    <td align="center" width="422" height="57"><font
size="1"><em><strong></strong></em></font><font color="#0000FF"
size="7">Banco
de Glendanthi</font><hr><hr></td>
  </tr>
  <tr>
    <td align="center" width="1" nowrap height="1"></td>
    <td align="right" valign="top" width="216" nowrap height="1"><font
size="2"></font></td>
    <td align="center" width="422" nowrap height="1"><font
size="1"><em><strong></strong></em></font></td>
  </tr>
  <tr>
    <td align="center" width="1" height="527"></td>
    <td align="right" valign="top" width="216" height="527">
      <p align="left">Banco de Glendanthi was
      established in 1975 with headquarters in New York. Today, under the
      chairmanship of Marty Bates, the bank has spread across the world
      and has
      its regional headquarters in London, Paris, Istanbul, Cairo, Kuala
      Lampur,
```

```
        and Singapore. Broadly, the bank specializes in the following
        three activities:
        regular deposits, loans, and credit. Customers can open different
        types of
        accounts, such as personal accounts, commercial accounts, and
        certificates of deposit accounts with the bank. Any person can
        avail of the loan facility by registering
        with the bank, provided certain prerequisites are fulfilled. A
        customer
        can choose from the commercial loan, consumer loan, or mortgage
        loan schemes. The bank also offers a credit card facility and has
        ATM (Any Time Money) centers in most of
        its business branches.
        <p> </td>
    <td align="center" width="422" height="527"><img border="0"
src="C:/j2sdkee1.2.1/public_html/7044.jpg" width="387" height="294"><br>
        <br>
      </td>
    </tr>
    <td height="1" width="1">
  </table>

  </body>

  </html>
```

Identify the JSP Tags to Be Included in Order to Display the Hit Count

URL rewriting is used when browsers do not support cookies or contain disabled cookies. The drawback of using the URL rewriting method is that any user can view the information with the URL. In addition, the amount of information that can be sent with the URL is limited to 2KB.

To track sessions by using URL rewriting, you need to use the response object methods. Table 13.5 lists the methods used along with response objects.

Table 13.5 The Methods Used with Response Objects

METHOD NAME	USED TO...
String encodeURL(String url)	Encode the URL by appending the session ID to the URL. Implementation of the encodeURL() method depends on the configuration of the Web browser and the settings for session tracking. For example, if the Web browser supports cookies or if session tracking is turned off, URL encoding is not required.

METHOD NAME	USED TO...
`String encodeRedirectURL(string url)`	Encode the URL that is passed as parameter to the method. The encoded URL is used in the `sendRedirect()` method. The implementation of this method depends on whether encoding of the session ID is required.
`void sendRedirect(string url)`	Send a redirect message to the clients using the URL that is passed as a parameter to the method.

The following code uses the session object to display the hit count for a particular Web page. In addition, the `response.encodeURL()` method is used to embed the URL of the same page in order to retain the session while accessing the page again.

The complete code for tracking sessions by using both a session object and URL rewriting is as follows:

UrlTxtEg.jsp

```
<html>
<body bgcolor="#FFDFD7">
<center><h3> An example using URL encoding</h3></center>
<%
    if (session.getAttribute("count") == null)
        session.setAttribute("count", new Integer(0));
    int count=((Integer) session.getAttribute("count")).intValue();

    switch (count) {
        case 0:
%> <center>This is the first time you have accessed this page.
</center><%
            break;
        case 1:
%> <center>You have accessed the page once before.</center><%
            break;
        default:
%> <center>You have accessed the page <%= count %> times
before.</center><%
            break;
    }

    session.setAttribute("count", new Integer(count+1));
%>

<center><font face="Book Antiqua" size="2"><P>
```

```
Click
<A HREF="<%= response.encodeURL("UrlTxtEg.jsp") %>">here</A>
to visit the page again.
</center>
</body>
</html>
```

Figure 13.9 displays the screen output on executing the preceding code for the first time.

Clicking on the link provided in the page can subsequently increase the count of visits to the same page. The URL of the page is embedded by using the encodeURL() method in order to maintain the session and increment the count according to the number of visits to the page. Figure 13.10 displays the screen output on clicking the link three times.

Let's now identify the JSP elements to be included in the code to add the URL of the login page to the home page. The JSP elements in the code will consist of the following methods and statements:

- The encodeURL() method will be used along with the response object to encode the URL containing a referral ID associating the user with the session.

- The session ID can be obtained by using the getRequestedsessionId() method along with the request object.

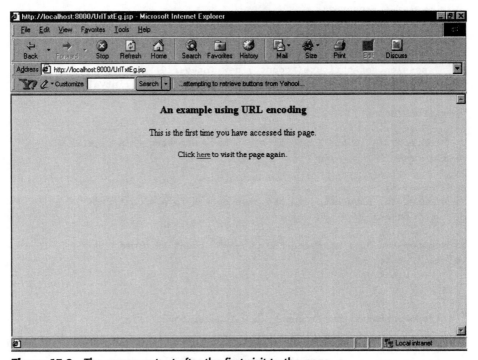

Figure 13.9 The screen output after the first visit to the page.

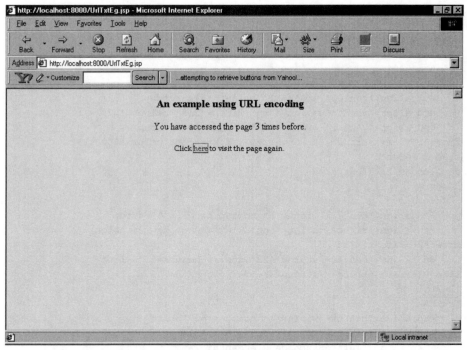

Figure 13.10 The screen output after visiting the page three times.

The code containing the JSP elements is as follows:

```
<%
String linkName = response.encodeURL("login.jsp");
String sessId = request.getRequestedSessionId();
%>
<a href = "<%= linkName %>"> Click here to Login</a>
<hr><center><%--The include directive is used here to add the elements
of the file Header.html to the login page--%>
<%@ include file="Copyright.html" %></center>
<center>
The session id is: <%= sessId %>
</center>
```

Write the Code for the JSP Page

The code for the user interface to accept customer-specific inputs is as follows:

```
<html>

<head>

<title>Banco de Glendanthi</title>
```

```
</head>

<body bgcolor="#FFDFD7">
<table border="0" cellpadding="3" cellspacing="0" width="661"
height="540">
  <tr>
    <td align="center" width="1" height="57"></td>
    <td align="right" valign="top" width="216" height="57"></td>
    <td align="center" width="422" height="57"><font
size="1"><em><strong></strong></em></font><font color="#0000FF"
size="7">Banco
de Glendanthi</font></td>
  </tr>
  <tr>
    <td align="center" width="1" nowrap height="1"></td>
    <td align="right" valign="top" width="216" nowrap height="1"><font
size="2"></font></td>
    <td align="center" width="422" nowrap height="1"><font
size="1"><em><strong></strong></em></font></td>
  </tr>
  <tr>
    <td align="center" width="1" height="527"></td>
    <td align="right" valign="top" width="216" height="527">
      <p align="left">Banco de Glendanthi was
      established in 1975 with headquarters in New York. Today, under the
      chairmanship of Marty Bates, the bank has spread across the world
      and has
      its regional headquarters in London, Paris, Istanbul, Cairo, Kuala
      Lampur,
      and Singapore. Broadly, the bank specializes in the following
      three activities:
      regular deposits, loans, and credit. Customers can open different
      types of
      accounts, such as current accounts, savings accounts, and credit
      accounts,
      with the bank. Any person can avail of the loan facility by
      registering
      with the bank, provided certain prerequisites are fulfilled. A
      customer
      can choose from the personal loan, car loan, housing loan, or
      business
      loan schemes. The bank also offers a credit card facility and has
      ATM (Any Time Money) centers in most of
      its business branches.
      <p> </td>
    <td align="center" width="422" height="527"><br>
      <img border="0" src="file:///C:/j2sdkee1.2.1/public_html/7044.jpg"
```

```
width="387" height="294">
    </td>
  </tr>
  <td height="1" width="1">
</table>

<%
String linkName = response.encodeURL("login.jsp");
String sessId = request.getRequestedSessionId();
%>
<a href = "<%= linkName %>"> Click here to Login</a>
<hr><center><%--The include directive is used here to add the elements
of the file Header.html to the login page--%>
<%@ include file="Copyright.html" %></center>
<center>
The session id is: <%= sessId %>
</center>
</body>
</html>
```

View the JSP Page

To view the JSP page, do the following:

1. Save the JSP file as **UrlEg.jsp**.
2. Copy the JSP file in the **C:/j2sdkee1.2.1/public_html directory**.
3. Initiate the server startup in verbose mode.
4. In the Internet Explorer address, type the location of the JSP file as **http://localhost:8000/filename.jsp** where the filename denotes the name of the JSP file.

Figure 13.11 displays a section of the screen output containing the session ID and a link to the login page.

> **NOTE** After clicking the link to the login page, you can follow the steps for validating the user login by referring to the steps of Chapter 11, "Building JDBC Applications."

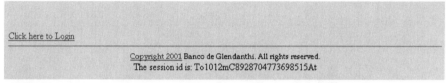

Figure 13.11 A section of the screen output containing the session ID and link.

Summary

The concepts discussed in this chapter dealt with the various approaches adopted to maintain a stateful interaction between the browser and the Web server. We used scenario-based examples to implement session tracking in the following ways:

- Cookies were used to create a hit count displaying the previous date of access to the Banco de Glendanthi Web site.

- Session objects were used to create a to-do list for bank personnel so that they are able to record their tasks for the day.

- URL rewriting was used to embed the login page in the home page.

It is important to understand that the use of session tracking adds state to the otherwise stateless HTTP request-response cycle. As a result, all interactions between the client and the server can be stored and retrieved for further processing.

With the growing acceptance of XML as an extensible markup language for Web applications, integrating XML with JSP will no doubt prove to be an advantage. Both HTML and XML have descended from SGML and are hence quite similar. In the next chapter, we'll discuss how an XML document can be used as a template for the output while using Java code for the underlying business logic. The Java code can be either written directly within the JSP page or called externally from the page to generate the dynamic portions of the document.

CHAPTER 14

JSP and XML

OBJECTIVES:

In this chapter, you will learn to do the following:

- ✔ Identify the basic features of XML
- ✔ Identify the benefits of XML
- ✔ Identify the SAX API
- ✔ Use XML in JSP

Getting Started

In today's world of growing competition, the usability of Web applications becomes the most basic requirement for the applications to survive. You cannot afford to have a Web application that has poor or mediocre usability. For example, consider an e-commerce application with poor or mediocre usability whose shortcomings can be discovered even before a customer pays. In the current times of tough competition (a fact not to be forgotten), you'll find, not to your surprise, that your customer moves to a competitor's Web site, which is just a click away.

In addition to usability, two other major requirements for the success of Web applications are interoperability and the ability of applications to deliver dynamic content. Interoperability is required because you cannot assume that all your customers and business clients use the same hardware and software platforms. Your Web applications should be able to work with different hardware and software platforms. You cannot afford to lose your potential customers and business clients because of differences in system compatibility. For your applications to be compatible with various platforms, you can rely on Java, which is ideal for producing portable programs that can run on any platform.

In addition to meeting the requirement for portable programs, applications need to disperse data to customers and clients located across the globe. Again, you cannot assume that different customers and clients use the same hardware and software platform, which is undoubtedly an impractical assumption! To present data on varied platforms, the data must be presented in a standard format that is compatible with all hardware and software platforms. Therefore, in addition to portable applications, there is an equal need for portable data. The task of presenting data in a standardized format to make it portable across platforms may seem enormous at the moment. You will, however, appreciate the ease with which this has been made possible through the technology called *Extensible Markup Language (XML)*. XML is a markup language defined by the World Wide Web Consortium (W3C), and it provides a format for describing structured data.

The second major requirement for successful Web applications is their ability to deliver dynamic content. You cannot afford to present static data on your Web site when business data changes. Your Web site must give users updated data, which may consist of updated inventory stocks or product prices. Such dynamic Web sites can be created using JSP, which uses Java as the server-side scripting language.

When developing solutions for the Web, you cannot afford to ignore any of these requirements. The success of your applications will depend on how well you can meet the requirements of usability, interoperability, and dynamic content. A combination of JSP and XML can help you meet all these requirements and enable you to develop Web applications that can pose a challenge to your competitors. By default, JSP pages present dynamic content by using the HTML format; however, you can use JSP pages to present XML pages as well. Additionally, you can consume XML data in JSP pages. You can use JSP pages to generate dynamic content using the XML format and to consume XML data.

This chapter begins with a brief introduction to XML. You'll learn about the basic features and benefits of XML. The chapter then discusses the Simple API for XML (SAX), the API used to consume XML data in JSP pages. Then, you'll implement JSP pages to generate dynamic content using XML. In the later sections of the chapter, you'll implement the SAX API in your JSP pages for the bank site.

Introducing XML

XML, a markup language specified by W3C, is used to describe data, which is presented in a structured format and stored in XML documents. Structured data includes both content and the information indicating the role of the content. For example, the content used in a section header has a different meaning when it used in another part of the document—say, the section footer. To illustrate the meaning of the preceding sentence, consider the content that presents a customer name, which is used in the section header and in the section footer of a document. In the header, the customer name may be used to present a brief history of the customer; in the footer, the customer name may simply present an identifying tag for the document.

The vision of developing XML has made it the de facto language used to describe data on the Web. XML is also gaining ground as a medium to describe portable data. Today, most upcoming software products have built-in support for XML. Therefore, we can say without any exaggeration that the future of the Web lies in XML.

Like relational databases, XML documents store data. How is XML different from relational data? As already mentioned, XML is a markup language specified by W3C. How is XML similar to or different from other markup languages, such as HTML and SGML? These are the questions we'll address in the following sections.

XML versus Relational Databases

Relational databases are excellent tools to store and manipulate data. In addition to storing data in a normal form, which reduces redundancy, they provide many advantages. To enable the performance of multiple and frequent data updates without any failures, databases usually support transactions. Database transactions enable concurrency without the corruption of data. In addition to supporting transactions, relational databases have several other features, such as a rich query language, optimized indexes, and proven scalability. In spite of these features, there are enough reasons to use XML for storing data. Some of these are listed here:

- Using relational databases requires you to have a separate server, which often requires installing and supporting a database administrator. In contrast, using XML requires no overhead for an extra server.

- Relational databases require you to learn and use Structured Query Language (SQL) to convert data from the relational format to object structure and vice versa. On the other hand, you can access and edit XML data by using text editors.

- When transporting data from relational databases, which store data in the relational format, the data must be converted into a format understood by a specific platform. On the other hand, XML data is stored in a hierarchical manner as plain text, which can be understood across platforms.

XML versus HTML

Like Hypertext Markup Language (HTML), XML uses tags to describe data; however, you must understand a basic difference between the two languages. The primary focus of HTML is data presentation; the primary focus of XML is data description. HTML uses a predefined set of tags to present data. For example, the `<I>... </I>` tags are used to italicize the text enclosed within the tag. When this data is presented in a browser, the browser displays the text in the italic format without bothering about what the data is. Thus, the primary focus of HTML is to present data.

On the other hand, in XML, there is no provision for predefined tags. You use your own tags to describe data. For example, to describe customer data, you can use the `<CustomerID>` tag to include Customer IDs within this tag. Thus, unlike HTML, the primary focus of XML is to define the structure of data.

To understand the demarcation between HTML and XML more clearly, let's look at the following example. Create an HTML file named Customers.html in Notepad to present customer details:

```
<HTML>
<HEAD> <TITLE> Customer Details </TITLE> </HEAD>
<BODY>
<OL>
    <LI> <I> Customer ID: </I> C001  <I> Customer Name : </I> Nancy
Brown </LI>
    <LI> <I> Customer ID: </I> C002  <I> Customer Name : </I> Mike Greg
</LI>
</OL>
</BODY>
</HTML>
```

When you open this HTML file in a browser, the output is displayed as shown in Figure 14.1.

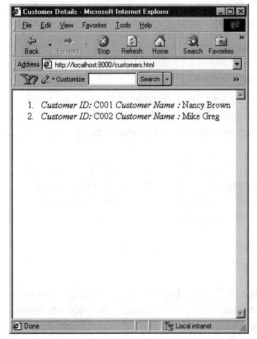

Figure 14.1 An HTML document in a browser.

Next, create an XML file named Customers.xml in Notepad to describe customer details as shown in the preceding code. Following is the XML code to describe customer details:

```xml
<?xml version="1.0"?>
<Customers>
    <Customer>
        <ID> C001 </ID>
        <LastName> Brown </LastName>
        <FirstName> Nancy </FirstName>
    </Customer>
    <Customer>
        <ID> C002 </ID>
        <LastName> Greg </LastName>
        <FirstName> Mike </FirstName>
    </Customer>
</Customers>
```

The first statement in the preceding code is called the *XML prolog*, which indicates that the document is an XML document. When you open this document in a browser, the output is displayed as shown in Figure 14.2.

As you can see in the figure, the entire data is displayed in a hierarchical manner in the form of a tree. The tags that contain other tags, also called child tags, can be expanded or collapsed.

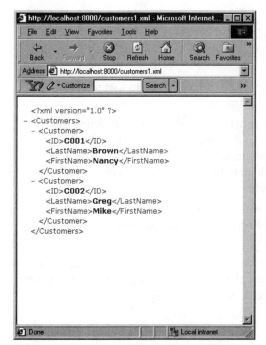

Figure 14.2 An XML document in a browser.

XML versus SGML

Standard Generalized Markup Language (SGML) is a powerful meta language that was designed by W3C to define other markup languages. HTML and XML both origi-nated from SGML; however, SGML is very large and complex, making it overkill for use in common applications. Therefore, to bring SGML to the Web with the least com-plexity but with most of its strengths, W3C defined XML.

XML contains almost all the powerful features of SGML and trims down the com-plex features. It therefore finds more favor with programmers than SGML. XML is faster than SGML, and since its release in 1996, XML has been a tremendous success.

Let's now explore the basic rules to create XML documents and learn to use Docu-ment Type Definition (DTD) in the next couple of sections.

Basic Rules to Create XML Documents

Now that you are familiar with XML and the way XML documents look, you must know the basic rules to create XML documents. All XML documents that conform to these basic rules are called *well-formed XML documents*. The rules are listed here:

- XML documents consist of elements. An element is identified by opening and closing tags. All opening tags must be closed. For example, the tag `<Customer>` must be closed by the corresponding `</Customer>` tag.

- All empty tags must be closed using the "/" character before the closing angu-lar bracket of a tag. For example, the following code represents the use of an empty tag.

  ```
  <Image src = "Welcome.gif" />
  ```

- Tag names are case-sensitive. The tag `<Customer>` is not the same as the tag `<customer>`.

- An XML document must always have a single root element that resides at the top of the tree structure of the document.

- An element defined by a tag might contain several attributes defining the behavior of the element. For example, the Image element defined by the `<Image>` tag contains the `src` attribute, which defines the path of the image. The values of the attributes of an element must be enclosed within quotes, as demonstrated in the previous bullet.

- The names of XML tags must start with a letter or an underscore. Then, you can use any number of letters, numbers, underscores, periods, and hyphens. You cannot use spaces in tag names.

- All inner tags must be closed before closing an outer tag. For example, the fol-lowing XML code is incorrect because the `<Customer>` tag, which is the outer tag, is closed before closing the inner tag, `<FirstName>`:

  ```
  <Customer>
      <ID> C001 </ID>
  ```

```
    <LastName> Brown </LastName>
    <FirstName> Nancy </Customer>
</FirstName>
```

Document Type Definition

Consider the `Create Table` SQL statement in a relational database. The `Create Table` statement is used to define the structure of a table indicating the columns that can be included in the table, data types for different columns, whether a column can contain null values, and so on. In a similar manner, in XML, Document Type Definition (DTD) represents a set of rules that defines the structure of XML documents. DTD documents (DTDs) define the tags and attributes that can be used in XML documents. DTDs use .dtd as an extension.

DTDs work with XML documents to validate them. If XML documents conform to a DTD, the XML document is said to be valid, and no error is reported when parsing the document. A DTD defines an element by using the element type declaration as shown here:

```
<!ELEMENT Element_Name (#PCDATA|#CDATA|ANY)>
```

In the preceding syntax:

- `Element_Name` is the element to be used in the XML document.
- The following are the values used to specify the type of element:
    - `#PCDATA`   This value indicates that the text within the element will be parsed.
    - `#CDATA`   This value indicates that the parser will ignore the text within the element. This type is useful when the text contains special characters, such as <, which the parser might interpret as markup tags.
    - `ANY`   This value indicates that the element can contain any tag.

In addition to elements, a DTD can also define the attributes of an element by using an attribute list declaration as shown here:

```
<!ATTLIST Element_Name Attribute_Name Data_Type Default>
```

In the preceding syntax, the following are the values used to define the attributes:

- `Element_Name` is the name of the element whose attribute is defined.
- `Attribute_Name` is the name of the attribute being defined.
- `Data_Type` can be any one of the several data types. Some of these are listed here:
    - CDATA, which is primarily used to represent non markup character data of the document. An XML processor treats such character data as parsed data

represented in the DTD as #PCDATA or as unparsed data represented as CDATA.

- Enumerated, which is a list of values separated by vertical bars. The value of the attribute can then be any one of these values.
- ID, which creates a unique ID for the attribute. Programs that need to process the document use it most often.

- The Default option can be any of the following values:
  - #REQUIRED   Indicates that the attribute must be included when the element is used.
  - #IMPLIED   Indicates that the attribute is optional. If the attribute is not used, no default value is provided.
  - #FIXED   ndicates that the attribute is optional; however, if the attribute is not used, a default value is provided. The syntax is this:

    ```
    <!ATTLIST Element_Name Attribute_Name #FIXED "value">
    ```
  - value   Indicates a value as the default value.

Apart from attributes, DTDs can contain entity declaration statements. An entity is an alias for a block of text in a document. When you want to use this block of text, you can call the block with the entity name by using entity declaration. To understand the use of entities, consider XML documents pertaining to customers who use the same DTD. A quick way to use a customer address in all these documents is to keep the address at a central place. In case there is any change in the address, you simply need to modify the address at this central location, and the change is automatically reflected in all the documents where the entity has been referenced. An entity can occur within the document (called internal entity) or outside the document (called external entity). For example, the following statement is an entity declaration statement for a customer's address:

```
<!ENTITY Address "!825 Eighth Avenue Los Angeles CA"
```

You can also use external entity declaration as follows:

```
<!ENTITY Address SYSTEM "Address.txt">
```

To enable XML documents to process outside information, you can use notation declaration as follows:

```
<!NOTATION Not_Name SYSTEM "Not_File.exe">
```

NOTE Usually an external information source is non-XML information.

To understand how DTDs work, let's create a DTD called Customers.dtd that defines the structure of the XML document used for specifying the customer details:

```
<!ELEMENT Customers (Customer)+>
<!ELEMENT Customer (ID, LastName, FirstName)>
<!ELEMENT ID (#PCDATA)>
<!ELEMENT LastName (#PCDATA)>
<!ELEMENT FirstName (#PCDATA)>
```

Each of the preceding element declaration statements defines an element name and the type of content of that element. For example, the first statement specifies the `Customers` element and the type of content for this element as `(Customer)+`, which indicates that the `Customers` element can contain one or more `Customer` elements. Similarly, the `Customer` element can contain three elements: `ID`, `LastName`, and `FirstName`. All three elements can contain data that will be parsed by the parser, which is represented as `#PCDATA`. If the elements are supposed to contain data that will not be parsed, use `#CDATA`. If the elements can contain any content, use `ANY`.

Next, to use the preceding DTD with the XML document defining the customer data, use the following statement:

```
<!DOCTYPE Customers SYSTEM "Customers.DTD">
```

The preceding statement is the document type declaration. In this statement, the following is true:

- `Customers` is the name of the DTD. This name must be the root element (the first element) of the XML document.

- `SYSTEM "Customers.DTD"` instructs the processor to fetch the Customers.DTD file to validate the XML document.

The complete XML code of **Customers.xml** including the document type declaration statement is specified here:

```
<?xml version="1.0"?>
<!DOCTYPE Customers SYSTEM "Customers.DTD">
<Customers>
    <Customer>
        <ID> C001 </ID>
        <LastName> Brown </LastName>
        <FirstName> Nancy </FirstName>
    </Customer>
    <Customer>
        <ID> C002 </ID>
        <LastName> Greg </LastName>
        <FirstName> Mike </FirstName>
    </Customer>
</Customers>
```

The preceding code, when parsed, generates no error because the XML document conforms to the DTD specification.

Before we proceed to the next section, it is important to know that you do not need to create DTDs for your XML documents. Consider a situation where, apart from you, certain external users also need to use the structure used in your XML documents. These external users can identify the structure of XML documents by just glancing at the DTDs defined for them. Therefore, DTDs can be of immense help to people who need to identify the structure of XML documents.

XML Namespaces

You create XML documents by defining your own elements to describe data. Additionally, you can use elements from outside an XML document. When using several elements in an XML document, you might sometimes face a situation wherein the same element is being used more than once, leading to name collision. For example, to define customer data, you might unknowingly use the same element, <Name>, to qualify a customer name and a city name. This might lead to name collision. You can avoid this situation by using the XML namespaces recommended by W3C. *XML namespaces* are sets of unique element names that you can refer to in your XML documents so that element names are not repeated.

You declare XML namespaces by using the xmlns keyword. When declaring a namespace, you need to use a Uniform Resource Identifier (URI) to identify the namespace. When you specify a namespace URI, the browser does not search the URI or the documents at the specified URI. The URI just serves as a unique identifier for tags from different vocabularies. For example, you can use the following code to declare a namespace that is a collection of all the elements related to a customer address:

```
xmlns:CustomerAddress="http://www.CustAddress.com/ca"
```

To use elements from the collection of elements specified in the namespace, you must prefix the elements with the alias CustomerAddress:

```
<CustomerAddress: Name>
```

XML Schemas

When using XML documents for data interchange across organizations, consistency among documents is one major concern. To create consistent XML documents, you need to follow a set of well-defined rules for elements, attributes, and data types. These well-defined rules that are shared among XML documents are called *XML schemas*. XML schemas can be used to check the validity of well-formed XML documents. Because XML schemas ensure consistency among XML documents, organizations can use them as a contract to exchange data between different applications. XML schema documents use the .xsd extension.

XML schemas might seem similar to DTDs. Actually, XML schemas are similar to DTDs, but they offer certain advantages over DTDs:

- When specifying elements in DTDs, you can specify whether the elements can be empty or contain character data or other elements. In XML schemas, you can specify the data type of an element as integer, float, or string.

- DTDs use their own syntax whereas XML schemas use XML syntax. Therefore, you do not need to learn any new syntax to create XML schemas.

XML schemas are recommended by W3C to define the elements, attributes, and data types to be used in XML documents. XML schema documents start with <schema> as the root element. To use the schema specification recommended by W3C, XML schema documents must contain the http://www.w3.org/2001/XMLSchema namespace. To understand this better, create an XML schema document named Customers.xsd for the Customers.xml document:

```
<?xml version="1.0" encoding="utf-8" ?>
<xsd:schema
    xmlns:xsd="http://www.w3.org/2001/XMLSchema">

</xsd:schema>
```

Within the schema, you can define elements, attributes, and data types. To define elements, you use the <xsd:element> tag. With this tag, you can specify several attributes to qualify the element being defined. Some of these attributes are listed here:

name.   The name of the element being defined.

type.   The data type of the element being defined.

minOccurs.   The minimum number of occurrences of the element. To make the element an optional element, set this attribute to 0.

maxOccurs.   The maximum number of occurrences of the element. Set this attribute to unbound if there is no limit on the number of occurrences of the element.

To define attributes, use the <xsd:attribute> tag. Some of the attributes that you can use to further qualify an attribute of an element are listed here.

name.   The name of the attribute.

type.   The data type of the attribute.

use.   The way the attribute should be used with the element in XML documents. This attribute can take one the following values:

- default   Indicates that the attribute takes a default value in case the attribute is not specified.

- fixed   Indicates that the attribute takes a fixed value.

- optional   Indicates that the attribute is optional and can take any value.

- prohibited   Indicates that the attribute cannot be used.

- required   Indicates that the attribute must be used with the element.

value.   The value that the attribute can take. This can be the default or fixed value, depending on the use of the property.

When you define elements or attributes, you also specify their data types. An element or an attribute can take built-in data types, such as integer, float, and string, specified by W3C. Additionally, you can use the complexType data type to define user-defined data types that can include other elements and attributes.

To understand how XML schemas are created and used, create the following XML schema document named Customers.xsd for the Customers.xml document:

```
<?xml version="1.0" encoding="utf-8" ?>
<xsd:schema xmlns:xsd="http://www.w3.org/2001/XMLSchema">
    <xsd:element name="Customers" type="CustomerInfo" />
      <xsd:complexType name="CustomerInfo">
          <xsd:sequence>
             <xsd:element name="Customer" type="Details" minOccurs="0"
maxOccurs="unbounded" />
          </xsd:sequence>
      </xsd:complexType>
      <xsd:complexType name="Details">
          <xsd:sequence>
             <xsd:element name="ID" type="xsd:string" />
             <xsd:element name="LastName" type="xsd:string" />
             <xsd:element name="FirstName" type="xsd:string" />
          </xsd:sequence>
      </xsd:complexType>
</xsd:schema>
```

The values for the various elements in the preceding code are as follows:

- <xsd:element> defines the element Customers with the type CustomerInfo, which is a user-defined data type.

- <xsd:complexType name = "CustomerInfo"> defines the CustomerInfo type. Notice that the elements included in this data type are included within the <xsd:sequence> element.

- In the element definition for ID, LastName, and FirstName, the data type has been specified as xsd:string, indicating that these elements can take only string values.

Extensible Stylesheet Language Transformations (XSL/T)

The basic purpose of XML is to describe data instead of presenting data. To present XML data, W3C has specified the use of Extensible Stylesheet Language Transformations (XSL/T) language. This styling has an advantage because you can apply different styles to the same XML data depending on the audience for the data. XSL/T is XML based and presents XML data in the HTML format. XSL/T files use either the .xsl or the .xslt extension.

When you want a set of rules to be used to process a list of source nodes (elements in an XML document), you can use the xsl:template element. For example, to specify a set of rules for all elements within the root element of an XML, use the match attribute as follows:

```
<xsl:template match="/">
```

To specify a set of style rules for each occurrence of an element, use the <xsl:for-each> tag. The select attribute is used to specify the element as follows:

```
<xsl:for-each select = 'Customers/Customer'>
```

In the preceding code, Customers/Customer is used to specify the Customer element within the Customers element.

To substitute the text value of an element in an XML document, use the <xsl:value-of> tag as follows:

```
<xsl:value-of select = 'ID'>
```

To understand XSL/T better, create the XSL/T document named Customers.xslt for the Customers.xml document as follows:

```
<xsl:stylesheet version="1.0"
xmlns:xsl="http://www.w3.org/1999/XSL/Transform"
xmlns="http://www.w3.org/TR/xhtml1/strict">
<xsl:output method="xml" encoding="iso-8859-1" />
<xsl:template match="/">
    <OL>
        <xsl:for-each select='Customers/Customer'>
            <LI>
                <b>
                    Customer ID :
                    <xsl:value-of select='ID' /> <br />
                </b>
                Last Name :
                    <xsl:value-of select='LastName' /> <br />
                First Name :
                    <xsl:value-of select='FirstName' /> <br />
                <hr />
            </LI>
        </xsl:for-each>
    </OL>
</xsl:template>
</xsl:stylesheet>
```

The definitions for the various elements in the preceding code are as follows:

- The XSL/T document begins with the <xsl:stylesheet> element. The XSL/T namespaces (specified by W3C) are also specified with this element.

- `<xsl:output method="xml" encoding="iso-8859-1" />` specifies the method and encoding for the stylesheet.

- `<xsl:template match="/">` specifies that the template specifies rules for all the elements or nodes within the root element of the XML document. Notice that within this template, HTML tags are used for formatting.

- `<xsl:for-each select='Customers/Customer'>` specifies that the rules specified within this tag apply for each occurrence of the Customer element, which exists with the Customers element.

Benefits of XML

Now that you know the basics of XML, let's identify its benefits.

Plain-text format.   XML data is stored in text files that are easy to read and edit. You can use any text editor or visual development editor to read and modify XML data.

Data description.   As already mentioned, XML focuses on describing data rather than presenting data. Because XML data is identified and broken down into different parts through several markup tags, different parts of XML data can be used in different ways by different applications. For example, data defined by an XML document can be processed by an email program, by a search program to identify a particular person to which a message has been sent, and by an address book to extract address information from the rest of a message.

Easy processing.   For XML data to be read by XML parsers, the XML document must be well formed. Recollect that a well-formed XML document is one that conforms to the basic rules to creating XML documents. These restrictions lead XML to have regular and consistent tags, which, in turn, allow XML data to be easily processed. Because XML is vendor neutral, you can choose any of the available XML parsers.

Hierarchical format.   XML data is arranged in a hierarchical manner, which is easy to rearrange and quickly accessible. The accessibility is faster because you can track down the element you want just as you do in a table of contents. Because each element is delimited it is easy to rearrange.

Extensibility.   Because XML defines its own tags to describe data, XML can be used to create its own markup languages. For example, Wireless Markup Language (WML) has originated from XML.

The combination of XML and JSP is great simply for the reason that this combination uses the strengths of XML (portable data) and JSP (portable programs that generate dynamic content). You can use XML in JSP pages in one of two ways:

- To generate dynamic content in the XML format
- To consume XML data

Let's first use the Banco de Glendanthi scenario to understand how XML is used in a JSP page to generate dynamic content.

As already mentioned, JSP is typically used to generate dynamic content by using the HTML format. You can also use JSP to generate dynamic content by using the XML format, which is considered to be the future of the Web. Recollect from Chapter 2, "Introducing Java Server Pages," that in the traditional model (using HTML), JSP pages are very much similar to HTML pages with some additional tags. These additional tags enable you to embed Java code in JSP pages. When a JSP page is requested, the Web application server preprocesses the page to extract all JSP tags and any embedded Java code, leaving behind only HTML. The JSP tags and the embedded Java code are used to build a Java servlet. The Java servlet then runs on the server, and the result is inserted back to the original place in the JSP page where the JSP tags were used. Finally, the result is pure HTML.

The same principal applies to the JSP pages that generate XML pages. Before an XML page is displayed in a browser, all JSP tags and embedded Java code are extracted by a Web application server to build a Java servlet, which runs on the server and then inserts the results back to the original place in the JSP page where the JSP tags were used. Finally, the result is pure XML.

Generating Dynamic Content in the XML Format

Problem Statement

A faction of the technical team developing the application for Banco de Glendanthi is in favor of using the XML format for storing customer-related information so that the transfer of data is fast on the Web. The development team is already using JSP technology to create Web applications for the bank. As a result, the team can use XML to present customer information in the XML format using JSP. Bryan, the project manager of the team, has decided to use XML to generate information regarding the maturity dates of the various certificates of deposit accounts. Apart from static information, such as customer IDs and customer names, dynamic information, such as the date of maturity of a fixed deposit, needs to be generated using an XML format.

Task List

✔ **Identify the customer details to be included in the XML document.**

✔ **Identify the tags to be added to the XML document.**

✔ **Identify the JSP tag to be added to the document.**

✔ **Identify the Java code to be added to the document.**

✔ **Write the code for the XML document.**

✔ **Write the code for the JSP page.**

✔ **View the JSP page.**

Identify the Customer Details to Be Included in the XML Document

Customer information includes the following details:

- Personal details
  - ID
  - LastName
  - FirstName
- Deposit details
  - Document number for a fixed deposit
  - Date of a fixed deposit
  - Days for which the amount is deposited
- Date of maturity

Identify the Tags to Be Added to the XML Document

The customer details will be defined using XML tags at two levels. The personal details of a customer will be enclosed within <Personal> and </Personal> tags, and deposit details will be enclosed within <Deposit> and </Deposit> tags. Table 14.1 lists the broad-level XML tags to be used to define the customer details.

Table 14.2 lists the tags to be used within <Personal> and </Personal> tags to define a customer's personal details.

Table 14.1   The Broad-Level XML Tags Used to Define the Customer Details

XML TAGS	USED TO DEFINE...
<Customers>	Highest-level tag for the customer details
<Customer>	Second-level tag for defining the details of a customer
<Personal>	Personal details of the customer
<Deposit>	Details of the certificate of deposit

Table 14.2   The XML Tags Used to Define the Customer's Personal Details

XML TAGS	USED TO DEFINE...
<ID>	A unique identification number for a customer
<LastName>	The first name of a customer
<FirstName>	The last name of a customer

Table 14.3 The XML Tags Used to Define a Customer's Deposit Details

XML TAGS	USED TO DEFINE...
`<DocumentNumber>`	The number of a certificate of deposit
`<StartDate>`	The date of a deposit
`<Days>`	The number of days for a deposit
`<MaturityDate>`	The date a deposit matures

Table 14.3 lists the tags to be used within the `<Deposit>` and `</Deposit>` tags to define a customer's deposit details.

Identify the JSP Tag to Be Added to the Document

By default, a JSP compiler assumes that the page content is HTML. If you want the JSP page to display content in the XML format, you need to specify this in the page. To do this, you need to use the `Page` directive as follows:

```
<%@ page contentType="text/xml;charset=ISO-8859-1" %>
```

In XML documents, the XML version tag must be on the first line. Therefore, add the preceding `Page` directive after the XML version tag in the XML document. After adding the page directive to XML code, you'll need to save the document as a JSP page. The `Page` directive specification will be as follows:

```
<?xml version="1.0" encoding="ISO-8859-1" ?>
<%@ page contentType="text/xml;charset=ISO-8859-1" %>
```

Identify the Java Code to Be Added to the Document

Next, add Java code to the Customers.jsp page to add functionality. You can add Java code between the scriptlet tags (`<%...%>`) in the page.

In the Customers.jsp page, the date of maturity of the fixed deposit should be calculated automatically based on the date the fixed deposit is made and the number of days for which it is deposited. To implement this, you need to use the `Calendar` class of the `java.util` package. The `getInstance()` method of the `Calendar` class is used to create an instance of the `Calendar` class that sets the instance to the current date and time:

```
<% java.util.Calendar cal = java.util.Calendar.getInstance(); %>
```

The getInstance() method returns the Calendar object, and this object can be manipulated via the individual fields of the object. Some of the field names may include YEAR, MONTH, or DATE. The YEAR field represents the year of the date, the MONTH field represents the month of the date, and the DATE field represents the days of the date. The set() method of the Calendar class is used to set the fields to specific values. The set() method takes two arguments as follows:

```
set(field, value)
```

The add() method of the Calendar class is used to add a specific value to a field of the date. The syntax of the add() method is given here:

```
add(field, value)
```

For each customer, you need to calculate the date of maturity of a fixed deposit by adding days to the start date of the fixed deposit. To do this, you first need to set the date of the Calendar object to the start date of a fixed deposit. Second, you need to add the days for which the amount is deposited to the Calendar object. Finally, you need to display the date (after calculation) in the Calendar object. The code for calculating the date of maturity of a fixed deposit is given here:

```
cal.set(java.util.Calendar.YEAR, 2001);
cal.set(java.util.Calendar.MONTH, java.util.Calendar.DECEMBER);
cal.set(java.util.Calendar.DATE, 12);
cal.add(java.util.Calendar.DATE, 91);
out.print(cal.getTime().toString());
```

Write the Code for the XML Document

To store the customer information, create the XML document called Customers.xml. Initially, the document will contain static details for only two customers. The code for the XML document is given here:

```
<?xml version="1.0" encoding="ISO-8859-1" ?>
<Customers>
 <Customer>
   <Personal>
       <ID> C001 </ID>
       <LastName> Brown </LastName>
       <FirstName> Nancy </FirstName>
   </Personal>
   <Deposit>
       <DocumentNumber> FD00025 </DocumentNumber>
       <StartDate> 12/12/2001 </StartDate>
       <Days> 91 </Days>
       <MaturityDate> 03/13/2002 </MaturityDate>
   </Deposit>
```

```
    </Customer>
    <Customer>
      <Personal>
           <ID> C002 </ID>
           <LastName> Greg </LastName>
           <FirstName> Mike </FirstName>
      </Personal>
      <Deposit>
           <DocumentNumber> FD00030 </DocumentNumber>
           <StartDate> 6/12/2001 </StartDate>
           <Days> 182 </Days>
           <MaturityDate> 12/20/2001 </MaturityDate>
      </Deposit>
    </Customer>
</Customers>
```

Write the Code for the JSP Page

The code for Customers.xml with the JSP-specific tags containing the Java code is given here:

```
<?xml version="1.0" encoding="ISO-8859-1"?>
<%@ page contentType="text/xml;charset=ISO-8859-1" %>
<% java.util.Calendar cal = java.util.Calendar.getInstance(); %>
<Customers>
 <Customer>
   <Personal>
        <ID> C001 </ID>
        <LastName> Brown </LastName>
        <FirstName> Nancy </FirstName>
   </Personal>
   <Deposit>
        <DocumentNumber> FD00025 </DocumentNumber>
        <StartDate> 12/12/2001 </StartDate>
        <Days> 91 </Days>
        <MaturityDate>
        <%
         cal.set(java.util.Calendar.YEAR, 2001);
         cal.set(java.util.Calendar.MONTH, java.util.Calendar.DECEMBER);
         cal.set(java.util.Calendar.DATE, 12);
         cal.add(java.util.Calendar.DATE, 91);
         out.print(cal.getTime().toString());
        %>
        </MaturityDate>
   </Deposit>
 </Customer>
 <Customer>
   <Personal>
```

```
        <ID> C002 </ID>
        <LastName> Greg </LastName>
        <FirstName> Mike </FirstName>
    </Personal>
    <Deposit>
        <DocumentNumber> FD00030 </DocumentNumber>
        <StartDate> 6/21/2001 </StartDate>
        <Days> 182 </Days>
    <MaturityDate>
     <%
      cal.set(java.util.Calendar.YEAR, 2001);
      cal.set(java.util.Calendar.MONTH, java.util.Calendar.JUNE);
      cal.set(java.util.Calendar.DATE, 21);
      cal.add(java.util.Calendar.DATE, 182);
      out.print(cal.getTime().toString());
     %>
    </MaturityDate>
    </Deposit>
    </Customer>
</Customers>
```

Rename the Customers.xml file as Customers.jsp so that the Web application server knows how to process the file.

View the JSP Page

To view the JSP page, do the following:

1. Copy Customers.jsp in the C:/j2sdkee1.2.1/public_html.

2. Start j2ee in verbose mode.

3. In the Internet Explorer address, type the location of the .jsp file as
   http://localhost:8000/Customers.jsp.

The output of the JSP page is displayed in the browser. For better readability, the output has been shown in two figures. Figure 14.3 displays the output for Nancy Brown, and Figure 14.4 displays the output for Mike Greg.

```
<?xml version="1.0" encoding="ISO-8859-1" ?>
- <Customers>
  - <Customer>
    - <Personal>
        <ID>C001</ID>
        <LastName>Brown</LastName>
        <FirstName>Nancy</FirstName>
      </Personal>
    - <Deposit>
        <DocumentNumber>FD00025</DocumentNumber>
        <StartDate>12/12/2001</StartDate>
        <Days>91</Days>
        <MaturityDate>Wed Mar 13 11:55:39 GMT+05:30 2002</MaturityDate>
      </Deposit>
    </Customer>
```

Figure 14.3 Nancy's record displaying dynamic content in XML.

```
- <Customer>
  - <Personal>
      <ID>C002</ID>
      <LastName>Greg</LastName>
      <FirstName>Mike</FirstName>
    </Personal>
  - <Deposit>
      <DocumentNumber>FD00030</DocumentNumber>
      <StartDate>6/21/2001</StartDate>
      <Days>182</Days>
      <MaturityDate>Thu Dec 20 11:55:39 GMT+05:30 2001</MaturityDate>
    </Deposit>
  </Customer>
</Customers>
```

Figure 14.4   Mike's record displaying dynamic content in XML.

That surely was exhilarating, wasn't it? The date of maturity of a particular deposit can actually be calculated within minutes. Let's now look at how XML data can be accessed using a JSP page.

APIs to Access XML Data

To use XML data in JSP pages, you need to convert XML elements to server-side objects. Then, you need to extract the properties of these server-side objects to JSP pages. The conversion of XML elements to server-side objects does not occur automatically. Instead, you need to manually create an XML parser to parse an XML document and encapsulate it in a JavaBean component.

To implement parsers, two application-programming interfaces (APIs) are available:

Document Object Model (DOM).   DOM is a tree-based API that maps a complete XML document to an internal tree in the memory. An application can then access different XML elements by navigating this tree.

Simple API for XML (SAX).   SAX is an event-based API that generates parsing events when parsing each element of an XML document. For example, a parsing event is generated when the parser starts with the document, reaches the beginning of an element, identifies character data, reaches the end of an element, or reaches the end of the document. The different events are reported directly to the application through callbacks. The application can access the XML data by handling different parsing events.

Therefore, these APIs enable your applications to use XML data. The question that arises now is why do two APIs exist in the first place. What is the need to have two APIs when their purpose is the same? As you know, DOM stores an entire document as a tree in the memory. Therefore, situations might arise in which the memory is reduced because of the large size of XML documents. In addition, using DOM to access XML elements is quite clumsy because you need to navigate the tree even if you want to access only a few XML elements. Figure 14.5 demonstrates DOM processing.

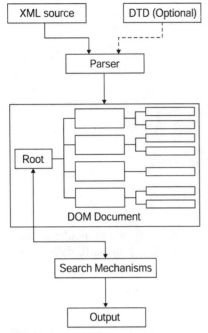

Figure 14.5   DOM processing.

The SAX API, being event based, does not create any internal tree in the memory. Therefore, the memory requirement does not depend on the size of XML documents. Instead, applications can handle parsing events and access the data there and then. This is also a convenient way to access data because it does not require you to navigate a tree. Figure 14.6 demonstrates the SAX processing.

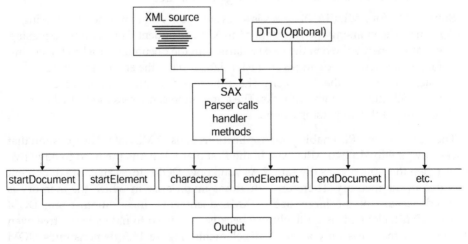

Figure 14.6   SAX processing.

Document Object Model

As already mentioned, DOM is a tree-based API that maps an entire XML document to a tree in memory. To represent XML documents, DOM specifies interfaces. These interfaces can be implemented in a programming language to process XML documents.

In DOM, you can visualize an entire XML document as the Document object consisting of several nodes—each node is a tree in itself. The node that contains several other nodes is called the parent node, and the nodes contained are called children nodes. Table 14.4 describes the different types of nodes in a DOM tree.

Table 14.4 Types of Nodes

NODE	DESCRIPTION	CAN CONTAIN
Document	Represents the entire XML document. The Document node is the root of an entire document.	Element (at most one), ProcessingInstruction, Comment, DocumentType
DocumentFragment	Is a minimal Document object and is used to extract a portion of a document tree or create a new fragment of a document.	Element, Processing-Instruction, Comment, Text, CDATASection, EntityReference
DocumentType	Provides an interface to the list of entities defined for a document. Each document has a doctype attribute that takes either a null value or a DocumentType object.	No children
EntityReference	Use this interface when the source document has an entity reference or when you want to insert an entity reference in the document.	Element, Processing-Instruction, Comment, Text, CDATASection, EntityReference
Element	Represents elements other than text within XML documents.	Element, Text, Comment, ProcessingInstruction, CDATASection, EntityReference
Atrr	Represents an attribute of an Element object.	Text, EntityReference

(continues)

Table 14.4 Types of Nodes *(Continued)*

NODE	DESCRIPTION	CAN CONTAIN
Processing-Instruction	Used to keep processor-specific information in a document.	No children
Comment	Represents the content within comment elements (within '`<!--`' and '`-->`').	No children
Text	Represents the textual content within the Element and Attrib objects.	No children
CDATASection	Escapes the blocks of text containing character data that is otherwise treated as markup.	No children
Entity	Represents a parsed or unparsed entity in the document.	Element, ProcessingInstruction, Comment, Text, CDATASection, EntityReference
Notation	Represents a notation declared in a DTD.	No children

Simple API for XML

As already mentioned, the SAX API is an event-based API used to create XML parsers. This API contains several classes and interfaces that enable you to create XML parsers and access XML data programmatically. SAX API interfaces are contained within the following packages:

org.xml.sax. This package contains the core SAX interfaces. Some of the classes, interfaces, and exceptions in this package are the following:

ContentHandler interface. This is the main interface that must be implemented in the application so that the application can receive notifications of the various parsing events. Then, the application must register the instance of the parser by using the setContentHandler method of the XMLReader interface. Otherwise, the application will silently ignore the parsing events in spite of receiving notifications.

DTDHandler interface. This interface must be implemented in the application if the application needs to receive notifications of DTD-related events. Then, the application must register the instance of the parser by using the setDTDHandler method of the XMLReader interface.

EntityResolver interface. This is the basic interface to implement customized handling for external entities in XML documents. In addition, the application is required to register an instance of the parser by using the `setEntityResolver` method of the `XMLReader` interface.

ErrorHandler interface. This is the basic interface to implement customized error handling. After the interface is implemented, the application must register the instance of the parser by using the `setErrorHandler` method of the `XMLReader` interface.

Locator interface. This interface is used when your application needs to associate SAX events with the document location. Then, the application needs to pass this instance to the `setDocumentLocator` method of the `ContentHandler` interface.

XMLReader interface. This interface must be implemented to read XML documents by using callbacks. The `parse()` method instructs the `XMLReader` instance to begin parsing an XML document from any valid input source.

InputSource class. The instance of this class encapsulates information regarding input source, which can include character stream, a binary stream, and a URI.

SAXParserException class. The instance of this class encapsulates information for locating an error in the original XML document.

org.xml.sax.ext. This package contains interfaces that conformant SAX drivers might not support.

org.xml.sax.helpers. This package contains helper classes that help bootstrapping SAX-based applications. The `DefaultHandler` class in this package implements `ContentHandler`, `DTDHandler`, `EntityResolver`, and `ErrorHandler` interfaces. Therefore, instead of these interfaces, you can use the `DefaultHandler` class in your application.

Consuming XML Data

Problem Statement

The customers of Banco de Glendanthi are growing rapidly in number. The bank is committed to providing customized online services to its customers. Therefore, the bank has switched to data storage in the XML format to ensure portability of data. The development team must develop an application that displays only the deposit details for customers. Because only deposit details are needed, you do not need to scroll through all the elements in the XML source document. Therefore, in this case, you simply need to display the data when the parser encounters the `Deposit` element. Therefore, instead of DOM, which will be cumbersome to use in this case, the development team uses the SAX API.

Task List

✔ **Identify interfaces, classes, and methods.**

✔ **Write the code to implement handlers.**

✔ **Test the code.**

✔ **Use the parser bean from a JSP page.**

✔ **View the JSP page.**

Identify Interfaces, Classes, and Methods

To display XML data from the **Customers.xml** document in a JSP page, you need to use the SAX API. This API provides several interfaces, classes, and methods that can be used to handle the events that are generated when the XML document is parsed. To implement this functionality, the following interfaces, classes, and methods are required:

The `DefaultHandler` class.   This class resides in the `org.xml.sax.helpers` package. This class implements many interfaces, including `ContentHandler`, `DTDHandler`, `EntityResolver`, and `ErrorHandler` interfaces. Therefore, instead of implementing these many interfaces separately, you simply need to inherit from the `DefaultHandler` class.

The `java.io.Serializable` interface.   It is a marker interface specifying that a particular class is serializable.

The `XMLReader` interface.   This interface resides in the `org.xml.sax` package. This interface must be implemented to read XML documents using callbacks. The `parse()` method instructs the `XMLReader` instance to begin parsing an XML document from any valid input source.

The `InputSource` class.   The instance of this class encapsulates information regarding an input source, which can include a character stream, a binary stream, and a URI.

Event handlers for parsing events.   These handlers include methods that must be implemented to perform the desired processing when specific parsing events are generated. Some of these event handlers are `startElement`, `characters`, and `endElement`.

Write the Code to Implement Handlers

Write the following code to implement handlers:

```
package saxbean;

import java.io.*;
import java.util.*;
```

```
import org.xml.sax.*;
import org.xml.sax.helpers.DefaultHandler;
import org.xml.sax.helpers.*;
import javax.xml.parsers.SAXParserFactory;
import javax.xml.parsers.SAXParser;

public class MyParserBean extends
DefaultHandler implements java.io.Serializable
{
    private String text;
    private Vector vector = new Vector();
    private MyElement current = null;

    public MyParserBean()
    {

    }
public Vector parse(String filename) throws
Exception
{
    SAXParserFactory spf = SAXParserFactory.newInstance();
    spf.setValidating(false);
    SAXParser saxParser = spf.newSAXParser();
    // create an XML reader
    XMLReader reader = saxParser.getXMLReader();
    FileReader file = new FileReader(filename);
    // set handler
    reader.setContentHandler(this);
    // call the parse method on an input source
    reader.parse(new InputSource(file));
    return vector;
}


// receive notification of the beginning of an element
public void startElement (String uri, String name, String qName,
Attributes atts)
{
    current = new MyElement(
    uri, name, qName, atts);
    vector.addElement(current);
    text = new String();
}

// receive notification of the end of an element
public void endElement (String uri, String name, String qName)
{
    if(current != null && text != null)
      { current.setValue(text.trim());
      }
      current = null;
```

```
    }
    // receive notification of character data
    public void characters (char ch[], int start, int length)
    {
        if(current != null && text != null)
        {
            String value = new String(ch, start, length);
            text += value;
        }
    }
}
```

Save the code as **MyParseBean.java**. After successfully compiling the code, write the following code to create the JavaBean named **MyElement.java**:

```
package saxbean;

import org.xml.sax.Attributes;

public class MyElement implements
java.io.Serializable
{
    String uri;
    String localName;
    String qName;
    String value=null;
    Attributes attributes;

    public MyElement(String uri, String localName, String qName,
Attributes attributes)
    {
        this.uri = uri;
        this.localName = localName;
        this.qName = qName;
        this.attributes = attributes;
    }

    public String getUri()
    {
        return uri;
    }

    public String getLocalName()
    {
        return localName;
    }

    public String getQname()
    {
        return qName;
    }
```

```
    public Attributes getAttributes()
    {
        return attributes;
    }

    public String getValue()
    {
        return value;
    }
    public void setValue(String value)
    {
        this.value = value;
    }
}
```

Compile the JavaBean and move to the next step to test the code.

Test the Code

Before implementing the JavaBean in a JSP page, it is recommended that you test the bean first. To test the bean from the command prompt, write the following code and save the file as **Test.java**:

```
import java.io.*;
import java.util.*;

public class Test
{
    public static void main(String argv[])
    {
        String file = new String(argv[0]);
        MyParserBean p = new MyParserBean();
        String str = null;
        try {
            Collection v = p.parse(file);
            Iterator it = v.iterator();
            while(it.hasNext())
              {
                MyElement element =
                (MyElement)it.next();
                String tag = element.getLocalName();

                if(tag.equals("ID"))
                {
                    System.out.println("ID:
                    " + element.getValue());
                } else if(tag.equals("DocumentNumber"))
                {
                    System.out.println("Document Number: "
                    +element.getValue());
                } else if (tag.equals("StartDate"))
```

```
          {
            System.out.println("Start Date: "
            +element.getValue());
          } else If (tag.equals("Days"))
          {
            System.out.println("Days: "
            +element.getValue());
          } else If (tag.equals("MaturityDate"))
          {
            System.out.println("Maturity Date: "
            +element.getValue());
          }
        }
      } catch (Exception e)
      {
      }
    }
  }
}
```

After successful compilation of the preceding code, run the code at the command prompt as follows:

```
java Test Customers.xml
```

Use the Parser Bean from a JSP Page

After successfully testing the parser, you need to use the parser in a JSP page. To do this, write the following code:

```
<html>
<head>
<title>sax parser</title>
<%@ page import="java.util.*" %>
<%@ page import="saxbean.*" %>
</head>

<body bgcolor="#FFDFD7">
<jsp:useBean id="saxparser" class="saxbean.MySAXParserBean" />

<%
Collection customers =
saxparser.parse("c:/j2sdkee1.2.1/public_html/Customers.xml");
Iterator ir = customers.iterator();
%>

<center>
<h3>Certificate of Deposit details</h3>
<table border="2" width="50%">
 <tr>
```

```
  <th>Customer ID</th>
  <th>Document Number</th>
  <th>Start Date</th>
  <th>Days</th>
  <th>Maturity Date</th>
</tr>
  <tr>

<%
while(ir.hasNext()) {
  MyElement element = (MyElement) ir.next();
  String tag = element.getLocalName();
  if(tag.equals("ID"))
  {
%>
    <td><%= element.getValue() %></td>
<% } else if (tag.equals("DocumentNumber")) { %>
    <td><%= element.getValue() %></td>
<% } else if (tag.equals("StartDate")) { %>
    <td><%= element.getValue() %></td>
<% } else if (tag.equals("Days")) { %>
    <td><%= element.getValue() %></td>
<% } else if (tag.equals("MaturityDate")){ %>
    <td><%= element.getValue() %>
</td>
</tr>
<tr>
  <% } %>
<% } %>

</body>
</html>
```

Save the file as **CustomersDeposit.jsp**.

NOTE When using the parser bean from a JSP page, you need to extract the
sax.org.xml package and set the class path again. The package is available in
the donj2ee folder under C:\j2sdkee1.2.1\lib\classes. You'll have to extract the
j2ee.jar file to a folder and set the class path to the folder containing these
packages.

View the JSP Page

To view the output of the **CustomersDeposit.jsp** page, you need to copy the file in the
public_html folder in the C:\j2sdkee1.2.1 directory. Then, start the server by typing
start j2ee - verbose at the Command prompt. Finally, open the browser window and
type **http://localhost:8000/CustomersDeposit.jsp** in the address bar to execute the JSP
code. Figure 14.7 displays the output of the CustomersDeposit.jsp page.

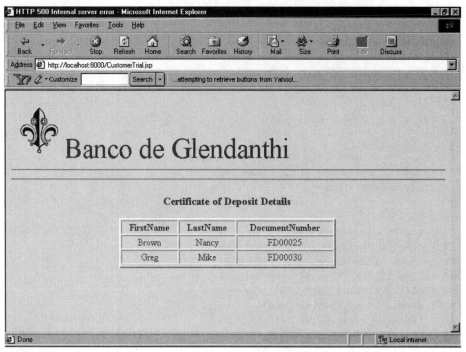

Figure 14.7 The output of the CustomersDeposit.jsp page.

Summary

In addition to portable applications, portable data is a major focus in the field of application development for the Web. JSP enables the development of portable applications to generate dynamic content. XML enables the presentation of portable data. Therefore, the combination of JSP and XML is certainly great. It enables you to develop Web applications that can pose immense challenges to your competitors.

In this chapter, we introduced you to XML. Although XML is too wide a topic to be covered in just one chapter, we discussed some of its basic features to help you understand its significance and applicability. Then, we talked about the usage of XML in JSP. We walked you through using XML and JSP together to generate dynamic content in the XML format. Also, we told you about the two APIs, Document Object Model (DOM) and Simple API for XML (SAX), which are used to consume XML data in JSP pages. Finally, we worked through an example to demonstrate how to consume XML data in JSP pages using the SAX API.

We have frequently restated the use of JSP in segregating the profiles of an author and a programmer. We have already discussed one of the methodologies, the useBean tag, used to implement this segregation. The next chapter discusses the use of custom tags for segregating the static and dynamic content of a JSP page.

CHAPTER

15

Developing Custom Tags

OBJECTIVES:

In this chapter, you will learn to do the following:

- ✔ Identify the need to for using custom tags
- ✔ Identify the various components of a tag library
- ✔ Create a tag handler to extract records from a database
- ✔ Use a custom tag to display the extracted database records

Getting Started

Although JSP has contributed to freeing designers from becoming involved in the intricacies of programming constructs, developers still need to be involved in writing lengthy and complex code. Generally, some sections of the code are repetitive and require rewriting. An ideal situation under such circumstances would be to use a technique or mechanism to encapsulate and simplify such tedious and recurring tasks.

Man is empowered with intellectual superiority and has forever been searching for innovative ways to simplify tasks. For example, today, we cannot imagine beginning a day without the aid of a coffee maker, a toaster, and other such appliances that automate and simplify household chores. Similarly, a task such as making multiple copies of documents was done manually before the invention of the copier.

Thankfully, the challenge to encapsulate recurrent tasks in JSP is met using JSP-specific tags such as the useBean tag and the custom tags. We have already discussed the useBean tag in Chapter 9, "JSP and JavaBeans." In this chapter, we'll look at the other mechanism that allows Java developers to encapsulate recurrent tasks by creating a library of customized, user-defined tags that can be mixed with both JSP and HTML tags. The tag library has proved a boon for the development of Web applications because programmers can now focus on data manipulation and retrieval while the designers focus on the presentation. Does the creation and implementation of this mechanism require additional skills? No! In fact, the only skill that you need to build a tag library is the ability to program a JSP page. You may recall the use of the JSP action element useBean that facilitates the reuse of existing beans. Custom tags also facilitate reusability, thereby increasing productivity. It is important to remember, though, that only JSP 1.1 supports custom tags.

This chapter discusses the importance and application of tag libraries. The chapter begins with an introduction to the application and use of custom tags. Next, we discuss the various components of the tag library. In the final section of the chapter, we apply the concepts by using a scenario-based example to create and implement custom tags in JSP.

Custom Tags

What exactly is the functionality of custom tags? Before learning about the functional scope of tags, let's first understand the definition, implementation, and structure of custom tags. Custom tags are user-defined tags that are very similar to XML tags and explicitly render information about the type of data they represent. These tags encapsulate reusable Java code that is implemented using an XML-based interface for the JSP page.

Custom tags are implemented in two ways. The first implementation directs the JSP engine to sequentially execute the various components of the tag library. To understand this mechanism, let's consider the simple example of a library. Been to a library and requested a book or video lately? Have you wondered how, from the never-ending rows of books or videos, within a very short time, the librarian or attendant is able to hand you the book or video you requested? The answer is the universally used catalog or indexed list in which the name of the book or video tape is associated with a number or easily distinguishable section of the library. In other words, the tedious task of physically searching for the book or video is made easier by using the catalog. In this case, the indexed catalog can be mapped to a custom tag in a JSP file that maps the name of the tag library to its executable components. As a result, on execution, the components associated with the specified tag are automatically and sequentially executed to display the required results. The details of the methodology used for implementation of custom tags are covered in the later sections of this chapter.

The second implementation of custom tags is its user-defined feature like XML. As a result, custom tags easily distinguish the encapsulated data. When defining custom tags, we have repeatedly used the terms "very similar to XML tags" or "like XML tags." You'll recollect the definition and use of Extensible Markup Language to create custom or user-defined tags. Considering the acceptance, presence, and support for HTML in defining tags, an inevitable query is the need to use a new tag definition system (similar to XML) for custom tags. Let's consider a simple example to appreciate the need for using the XML type of tag definition to identify custom tags in JSP despite the availability of HTML.

Need for XML

In Chapter 14, "JSP and XML," we discussed the ways in which XML can be integrated with the presentation content of a JSP page in a Web application. To highlight the advantages of using customized tags in JSP, consider the following example. We will use examples of both HTML and XML code to display customer information to draw attention to the preference in using XML-like tags for defining custom tags. The basic customer information records of an organization store data in the form of the details of the customer's personal information. The following code snippet illustrates the use of HTML tags to display the customer information:

```
<tr>
<td>Ms Anne Brown</td>
<td>9, Sunley House, Gunthorpe Street</td>
<td>London E1-7RW</td>
</tr>
```

The output appears as any textual data with no additional information about the type and importance of each section of the data input. In other words, the output generated using HTML is only presentation or display based, instead of being information based. As a result, by using predefined HTML tags, details about the type of data are lost. Figure 15.1 displays the presentation-centric display of customer details by using HTML tags.

Figure 15.1 The presentation-centric HTML output.

On the other hand, consider the same example written using user-defined XML tags. The following code snippet illustrates the use of XML tags to display the customer information:

```
<customerdetails>
<name>
<title>Ms</title>
<firstname>Anne</firstname>
<lastname>Brown</lastname>
</name>
<address>
<aptname>9, Sunley House</aptname>
<streetname>Gunthorpe Street</streetname >
<city>London</city >
<zip>E1-7RW</zip>
</address>
</customerdetails>
```

The specific use of personalized tags to define customer details presents the input data in a better format with an emphasis on the type of data. As a result, using specific tags such as firstname, lastname, street, and zip makes it comparatively easy to differentiate the data. Figure 15.2 displays the data-centric display of the customer details by using XML tags.

It is evident from the preceding figure that the tag <city>London</city> defines the enclosed data as that of the country of the customer. For that reason, although the presentation of this data is similar to that written in HTML, the code for XML is more data centered. The use of XML in defining custom tags thus facilitates the use of tag names that can be easily distinguished and added to a JSP page.

The following list summarizes the advantages of using XML-like tags for custom tag definitions:

Easy coding. Being similar to HTML, XML is easy to code except for the inclusion of custom tags.

Easy data interchange. Translating the contents of an XML document is easy due to the use of explicit customized tags. Therefore, data exchange occurs at different levels without the need to decode or interpret its structure.

```
- <XML>
  - <CUSTOMERDETAILS>
    - <NAME>
        <TITLE>Ms</TITLE>
        <FIRSTNAME>Anne</FIRSTNAME>
        <LASTNAME>Brown</LASTNAME>
      </NAME>
    - <ADDRESS>
        <APTNAME>9, Sunley House</APTNAME>
        <STREETNAME>Gunthorpe Street</STREETNAME>
        <CITY>London</CITY>
        <ZIP>E1-7RW</ZIP>
      </ADDRESS>
    </CUSTOMERDETAILS>
  </XML>
```

Figure 15.2 The data-centric XML output.

After learning about the need for a new tag definition for the custom tags and the advantages of their use, let's now look at the advantages of using a tag library before identifying its components.

Advantages of Tag Libraries

The advantage of using tag libraries has enhanced the choice of JSP as a primary server-side programming solution. The main advantages of using these libraries are easy maintenance of applications and high development speed. The tag libraries simplify the task of using, inserting, and debugging tag components. What are these advantages, and how have they helped JSP gain an edge over equivalent and similar server-side Web application development tools? To understand this, let's list the advantages of using tag libraries:

Portability. Tags can be used across projects because the packaging of tags as JAR or WAR files enables tags and the encapsulated Java code to be reused in any JSP project.

Maintainability. Web applications are better maintained using JSP custom tags for these reasons:

- The business logic of the application is located in separate Java files that can be easily updated. Therefore, changes to the business logic require updating of only one file instead of all the pages of the application.

- The addition of new functionality can be controlled using attributes of the tag. Therefore, existing features can be retained despite the additions.

- Because the code of the tags is tested and reused, the chances of encountering bugs in JSP pages is substantially lowered.

Productivity. The mechanism of reusing code by using custom tags contributes to decreasing the time spent in code development and can be added to that spent in designing the Web application.

Well, that completes all the theoretical concepts. Before we actually begin to develop and implement a custom tag, let's look at the structure of a tag and the components of the tag library required to develop the application.

Structure of a Custom Tag

Like the tags of XML and HTML, the custom tags in JSP consist of container tags that have both the start and end tags. The content that is written within the start and end tag is known as the body of the tag. In addition, a tag contains attributes that define parameters to customize the tag behavior. Custom tags in JSP can be categorized into the following four types of tags:

Simple tags. A simple tag is a tag without body or attributes. The syntax of the structure of a simple custom tag can be represented as the following:

```
<start tag>
body
</end tag>
```

Tags with attributes.   Attributes are used to parameterize tags and implement context-specific behavior. The attribute is identified by a name, and its requirement is specified by the use of a Boolean parameter. The syntax of the structure of a custom tag with attributes can therefore be represented as the following:

```
<start tag attribute1="value" attribute2="value"...>
</end tag>
```

Body tags.   A body tag consists of body content that is written between the start and end tags. The syntax of the structure of a custom tag with a body tag can therefore be represented as the following:

```
<start tag>
body
</end tag>
```

Nested tags.   A nested tag contains tags of various levels, which simulate nested loops. The syntax of the structure of a nested custom tag can therefore be represented as the following:

```
<start tag of first tag>
<start tag of second tag>
</end tag of second tag>
</end tag of first tag>
```

Components of a Tag Library

To be able to use the custom tags, it is important to define the following three components of the tag library:

- The tag handler class
- The Tag Library Descriptor (TLD) file
- The JSP file

The Tag Handler Class

The tag handler class, as the name suggests, handles the Java class file that contains the business logic of the application that defines the working of the custom tags. In principle, the tag handler is used to define a Java class that directs the system to perform specific tasks after it comes across a custom tag in a JSP file. This class file derives its methods from the `javax.servlet.tagext` package and implements the `TagSupport` or

BodyTagSupport interface. The TagSupport interface is implemented for tags with an empty body, and the BodyTagSupport interface is used for tags that use a body. The tag handler class file definition can also include classes from other packages, such as javax.servlet.jsp and java.io. It is essential to add the corresponding import statements for the tag implementations.

The Tag Library Descriptor File

The Tag Library Descriptor (TLD) file is an XML file that is used to describe the contents of a tag library. It consists of custom tags that are used to document fixed information regarding the properties and location of a tag handler file. The JSP engine uses the TLD file to identify the class of the Java file with a particular tag name.

The JSP file

The JSP file uses the custom tags of the tag library. A JSP page using custom tags from the tag library specifies the tag usage with the taglib directive. The syntax for the taglib directive is as follows:

```
<% @taglib uri="............" prefix="........." %>
```

The two attributes for the taglib directive are uri and prefix. These attributes are used to specify a unique identifier and a reference name for the particular tag library. The Universal Resource Identifier (URI) can be defined as an amalgamation of the Universal Resource Name (URN) and the Universal Resource Locator (URL). The URN is used to specify the Web placement of an object. The URL is used to specify strings such as http and ftp, which are passed to the browser to locate an object on the Web. When the JSP engine encounters insertion of the taglib directive, it uses the uri to locate the descriptor file for a particular library.

By now, you are conversant with the implementation, definition, and components of custom tags and tag libraries. The following list can be used to summarize the declarations needed for the implementation of a custom tag:

- Create a tag handler class file containing Tag and bodyTag interfaces.
- The tag handler file should define the tasks to be performed by the tags.
- Map the tags and the tag handler file by using the Tag Library Descriptor (TLD) file.
- The TLD file should define the inputs for the tag handler.
- The JSP file should include the taglib directive specifying the use of tags and the definition for the tag.

Considering this structure, it is evident that the developer is responsible for writing the code for the tag handler and the TLD file. The Web designer, on the other hand, writes the code for the static content of the Web page. The custom tag declaration is then added to the JSP file. The custom tag feature of JSP enhances the productivity of quality Web applications by separating the work profiles of the Web designer and the developer.

Developing Simple Tags

Problem Statement

The welcome page of the Banco de Glendanthi application is displayed after the validation of the user login. The page design includes a personalized welcome message along with the login name. In addition, the design of the page requires the current date and time to be displayed along with the welcome message. The date and time code is used throughout most of the pages of the application. Ideally, the code can be written once and reused throughout the pages of the application.

The development team has decided to encapsulate the code for displaying the date and time in JSP-specific tags and reuse it through the pages of the application. Therefore, the JSP-specific tag used for this task is the custom tag. The components of the tag library enable encapsulation of Java code in the tag handler. In addition, the entire code can be represented in the JSP page by using a custom tag supported by a TLD file. As a result, the only change necessitated for the reuse of the code is the change in the supporting message and corresponding changes in the presentation content of the HTML. The use of this mechanism saves coding time that would be otherwise lost in rewriting the code for the current date and time for the pages of the application.

Task List

✔ **Identify the components of the tag library.**

✔ **Identify the structure of the tag handler class.**

✔ **Identify the structure of the TLD file.**

✔ **Identify the additional inclusions in the JSP file.**

✔ **Write the code for the tag handler class.**

✔ **Write the code for the TLD file.**

✔ **Write the code for JSP file.**

✔ **Compile the tag handler class**

✔ **Deploy the tag library.**

✔ **View the JSP page.**

Identify the Components of the Tag Library

Because the application will use custom tags, a tag library has to be defined. Table 15.1 lists the components of the tag library.

Table 15.1 The Attributes of a Custom Tag

COMPONENT	FEATURES
Tag Handler class	Contains definitions of the classes and methods to be used to display the welcome message and the current date and time
Tag Library Descriptor (TLD) file	Contains tag specifications in a file similar to an XML file that describes the custom tag
JSP file	Contains HTML elements and the custom tag declaration

Identify the Structure of the Tag Handler Class

The contents of a custom tag can be classified as a simple tag without a body, a tag with a body, or a tag with attributes. The methods to be implemented in the tag handler class file will therefore depend on the structure of the tag. Table 15.2 lists the various methods that are implemented according to the structure of the tag handler.

The functionality of the tag library is defined using the methods from the abstract class Tag. Table 15.3 lists the methods of the Tag class.

Table 15.2 The Tag Handler Methods

STRUCTURE OF THE TAG HANDLER	METHODS TO BE IMPLEMENTED
Simple tag with no body and no attributes	doStartTag, doEndtag, and release()
Tag with a body	doStartTag(), doAfterBody(), and doBeforeBody()
Tag with attributes	doStartTag, doEndtag, and the setXXX() and getXXX() methods for each of the attributes defined

Table 15.3 The Methods of the Tag Class

METHOD	DESCRIPTION
doStartTag()	Initializes the tag handler and establishes connectivity with a database if required
doEndTag()	Performs post-tag tasks, such as writing the output and closing the database connection
release()	Used to remove the instance of the tag handler class
doAfterBody()	Invoked after the completion of the evaluation of the body tag
doBeforeBody()	Invoked before the evaluation of the body tag

Table 15.4 tabulates the methods returned by doStartTag().
Table 15.5 tabulates the methods returned by doEndTag().

Table 15.4 The Methods Returned by doStartTag()

METHOD	DESCRIPTION
SKIP_BODY	Used in empty tags and directs the JSP engine to skip the body of the tag. The next method, namely the doEndTag(), is subsequently invoked.
EVAL_BODY_INCLUDE	Used to direct the JSP engine to process the body content of a tag. This method is used only if the interface implemented is javax.servlet.tagext.Tag.
EVAL_BODY_TAG	Used to direct the JSP engine to process the body of a tag. This method is used only if the interface implemented is javax.servlet.tagext.BodyTag.

Table 15.5 The Methods Returned by doEndTag()

METHOD	DESCRIPTION
SKIP_PAGE	Used to specify skipping or omission of evaluation of the rest of the JSP page
EVAL_ PAGE	Used to specify evaluation of the rest of the JSP page

In addition to these methods, the tag handler includes the following classes and methods:

- The `JspWriter()` method has to be explicitly mentioned in the tag to write the output to a JSP page.

- The `getAttribute()` and `setAttribute()` methods are used to retrieve variable values from scriplets. After processing the variable, its value is then set using the `setAttribute()` method. When using the `getAttribute()` and `setAttribute()` methods, the details about the scripting variable also need to be specified using the `TagExtraInfo` class.

- The `TagExtraInfo` class uses the `getVariableInfo()` method to return information about the scripting values retrieved from the scriplets `TagExtraInfo()` method, which is the default constructor for this class, and the `setTagInfo()` and `getTagInfo()` methods to set and get the `TagInfo` object for this class.

Figure 15.3 illustrates the sequence of the execution of a JSP file containing custom tags.

The steps to execute the JSP file areas follows:

1. When the JSP engine comes across the `taglib` directive in a JSP page, it recognizes the presence of a custom tag associated with the JSP file. The `uri` and `prefix` attributes for a tag act as referential data for specifying the unique URI and name for the tag.

2. The specified tag handler is initialized.

3. The `getXXX()` and `setXXX()` methods for each of the attributes are then executed.

4. The `doStartTag()` method is invoked and used to perform tasks such as establishing a connection with the database.

5. The tag body is evaluated next but is skipped if the `SKIP_BODY` field constant is specified. In that case, the method invoked is `doEndTag()`.

6. The `setBodyContent()` method is then invoked to store the output of the tag in a special print writer called `JspWriter`. The `pageContext.get.Out()` is used for this so that the contents are available for the subsequent methods. The output is not forwarded to the client at this stage.

7. Next, the `doAfter()` method is invoked to work on the content generated after the evaluation of the tag body. The field constants `SKIP_BODY` and `EVAL_BODY_TAG` field constants can be returned to estimate the exact stage of the life cycle.

8. The `doEndTag()` method is invoked next. All connections established earlier are closed, and the output is directed to the browser.

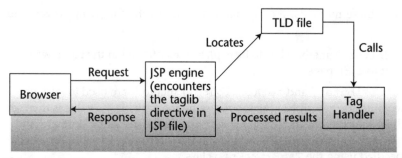

Figure 15.3 The execution cycle of a JSP file with custom tags.

The tag handler file for the simple tag will consist of the following statements and methods:

1. The import statements for importing all relevant packages
2. Inclusion of the interface that has to be extended
3. The doStartTag () method to initialize the tag handler
4. The doEndTag () containing the message string and the method to extract the current date and time

Identify the Structure of the TLD File

The TLD file is an XML file that contains the tag library description. It contains a list and description of all the custom tags in the library that are used as a reference to validate the existence of the respective tags. The components of a TLD file can be broadly classified into two groups. The first group comprises the elements of the root tag of the TLD file or the taglib tag written as <TAGLIB>. The second group placed within the taglib tag comprises the elements that are a part of the tag element written as <TAG>.

Table 15.6 lists the elements of the TLD file at the taglib level.

Table 15.6 The Elements of the TLD File at the taglib Level

ELEMENT	SPECIFIES...
<tlibversion>	The version of the tag library, such as <tlibversion>1.0</tlibversion>
<jspversion>	The version of JSP that the tag library depends on, such as <jspversion>1.1</jspversion>
<uri>	The Universal Resource Identifier, which is an optional component that is a unique ID for the tag library
<info>	The detailed information about the tag library
<shortname>	The name of the tag library

NOTE A practice prevalent among developers is the use of the `<URN></URN>` tag instead of the `<URI>` tag. These tags are often specified as empty tags because they are ignored by most of the application servers.

Table 15.7 lists the elements of the TLD file at the tag level.
The steps to create the TLD file are as follows:

1. In a text editor such as Notepad, include the following definitions for the document type and its definition (DTD) as the header:

```
<!DOCTYPE taglib PUBLIC "-//Sun Microsystems, Inc.//DTD JSP Tag
Library 1.1//EN" "web-jsptaglib_1_1.dtd">
```

NOTE The detailed rules and specifications followed in the XML code are written in Document Type Definition (DTD). DTD defines the tags, tag structures, attributes, and values that are used in a particular document.

In the preceding definition, the tag `DOCTYPE` specifies the use of the `taglib` element as the root tag in the DTD file.

Table 15.7 The Elements of the TLD File at the Tag Level

ELEMENT	SPECIFIES...
`<name>`	A name for the tag.
`<tagclass>`	The name of the tag handler class. The format for this specification is `<tagclass>` package.class.name`</tagclass>` or simply `<tagclass>` class filename `</tagclass>`.
`<teiclass>`	The optional class of `javax.servlet.jsp.` `tagext.Tag`. The format for this specification is `<teiclass>`package.class.name`</teiclass>` or simply `<teiclass>` class filename `</teiclass>`.
`<info>`	Additional information about the tag and its functionality.
`<attribute>`	The attribute name and requirement specification for the tag. This tag, in turn, defines a tag `<required></required>` that values `true` or `false`.
`<bodycontent>`	The definition for the body of the tag. The value of the attribute is specified as `empty` if the tag is an empty tag, `JSP` if the body content is in JSP, and `tagdependent` if the body content is non-JSP. The default value for the body content is `JSP`.

2. Add the `tlibversion`, `jspversion`, `uri`, and `info` tags with their relevant information within `<taglib>` and `</taglib>`.

```
<taglib>
    <tlibversion>1.0</tlibversion>
    <jspversion>1.1</jspversion>
    <shortname>name of the tag library</shortname>
    <info>.....................................</info>
```

3. Add the tag-specific definitions within `<tag>` and `</tag>`.

```
    <tag>
        <name>Welcome</name>
        <tagclass>name of the class file to be used</tagclass>
        <bodycontent>empty</bodycontent>
        <info>..............................................</info>
    </tag>
```

4. Add the end tag for `taglib`.

```
    </taglib>
```

NOTE The tags of the TLD file are always written using lowercase letters only. An oversight in this case results in the nonrecognition of the tag that is represented by the error message "Unable to open taglibrary SimpleTag.tld: More than one taglib in the TLD."

The TLD file consists of the following:

- The tags to be included at the `taglib` level are `tlibversion`, `jspversion`, `shortname`, and `info` tags. The name for the tag library will be `firstTag-Library`.

- The tags to be included at the tag level are `name`, `tagclass`, `bodycontent`, and `info` tags. The name for the tag will be `SimpleTag`.

Identify the Additional Inclusions in the JSP File

How does the JSP file associate the specifications for the existence of the tag handler and TLD file? After the tag handler and TLD files are written, to specify inclusion of a tag in the JSP file, you need to specify the names of the tag and the tag library. These specifications are defined in the TLD file. The syntax to indicate the use of a custom tag in a JSP file is represented as follows:

```
<Name of tag library:Name of custom tag>
</Name of tag library:Name of custom tag>
```

This specification can also be written this way:

```
<Name of tag library:Name of custom tag />
```

In addition to the HTML content, the JSP file will contain the following tag specification:

```
<firstTagLibrary:SimpleTag />
```

The `taglib` directive has to be added at the beginning of the JSP page. If the TLD file is saved as `TestTaglib.tld`, then the specification for the `taglib` directive will be written as:

```
<% @taglib uri=" TestTaglib.tld" prefix="firstTagLibrary" %>
```

Write the Code for the Tag Handler Class

The code for the tag handler file is as follows:

```
import java.io.IOException;
import java.util.Date;
import javax.servlet.jsp.*;
import javax.servlet.jsp.tagext.*;
//Implementing the tag generates the HTML
public class TestTag extends TagSupport
{
//This is the start of the tag
   public int doStartTag() throws JspTagException
   {
       String dateString=new Date().toString();
       try
       {
          JspWriter out = pageContext.getOut();
          out.println("Welcome to the Loan Dept" + " <br>");
          out.println("Today is: " + dateString + "<br>");
          return SKIP_BODY;
       }catch(IOException ee) {
          throw new JspTagException("Error encountered");
       }
   }
//This is the end of the tag
   public int doEndTag() throws JspTagException {
//This return value evaluates the rest of the page
return EVAL_PAGE;
   }
}
```

Write the Code for the TLD File

The code for the TLD file is as follows:

```
<?xml version="1.0" encoding="ISO-8859-1" ?>
<!DOCTYPE taglib PUBLIC "-//Sun Microsystems, Inc.//DTD JSP Tag Library
```

```
1.1//EN"
"http://java.sun.com/j2ee/dtds/web-jsptaglibrary_1_1.dtd">
<taglib>
    <tlibversion>1.0</tlibversion>
    <jspversion>1.1</jspversion>
    <shortname>firstTagLibrary</shortname>
    <urn></urn>
    <info>Example of a tag</info>
    <tag>
        <name>simpleTag</name>
        <tagclass>TestTag</tagclass>
        <bodycontent>JSP</bodycontent>
        <info>An example</info>
    </tag>
</taglib>
```

Write the Code for the JSP File

The code for the JSP file is as follows:

```
<html>

<head>

<title>Banco de Glendanthi</title>
</head>
<body bgcolor="#FFDFD7">

<%@ taglib uri="TestTaglib.tld" prefix="firstTagLibrary" %>

<p><font size="7" color="#0000FF"><img border="0"
src="dd00448_1.gif">Banco de Glendanthi</font></p>
<hr>

<font face="Arial" color="#0000CC" size="5">
Welcome,
</font><br><font face="Arial" color="#0000CC"><h5 style="margin-top: 0;
margin-bottom: 0

<firstTagLibrary:SimpleTag />

</h5></font>
<hr>
<h4><font color="#0000FF">Tells what you would like to do
(Click icon-specific button to view the page)?</h4>

<p>          &nb
sp;          
</p>

<p>      <img border="0" src="bs00508_new.gif"
```

```
width="95" height="63">       
<img border="0" src="bd06517_new.gif " width="99"
height="65">       
<img border="0" src="bd07153_new.gif " width="97"
height="68">       
<img border="0" src="bs02064_new.gif " width="101"
height="68">       
<img border="0" src="sy01265_new.gif " width="83" height="68"></p>

<p>      </p>

<form method="POST" >
    <p>      <input type="button"
value="Deposit "
name="B3">          &n
bsp;   
  <input type="button" value="Withdraw "
name="B4">          
  <input type="button" value="Transfer "
name="B5">          &n
bsp;  
  <input type="button" value="Balance "
name="B6">          &n
bsp;  
  <input type="button" value=" Home" name="B7"></p>
</form>
<p>           &nb
sp;           
</p>
<h4> Not banking with us as yet? To
open a new account, click <a
href="http://registration.jsp">HERE</a></h4>

</body>

</html>
```

Compile the Tag Handler Class

Before deploying the tag library, you'll need to complete the following tasks:

1. Save the tag handler class as **TestTag.java**.
2. Compile the tag handler class.
3. Copy the class file into **C:\j2sdkee1.2.1\lib\Classes**.

Deploy the Tag Library

The tag library is deployed after constructing the tag handler for the TLD and the JSP files. This implies that you'll need to organize and position the tag library to be able to view the output of its implementation. Depending on the mode of deployment you choose, certain changes are also made to the `taglib` directive specification in the JSP file.

Deployment involves placement and execution of the TLD file that is executed in the following three ways:

1. Deployment by using no packaging: This procedure involves placing the TLD file under the document root of the server. The class file is implemented in the class-path. The `uri` in the `taglib` directive is replaced with the path of the TLD file.

2. For example, the `taglib` directive specification for a TLD file named example.tld that is deployed without any packaging would be specified as follows:

   ```
   <%@ taglib uri="./example.tld" prefix="first" %>
   ```

3. Deployment using a JAR file (Java ARchive): This procedure involves the creation of a META_INF subdirectory in the JAR file. The TLD file is placed in the META_INF directory, and the class files are placed in the JAR file. To create a JAR file:

   - At the command prompt, type:

     ```
     jar -cfv try.jar tagexample/*.class META_INF
     ```

   - In the preceding example, `try.jar` is the name of the JAR file and `tagexample` is the name of the package that will contain the class files.

   - To confirm the packaging of the files in the JAR file, at the command prompt, type:

     ```
     jar -tvf
     ```

   - The -v option enables the inclusion of the manifest file in the JAR file.

   - For example, the `taglib` directive specification for a TLD file named example.tld deployed using the preceding JAR file would be specified as follows:

     ```
     <%@ taglib uri="tagexample/example.tld" prefix="first" %>
     ```

4. Deployment by using a Web ARchive file (WAR): This procedure involves placement of the TLD file, the Java class file, and the JSP files in a WAR file. A WAR file is a JAR file that contains a WEB_INF directory with a special file called web.xml. The web.xml file contains details about the `uri` and the location of the TLD file. The WEB_INF directory, in turn, consists of a classes folder for the class files and a lib folder for the additional class files.

5. For example, the `taglib` directive specification for a TLD file named example.tld deployed using a WAR file would be specified as follows:

   ```
   <%@ taglib uri="example" prefix="first" %>
   ```

NOTE In the preceding example, the extension for the TLD file need not be specified because it is available from the web.xml file.

To deploy the tag library by using no packaging, copy both the JSP file and the TLD file in the C:\j2sdkee1.2.1\public_html folder.

To deploy the tag library using no packaging, do the following:

1. Save the TLD file as **TestTaglib.tld.**

2. Save the JSP file as **WelcmPg.jsp**.

3. Copy the TLD and JSP file in **C:/j2sdkee1.2.1/public_html**.

NOTE In case you are using a user-defined folder to contain the tag handler class file, map the `j2ee_classpath` **environment variable to the folder containing the class file.**

View the JSP Page

To view the JSP page, do the following:

1. Start j2EE in verbose mode.

2. In the Internet Explorer address, type the location of the JSP file as **http://localhost:8000/filename.jsp** where the filename denotes the name of the JSP file.

3. Compare and verify the screen display. Figure 15.4 displays the output that is implemented using a custom tag.

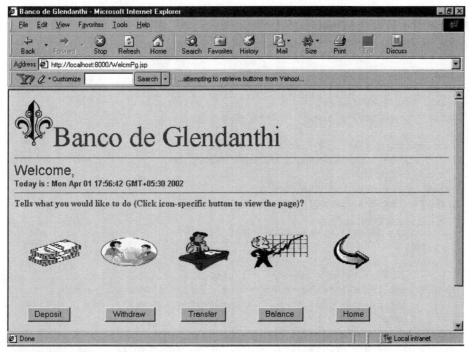

Figure 15.4 The screen output.

In the preceding example, we used a simple tag to display the current date and time in the welcome page of the bank site. Let's now use a few examples to understand the structure and components of tags that define body content and attributes.

Tag with a Body

In the previous example for the Web site of the bank, we used a simple tag to display a welcome message with the current date and time. The tag declaration in the JSP file defined the opening and closing tags for the particular task. As a result, when the JSP engine encounters the `taglib` directive, it is made aware of the inclusion of the content from the tag handler file. In the beginning of this chapter, we defined a tag with a body as a tag that contained content within the opening and closing tags. In other words, the tag can structurally be represented as follows:

```
<start tag>
body content
</endtag>
```

The components of the tag library remain the same and consist of the tag handler file, the TLD file, and the JSP file. A question that immediately comes to mind is the composition of the body content. What is the content of the body? The content can be anything from a simple message to scripting elements used to specify the output of the classes in the tag handler. For example, let's observe the output of a simple message tag example with body content. The code for the components for the tag library will remain the same. Let's specify the code for each component one by one.

Code for the Tag Handler

The tag handler will display the data and time with a simple message:

```
import java.io.IOException;
import java.util.Date;
import javax.servlet.jsp.*;
import javax.servlet.jsp.tagext.*;

//Implementing the tag generates the HTML
public class SimpleTagExample extends TagSupport
{
//This is the start of the tag
   public int doStartTag() throws JspTagException
    {
        String dateString=new Date().toString();
        try
        {
            JspWriter out = pageContext.getOut();
            out.println("Welcome to custom tags" + " <br>");
            out.println("Today is: " + dateString + "<br>");
            return SKIP_BODY;
        }catch(IOException ee) {
            throw new JspTagException("Error encountered");
```

```
        }
    }
//This is the end of the tag
    public int doEndTag() throws JspTagException {
//This return value evaluates the rest of the page
return EVAL_PAGE;
    }
}
```

Code for the TLD File

The code for the TLD file remains the same except for the change in the names of the tag library and the tag:

```
<?xml version="1.0" encoding="ISO-8859-1" ?>
<!DOCTYPE taglib PUBLIC "-//Sun Microsystems, Inc.//DTD JSP Tag Library
1.1//EN"
"http://java.sun.com/j2ee/dtds/web-jsptaglibrary_1_1.dtd">
<taglib>
    <tlibversion>1.0</tlibversion>
    <jspversion>1.1</jspversion>
    <shortname>Simple</shortname>
    <urn></urn>
    <info>Example of a tag</info>
    <tag>
        <name>TagBody</name>
        <tagclass>SimpleTag</tagclass>
        <bodycontent>JSP</bodycontent>
        <info>An example of body tag</info>
    </tag>
</taglib>
```

Code for the JSP File

The code for the JSP file will contain a body between the opening and closing tags. The code for the JSP file can therefore be written as follows:

```
<html>
<head>
<title>A tag with body content</title>
</head>

<body bgcolor="#FFDFD7">
<%@ taglib uri="SimpleTagExample.tld" prefix="Simple" %>
<p><font size="7" color="#0000FF"><img border="0"
src="dd00448_1.gif">Adding a body to the custom tag-an
example</font></p><hr>
<hr>

<Simple:TagBody>
This content comes from within the tag body "Hello World"
```

```
</Simple:TagBody>
</body>
</html>
```

After saving and placing the files in their respective directories, the JSP filename can be specified in the Internet Explorer address bar. Figure 15.5 displays the output of a tag with the body content.

In the preceding example, we used the processing of the tag handler to generate the date and time as the output; however, the same output can also be generated by URL using JSP scripting elements. Let's use an example to include body content in the form of scripting elements.

Let's create a tag with a body content to display the bank name, the tag name, the class name, and the date as output. In the earlier task, we used a tag handler file to display the current date and time. In this example, we'll use the tag body to display the specific information. Similar to the previous task, the tag library using a body tag will consist of the usual components, namely the tag handler class, the TLD file, and the JSP file. We'll use scripting elements, especially the expression statement, to display the information within the tag as a part of the body content. As a result, in addition to using the tag handler class, we'll define an extra class file called the `TagExtraInfo` class to define the use of the scripting elements. The use of scripting elements in the body content of a tag extends freedom to present the output without performing any process to determine the content. The structure of the tag handler, the TLD, and the JSP files remains the same. Therefore, let's look at the additional class that you need to define to include scripting elements as a part of the body content.

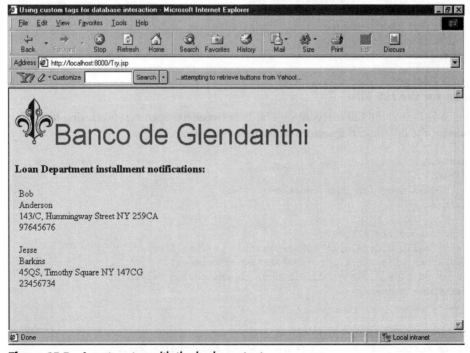

Figure 15.5 A custom tag with the body content.

You need to include a `TagExtraInfo` class file to define the variables that will be available to the JSP page when using the particular tag. Let's look at the structure and declarations in the `TagExtraInfo` class. The implementation of this class file is achieved by following three steps:

1. Use the `<teiclass>` tag in the TLD file to specify the name of the `TagExtraInfo` class filename to indicate the inclusion of the `TagExtraInfo` class as an additional component of the tag library.

2. Define the name and type of the various variables in the `TagExtraInfo` class file.

3. Use the `PageContext` object to add the variables to the tag handler class.

Let's look at the code for the various components for this example.

Code for the TagExtraInfo Class

The code for the `TagExtraInfo` class is as follows:

```
import javax.servlet.jsp.tagext.*;

public class BodyTagExtraInfo extends TagExtraInfo {
public VariableInfo[ ] getVariableInfo(TagData data) {
return new VariableInfo[ ] {
//The use of NESTED ensures that the scripting variables are available
Inside the particular tag only
new VariableInfo("name", "java.lang.String", true, VariableInfo.NESTED),
new VariableInfo("className", "java.lang.String", true,
VariableInfo.NESTED),
new VariableInfo("date", "java.util.Date", true, VariableInfo.NESTED)
};
}
}
```

Code for the TagHandler Class

The code for the `TagHandler` class is as follows:

```
import java.io.*;
import javax.servlet.jsp.*;
import javax.servlet.jsp.tagext.*;
import javax.servlet.*;
import java.util.*;

public class SimpleBodyTag extends TagSupport {

private String name;

public String getName() {
return name;
}

public void setName (String name) {
```

```
    this.name = name;
}

public int doStartTag() throws JspTagException {
    pageContext.setAttribute("name", name);
    pageContext.setAttribute("className", getClass().getName());
    pageContext.setAttribute("date", new Date());
    return EVAL_BODY_INCLUDE;
}
}
```

Code for the TLD File

The code for the TLD file is as follows:

```
<?xml version="1.0" encoding="ISO-8859-1" ?>
<!DOCTYPE taglib PUBLIC "-//Sun Microsystems, Inc.//DTD JSP Tag Library
1.1//EN"
"http://java.sun.com/j2ee/dtds/web-jsptaglibrary_1_1.dtd">
<taglib>
<tlibversion>1.0</tlibversion>
<jspversion>1.1</jspversion>
<shortname>third</shortname>
<urn></urn>
<info>Example of a  body tag</info>
<tag>
<name>BodyExample</name>
<tagclass>SimpleBodyTag</tagclass>
<teiclass>BodyTagExtraInfo</teiclass>
<bodycontent>JSP</bodycontent>
<info>A simple tag with an attribute</info>
<attribute>
<name>name</name>
<required>true</required>
<rtexprvalue>true</rtexprvalue>
</attribute>
</tag>
</taglib>
```

Code for the JSP File

The code for the JSP file is as follows:

```
<%@ taglib uri="Body.tld" prefix="third" %>
<html>
<head>
<title>Example of a  tag with a body</title>
</head>
<body bgcolor="#FFDFD7">
<h3>An example of using a body tag</h3>
<hr>
<font face="Arial" color="#0000CC" size="5">
```

```
</font><br>
<i><third:BodyExample name = "Banco de Glendanthi">
Welcome to <%= name %>.</br>
The tag being used is <%= className %>. </br>
The date today is <%= date %>. <p/>
</third:BodyExample>
</i>
<hr>
</body>
</html>
```

After saving and placing the files in their respective directories, the JSP filename can be specified in the Internet Explorer address bar. Figure 15.6 displays the output of a tag with body content specifying the output by using scripting elements.

That was quite interesting, wasn't it? The use of body content in a tag! In addition to body tags, you can specify parameters for tags in the form of attributes. Let's now look at an example of a custom tag with attributes.

When attributes are specified for a tag, they are mapped to the bean properties (getXXX() and setXXX() methods) of the tag handler. As a result, the inclusion of the attribute controls the tag behavior at run time. This type of approach ensures that the tag is generic and can be reused in other contexts. The only addition required in the tag handler is the inclusion of the getXXX() and setXXX() methods for the particular attribute. In addition, Table 15.8 defines the specifications for the additional tags in the TLD file.

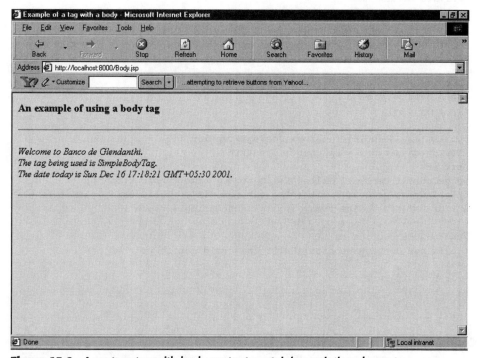

Figure 15.6 A custom tag with body content containing scripting elements.

Table 15.8 The Specifications for the Tag Attributes

ATTRIBUTE SPECIFICATIONS	DESCRIPTION
Name	Used to specify the name to be used within the tag
required	Used to specify the tag requirement. The values that this attribute accepts are true, false, yes, or no

Let's now look at the code for the various components for this example.

Code for the Tag Handler

The code for the tag handler is as follows:

```
import java.io.*;
import javax.servlet.jsp.*;
import javax.servlet.jsp.tagext.*;
import javax.servlet.*;
import java.util.*;

public class AttribTag extends TagSupport {

public int doStartTag() throws JspTagException {
     return EVAL_BODY_INCLUDE;
}

private String name;

public String getName() {
return name;
}

public void setName (String name) {
this.name = name;
}

public int doEndTag() throws JspTagException {
String dateString = new Date().toString();
try {
pageContext.getOut().write("Hello <b>" + name + "</b></br>");
pageContext.getOut().write("The tag name is " + getClass().getName() +
"</br>" + " The date today is  " + dateString + "<p/>");
}
catch (IOException ex) {
throw new JspTagException("Hello tag could not be written");
}
return EVAL_PAGE;
}
}
```

Code for the TLD File

The code for the TLD file is as follows:

```
<?xml version="1.0" encoding="ISO-8859-1" ?>
<!DOCTYPE taglib PUBLIC "-//Sun Microsystems, Inc.//DTD JSP Tag Library
1.1//EN"
"http://java.sun.com/j2ee/dtds/web-jsptaglibrary_1_1.dtd">
<taglib>
<tlibversion>1.0</tlibversion>
<jspversion>1.1</jspversion>
<shortname>second</shortname>
<urn></urn>
<info>Example of a tag</info>
<tag>
<name>AttribExample</name>
<tagclass>AttribTag</tagclass>
<bodycontent>JSP</bodycontent>
<info>A simple tag with an attribute</info>
<attribute>
<name>name</name>
<required>true</required>
<rtexprvalue>true</rtexprvalue>
</attribute>
</tag>
</taglib>
```

Code for the JSP File

The code for the JSP file is as follows:

```
<%@ taglib uri="Attrib.tld" prefix="second" %>

<html>
<head>
<title>Example of a  tag with an attribute</title>
</head>
<body bgcolor="#FFDFD7">
<h3>An example of using an attribute</h3>
<hr>
<font face="Arial" color="#0000CC" size="5">
</font><br>
<i><second:AttribExample name = "Banco de Glendanthi">
</second:AttribExample>
</i>
<hr>
</body>
</html>
```

After saving and placing the files in their respective directories, the JSP filename can be specified at the Internet Explorer address bar. Figure 15.7 displays the output of a tag with body content specifying the output by using scripting elements.

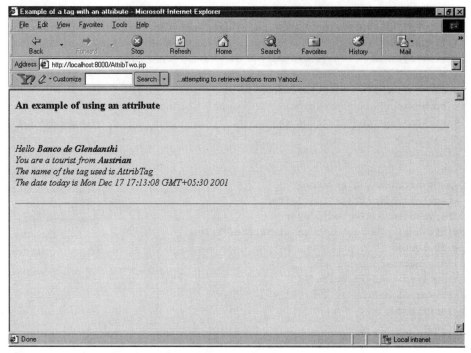

Figure 15.7   A custom tag with attribute values.

Now that we are conversant with the structure and implementation of custom tags, let's try to use the tags for database interaction. The mode that we will follow for understanding the components will be more concise now that you can identify with the basics of custom tags. Continuing with the scenario for Banco de Glendanthi, let's take a look at the various tasks and files required to achieve this database interaction.

Developing a Tag for Database Interaction

Problem Statement

A large number of the customers at Banco de Glendanthi choose to get loans from the bank for personal and professional needs. The applications for the loans are scrutinized, and loans are granted to only those applicants who meet the bank's requirements. The management at Banco de Glendanthi has decided to send a postal notification to the loan account holders who have only two or fewer installments left to pay.

The system administrator has shown interest in regularizing such notifications for other customers with loan accounts, too. To facilitate the reuse of code, your project manager is enthusiastic about using custom tags in the application. As a result, with minor changes to the code in relation to the increase in the number of installments, the same code can be reused by a simple insertion of the corresponding custom tag.

You have been assigned the task of writing the application that will display a list of the accounts that have two or fewer installments to pay. The list should contain the name, address, and phone number of these accounts to facilitate the notifications. The details for the applicant have to be retrieved from the corresponding tables of the database.

Task List

✔ **Identify the components of the tag library.**

✔ **Identify the structure of the tag handler class.**

✔ **Identify the structure of the TLD file.**

✔ **Identify the additional inclusions in the JSP file.**

✔ **Write the code for the tag handler class.**

✔ **Write the code for the TLD file.**

✔ **Write the code for the JSP file.**

✔ **Compile the tag handler class.**

✔ **Deploy the tag library.**

✔ **View the JSP page.**

Identify the Components of the Tag Library

The components of the tag library are the tag handler class, theTLD file, and the JSP file.

Identify the Structure of the Tag Handler Class

The tag handler file for the simple tag will consist of the following:

- The `import` statements for importing all relevant packages
- The interface that has to be extended
- The `doStartTag()` method to initialize the tag handler
- The `doEndTag()` method containing the methods and classes to implement database interaction

Identify the Structure of the TLD File

The TLD file will consist of the following:

1. In a text editor such as Notepad, include the following definitions for the document type and its definition (DTD) as the header:

```
<!DOCTYPE taglib PUBLIC "-//Sun Microsystems, Inc.//DTD JSP Tag
Library 1.1//EN" "web-jsptaglib_1_1.dtd">
```

2. Add the `tlibversion, jspversion, uri,` and `info` tags with relevant information within `<taglib>` and `</taglib>`:

```
<taglib>
    <tlibversion>1.0</tlibversion>
    <jspversion>1.1</jspversion>
    <shortname>secondTagLibrary</shortname>
    <info>.....................................</info>
```

3. Add the tag definitions separating each within `<tag>` and `</tag>`:

```
    <tag>
        <name>DatabaseTag</name>
        <tagclass>LoanDetails</tagclass>
        <bodycontent>empty</bodycontent>
        <info>...............................................</info>
```

4. The database interaction will use the loan ID in the `Loan_Details` table to extract the personal details of the customer from the `Loan_Registration` table. As a result, an additional tag, `<attribute>`, is added at the tag level:

```
        <attribute>
        <name>LoanId </name>
        <required>True</required>
        </attribute>
    </tag>
```

5. Add the end tag for `taglib`.

```
    </taglib>
```

Identify the Additional Inclusions in the JSP File

Other than the HTML content, the JSP file will contain the following tag specification:

```
<secondTagLibrary:DatabaseTag />
```

In addition, the `taglib` directive has to be added at the beginning of the JSP page. If the TLD file is saved as tryjsp-taglib.tld, then the specification for the `taglib` directive will be written as follows:

```
<% @taglib uri="tryjsp-taglib.tld" prefix="secondTagLibrary" %>
```

Write the Code for the Tag Handler Class

The code for the tag handler class is as follows:

```
import javax.servlet.jsp.*;
import javax.servlet.jsp.tagext.*;
import java.io.*;
```

```
import java.sql.*;
import java.util.*;
import java.math.*;
public class BankAccountTag extends TagSupport
{
    protected String sLoanId="";
    Connection connect = null;
    Statement state = null;
    ResultSet result = null;
    public BankAccountTag() throws ClassNotFoundException
    {
        Class.forName("sun.jdbc.odbc.JdbcOdbcDriver");
    }
    public int doStartTag() throws JspTagException
    {
        return EVAL_BODY_INCLUDE;
    }
    public int doEndTag() throws JspTagException
    {
        try
        {
            JspWriter out=pageContext.getOut();
            connect=DriverManager.getConnection("jdbc:odbc:
            MyDataSource","sa","");
            String strQuery = " Select cFirst_name,cLast_name,
            cAddress,cPhone from Loan_Registration LR,Loan_Details LD
            where LD.intBal_no_installments<=2 and
            LD.cLoan_registration_id=LR.cLoan_registration_id " ;
            System.out.println("Query: "+strQuery);
            state = connect.createStatement();
            ResultSet result = state.executeQuery(strQuery);
            String sFirstName = null;
            String sLastName = null;
            String sAddress = null;
            String sPhone = null;
            Vector v=new Vector();
            while(result.next())
            {
                sFirstName = result.getString(1);
                sLastName  = result.getString(2);
                sAddress   = result.getString(3);
                sPhone=result.getString(4);
                v.add(sFirstName);
                v.add(sLastName);
                v.add(sAddress);
                v.add(sPhone);
            }
            for(int i=0;i<v.size();i++)
            {
                String str=(String)v.elementAt(i);
                pageContext.getOut().write(str);
```

```
            if(i==3)
            {
                pageContext.getOut().write("<BR>");
            }
            pageContext.getOut().write("<BR>");
        }
    }catch(Exception ioe)
    {
        System.out.println(" Error in getting
        results"+ioe.toString());
    }
    return EVAL_PAGE;
    }
}
```

Write the Code for the TLD File

The code for the TLD file is as follows:

```
<?xml version="1.0" encoding="ISO-8859-1" ?>
<!DOCTYPE taglib PUBLIC "-//Sun Microsystems, Inc.//DTD JSP Tag Library
1.1//EN"
"http://java.sun.com/j2ee/dtds/web-jsptaglibrary_1_1.dtd">
<taglib>
    tlibversion>1.0</tlibversion>
    <jspversion>1.1</jspversion>
    <shortname>second</shortname>
    <urn></urn>
    <info>A Tag library for the bank details</info>
    <tag>
        <name>databaseTag</name>
        <tagclass>BankAccountTag</tagclass>
        <info>Outputs of the bank details</info>
        <bodycontent>JSP</bodycontent>
        <attribute>
        <name>LoanId</name>
        <required>false</required>
        </attribute>
    </tag>
</taglib>
```

Write the Code for the JSP File

The code for the JSP file is as follows:

```
<HTML>
<HEAD>
```

```
<TITLE> Using custom tags for database interaction</TITLE>
</HEAD>
   <BODY bgcolor="#FFEAFF">
      <%@ taglib uri="tryjsp-taglib.tld" prefix="second" %>
      <FONT size="7" color="#0000FF">
         <FONT face="Arial">Banco de Glendanthi</FONT>
         <IMG border="0" src="dd00448_1.gif" width="89"
         height="99">
      </FONT></P>
      <H3>Loan Deparment installment notifications:</H3>
      <TABLE>
      <TR>
      <TD></TD>
      <TD><second:databaseTag/></TD>
      <TABLE>
   </BODY>
</HTML>
```

Compile the Tag Handler Class

Before deploying the tag library, you'll need to complete the following tasks:

1. Save the tag handler class as **BankAccountTag.java**.

2. Compile the tag handler class.

3. Copy the class file into **C:\j2sdkee1.2.1\lib\Classes**.

Deploy the Tag Library

To deploy the tag library, do the following:

1. Save the TLD file as **tryjsp-taglib.tld**.

2. Save the JSP file as **Try.jsp**.

3. Copy the TLD and JSP file in the **C:/j2sdkee1.2.1/public_html**.

View the JSP Page

To view the JSP page, do the following:

1. Start j2EE in verbose mode.

2. In the Internet Explorer address, type the location of the .jsp file as **http://localhost:8000/filename.jsp**.

3. Compare and verify the screen display.

Figure 15.8 displays the output that is implemented using a custom tag.

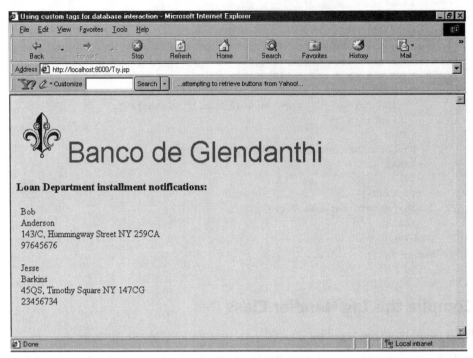

Figure 15.8   The screen output.

Summary

Even though the advantages of using the JSP tag libraries are clear, this methodology is quite underutilized in JSP. The apprehension about using tag libraries is slowly but surely wearing off. As a result, tag libraries have recently become a common feature in most JSP projects.

We have talked about the use of custom tags in encapsulating Java code snippets. You will recollect that in Chapter 8, "Using Scripting Elements," we discussed how scriplets in JSP are used to encapsulate Java code. Scriplets and custom tags, though functionally similar, are implemented in different ways. The discussion about this difference did not fit in well between the concepts of tag libraries and custom tags. Therefore, before summing up this chapter, let's also look at the advantages of using custom tags over scriplets:

Reduction of scriplets in the code.   The attributes of a custom tag can be used to accept parameters. Therefore, inclusion of declarations to define variables and scriplets to set properties of Java components can be avoided or reduced.

Reusability.   Contrary to scriplets that are nonreusable Java code snippets, custom tags can be reused. This saves time in the development and deployment of the codes.

Easy maintainability of Web applications.   By providing a simple interface, custom tags contribute to segregating the work profiles of Web designers and developers. As a result, application development is more team-oriented.

Due to its versatility, portability, and reusability, the use of tag libraries can give a boost to JSP to make it the most dynamic Web programming environment available today. All that you need to do is add a little imagination and innovation. In the next chapter, we'll discuss the contribution and usage of JSP in JavaMail services.

CHAPTER

16

JavaMail

OBJECTIVES:

In this chapter, you will learn to do the following:

- ✔ Identify the protocols of the JavaMail API
- ✔ Identify the various classes and methods of the JavaMail API
- ✔ Send messages using JavaMail
- ✔ Use JavaMail in JSP

Getting Started

Today communication within states, across countries, and across continents by using traditional mail services is passé. In its place, people use the easy, convenient, reliable, and faster mode of communication called email. As a result, it comes as no surprise that people use Internet mail services instead of the customary mail services for the exchange of letters and greeting cards. Electronic mail (email) is the most frequently used service of the Internet. Although the task of sending messages to friends and relatives seems simple, it involves a lot of complex behind-the-scenes activities. Countless protocols and multiple APIs are used for packaging, sending, and receiving emails. The addition of these protocols incorporates mailing functionality into applications.

The traditional approach for building interactions with a mail server from within application code required the addition of socket code, which involved a good amount of string parsing. As a result, the code was messy and required long wait periods for the completion of the request-response cycle. The JavaMail API, on the other hand, provides simple abstract classes to define an easy-to-use, general mail system. Java programmers are therefore better equipped with an interface designed to add messaging and mailing functionality in applications.

This chapter begins with a brief discussion of the advantages of using the JavaMail API. In later sections, we discuss the JavaMail API in detail, summing up with a task-based scenario example for sending mail messages.

Introduction to the JavaMail API

Internet mail service has set standards specifying the formats of a message and the process of handling the messages. Accordingly, the JavaMail API also uses providers for implementing the messaging functionality. Because the defined abstract interfaces and classes are not directly usable, using specific protocols the JavaMail's providers implement the messaging functionality in applications. The different providers specified by Sun include Simple Mail Transfer Protocol (SMTP), the Post Office Protocol (POP3), the Multipurpose Internet Mail Extensions (MIME), and the Internet Message Access Protocol (IMAP4). Providers implement the following two protocol services for sending and receiving mail:

Transport services. The transport services are basically responsible for accepting the message and sending it to the specified recipient.

Store services. The store services are used to manipulate the storage of mails. You'll surely be able to understand this functioning by mapping it to the mailboxes represented by the inbox. The mailboxes in JavaMail are referred to as folders. The folders of JavaMail are similar to the structure of normal folders, which can contain other folders and files. As a result, a JavaMail folder also contains other folders, messages, or both.

These two services are generic terms used by Sun to define the protocols for implementing mailing services using the JavaMail API. The Internet mail service uses the Simple Mail Transfer Protocol (SMTP) to implement the transport services and the Post Office Protocol (POP3) and the Internet Message Access Protocol (IMAP4) to implement the store services.

The jdk1.3 specification contains the `mail.jar` file with the necessary packages for implementing mailing services. Because we are using jdk1.3 along with the Enterprise edition of the Java 2 Platform, no separate download is required; however, you can also download the reference implementation from the Sun's JavaMail site at http://java.sun.com/products/javamail/. Extract the content of the archive, and add the path of the `mail.jar` to the `CLASSPATH` variable.

Let's use the bank scenario to create an application implementing mailing services for improved interdepartmental communication.

Using JavaMail in JSP

Problem Statement

Each type of account at Banco de Glendanthi is managed by a dedicated group of executives responsible for handling the accounts, their updates, and customer queries. In other words, each of these groups of executives is a part of a department, headed by a Chief Governing Officer (CGO). This is just one sector for the implementation of in-house mail services. Customer updates, such as intimation of increase or decrease of interest rates and launching of new products, can also use mailing services for updating registered customers with the latest banking news. As a result, the inclusion of an in-house mailing service will serve the following two purposes:

- Facilitate mail communication between the executives of various departments within the bank.

- Facilitate sending the latest updates to registered account holders of the bank. The updates will primarily contain details about bank accounts.

Most customers of Banco de Glendanthi prefer to open Personal Checking Accounts with the bank because the minimum amount required to open the account is $100 with a nominal monthly maintenance charge of $7. To encourage customers to open Personal Checking Accounts, the administration of the bank has decided to lower the maintenance charges from $7 to $5.

The development team headed by Janice Griffin has been assigned the task of creating an application that will mail the latest updates to registered customers. The task requires sending a message informing customers of the decrease in the maintenance charges of Personal Checking Accounts. Let's look at the approach and methodology adopted to add such functionality to the application.

Task List

✔ **Identify the elements of the HTML page to accept the details of the mail.**

✔ **Identify the elements of the JSP page to add the JavaMail functionality to the application.**

✔ **Write the code for the HTML page.**

✔ **Write the code for the JSP page.**

✔ **View the JSP page.**

Identify the Elements of the HTML Page to Accept the Details of the Mail

The standardized format for composing a mail consists of the following HTML controls:

- The header elements consisting of the bank name and logo.
- Text controls for accepting the email addresses of the sender and recipient and the subject of the mail.
- A text area that contains the mail message.
- Submit and reset buttons to submit the mail form. The reset button can be used to clear the contents of the text controls and reenter new values in them.

To create a format similar to the commonly used standardized format, each of the individual text controls and buttons will be placed within a table. Table 16.1 lists the HTML tags to be used for designing the mail form.

Table 16.1   HTML Forms of the Mail Form

INPUT FIELD	SPECIFICATIONS

Text controls for the sender's and recipient's email address and the subject of the mail	`<td width="118">To:</td>`
	
	`<td width="468">`
	
	`<input tye="text" name="receipient" size="63">`
	
	`</td>`
	
	`</tr>`

Text area for the mail message	`<td colspan ="2" width="598">`
	
	`<textarea cols="71" rows="15" name="message" size="30">`
	
	`</textarea>`
	
	`</td>`
	
	`</tr>`

Submit and reset buttons	`<td width="118">`
	
	`<p align="center">`
	
	`<input type="submit" value="Send" name="send">`
	
	`<input type="reset" value="Reset" name="reset">`

To add the header elements to the mail form, you can use HTML-specific tags or the `include` directive specifying the name of the file containing the header elements (**Header.html**). In case you use the `include` directive, add the following code to the HTML page and be sure to save it as an JSP page (not HTML):

```
<%--The include directive is used here to add the elements of the file
Header.html to the login page--%>
<%@ include file="Header.html" %>
```

Figure 16.1 displays the output of the HTML mail form.

Let's look at the JSP page that contains the JavaMail API specifications for creating the mail session and transporting the mail to the intended recipient.

Identify the Elements of the JSP Page to Add the JavaMail Functionality to the Application

In the preceding sections, we discussed the protocol and services used by JavaMail to send and receive mail. Bear in mind that with advances in technology , the existing list of protocols will expand. Therefore, it is important to equip the mailing system with a feature to accommodate new protocols. This feature ensures that, with minor changes, the preexisting JavaMail applications can adapt and use the new protocols. JavaMail applications use the Provider Registry to detect the available providers. As a result, it would not be wrong to describe JavaMail as an extensible, adaptable, and usable mailing system.

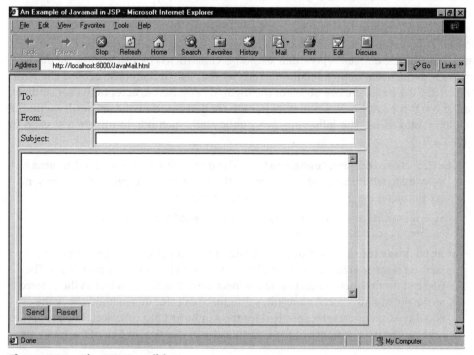

Figure 16.1   The HTML mail form.

To access the names of the providers available to an application, JavaMail first looks for the Provider Registry in the lib directory. The registry is actually a single file named javamail.Providers. In case the file is missing from the lib directory, JavaMail subsequently looks for the file in the META-INF directory. Once found, javamail. Default.providers is used to extract the names of the providers and add them to the previous list of providers.

Although the JavaMail API contains specifications for many packages, we'll not discuss all of them. Let's look at the most commonly used packages of the JavaMail API:

- The javax.mail.Session package contains class and method definitions for creating a mail session and setting the properties of the mail environment.

- The javax.mail.message contains class and method definitions for composing the mail.

javax.mail.Session

From the discussions in the preceding chapters, we need not stress the importance of a session in a Web interaction. Similarly, a JavaMail session needs to be initiated before the mail is sent. The transport and store services are initiated by the implementation of javax.mail.Session. The session object of javax.mail.Session is different from that initiated by the javax.servlet.HTTPSession object. You'll recall that by using a session object the otherwise stateless session was able to store information from previous sessions. The javax.mail.Session object serves as an object for associating a set of user-specified properties with a provider. A JavaMail session is a user-oriented session that begins and ends with the user login, authentication, and logoff. A JavaMail session is stored as a servlet session object to retrieve the store and transport objects. A JavaMail session is constructed by using static methods in contrast to the usual implementation of classes that use public constructors. The parameters for the Properties object of the methods are used to accept the user settings, and those for the Authenticator object are used to associate the properties with the session. You can use the following two public static methods to initiate a session in JavaMail:

static Session getInstance(). The getInstance() method returns a new unshared instance of Session with all the specified properties. The syntax for using the getInstance() method is this:

```
static Session getInstance(Properties nameOfPropertyObject,
Authenticator nameOfAuthenticatorObject)
```

static Session getDefaultInstance(). The getDefaultInstance() method returns a shared instance of Session with the specified properties. The first call for this method creates a new instance of the object, which is then stored as the default instance. As a result, subsequent calls for this method check the equality of the parameter specified for the Authenticator object. The properties are ignored if the instance of the authenticator is identical to that of the previous

call and the same instance is returned repeatedly. The syntax for using the
getInstance() method is this:

```
static Session getDefaultInstance(Properties nameOfPropertyObject,
Authenticator nameOfAuthenticatorObject)
```

To add specific properties to the getInstance() and getDefaultInstance()
methods, invoke the System.getProperties() method of java.util.
Properties object. The value of the java.util.Properties object is subsequently passed on to the getInstance() and getDefaultInstance()
methods. Table 16.2 lists the properties that a user can set for a JavaMail session.

For example, the following code can be used to set the properties for the host and
transport protocols:

```
Properties prop = System.getProperties();
prop.put("mail.transport.protocol", "smtp");
prop.put("mail.smtp", "mail.bancoG.com");
Session sess = Session.getInstance(prop, null);
```

Using the methods of javax.mail.Session helps to manage and configure the
user's mail settings. In addition, these methods also handle the authentication for various services that are used during a mail session. Once the mail environment or settings are configured, the focus shifts to writing or composing the mail before it is sent
to the intended recipient. What inputs do you need to provide for this? First, you need
to specify the mail address of the recipient, the subject of the mail, and the body of the
mail or the mail text. The abstract class javax.mail.message is used to define the
properties of the mail contents.

Table 16.2 The JavaMail Session Properties

PROPERTY NAME	USED TO SPECIFY...
mail.transport.protocol	The value of the default transport protocol.
mail.store.protocol	The value of the default store protocol.
mail.host	The name of the default host for both the transport and store protocols. The default value accepted is usually that of the local machine.
mail.user	The name of the default user for both the transport and store protocols.
mail.from	The email address of the user.
mail.debug	The default debug setting for a particular session. The setting of the debug property ensures that the debug messages are output to both the session and its providers.

javax.mail.message

The actual implementation of the mail messages is achieved by using a few interfaces and abstract class definitions. The abstract class `Message` uses the class `MimeMessage` to ensure that the composed message adheres to Internet email standards. As a result, before a mail is forwarded to the recipient, the message and its headers are formatted according to the standards.

Each message cycle begins by sending a mail, which is initiated by a session. Subsequently, the sender receives a reply that, in turn, returns a new message. The following are the two ways used to implement the `Message` class:

- The `MimeMessage (Session)` constructor is used to create a new `Session` containing the `MimeMessage` class. The `MimeMessage` created contains empty headers and content.

- The `reply(boolean)` method is used to return a new message containing appropriate headers as a reply to the sent message.

Before we move any further, let's clear up the definitions of the much-used terms "headers" and "content." A typical Internet message consists of the following details:

- Message ID displayed as Message-ID: <54316478347>
- The date the message was sent displayed as Date: Thurs, 15 Nov 2000 10:53:12
- Sender's email address displayed as From: johndoe@serviceprovider.com
- Recipients email address displayed as To: Seanp@serviceprovider.com
- Subject of the mail displayed as Subject: What's wrong? No mails?
- Version of the MIME type displayed as Mime-Version: 1.0
- Content type of the mail displayed as Content-Type: text/plain
- The body of the message displayed as What's up Sean...I have waited all week for a mail. Hope you are not unwell?

The source for each mail consists of two parts, the headers and content. The headers consist of the header name and value separated by a colon. The content entry containing the body text is separated from the header entries by a double return. For example, the source for the specification in the preceding list will be displayed in the following format:

```
Message-ID: <35476575847.JavaMail.Administrator@BancoG
Date: Thurs, 15 Nov 2000 10:53:12
From: johndoe serviceprovider.com
To: Seanp serviceprovider.com
Subject: What's wrong? No mails?
Mime-Version: 1.0
Content-Type: text/plain

What's up Sean...I have waited all week for a mail.
Hope you are not unwell?
```

You'll easily differentiate that Message-ID, Date, From, To, Subject, Mime-Version, and Content-Type are the headers and the content is separated by the double return. The most commonly used formats for messages are specific to RFC 822 and the RFC 2045-2049 MIME extension. Let's look at the commonly used headers in detail.

The From Header

In the preceding mail headers and content example, when Jeannie sent the mail to Sean, the From header contained the address of John Doe. The value of the From header is sourced from the sender's email address. The default Session properties of the Message class are used with the setFrom() method to set the value of the From header in the following ways:

- The From header can be set by using the address that is specified in the session's mail.user. The following specification for the From header uses the Session's mail.user specification:

```
void setFrom()
```

- The From header can also be explicitly set by passing an Address object. The syntax for explicitly setting the From header is this:

```
void setFrom(Address add)
```

- The From header can also include multiple addresses for which an array of type Address is declared with the addForm() method. This is followed by the declaration for the getForm() method to return the value of the array. The syntax for setting multiple addresses for the From header is this:

```
void addFrom(Address[] add)
Address[] getFrom()
```

- The multiple addresses in the From header are separated by commas that can cause parsing errors. Therefore, in addition to the standard constructor, the InternetAddress class has been added to the JavaMail API to enable parsing of the comma separators of the multiple addresses in the From header. The following code uses the InternetAddress class as a convenient factory method for accepting a list of addresses:

```
mess.setFrom(new InternetAddress "celina@bancoG.org"));
mess.addFrom(InternetAddress.parse "jonathan@bancoG.org,
Isabella@bancoG.org"));
```

The To Header

The preceding mail headers and content example accepted the address of Sean as a *Normal receipient* denoted by the To header. Situations may require copies of the mail to be sent to additional recipients. For example, a memo intended for a supervisor in a department can also be sent to the departmental head for reference. Do you send individual copies of the mail to each of the two personnel? No! An easier method adopted for sending the same mail to two or more individual is the addition of a *Carbon copied recipient* (Cc header) for the same mail. The supervisor in this case is the primary recipient while the department head is the secondary recipient. Similarly, the name of one or more of the intended recipients can be excluded from the list of the primary and secondary recipients. The addition of a *Blind carbon copied* (Bcc header) recipient ensures that the address of an intended recipient is hidden from the list of other recipients.

The Message class defines an inner class recipientType, which can be used to specify the type of header of the recipient. The syntax for specifying the various types of recipients is this:

```
SetRecipient(Message.RecipientType type, Address address)
```

For example, the following code sets the header type of a recipient as Normal:

```
SetRecipients(Message.Recipienttype.TO,address);
```

The Subject and Date Headers

The subject of a mail message summarizes the intent of the mail. Some mail formats also include the Date header to specify the date of the mail. The message class consists of the setter and getter methods for the value of the subject and date of the mail. The syntax for setting and getting the value of the subject and date of a mail is this:

```
void setSubject (String sub)
String getSubject()
void setSentDate (Date date)
String getSentDate()
```

Next, let's move on to discussing the presentation of the message text or the content of a mail. The Part interface is used to retrieve the content of a mail. This type of retrieval operates at a very low level by manipulating DataHandlers.

That completes this section on the various methods and classes used for composing a mail. Let's identify the various sections of the code for the JSP that will set the mail environment and perform functions related to sending the mail to the registered customers of the bank. Let's look at the method and class definitions in each section.

We'll begin with the instantiation of a default session that will be used to retrieve the values of the system properties. The following code specifies the various properties of javax.mail.*:

```
String host = "server.host.com";
String rec = request.getParameter("receipient");
String sen = request.getParameter("sender");
String sub = request.getParameter("subject");
String mess = request.getParameter("message");
boolean sessionDebug = false;
```

```
//creating a default session and building its properties
Properties prop = System.getProperties();
prop.put("mail.host", host);
prop.put("mail.transport.protocol", "smtp");
Session mailsess = Session.getDefaultInstance(prop, null);
```

An HTML form is used to accept the various headers and the content of the mail. In addition, the request object is used to retrieve the values of the various HTM controls used to accept the details of the mail. As a result, we do not require any additional variable definitions to specify the To, From, and Subject headers. We also do not need to explicitly define the message text. Next, we'll create a mail message to send it to the intended recipient:

```
mailsess.setDebug(sessionDebug);
Message msg = new MimeMessage(mailsess);
msg.setFrom(new InternetAddress(sen));
InternetAddress[] address = {new InternetAddress(rec)};
msg.setRecipients(Message.RecipientType.TO, address);
msg.setSubject(sub);
//msg.setSentDate(newDate());
msg.setText(mess);
```

That's all; the code for the mail needs to be put together for sending. Let's look at the complete codes for the HTML form and the JSP page.

Write the Code for the HTML Page

The code for the HTML page containing both the HTML and JSP elements is as follows:

```
<html>
<head><title>An Example of Javamail in JSP</title></head>
<body  bgcolor="#FFDFD7">
<form  method="Post" action="Javamail.jsp">
<table cellspacing="3" cellpadding="3" border="2" width="618">
<tr>
<td width="118">To:</td>
<td width="468">
<input tye="text" name="receipient" size="63">
</td>
</tr>
<tr>
<td width="118">From:</td>
<td width="468">
<input tye="text" name="sender" size="63">
</td>
</tr>
<tr>
<td width="118">Subject:</td>
<td width="468">
```

```
<input type="text" name="subject" size="63">
</td>
</tr>
<tr>
<td colspan ="2" width="598">
<textarea cols="71" rows="15" name="message" size="30">
</textarea>
</td>
</tr>
<tr>
<td width="118">
<p align="center">
<input type="submit" value="Send" name="send">
<input type="reset" value="Reset" name="reset">
  
</p>
</tr>
</table>
</body>
</html>
```

Write the Code for the JSP Page

The code for the JSP page containing both the HTML and JSP elements is as follows:

```
<html>
<head><title>Java mail example</title></head>
<body bgcolor="#FFDFD7">
<%--The include directive is used here to add the elements of the file
Header.html to the login page--%>
<%@ include file="Header.html" %>
<%@ page import="java.util.*" %>
<%@ page import="javax.mail.*" %>
<%@ page import="javax.mail.internet.*" %>
<%@ page import="javax.activation.*" %>
<h4><font face="Arial" color="#0000CC" size="4">Confirmation page of
mail</font></h4>

<%
String host = "name of the mail host";
String rec = request.getParameter("receipient");
String sen = request.getParameter("sender");
String sub = request.getParameter("subject");
String mess = request.getParameter("message");
boolean sessionDebug = false;
//creating a default session and building its properties
Properties prop = System.getProperties();
prop.put("mail.host", host);
prop.put("mail.transport.protocol", "smtp");

Session mailsess = Session.getDefaultInstance(prop, null);
```

```
mailsess.setDebug(sessionDebug);

Message msg = new MimeMessage(mailsess);
msg.setFrom(new InternetAddress(sen));
InternetAddress[] address = {new InternetAddress(rec)};
msg.setRecipients(Message.RecipientType.TO, address);
msg.setSubject(sub);
msg.setText(mess);

Transport.send(msg);
%>
<font face="Arial" color="#0000CC" size="4">
<%out.println("Recipient: " + rec + "<br>");
out.println(" Sender: " + sen + "<br>");
//out.println(" Mail host: " + host + "<br>");
%>

</body>
</html>
```

View the JSP Page

To view the JSP page, do the following:

1. Specify the name of the mail host in the corresponding line of the JSP code:

   ```
   String host = "server.host.com";
   ```

2. Save the HTML and JSP file as JavaMail.html and JavaMail.jsp, respectively.

3. Copy both the files in the public_html directory.

4. Initiate the server startup in verbose mode.

5. In the Internet Explorer address, type the location of the HTML file as **http://localhost:8000/filename.html** where the filename denotes the name of the HTML file.

NOTE Before viewing the JSP page, we need to take into account certain policy issues that can prevent delivery of the mail. By default, the permissions for **javax.util.PropertyPermission** is set to read. As a result, the application encounters a no-read permission-error on execution. We need to change the property permission to read and write. To change the property, navigate to C:\j2sdkee1.2.1\lib\security and open the server.policy file in Notepad. Edit the permissions for **javax.util.PropertyPermission** to read, write. Save the file.

6. In the To box, enter the address of the recipient as **melaniew@ serviceprovider.com**.

7. In the From box, enter the address of the sender as **johndoe@ serviceprovider.com**.

8. In the Subject box, enter the subject of the mail as **Reduction in the maintenance charges of Personal Checking Accounts**.

9. Compose the mail message to reflect the reduction in charges from $7 to $5.

10. Click Send to submit the form.

NOTE The output of the JSP page will vary according to the difference in the entries for the various controls of the HTML page. The output displayed in Figure 16.2 is a generic figure displaying fictitious values.

Figure 16.2 displays the confirmation message containing the names of the recipient, sender, and the mail host used for sending the mail. You can send a mail to yourself to check for the execution of the code.

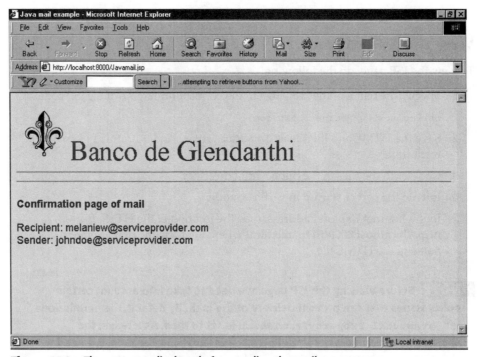

Figure 16.2 The message displayed after sending the mail.

Summary

The importance of email in our lives today needs no separate introduction. The JavaMail API can be used to add mailing functionality in a Web application. As a result, developers of JSP pages can use the JavaMail specification to create a general mailing system. In this chapter, we discussed the various interfaces and abstract classes of the JavaMail API that provide a channel of textual communication by using specific protocols.

In the course of the preceding chapters, we created Java Server Pages that illustrated the clear separation of the application logic from the presentation logic. In contrast to the pure Java code content of servlets, a JSP page includes both HTML code and Java code that are compiled to generate a servlet. As a result, it would not be wrong to say that JSP provides a powerful platform backed by both Java and servlet specifications.

Index

SYMBOLS

& (ampersand), 109
<> (angle brackets), 58, 59, 75
* (asterisk), 112
: (colon), 402
/ (forward slash), 332
% (percent sign), 28, 58
? (question mark), 109
; (semicolon), 28

A

accessor methods, 177
AccountBean.java, 196
AccountHolder JavaBean, 178–185
AccountValidate class, 178
AccountValidate() method, 240
Acknowledgement page, 64–66, 149–153
Acknowledgement.jsp, 65–66
action attribute, 107, 108
actions
  described, 87–101
  <jsp:forward> action, 86, 89–91
  <jsp:getProperty> action, 86, 89–90,
    188–189, 191–193
  <jsp:include> action, 86, 91–95, 98, 99
  <jsp:param> action, 86, 91–92
  <jsp:plugin> action, 86, 91, 96–97

<jsp:setProperty> action, 86, 89, 188–190,
  192–193, 241
<jsp:useBean> action, 86, 88, 145,
  188–189, 192, 241
Active Server Pages. *See* ASP (Active
  Server Pages)
addCookie() method, 298, 301
add() method, 344
addressing schemes, 8–9, 65
address location bar, 11–12, 14
ampersand (&), 109
angle brackets (<>), 58, 59, 75
ANSI (American National Standards
  Institute), 202
Apache Web Server, 20, 23, 48
APIs (Application Programming
  Interfaces), 39, 137, 207, 293–295
  JavaMail and, 395–397, 399
  JDBC and, 210–211
  XML and, 328, 347–351
applets, embedded, 96–97
application object, 138, 143
Application Programming Interfaces.
  See APIs (Application Programming
  Interfaces)
application scope, 146
ASP (Active Server Pages), 18–19, 23–25,
  37, 44–45